Get the eBook FREE!
(PDF, ePub, Kindle, and liveBook all included)

We believe that once you buy a book from us, you should be able to read it in any format we have available. To get electronic versions of this book at no additional cost to you, purchase and then register this book at the Manning website.

Go to https://www.manning.com/freebook and follow the instructions to complete your pBook registration.

That's it!
Thanks from Manning!

T0076134

Evolutionary Deep Learning

Evolutionary Deep Learning

GENETIC ALGORITHMS AND NEURAL NETWORKS

MICHEAL LANHAM

MANNING
SHELTER ISLAND

Manning Publications Co.
20 Baldwin Road
PO Box 761
Shelter Island, NY 11964

Development editor:	Patrick Barb
Technical development editor:	Adam London
Review editor:	Adriana Sabo
Production editor:	Keri Hales
Copy editor:	Christian Berk
Proofreader:	Jason Everett
Technical proofreader:	Ninoslav Čerkez
Typesetter:	Gordan Salinovic
Cover designer:	Marija Tudor

ISBN 9781617299520
Printed in the United States of America

I would like to dedicate this book to my mother, Sharon Lanham.
She taught me at an early age how to think outside the box and believe in myself.

brief contents

contents

preface

When I started my career in machine learning and artificial intelligence 25+ years ago, two dominant technologies were considered the next big things. Both technologies showed promise in solving complex problems and both were computationally equivalent. Those two technologies were evolutionary algorithms and neural networks (deep learning).

Over the next couple of decades, I witnessed the steep decline of evolutionary algorithms and explosive growth of deep learning. While this battle was fought and won through computational efficiency, deep learning has also showcased numerous novel applications. On the other hand, for the most part, knowledge and use of evolutionary and genetic algorithms dwindled to a footnote.

My intention for this book is to demonstrate the capability of evolutionary and genetic algorithms to provide benefits to deep learning systems. These benefits are especially relevant as the age of DL matures into the AutoML era, in which being able to automate the large and wide-scale development of models is becoming mainstream.

I also believe that our search for generalized AI and intelligence can be assisted by looking at evolution. After all, evolution is a tool nature has used to form our intelligence, so why can't it improve artificial intelligence? My guess is we are too impatient and arrogant to think humanity can solve this problem on its own.

By writing this book, I wanted to showcase the power of evolutionary methods on top of deep learning as a way of thinking outside the norm. My hope is that it demonstrates the basics of evolutionary methods in fun and innovative ways, yet also ventures into the advanced territory of evolving deep learning networks (aka NEAT) to instinctual learning. Instinctual learning is my take on how we should be paying more attention to how biological life evolved and mirroring those same characteristics in our search for more intelligent artificial networks.

acknowledgments

I would like to thank the open source community and, especially, the following projects:

- Distribution Evolutionary Algorithms in Python (DEAP)—https://github.com/DEAP/deap
- Gene Expression Programming Framework in Python (GEPPY)—https://github.com/ShuhuaGao/geppy
- NeuroEvolution of Augmenting Topologies in Python (NEAT Python)—https://github.com/CodeReclaimers/neat-python
- OpenAI Gym—https://github.com/openai/gym
- Keras/TensorFlow—https://github.com/tensorflow/tensorflow
- PyTorch—https://github.com/pytorch/pytorch

Without the work and time others have tirelessly spent developing and maintaining these repositories, books like this wouldn't be possible. These are also all excellent resources for anyone interested in improving their skills in EA or DL.

Thanks especially to my family for their ongoing support of my writing, teaching, and speaking endeavors. They are always available to read a passage or section and give me an opinion, be it good or bad.

A huge thanks must go to both the editorial and the production teams at Manning who helped create this book.

Thanks to all the reviewers: Al Krinker, Alexey Vyskubov, Bhagvan Kommadi, David Paccoud, Dinesh Ghanta, Domingo Salazar, Howard Bandy, Edmund Ronald, Erik Sapper, Guillaume Alleon, Jasmine Alkin, Jesús Antonino Juárez Guerrero, John Williams,

Jose San Leandro, Juan J. Durillo, kali kaneko, Maria Ana, Maxim Volgin, Nick Decroos, Ninoslav Čerkez, Oliver Korten, Or Golan, Raj Kumar, Ricardo Di Pasquale, Riccardo Marotti, Sergio Govoni, Sadhana G, Simone Sguazza, Shivakumar Swaminathan, Szymon Harabasz, and Thomas Heiman. Your suggestions helped make this a better book.

Finally, I would also like to thank Charles Darwin for his inspiration and courage to write his seminal work, *On the Origin of Species*. Being a very religious man, Charles wrestled internally for two decades, fighting between his beliefs and observation before deciding to publish his book. In the end, he demonstrated his courage and trust in science and pushed beyond his beliefs and the mainstream thought of the time. This is something I took inspiration from when writing a book that combines evolution and deep learning.

about this book

This book introduces readers to evolutionary and genetic algorithms, from tackling interesting machine learning problems to pairing the concepts with deep learning. The book starts by introducing simulation and the concepts of evolution and genetic algorithms in Python. As it progresses, the focus shifts toward demonstrating value, with applications for deep learning.

Who should read this book

You should have a strong background in Python and understand core machine learning and data science concepts. A background in deep learning will be essential for understanding concepts in later chapters.

How this book is organized: A road map

This book is organized into three sections: Getting started, Optimizing deep learning, and Advanced applications. In the first section, Getting started, we begin by covering the basics of simulation, evolution, and genetic and other algorithms. From there, we move on to demonstrating various applications of evolution and the genetic search within deep learning. Then, we finish the book by looking at advanced applications in generative modeling, reinforcement learning, and generalized intelligence. The following is a summary of each chapter:

- Part 1: Getting started
  - *Chapter 1: Introducing evolutionary deep learning*—This chapter introduces the concept of pairing evolutionary algorithms with deep learning.

- *Chapter 2: Introducing evolutionary computation*—This chapter provides a basic introduction to computational simulation and how evolution can be enlisted.
- *Chapter 3: Introducing genetic algorithms with DEAP*—This chapter introduces the concepts of genetic algorithms and using the framework DEAP.
- *Chapter 4: More evolutionary computation with DEAP*—This chapter looks at interesting applications of genetic and evolutionary algorithms, from the traveling salesman problem to generating images of the Mona Lisa.
- Part 2: Optimizing deep learning
  - *Chapter 5: Automating hyperparameter optimization*—This chapter demonstrates several methods for optimizing hyperparameters in deep learning systems with genetic or evolutionary algorithms.
  - *Chapter 6: Neuroevolution optimization*—In this chapter, we look at network architecture optimization of deep learning systems using neuroevolution.
  - *Chapter 7: Evolutionary convolutional neural networks*—This chapter looks at an advanced application of optimizing convolutional neural networks architectures using evolution.
- Part 3: Advanced applications
  - *Chapter 8: Evolving autoencoders*—This chapter introduces or reviews the basics of generative modeling with autoencoders. Then, it demonstrates how evolution can develop evolving autoencoders.
  - *Chapter 9: Generative deep learning and evolution*—This chapter continues where the previous one left off by introducing or reviewing the generative adversarial network and how it can be optimized with evolution.
  - *Chapter 10: NEAT: NeuroEvolution of Augmenting Topologies*—This chapter introduces NEAT and covers how it can be applied to various baseline applications.
  - *Chapter 11: Evolutionary learning with NEAT*—This chapter discusses the basics of reinforcement and deep reinforcement learning and then showcases using NEAT to solve some difficult problems on the OpenAI Gym.
  - *Chapter 12: Evolutionary machine learning and beyond*—This final chapter looks at the future of evolution in machine learning and how it may provide insights into generalized AI.

While this book is intended to be read from cover to cover, not all readers may have the time, background, or interest to benefit from all the material. The following is a quick guide that may help you pick which sections or chapters you want to focus on:

- *Part 1: Getting started*—Be sure to read this entire section if you are new to simulation and evolutionary or genetic computation. This section can also be a useful review and demonstrates several entertaining applications.
- *Part 2: Optimizing deep learning*—Read this section or specific chapters therein if you have a real need to optimize deep learning systems for neuroevolution or hyperparameter tuning.

- *Part 3: Advanced applications*—The chapters in this section are broken up into three subsections: evolutionary generative modeling (chapters 8 and 9), NEAT (chapters 10 and 11), and instinctual learning (chapter 12). Each of these subsections can be tackled independently.

About the code

All the code for this book has been written with Google Colab notebooks and can be found in the author's GitHub repository: https://github.com/cxbxmxcx/Evolution aryDeepLearning. To run the code, you just need to navigate to the GitHub repository in your browser and find the relevant code sample. All code samples have been identified with a prefix for the chapter number and then an example number—for example, EDL_2_2_Simulating_Life.ipynb. From there, just click the Google Colab badge to launch the notebook in Colab. Any dependencies will either be preinstalled on Colab or installed as part of the notebook.

This book contains many examples of source code both in numbered listings and in line with normal text. In both cases, source code is formatted in a `fixed-width font like this` to separate it from ordinary text. Sometimes code is also **in bold** to highlight code that has changed from previous steps in the chapter, such as when a new feature adds to an existing line of code.

In many cases, the original source code has been reformatted; we've added line breaks and reworked indentation to accommodate the available page space in the book. In rare cases, even this was not enough, and listings include line-continuation markers (➥). Additionally, comments in the source code have often been removed from the listings when the code is described in the text. Code annotations accompany many of the listings, highlighting important concepts.

You can get executable snippets of code from the liveBook (online) version of this book at https://livebook.manning.com/book/evolutionary-deep-learning. The complete code for the examples in the book is available for download from the Manning website at https://www.manning.com/books/evolutionary-deep-learning, and from GitHub at https://github.com/cxbxmxcx/EvolutionaryDeepLearning.

liveBook discussion forum

Purchase of *Evolutionary Deep Learning* includes free access to liveBook, Manning's online reading platform. Using liveBook's exclusive discussion features, you can attach comments to the book globally or to specific sections or paragraphs. It's a snap to make notes for yourself, ask and answer technical questions, and receive help from the author and other users. To access the forum, go to https://livebook.manning.com/book/evolutionary-deep-learning/discussion. You can also learn more about Manning's forums and the rules of conduct at https://livebook.manning.com/discussion.

Manning's commitment to our readers is to provide a venue where a meaningful dialogue between individual readers and between readers and the author can take place. It is not a commitment to any specific amount of participation on the part of the author, whose contribution to the forum remains voluntary (and unpaid). We suggest you try asking the author some challenging questions lest his interest stray! The forum and the archives of previous discussions will be accessible from the publisher's website as long as the book is in print.

about the author

MICHEAL LANHAM is a proven software and tech innovator with 25 years of experience. During that time, he has developed a broad range of software applications in areas including games, graphics, web, desktop, engineering, artificial intelligence, GIS, and machine learning applications for a variety of industries as an R&D developer. At the turn of the millennium, Micheal began working with neural networks and evolutionary algorithms in game development. He has used those skills and experiences working as a GIS and big data/enterprise architect to enhance and gamify a variety of engineering and business applications. Since late 2016, Micheal has been an avid author and presenter, giving his knowledge back to the community. Currently, he has completed numerous books on augmented reality, sound design, machine learning, and artificial intelligence. He is known for many areas in AI and software development but currently specializes in generative modeling, reinforcement learning, and machine learning operations. Micheal resides with his family in Calgary, Canada and is currently writing, teaching, and speaking about AI, machine learning operations, and engineering software development.

about the cover illustration

The figure on the cover of *Evolutionary Deep Learning* is "Homme Kourilien," or "Kuril Island Man," taken from a collection by Jacques Grasset de Saint-Sauveur, published in 1788. Each illustration is finely drawn and colored by hand.

In those days, it was easy to identify where people lived and what their trade or station in life was just by their dress. Manning celebrates the inventiveness and initiative of the computer business with book covers based on the rich diversity of regional culture centuries ago, brought back to life by pictures from collections such as this one.

Part 1

Getting started

Evolutionary and genetic algorithms have been around for several decades. Computationally, evolutionary methods for machine learning are not nearly as powerful as deep learning. However, evolutionary methods can provide us with unique tools to assist in a wide variety of optimization patterns, from hyperparameter tuning to network architectures. But before we discuss these patterns, we need to introduce evolutionary and genetic algorithms.

In chapter 1, we introduce the concept of using evolutionary methods for optimizing deep learning systems. Since the deep learning optimization methods we cover in this book fall under automated machine learning, we also introduce AutoML with evolution.

Chapter 2 then introduces life simulation from Conway's Game of Life, using a simple scenario that is later evolved with genetic algorithms. From there, chapter 3 introduces genetic algorithms in various forms, using distributed genetic algorithms in Python (DEAP). Finally, in chapter 4, we round out the section of chapters by introducing other diverse forms of evolutionary methods.

Introducing evolutionary deep learning 1

This chapter covers

- What evolutionary computation is and how it can be integrated into deep learning systems
- Applications of evolutionary deep learning
- Establishing patterns for optimizing deep learning networks
- The role automated machine learning plays in optimizing networks
- Applications of evolutionary computational methods to enhance deep learning development

Deep learning (DL) has become the ubiquitous technology most associated with artificial intelligence (AI) and the explosion of machine learning (ML). It has grown from being considered a pseudoscience (see *The Deep Learning Revolution* by Terrence J. Sejnowski, 2018, MIT Press) to being used in mainstream applications for everything from diagnosing breast cancer to driving cars. While many consider it a technology of the future, others take a more pragmatic and practical approach to its growing complexity and thirst for data.

As DL becomes more complex, we force-feed it more and more data, in the hopes of having some grand epiphany in a particular domain. Unfortunately, this is rarely the case, and all too frequently, we are left with bad models, poor results, and angry bosses. This is a problem that will continue to persist until we develop efficient processes for our DL systems.

The process of building effective and robust DL systems mirrors—or should mirror—that of any other ML or data science (DS) project. While some phases may vary in required resources and complexity, all steps will remain the same. What is often lacking in the relatively new DL world is a tool belt that can help automate some of those processes.

Enter *evolutionary deep learning* (EDL). EDL is such a tool belt or set of patterns and practices that can help automate the development of a DL system. The term *EDL* used in this book encompasses a broad spectrum of evolutionary computational methods and patterns applied to various aspects of DL systems across the ML process.

1.1   *What is evolutionary deep learning?*

Evolutionary deep learning, a term first described in this book, is a general categorization and grouping of a set of techniques that combine evolutionary methods with DL. These methods can be used to optimize a DL system, from the collection of data to validation. EDL is not new; tools for combining evolutionary methods with DL have gone by many names, including Deep Neural Evolution, Evolutionary Neural AutoML, Neuroevolution, Evolutionary AI, and others.

EDL is the merger of two unique subfields of AI: evolutionary computation (EC) and the application of DL to automate and improve models. EC itself is a family of methods by which biological or natural processes are simulated to solve complex problems. That, in turn, can be applied on top of DL to automate and optimize solutions but has the potential to uncover new strategies and architectures.

The broad category of methods we will encompass under EDL is by no means new, having been around for over 20 years. While much of that research has shown to be successful in auto-tuning DL models, it has received secondary attention behind the AI hype of more cutting-edge, handcrafted examples. In many papers, the authors discuss the extensive time taken to data or feature engineer and hyperparameter tune an innovative model.

However, for many now embracing DL, the challenge of building robust, high-performance models is daunting and riddled with challenges. Many of these challenges require advanced and sophisticated knowledge of all the options and quirks of one's chosen DL framework to understand when the model may just be incorrectly fitting. EDL as an automated machine learning (AutoML) solution is presented here to address most of the problems practitioners—experienced or novice—will face.

EDL's purpose is to provide a better mechanism and tool set for providing optimizations and AutoML for building DL solutions. Evolutionary methods are an excellent and relatively easy mechanism to provide a broad set of optimization tools that can be applied to DL. While there is potential that evolutionary techniques could automate the construction of more advanced AI, that is not the current intent of EDL or this book.

Instead, we focus on building better-optimized networks using evolutionary techniques. Before we do that though, we cover the operations and discuss the use of EC and evolutionary algorithms (EAs) to get aquatinted with the basic concepts in significant depth, starting with a brief introduction to evolution and evolutionary processes in the next section.

1.1.1 Introducing evolutionary computation

Evolutionary computation is a subfield of AI that uses biological and naturally inspired processes to solve complex problems. The word *evolution* is used to describe this family of algorithms, since many use the theory of natural selection as a base.

The theory of natural selection, developed by Charles Darwin in his book *On the Origin of Species* (1859, John Murray), defined the evolutionary process of life on Earth. It describes how the strongest and fittest of life will continue to grow, while the weak or ill-equipped will die and become extinct. He developed this theory from his experience as a naturalist aboard the *HMS Beagle* as it circumvented South America circa 1837. Darwin, being deeply religious, would wrestle with his findings for another 22 years before publishing the famous work.

Based on Darwin's theory, a cornerstone of EC is the concept of simulating an individual or population of individuals in a system to find the best. The purpose is to derive or evolve an individual who can survive and thrive in such an artificial environment by allowing them to change. This mechanism of an individual's change will vary by EC method, but in all cases, we require a mechanism that quantifies how well an individual is surviving.

The term we use to quantify how well an individual may survive or thrive is called *fitness*. This is a universal term used across EC that defines how well an individual can survive or perform in an environment. Fitness can be measured in a multitude of ways, but in all cases, it is the grand determiner of how efficient an individual or population of individuals is at solving a problem.

The concepts of natural selection and fitness have been used as the cornerstones of several computational methods developed to replicate the biological process of reproduction, either loosely or in great depth. Some of these methods even simulate the genetic mitosis in cells that takes place during the division of chromosomes and sharing of DNA. The following list is a summary of current notable EC algorithms:

- *Artificial life*—Going back as far as Conway's Game of Life and the Von Neumann cellular automaton, these processes simulate the artificial process of life itself, using agents. In this algorithm, agents often move, flow, live, or die based on their proximity to other agents or environments. While agent simulation is often done to mimic the real world, it can also be used to optimize processes.
- *Differential evolution*—A process in which search is optimized by combining differential calculus with evolutionary algorithms. This technique will often be

layered in with another EC method, like artificial life. In this algorithm, agents evolve or change by taking the vector differences and reapplying them to the population.

- *Evolutionary algorithms*—A broader category of EC methods that apply evolution, in the form of natural selection, to a problem. These methods often focus on simulating a population of individuals.

- *Evolutionary programming*—A specialized form of evolutionary algorithms that create algorithms using code. In this algorithm, an individual is represented by a block of code, and its respective fitness is measured to some optimal value generated by running the code. There are several ways of implementing code generation for EP, and in many cases, we will defer to more specific methods, like gene expression.

- *Genetic algorithm*—This algorithm uses the low-level cellular mitosis we see in organisms that allows for the passing of genetic traits to offspring. A genetic algorithm (GA) is the simulation of this process by encoding an individual's characteristics into a gene sequence, where this arbitrary gene sequence, which could be as simple as a sequence of 0s or 1s, evaluates to some fitness metric. That fitness is used to simulate the biological selection process and mating of parent individuals to produce new combined offspring.

- *Genetic programming*—This algorithm builds programming code using GA. In GA, an individual's traits are more generic, but in genetic programming (GP), a trait or gene could represent any number of functions or other code logic. GP is a specialized technique that allows new algorithmic code to be developed. Examples of this have been used to write agent simulation code that could solve a maze or create pictures.

- *Gene expression programming*—This algorithm is a further extension of genetic programming that develops code or mathematical functions. With GP, code is abstracted to high-level functions, whereas in gene expression programming (GEP), the purpose is to develop specific mathematical equations. A key difference between GEP and GP is the use of expression trees to represent functions. While in GP, expression trees represent code, in GEP expressions, they represent a mathematical expression tree. The benefit is that the code will follow a well-defined order of operations based on placement.

- *Particle swarm optimization*—This falls under a subset of artificial life and is the simulation of artificial and somewhat-smart particles. In this algorithm, each particle's fitness is evaluated, and the best particle becomes the focus for the remaining particles to swarm around.

- *Swarm intelligence*—This algorithm is a search method that simulates the behavior of swarm insects or birds to find peak values for optimization problems. It is very similar to particle swarm optimization (PSO) but varies in implementation, depending on the evaluation of fitness.

Figure 1.1 shows a hierarchy of EC methods used throughout this book for the application of EDL. Several other methods of EC could be used to improve DL models, but as an introduction, we will cover the basic methods in the figure, focusing on the areas of life and genetic simulation.

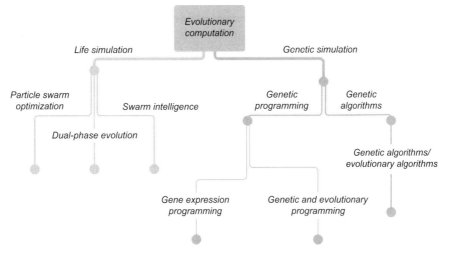

Figure 1.1   Subset of EC used to apply EDL

Life simulation is a specific subset of EC that takes an approach to simulate observed natural processes we see in nature, such as the way particles or birds swarm. Genetic simulation, on the other hand, mimics the process of cellular mitosis we observe in biological life. More specifically, it simulates the genetic transference of genes and chromosomes through an organism's evolution.

1.2   *The why and where of evolutionary deep learning*

Evolutionary deep learning is as much a concept as a set of tools and techniques for DL optimization. Conceptually, EDL is the pattern and practice of employing EC for the optimization of DL networks. Yet it also presents a set of tools that can be layered on top of DL—or even act as a replacement for DL.

Why and where you would use EDL depends on not only your level of expertise in DL but also your need to push the limits. That doesn't mean novices of DL could not benefit from using EDL. Indeed, this book explores many nuances of neural networks that are exposed with EDL and can be of benefit to any practitioner.

The answer to where EDL can be used is simple: anywhere. It can be used for basic hyperparameter optimization, neural weight search for discontinuous solutions, balancing adversarial networks in generative adversarial networks, and even replacing deep reinforcement learning. You really can apply the techniques presented in this book to any DL system.

Answering the *why* of EDL comes down to necessity. Evolutionary methods provide an option for further optimization or enhanced solution to any DL system. Yet EDL is computationally intensive and may not be appropriate for simpler systems. However, for complex or novel problems, evolution presents a new bag of tricks to any DL practitioner.

1.3 *The need for deep learning optimization*

DL is a powerful, yet somewhat new and oft-misunderstood, technology that provides a plethora of benefits as well as downsides. One such downside is the requirement to understand and optimize a model. This is a process that may require hours of data annotation or model hyperparameter tuning.

In almost all cases, we can never use a model directly out of the box, and we often need to optimize various aspects of the DL system, from tuning the learning rate to choosing the activation function. Optimizing a network model often becomes the primary exercise, and if done manually, this can take some substantial effort.

Optimizing a DL network can encompass a wide variety of factors. Aside from the usual hyperparameter tuning, we also need to look at the network architecture itself.

1.3.1 *Optimizing the network architecture*

As a network becomes more sophisticated with the addition of layers or various node types, it directly affects how the loss/error is backpropagated through it. Figure 1.2 demonstrates the most common problems encountered when growing more complex and larger DL systems.

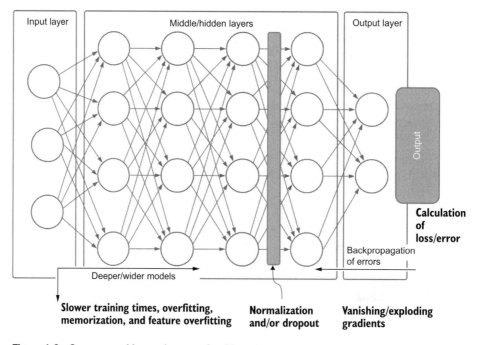

Figure 1.2   Common problems when growing DL systems

In larger networks, the amount of loss needs to be divided into smaller and smaller components that eventually approach zero. When these loss components or gradients approach zero, we call it a *vanishing gradient* problem, which is often associated with deep networks. Conversely, components may also get exceptionally large by passing through successive layers that magnify those input signals. This results in gradient components getting large, or what are called *exploding gradients*.

Both gradient problems can be resolved using various techniques, like normalizing input data and, again, through the layers. Special types of layer functions called *normalization* and *dropout* are shown in figure 1.2. These techniques add to the computational complexity and requirements for the network and may also overtly smooth over important and characteristic features in data. Thus, larger and more diverse training datasets are required to develop good network performance.

Normalization may solve the vanishing and exploding gradient problems of deep networks, but as models grow, these manifest other concerns. As they grow, models' ability to digest larger sets of input and images, for example, increases. However, this may cause a side effect known as *network memorization*, which can occur if the input training set is too small. This occurs because the network is so large that it may start to memorize sets of input chunks or even whole images or sets of text.

The cutting-edge DL models you may have heard about, like the GPT-3, a natural language processor from OpenAI, suffer in part from memorization. This problem comes up even after billions of documents representing multiple forms of text have been fed into such models. Even with such diverse and massive training sets, models like GPT-3 have been shown to replay whole paragraphs of remembered text. This "problem" may be an effective feature for a database that doesn't fit well into a DL model.

There have been workarounds developed for the memorization problem called *dropout*, a process by which a certain percentage of the nodes within network layers may be deactivated through each training pass. As a result of turning nodes off and on within each pass, a more general network is created. This, however, is at the cost of requiring the network to now be 100% to 200% larger.

On top of these problems, the addition of more layers to deeper networks adds more weights—weights that need to be individually trained over billions and trillions of iterations. Exponential growth in computational power is required to train such models, and many of the top, cutting-edge models are now only developed within organizations that can afford this high cost.

Many see the trend of wider and deeper networks soon reaching a plateau for most DL practitioners, leaving any future cutting-edge development to the AI giants, like Google DeepMind. The simple solution is to, therefore, look at alternative approaches that can streamline the development of such large networks. This is where we come back to applying EC to DL to optimize the network architecture, weights, or both.

Fortunately, EDL provides several potential methods, in that it can automatically optimize the size and form of a network for a variety of problems we will look at in this book. Automatic optimization is a cornerstone of EDL and will be a focus of many exercises demonstrating these techniques in this book.

Since evolutionary algorithms provide for several optimization patterns that can solve a multitude of problems, EDL can work across various aspects of the ML development process. These include tuning model hyperparameters to data or feature engineering, model validation, model selection, and architecture.

1.4   *Automating optimization with automated machine learning*

EDL provides a set of tools to help automate the optimization of DL systems for more robust models. As such, it should be considered an AutoML tool. Many commercial AutoML platforms, such as Google AutoML, use various evolutionary methods to develop models.

Before we continue, we also need to discuss the branding or misnaming of the terms *automated machine learning* and *AutoML*. In this book, we will interchange between using *AML* and *AutoML*; they are often considered the same, and for our purposes, they are. However, AML and AutoML may be considered different in that the former is often used to describe a black box system that produces optimized models.

Automating the optimization and development of any AI/ML model is considered the next step in the development process for any research and development project. It is the evolution of moving beyond research and development and formalizing the model-building process, which allows practitioners to take models into full-scale commercialization and productization.

1.4.1   *What is automated machine learning?*

Automated machine learning, or AutoML, is a tool or set of tools used to automate and enhance the building of AI/ML. It is not a specific technology but a collection of methods and strategies in which evolutionary algorithms or evolutionary optimization methods would be considered a subset. It is a tool that can be used throughout the AI/ML workflow, as depicted in figure 1.3.

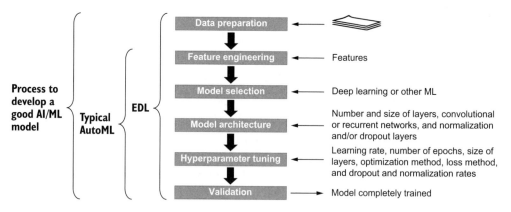

Figure 1.3   Steps for developing a good AI/ML model with AutoML and/or EDL

AutoML tools

The following is a list of tools and platforms that provide AutoML:

- *DataRobot*—Seen as the first platform and starting point of AutoML, Data-Robot provides a diverse set of tools to auto-build models.
- *Google Cloud AutoML*—This popular and robust platform is from the current main player in AI. This platform handles a diverse set of data, from images to structured data.
- *Amazon SageMaker AutoPilot*—This powerful platform is good for automating development models dependent on structured data.
- *H2O AutoML*—This tool provides various functions to automate the machine learning workflow.
- *Azure Machine Learning*—This platform provides automated processes of tuning models on diverse forms of data.
- *AutoKeras*—This excellent tool provides automated development of network architecture.
- *AutoTorch*—This tool provides automatic architecture search.

Many other tools and platforms are available, beyond the scope of this list.

Figure 1.3 depicts the typical AI/ML workflow for building a good model to be used for confident inference of new data. This workflow is often undertaken manually by various practitioners of AI/ML, but there have been various attempts to automate all steps. The following is a summary of each of these steps in greater detail, including how they may be automated with AML:

- *Data preparation*—Preparing data for AI/ML training is time-consuming and expensive. In general, preparing data and automating this task can dramatically increase the performance of data workflows critical for fine-tuning complex models. AutoML online services often assume the user has already prepared and cleaned data, as required by most ML models. With evolutionary methods, there are several ways to automate the preparation of data, and while this task is not specific to EDL, we will cover it in later chapters.
- *Feature engineering*—This is the process of extracting relevant features in data using prior domain knowledge, with experts selecting relevant features based on their intuition and experience. Since domain experts are expensive and opinionated, automating this task reduces costs and improves standardization. Depending on the AutoML tool, feature engineering may be included in the process.
- *Model selection*—As AI/ML has advanced, hundreds of model types that can solve similar problems have been created. Often, data scientists will spend days or weeks just selecting a group of models to further evaluate. Automating this process speeds up model development and helps the data scientist affirm they are using the right model for the job. A good AutoML tool may choose from dozens or hundreds of models, including DL variations or model ensembles.

- *Model architecture*—Depending on the area of AI/ML and deep learning, defining the right model architecture is often critical. Getting this right in an automated way alleviates countless hours of tuning architecture and rerunning models. Depending on the implementation, some AutoML systems vary in model architecture, but this is typically limited to well-known variations.

- *Hyperparameter optimization*—The process of fine-tuning a model's hyperparameters can be time-consuming and prone to errors. To overcome these problems, many practitioners rely on intuition and previous experience. While this has been successful in the past, increasing model complexity now makes this task untenable. By automating HP tuning, we not only alleviate work from the builders, but we also uncover potential flaws in the model selection or architecture.

- *Validation selection*—There are many options for evaluating the performance of a model, from deciding on how much data to use for training and testing to visualizing the output performance of a model. Automating the validation of a model provides a robust means of recharacterizing model performance when data changes and makes a model more explainable long-term. For online AutoML services, this is a key strength that provides a compelling reason to employ such tools.

The typical AML/AutoML workflow only attempts to tackle the feature engineering step and beyond, where the process is often done iteratively, either over a single step or multiple steps combined. Some steps, like hyperparameter tuning, are specific to model type and, in the case of DL, could require significant time to optimize the model.

While this new wave of commercial AutoML service is successful in processing a wide variety of data types and forms, the produced models lack innovation and can be quite expensive. It takes a substantial amount of computing power to crunch through all the tasks AutoML needs to perform to build a tuned model, and the models developed are essentially reconstructions of previous-generation benchmarks and often lack any novel insight into optimization.

Those AI/ML practitioners wanting more innovative automated models on a budget often turn to developing their AutoML solutions, with EDL being a prime candidate. As we will see in later chapters of this book, evolutionary methods can provide a wide variety of solutions to auto-building and optimizing DL models, hyperparameters, feature engineering, and network architecture.

1.5   *Applications of evolutionary deep learning*

Now that we understand *why* we would need to combine EC and DL into an AutoML solution, we can move on to *how*. That is, how can we apply methods like GAs on top of DL to improve working AI solutions? There are likely countless possibilities that would allow for EC to be merged with DL, but in this book, we will stick to some basic practical strategies.

Understanding these strategies will allow you to alter existing DL networks or create new combined EC/DL models of your own. This will allow you to create cutting-edge optimized networks in a shorter amount of time and with fewer resources, providing you the ability to pick and choose strategies or even develop new ones as your experience progresses.

To accomplish such lofty goals, we will explore the fundamentals of both DL and a specific subset of EC from the ground up. We will build basic models to solve problems with both subfields, and then in later chapters, we will look at how we may combine them for improved performance and automation.

EC can be applied to DL in several forms to cover various automated strategies wrapped in AutoML. Figure 1.4 demonstrates the various subsets of EC or EDL that can be applied to DL and where they may be applied across the AI/ML model development workflow.

1.5.1 Model selection: Weight search

As previously mentioned, the selected base model and layer types will often be dictated by the type of problem being solved. In most cases, optimizing the model selection can be done quickly and manually. However, model selection is not just about selecting the type of layers; it can also include the form of optimization, starting weights, and loss used to train a model.

By optimizing the model layer types, optimization mechanism, and even forms of loss, a network can be made more robust to learn more efficiently. We will look at examples where initial mode weights, types of optimizations, and measures of loss are tuned to fit a variety of problems.

1.5.2 Model architecture: Architecture optimization

Many times, when building DL networks, we often oversize the model or number of nodes and layers in a model. Then over time, we will scale the network back, so it becomes more optimal for the problem. In many cases, having too large of a network can result in the memorization of input data, resulting in overfitting. Conversely, a network that is too small to learn the variety and amount of data will typically suffer from underfitting.

To resolve over- and underfitting problems, we can apply GA to automatically prune a network to its lowest form. This not only improves model performance and limits over- or undertraining, but it also decreases training times by decreasing the network size. This is a technique that works well when trying to optimize larger, deeper networks.

1.5.3 Hyperparameter tuning/optimization

Hyperparameter tuning is a process we undertake in AI and ML that requires the optimization of a model by tweaking the various control variables that define it. In DL, parameters are used to denote the weights of the model; we differentiate between them by calling the control variables *hyperparameters.*

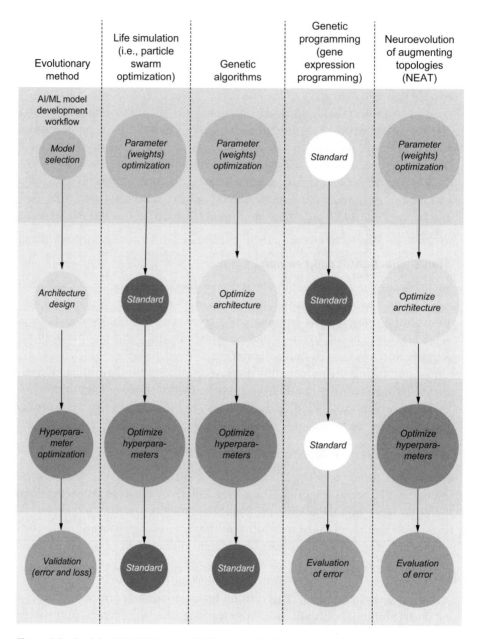

Figure 1.4   Applying EC (EDL) to the AI/ML model development workflow for DL

EC provides several alternative measures to add automatic HP optimization across a wide variety of models, including DL. Particle swarm optimization, differential evolution, and genetic algorithms have all been used with success. Each of these methods will be explored across a variety of frameworks to measure performance.

1.5.4 Validation and loss function optimization

When developing robust DL models, we often rely on several established patterns to generate quality networks. This may include validating a model's training and performance by reviewing training and test loss iteratively. We want to make sure both measures of loss don't diverge too far from one another.

In a typical supervised learning training scenario, we will often use established measures that align with label comparisons. With more advanced generative DL scenarios, opportunities to optimize the form of loss and even measures of validation become available.

Network architectures like autoencoders, embedding layers, and generative adversarial networks provide the opportunity to employ combinatory determinations of loss and model validation. Using EC, we can use methods to optimize these forms of networks in an AutoML manner.

1.5.5 Neuroevolution of augmenting topologies

Neuroevolution of augmenting topologies (NEAT) is a technique that combines hyperparameter and architecture optimization with weight search to automatically build new DL models that may also develop their method of loss and validation. While NEAT was developed almost 20 years ago, it wasn't until fairly recently that this technique has been applied to various applications of DL and deep reinforcement learning.

1.5.6 Goals

In this book, we look at the previously noted set of techniques and how they may be applied to DL. We focus on practical techniques that can be applied to a variety of problems using working solutions, paying particular attention to how various forms of AML/ AutoML may also be applied to optimizing DL systems and evaluating performance across techniques. Our focus also includes a broader range of techniques outside of evolutionary methods.

In the following chapters, we work through sections of the AutoML process that progressively introduce key concepts to someone familiar with DL. After covering the basics of EC, we move on to showcasing hyperparameter optimization and then data and feature engineering, model option selection, and model architecture. Finally, we progress to more complex examples that look to improve on generative DL and deep reinforcement learning problems.

By the end of this book, you should feel comfortable describing and using both DL and certain subsets of EC alone or in combination to optimize networks. You will be able to build models to solve problems using both subfields as well as understand which works better for specific classes of problems, including the ability to apply EC on top of DL models for various optimizations and applications of AutoML.

Summary

- DL is a powerful technology capable of solving many AI and ML tasks, but it is complex; requires significant amounts of data; and is expensive to develop, train, and optimize.

- EC is a subfield of AI and ML that is defined by the theory of natural selection. It has not matured as quickly as DL but still provides techniques for solving a wide variety of complex problems.

- EDL is a broad term encompassing the combination of evolutionary methods with DL. Neuroevolution, evolutionary hyperparameter optimization, and neuro-evolution of augmenting topologies are examples of EDL. EDL defines a subset of EC methods that may be used to automate and improve the development of DL models across many stages of the ML workflow.

- AML and AutoML define a set of tools and techniques that look to automate the entire AI and ML model development workflow. Many forms of evolutionary computation have been and can be used to automate the model development workflow. Google and other companies have invested significantly into developing AutoML to assist consumers in building robust models for their own needs. While these services are powerful, they often work like a black box and limit more agile customization of new cutting-edge models.

Introducing evolutionary computation

2

This chapter covers

- Exploring the Game of Life with Google Colaboratory
- Creating a simple cellular life simulation in Python
- Optimizing cell attributes by simulating life
- Applying the theory of evolution to a simulation
- Applying genetics and genetic algorithms to simulation optimization

In the last chapter, we introduced the concept of applying evolutionary computation on top of or as an optimization of DL. As a general all-encompassing term, we refer to this process as *evolutionary deep learning* (EDL). Before we start exploring the applications of EDL, we first need to understand what evolutionary computation or algorithms are.

Evolutionary computation is, likewise, a blanket term for a whole host of methods that borrow from life simulation in many forms, with evolution being just one of them. In this chapter, we present a gradual introduction to life simulation, what it is, what it does, and how it can optimize problems.

Life simulation is just one form of simulation we can use to explore and optimize problems. There are plenty of other forms of simulation that allow us to better model processes, from fires to financial markets and more. However, they do all have one thing in common: they find their origins in the computer version of Conway's Game of Life.

2.1 Conway's Game of Life on Google Colaboratory

The Game of Life is a simple cellular automation developed in 1970 by John Horton Conway; this "game" is attributed as the birth of the computer simulation. While the rules of the simulation are simple, the patterns and manifestations it can produce are an incredible testament to its eloquence.

This next exercise also helps us introduce Google Colaboratory, or Colab, as it is widely known. Colab is an excellent platform for performing all forms of ML, from evolutionary computation to DL. It is based on Jupyter Notebook, so it should be familiar to most Python developers with a notebook background. Furthermore, it is free and provides both CPU and GPU resources we use heavily later.

Begin the exercise by loading up the EDL_2_1_Conways_Game_of_Life.ipynb exercise in your browser. Please refer to the appendix for details on how to load the code from the GitHub repository to Colab.

After you open the notebook in Colab, you will see several text and code cells. Don't worry about any of the code in this exercise—just the steps on how to use Colab to execute the notebook and explore the results.

Next, select the first code cell in the notebook and click the Run Cell button in the top left or type Ctrl-Enter or Cmd-Enter to run the cell. This runs the code and sets up the `show_video` function to be used later. We employ this function to demonstrate a real-time visual output of the simulation.

> **Google Colaboratory: Colab and real-time output**
>
> Colab is an excellent platform and an incredible educational tool for quickly showcasing code to students. While it can be used to explore code quickly for various tasks, one downfall of Colab is that it doesn't provide a real-time graphic rendering output. To work around this, we use several tricks and techniques in this book to visualize real-time simulation graphic output.

Move down to the next cell, which implements the simple rules of life. Again, we don't explore the code here, but figure 2.1 pictorially explains the rules for Conway's Game of Life. Run the cell by pressing the Run button or using the keyboard shortcut.

> **The rules for Conway's Game of Life**
>
> The elegance of the Game of Life comes down to the simplicity of the rules used to mimic cellular simulation. Four simple rules were used to mimic or simulate the life of cells:

(continued)
- Any live cell with fewer than two live neighbors dies, as if by underpopulation.
- Any live cell with two or three live neighbors lives on to the next generation.
- Any live cell with more than three live neighbors dies, as if by overpopulation.
- Any dead cell with exactly three live neighbors becomes a live cell, as if by reproduction.

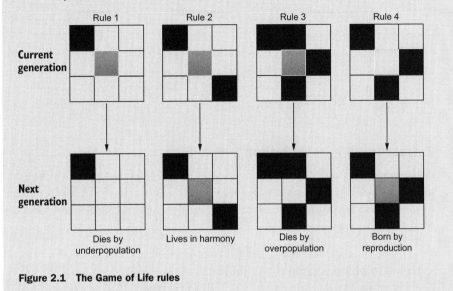

Figure 2.1 The Game of Life rules

Run the next cell, and observe the output, as shown in figure 2.2. For this simple life simulation, the starting cellular pattern is simple. There are a wide variety of other starting positions that can result in some fantastic animations and constructions.

Since we aren't interested in exploring the rest of the code, we can simply run the entire notebook using Runtime > Run All from the menu or typing Ctrl-F9, Cmd-F9. The second last cell that performs the simulation takes a couple of minutes to run, but as it does so, a progress bar is displayed. When the simulation is complete, the first function we set up, show_video, is used to show a short video clip in the output.

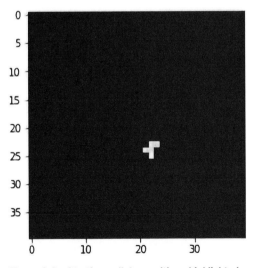

Figure 2.2 Starting cellular positions highlighted

Play the video after the process is complete, and watch how the cellular simulation runs. An excerpt from the video is shown in figure 2.3, which highlights how expansive the cellular network can grow to be.

The simplicity and elegance of the Game of Life showcased the power of computer simulation and birthed many disciplines. It showcased how simple rules could be used to mimic life but also generate new and unforeseen solutions, given some very basic rules and inputs.

Figure 2.3 Watching the simulation video

While the path life simulation has taken since looks significantly different now, we often try to adhere to the simple principle Conway extolled in this first simulation: derive a simple set of rules that simulate a greater process with the goal of uncovering some unforeseen pattern or solution. This goal helps orient us while learning about methods of EC in this and future chapters.

2.2 Simulating life with Python

Before we get into deriving more complex forms of life simulation using evolution or other methods, it is helpful to look at a simple contrived implementation. We continue looking at simulating cellular life, but this time, we only consider the attributes of a cell, ignoring the physical conditions.

Geospatial life and agent simulation

Simulations that use space or spatial representations, like the Game of Life, are still used to do all manner of modeling and predications, from traffic to a viral spread like COVID-19. These forms of simulation can be fun to explore and run but won't be our focus in EDL. Instead, our spatial focus is more mathematically driven, meaning we look more at analyzing vector or graph distances than physical space.

In the next exercise, we jump into Python code on Colab that demonstrates a simple cellular life simulation. Keep in mind this is a contrived example that is only meant to demonstrate some basic concepts and, in some ways, what not to do. As we move through the chapter, the sample evolves into a full evolutionary method.

Open notebook EDL_2_2_Simulating_Life.ipynb in your browser. Refer to the appendix if you need assistance.

As a rule, the first couple of cells in a notebook install or set up any additional dependencies and perform the general imports. Run the cell to perform the imports, as shown in the following listing.

Listing 2.1 EDL_2_2_Simulating_Life.ipynb: Using `import`

```
import random   ◁──── Used for creating random numbers
import time     ◁───┐
                    │ Used for tracking time and waiting
```

```
import matplotlib.pyplot as plt          ◁——— Used for displaying plots
from IPython.display import clear_output ◁———
                                              │ Used for clearing the notebook cell output
```

Move down to the next notebook cell. This block of code sets up a function to create a new cell as well as generate a list or set of cells based on the number of offspring desired. Run this cell, and you will see an example of the cells generated as a list of dictionaries, as shown in the following listing.

Listing 2.2   EDL_2_2_Simulating_Life.ipynb: Using `create_cell` and `birth`

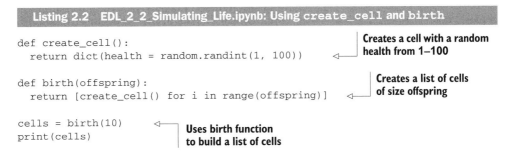

```
def create_cell():
  return dict(health = random.randint(1, 100))   ◁——┐ Creates a cell with a random
                                                      │ health from 1–100

def birth(offspring):
  return [create_cell() for i in range(offspring)]  ◁——┐ Creates a list of cells
                                                         │ of size offspring

cells = birth(10)      ◁———┐ Uses birth function
print(cells)               │ to build a list of cells
```

The following listing defines the reproduction and death code/rules. Unlike the Game of Life, this example uses a predefined parameter, called RPRD_RATE, to define the likelihood of new cells being created. Likewise, the code also checks for cell death based on a random evaluation.

Listing 2.3   EDL_2_2_Simulating_Life.ipynb: Reproduction and death

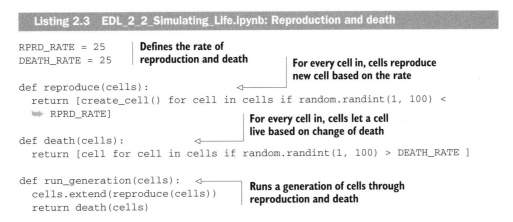

```
RPRD_RATE = 25    │ Defines the rate of
DEATH_RATE = 25   │ reproduction and death
                                        ┌ For every cell in, cells reproduce
                                        │ new cell based on the rate
def reproduce(cells):          ◁————————┘
  return [create_cell() for cell in cells if random.randint(1, 100) <
  ➡ RPRD_RATE]
                                ┌ For every cell in, cells let a cell
                                │ live based on change of death
def death(cells):              ◁┘
  return [cell for cell in cells if random.randint(1, 100) > DEATH_RATE ]

def run_generation(cells):   ◁———┐
  cells.extend(reproduce(cells))  │ Runs a generation of cells through
  return death(cells)             │ reproduction and death
```

Run the last code cell to create the reproduction and death functions; this sets up the base life simulation functions. At this stage, there won't be any output, since we are just setting up the functions.

Next, jump to the last cell. This cell performs the simulation, and our only goal now is to increase the cell `population`, as shown in the following listing.

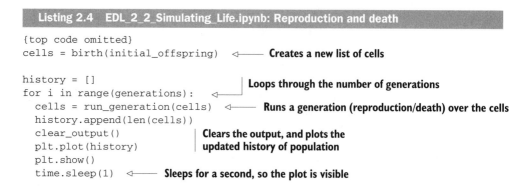

```
{top code omitted}
cells = birth(initial_offspring)     ◁——— Creates a new list of cells

history = []                                      | Loops through the number of generations
for i in range(generations):     ◁——┘
    cells = run_generation(cells)    ◁——— Runs a generation (reproduction/death) over the cells
    history.append(len(cells))
    clear_output()                     | Clears the output, and plots the
    plt.plot(history)                  | updated history of population
    plt.show()
    time.sleep(1)     ◁——— Sleeps for a second, so the plot is visible
```

Run this cell, and watch the simulation run. If the reproduction and death rates are set correctly, the population should show an increase. You can modify the parameters that drive the simulation using the Colab form sliders, as shown in figure 2.4. You can go back and alter the parameters and then run the last notebook cell again to see updated simulation results.

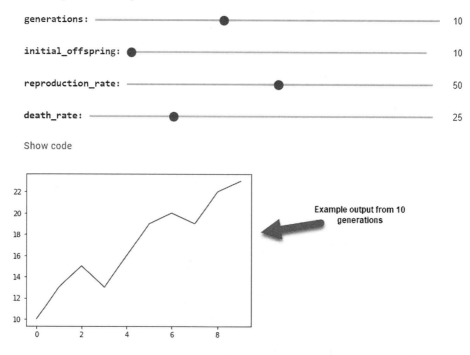

Figure 2.4   Running the simulation and changing parameters in Colab

The goal of this exercise is simply to set up a simple cellular simulation and try to get the population to grow. We define rates to control both the reproduction and death of the cells. There is very little elegance in this simulation, but it is easy to understand and use. Use the learning exercises in the next section to understand this basic life simulation.

2.2.1   Learning exercises

At the end of each section, there is a set of exercises to help you review the various sections' code and concepts. Taking the time to work through these exercises significantly aids your understanding of future concepts:

1. Modify the number of `generations` and `initial_offspring` parameters to see what effect that has on the results.
2. Modify the birth and death rates to see what effect this has on the final `population`.
3. See if you can find a reproduction and death rate that produces a decline in `population` growth.

Now that we understand how we can easily simulate life, we move on to understanding why we would want to in specific applications.

2.3   Life simulation as optimization

In this scenario, we use our previous simple example and elevate it to perform optimization of an attribute defined on the cells. There are many reasons we may develop simulations for all forms of discovery of behavior, optimization, or enlightenment. For most applications of evolutionary algorithms, our end goal is to optimize a process, parameters, or a structure.

In this notebook, we extend the attributes in each cell from `health` to include a new parameter called `strength`. Our goal is to optimize the cell strength of our entire `population`. The `strength` parameter is representative of any trait in an organism that makes it successful in its environment. That means in our simple example, our goal is to maximize `strength` across the entire `population`.

Open the notebook example EDL_2_3_Simulating_Life.ipynb in your browser. Check the appendix if you require assistance.

We use a useful real-time plotting library called LiveLossPlot for several examples in this book. This library is intended for plotting training losses for ML and DL problems, so the default graphs present terminology we would use in a DL problem. Nonetheless, it works perfectly well for our needs. The following listing demonstrates installing the package and importing the `PlotLosses` class.

> **Listing 2.5   EDL_2_3_Simulating_Life.ipynb: Installing `PlotLosses`**

```
!pip install livelossplot –quiet    ⟵——  Installs the livelossplot package into Colab

from livelossplot import PlotLosses    ⟵——  Loads the PlotLosses class for later use
```

The bulk of the code in this example is shared from the previous, and as such, we just look at the differences here. Starting with the first cell, we can see a few changes in the functions that define the life simulation shown in the following listing. The biggest change is that we now use the new `strength` parameter to derive the cell's `health`.

Listing 2.6   EDL_2_3_Simulating_Life.ipynb: Life functions updated

```
def create_cell():
  return dict(
      health = random.randint(1, 100),          Adds the strength
      strength = random.randint(1, 100)   ◁───   parameter to the cell
  )

def birth(offspring):
  return [create_cell() for i in range(offspring)]

def evaluate(cells):   ◁─── The new evaluate function calculates cell health.
  for cell in cells:
    cell["health"] *= cell["strength"]/100   ◁─┐ Cell health becomes a
  return cells                                   function of strength.
```

Likewise, the reproduction and death functions have been modified to not pick random cells to reproduce or die. Instead, the new functions determine whether a cell reproduces or dies based on the health attribute. Notice the addition of two new parameters—RPRD_BOUNDS and DEATH_BOUNDS—in the following listing. These new parameters control at what health level a cell can reproduce or when it should die.

Listing 2.7   EDL_2_3_Simulating_Life.ipynb: The new reproduction and death functions

```
                                  Reproduction now compares health against RPRD_BOUNDS.
def reproduce(cells):   ◁─┘
  return [create_cell() for cell in cells if cell["health"] > RPRD_BOUNDS]

                          Death compares cell health above DEATH_BOUNDS.
def death(cells):   ◁─┘
  return [cell for cell in cells if cell["health"] > DEATH_BOUNDS]

                              Cell health becomes a function of strength.
def run_generation(cells):   ◁─┘
  cells = evaluate(cells)   ◁─┐
  cells.extend(reproduce(cells))   Adds a new evaluation function to
  return death(cells)              update cell health based on strength
```

For this simulation, we have adapted explicit rules for determining when a cell dies or reproduces based on cell health. Remember the goal of our simulation is to optimize the cell's `population strength` attribute.

Jump down to the last code cell; we have made some additional changes to generating output, but otherwise, the simulation code remains mostly the same. The new code in the following listing uses the `PlotLosses` class to output a real-time plot of the simulation as it runs.

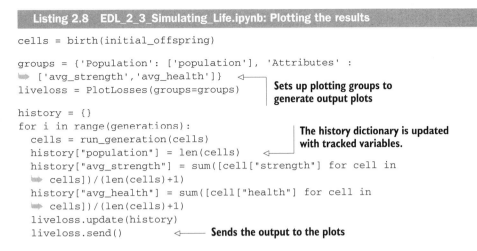

Listing 2.8   EDL_2_3_Simulating_Life.ipynb: Plotting the results

```
cells = birth(initial_offspring)

groups = {'Population': ['population'], 'Attributes' :
➡ ['avg_strength','avg_health']}
liveloss = PlotLosses(groups=groups)

history = {}
for i in range(generations):
  cells = run_generation(cells)
  history["population"] = len(cells)
  history["avg_strength"] = sum([cell["strength"] for cell in
➡ cells])/(len(cells)+1)
  history["avg_health"] = sum([cell["health"] for cell in
➡ cells])/(len(cells)+1)
  liveloss.update(history)
  liveloss.send()
```

Sets up plotting groups to generate output plots

The history dictionary is updated with tracked variables.

Sends the output to the plots

Go ahead and run the whole notebook using Run > Run All from the menu or Ctrl-F9, CMD-F9. Figure 2.5 shows the output of running the simulation for 25 `generations`. Notice in the Attributes plot on the left how the average strength and health are both trending upward.

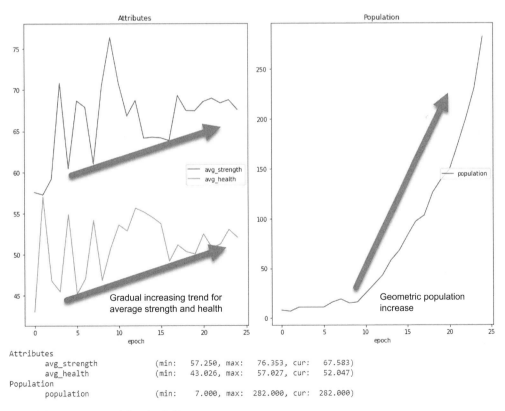

```
Attributes
        avg_strength            (min:   57.250, max:   76.353, cur:   67.583)
        avg_health              (min:   43.026, max:   57.027, cur:   52.047)
Population
        population              (min:    7.000, max:  282.000, cur:  282.000)
```

Figure 2.5   The output of the simulation run

By modifying our life simulation code, we were able to demonstrate the rough optimization of a single attribute: `strength`. While we can see a gradual increase in the `population`'s `strength` and `health` attributes, the results are not overwhelming. In fact, if our life sim was to replicate the real world, then it is likely we would have never evolved to be who we are.

The missing key to our life simulation is the ability of the cells to pass on their successful traits to offspring. Charles Darwin first observed that life passed on successful traits to its offspring in a process he termed *evolution*. As it turns out, this theory of evolution is a cornerstone to not only life on Earth but evolutionary computation.

2.3.1   Learning exercises

Use these quick exercises to help improve your understanding of the concepts:

1. Modify the death and birth rate parameters to see what effect this has on results.
2. Modify the `evaluate` function from listing 2.6 to alter the returned health parameter and then rerun the simulation and see what effect this has.
3. Alter the starting values of `health` and `strength` in the `create_cell` function from listing 2.6.

Simulation, as a form of optimization, is a diverse field, but our focus in the next section and the rest of the book is simulating evolution for optimization.

2.4   Adding evolution to the life simulation

Taking our life sim to the next level requires us to simulate evolution. While this may sound difficult, it is relatively simple to implement and elegant. In our next exercise, we borrow from many of the observations of Darwin and others to build our upgraded life sim.

2.4.1   Simulating evolution

Again, in this exercise we borrow much of the previous exercise code, modifying it to simulate evolution or the ability of the cells to pass on selective traits. This time, however, instead of using a single trait like strength, we are assigning three new traits, labeled a, b, and c. On top of that, we replace the `health` trait with a more generalized term called `fitness`.

Open notebook example EDL_2_4_Simulating_Evolution.ipynb in your browser. Consult the appendix if you need help doing this.

This code has several upgrades we inspect in detail, starting with the updated `create_cell` function. It is important to notice here that the function now takes two input cells or two cells to produce a single offspring. If there are no parents at the start of the sim, for instance, then random values are set for the traits. If there are parents, then the average of each trait becomes the child's new value, as shown in the following listing. Keep in mind that this averaging mechanism is just one possibility for creating the new child's trait values.

Listing 2.9   EDL_2_4_Simulating_Evolution.ipynb: Updating `create_cell`

```
def create_cell(parent1, parent2):        ◁──────  It now takes two parent
    if parent1 is None or parent2 is None:          cells to procreate.
        return dict(
            fitness = 0,
            a = random.randint(1, 100),    ◁──────  If there are no parents, traits are
            b = random.randint(1, 100),             initialized to random values.
            c = random.randint(1, 100)
        )
    else:
        return dict(
            fitness = 0,
            a = (parent1["a"] + parent2["a"])/2,
            b = (parent1[«b»] + parent2[«b»])/2,     The new trait value is the
            c = (parent1[«c»] + parent2[«c»])/2,     average of both parents.
        )
```

fitness
always
starts
at 0.

Next, we look at the updated `reproduce` function. A few things have changed here.
First, we sort the parent cells by `fitness` and then take the top half in a process
known as `selection`. Second, we loop over the remaining parents twice (two children
per parent) and randomly select two to mate. These two parents are then passed to
`create_cell` to bear a new child with shared traits from both parents. Lastly, the cells
are passed through a new `mutate` function before being returned. The form of reproduction `selection` we are using in the following listing is just one example; as we shall
see, there are many variations to this.

Listing 2.10   EDL_2_4_Simulating_Evolution.ipynb: Updating `reproduce`

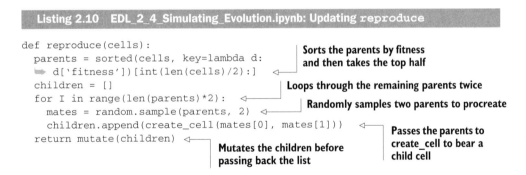

```
def reproduce(cells):
    parents = sorted(cells, key=lambda d:          Sorts the parents by fitness
      ⇨ d['fitness'])[int(len(cells)/2):]          and then takes the top half
    children = []                          ◁
    for I in range(len(parents)*2):        ◁────   Loops through the remaining parents twice
        mates = random.sample(parents, 2)  ◁────   Randomly samples two parents to procreate
        children.append(create_cell(mates[0], mates[1]))  ◁
    return mutate(children)   ◁──────                     Passes the parents to
                                    Mutates the children before    create_cell to bear a
                                    passing back the list          child cell
```

The last step in `reproduce` is calling the `mutate` function, shown in the following listing, which has a random chance of modifying the children. We add this function or
rule to simulate that random chance in life where organisms (cells) may `mutate`
beyond their parents' traits. Mutation is a key factor in evolution and is responsible for
all higher forms of life on Earth.

Listing 2.11   EDL_2_4_Simulating_Evolution.ipynb: The `mutate` function

```
def mutate(cells):
    for cell in cells:
```

```
if random.randint(1,100) < MUTATE_RATE:          ◁      Checks the random
  cell""""] = clamp(                                     chance the cell mutates
      cell""""] + random.randint
        ⮕ (-MUTATE_RNG, MUTATE_RNG), 1, 100)      ◁
  cell""""] = clamp(
      cell""""] + random.randint
        ⮕ (-MUTATE_RNG, MUTATE_RNG), 1, 100)      ◁      Adds a random number
  cell""""] = clamp(                                     from -+ MUTATE_RNG
      cell""""] + random.randint
        ⮕ (-MUTATE_RNG, MUTATE_RNG), 1, 100)      ◁
return cells
```

Next, we want to look at the updated `evaluate` function. This time we evaluate the value of traits a, b, and c using a simple equation that outputs the `fitness` of the cell. We can see this function places twice the value on trait a, places a negative value on trait b, and leaves trait c as is, as shown in the following listing. The goal of our evolutionary life sim is now to optimize these traits to maintain high `fitness`. Higher `fitness` contributes to a higher likelihood of reproducing, encouraging the passing of those successful traits further.

Listing 2.12 EDL_2_4_Simulating_Evolution.ipynb: The `mutate` function

```
def evaluate(cells):
  for cell in cells:
    cell""fitnes""] = 2 * cell""""]-- cell""""] + cell""""]      ◁      The updated
  return cells                                                          evaluate function
```

Notice that we removed the `death` function and instead focus on the `reproduce` function. We can do this because we now make the simple assumption that after reproducing, all the parents are not able to further reproduce; therefore, this is not a consideration. Thus, we no longer care about an increasing `population` but rather the breeding `population`. This assumption simplifies our process and the performance of the simulation and is one we continue to use in most cases. Obviously, you could also simulate breeding across multiple `generations`, but we consider that an advanced topic for now.

Lastly, we look at the `run_generation` function to see how it has been simplified. Inside the function, the first call is to `evaluate`, which updates the `fitness` of the cell. Next, the `reproduce` function is called to produce the next breeding `generation`. After this, we again call the `evaluate` function on the new `generation` to update the `fitness` values, as shown in the following listing.

Listing 2.13 EDL_2_4_Simulating_Evolution.ipynb: The `run_generation` function

```
def run_generation(cells):
    cells = evaluate(cells)    ◁
  ⤷ cells = reproduce(cells)          Evaluates the fitness of the
    cells = evaluate(cells)    ◁      current and new generations
    return cells
Reproduces a new breeding generation
```

Figure 2.6 shows the output of running all the code (Run > Run All from the menu or
Ctrl-F9, CMD-F9). Notice the sharp difference between figure 2.5 and 2.6, where there
is an obvious improvement in `fitness`, but the `population` remains at 10. Also notice
how the traits a, b, and c are all showing well-defined optimizations. In the case of trait
a, we see a definite increase, and with trait b, we see a decrease. This is a direct result of
the `evaluate` function and the way we defined those traits in the `fitness` equation.

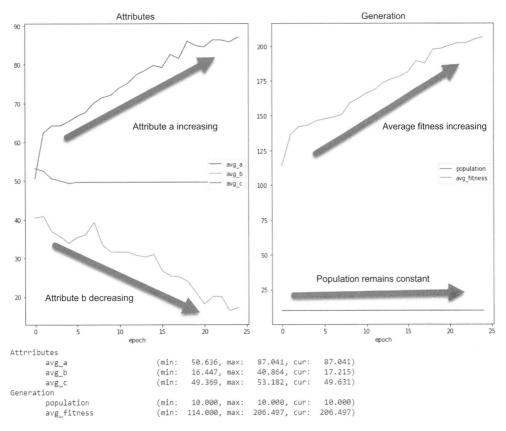

```
Attrributes
        avg_a                        (min:    50.636, max:    87.041, cur:    87.041)
        avg_b                        (min:    16.447, max:    40.864, cur:    17.215)
        avg_c                        (min:    49.369, max:    53.182, cur:    49.631)
Generation
        population                   (min:    10.000, max:    10.000, cur:    10.000)
        avg_fitness                  (min:   114.000, max:   206.497, cur:   206.497)
```

Figure 2.6   The results of running the evolution life sim

We can see that by adding the concept of evolution to the life sim, we are able to see a
strong correlation between `fitness` and trait optimization. Not only is this modified
simulation more elegant, but it is also more robust and scalable. It's so elegant, in fact,
that the simple concept of evolution is now the backbone of a whole class of algorithms, many of which we explore in later chapters.

2.4.2 *Learning exercises*

Use these exercises to improve your understanding:

1 Modify the `fitness` calculation in the `evaluate` function shown in listing 2.12. Rerun the evolution to confirm the new equation optimizes different values.

2 Add a new attribute, `d`, to the cell. This requires you to modify listings 2.9, 2.11, and 2.12.

3 Alter the `mutation` rate, `MUTATE_RATE`, to a new value between 0 and 1. Try this a few times and then after each change, rerun the notebook. Observe what effect `mutation` has on the evolution of the cells.

2.4.3 *Some background on Darwin and evolution*

Charles Darwin formed his initial concepts and theory of natural selection from his voyages around the continent of South America. From Darwin's work, our thirst for understanding evolution drove our exploration into how life on Earth shares and passes on selective traits using genetics.

Taking two decades to write, in 1859, Darwin published his most famous work, *On the Origin of Species* (published by John Murray), a seminal work that uprooted the natural sciences. His work challenged the idea of an intelligent creator and formed the basis of much of our natural and biological sciences to this day. The following quote from that book describes the theory of natural selection in Darwin's words: "One general law, leading to the advancement of all organic beings, namely, multiply, vary, let the strongest live and the weakest die."

From this law, Darwin constructed his theory of evolution and the need for life to survive by passing on more successful traits to offspring. While he didn't understand the process of cellular mitosis and genetics, he did observe the selective passing of traits in multiple species. It wasn't until 1865 that a German monk named Gregor Mendel would outline his theories of gene inheritance by observing seven traits in pea plants.

Mendel used the terms *factors* or *traits* to describe what we now understand as genes. It took nearly another three decades before his work was recognized and the field of genetics was born. Since then, our understanding of genetics has grown to include such fields as gene therapy and hacking to solving complex problems and evolving code.

2.4.4 *Natural selection and survival of the fittest*

The term *survival of the fittest* is often thrown around to define evolution and, subsequently, evolutionary computation. While the term is often incorrectly attributed to Darwin, it was first used by an earlier naturalist Herbert Spencer, who is attributed with coining the phrase 7 years earlier. Spencer, a misguided social evolutionist, would continue to be a critic of Darwin and his interpretation of evolution.

> **DEFINITION** *Social Darwinism*—The idea, often attributed to Herbert Spencer, that social success breeds success and those who socially fail are born to fail.

What Spencer and others missed from Darwin's greater theory of evolution was that survival was only a consequence of change. Darwin explains this concept well: "It is not the strongest of the species that survives, nor the most intelligent, but the ones most responsive to change."

As we move through the chapters in this book, there is no better idea to keep in mind than that Darwin quote. Evolution is not about developing the strongest or fittest but the one that can best adapt to change. What this means, in practical terms, is that while we focus on developing algorithms that produce the most `fitness`, our real goal is developing evolutionary change.

Evolutionary change, in computation, is applied to our algorithms by making sure not just the fittest or best survive. This means we employ methods to make sure a `population` of `individuals` is not just the best but, rather, the most diverse. Encouraging diversity in `populations` often allows us to solve problems more quickly.

> **Biology applied to evolutionary computation**
>
> Evolutionary computation borrows from biology and the theory of evolution. And like DL (neural networks) comparisons to the brain, not all terminology is transferable. In several cases, attempts are made to use terminology that resembles or matches the biological equivalent. In many cases, the biological terms have been significantly simplified for easier understanding. This was done not to incite biologists, geneticists, or evolutionists but to make the terminology more accessible.

2.5 Genetic algorithms in Python

GAs are the simulation of life in code, borrowing from the concepts of evolution, natural selection, and the passing of successful traits through genetics. These algorithms simulate the biological cell-level meiosis that occurs in higher-level organic reproduction. While you don't have to be a geneticist to use GAs, it may be helpful to understand biological relationships.

In the next section, we review some important base concepts of genetics and the process of meiosis. This is intended to demonstrate the relationship and mimicry of genetics in code. Certainly, if you already have a strong grounding in genetic theory and meiosis, feel free to quickly scan the section.

2.5.1 Understanding genetics and meiosis

GAs simulate the evolution of life at the genetic level. However, this simulation is more specific to higher forms of life—like us. We also make several simplifications in the genetic process (meiosis). As such, the concepts we cover in this section are intended to be at the same high level.

Anytime we talk about genetics, we need to start with *deoxyribonucleic acid*, commonly known as DNA. DNA strands are often referred to as the blueprint of life. Everything about us, down to our cells, is defined within our DNA.

DNA itself is composed of four base pairs that are arranged into patterns. Figure 2.7 shows how DNA is formed and wrapped into double-helix structures that are then folded into chromosomes. These chromosomes are housed in the nucleus of every cell, as shown in the figure.

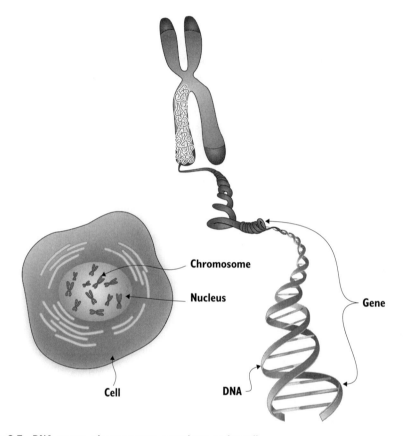

Figure 2.7   DNA, genes, chromosomes, a nucleus, and a cell

Genes, those things Mendel first defined, can be identified at the DNA level. A *gene* is a sequence of DNA that defines some characteristic or attribute of an organism. From 1990 to 2003, the Human Genome Project studied and classified all the genes within our chromosomes.

Chromosomes, as shown in figure 2.7, are containers for these sequences of genes. A single chromosome could contain hundreds or thousands of genes. Each gene itself could be comprised of hundreds to thousands of DNA base pairs. This all sounds quite complicated, but fortunately, in GA, we only worry about genes and chromosomes.

The simulation of genetic evolution itself is done by mimicking the process of meiosis. *Meiosis* is the sexual reproduction of cells from a sperm and egg, not to be confused with *mitosis*, which is the process of basic cellular division.

Meiosis is the process by which half an organism's genetic material is combined with half of another organism's genetic material. In humans, this is the story of the sperm in an egg, in which the male combines half its DNA (the sperm cell) with half of the female's DNA (the egg).

Figure 2.8 shows an excerpt from the meiosis process, in which chromosomes from mating organisms are combined. In this process, the homologous chromosome pairs (i.e., alike chromosomes) are first aligned. Then, a crossover, or sharing of genetic material, happens. The resulting recombined chromosomes are used to define the new organism.

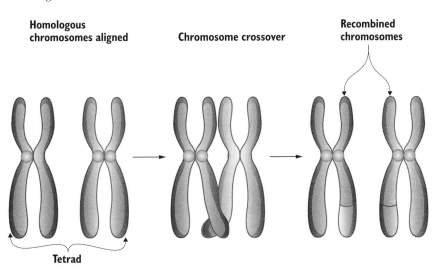

Figure 2.8   An excerpt of the meiosis process, showing chromosome crossover

In GAs, we simulate genes, chromosomes, and this mating or crossover process at the cellular level. We also need to simulate a couple other factors, as we discover in the next section.

2.5.2   Coding genetic algorithms

At the heart of GA is the gene that describes the various traits, good or bad, an individual possesses. In GA, we think of an individual as composed of one or more sequences of genes contained within a chromosome. We can also simulate multiple chromosomes, but typically, we stick with one.

Figure 2.9 shows a population of individuals, each with a sequence of genes in a chromosome. Each gene is described by a number or Boolean value, representing a 0 or 1 in this case. A gene may contain any information, including text characters, colors, or whatever else you want to use to describe the traits of an individual.

Population

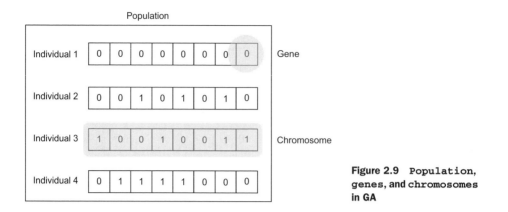

Figure 2.9 **Population, genes, and chromosomes in GA**

Genes and chromosomes

A `gene` may map to a single array value or could be defined by multiple values. Likewise, you may want to define a single `chromosome` or multiple. In most cases, we define only a single `chromosome` in this book.

2.5.3   *Constructing the population*

GA can be quite abstract and difficult to envision, so to assist with our understanding, in this section, we work through some example code in Python that will likely make these concepts more tangible. You can follow along by opening the notebook EDL_2_5_GeneticAlgorithms.ipynb in Google Colab in your browser. Refer to the appendix if you need assistance loading this notebook. When the notebook is loaded, use the menu to select Runtime > Run All to run all cells.

We can start by looking at the first code cell in the notebook, which sets up a `population` of `individuals` using a NumPy array. Everyone in the `population` is composed of a single *n*-dimensional vector with the size of `genes`. The entire `population` is constructed into a NumPy tensor using the `randint` function, with `0,2` as the inputs and the size of the tensor as (`population,genes`). This results in an output tensor, where each row represents a vector with the size of `genes`, as shown in the following listing.

Listing 2.14   **EDL_2_5_Genetic_Algorithms.ipynb: Creating the `population`**

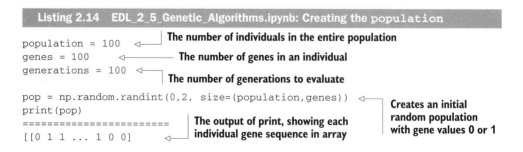

```
[1 1 0 ... 1 1 0]
[1 0 0 ... 1 0 1]
 ...
[1 0 1 ... 0 0 1]
[1 0 0 ... 0 1 0]
[1 0 0 ... 0 0 1]]
```

2.5.4 *Evaluating fitness*

Within a population of individuals, we want to determine which is the fittest or most likely to survive or solve a problem. In this simple example, our goal is to evolve individuals, so all their gene values are 1. This is known as the max one problem in GA and is a common first problem introduced to newcomers.

To determine the fitness of an individual, we typically derive a fitness function or way to calculate how close an individual is to reaching a target goal. Often, that goal is the maximization or minimization of a target value. In this example, our goal is to maximize the sum of all the genes in an individual. Since each gene is just a 0 or 1, a maximized sum represents an individual with all genes set to 1, as shown in listing 2.15.

With NumPy, the code to do this with our population already defined in a tensor is quite simple and can be done with a single line of code. Scrolling down to the next cell in the notebook, you can see the call to np.max taking as input the population pop tensor and the axis=1. The following code listing demonstrates how to calculate fitness, simply by using np.sum.

> **Listing 2.15 EDL_2_5_Genetic_Algorithms.ipynb: Calculating `fitness`**

```
fitness = np.sum(pop,axis=1)     ⟵──── The sum of all individuals (axis 1)
plt.hist(fitness)
```

Figure 2.10 shows the histogram output of the population's initial randomized individual fitness. As we might expect, the output resembles a normal distribution of the values, centered at approximately 50. For this example, since everyone has a single chromosome with 100 genes, each with a value of 0 or 1, the maximum ideal fitness score is 100.

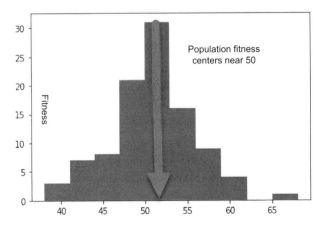

Figure 2.10 A histogram of the initial population fitness

2.5.5 Selecting for reproduction (crossover)

After evaluating the `fitness` of the `population`, we can determine which parents to use for mating to produce offspring. Just like in real life, we simulate the mating selection and reproduction of individuals. In nature, we typically see the strong, or more fit, individuals survive and reproduce to produce offspring that share some of their genetic code.

In GAs, we simulate this by first determining which `individuals` in our `population` are fit enough to produce offspring. There are several strategies we can use to make this `selection`, but for this simple example, we take the two fittest `individuals` to use as parents for the entire next `generation` of offspring. This form of `selection` is known as *elite selection*, and the code to perform it is shown in the following listing.

> **Listing 2.16 EDL_2_5_Genetic_Algorithms.ipynb: Selecting the fittest**

```
def elite_selection(fitness):
    return fitness.argsort()[-2:][::-1]      ◁── Sorts by fitness and then
                                                  returns the top two individuals
parents = elite_selection(fitness)
print(pop[parents[0]])
```

The `elite_selection` function takes as input the `population` `fitness` we calculated previously and returns indexes for the top two parents. It does this by sorting the `fitness` values using the `argsort` function and then indexing to the top two parents to return the indexes. These returned indexes can then be used to extract the `individuals` from the `population` using `pop[parents[idx]]`, with `idx` being 0 or 1.

For this simple example, *elite selection*, or selecting the best `individuals` to reproduce, works well, but in more complex problems, we often use more diverse `selection` methods. Diversity in parents and mating `selection` allows `individuals` to propagate traits that may not be beneficial in the interim but may develop to longer-term solutions. This is akin to solving for a global maximum and getting stuck at a local minimum.

2.5.6 Applying crossover: Reproduction

After the parents are selected, we can move on to applying `crossover` or, essentially, the reproduction process of creating offspring. As in the cellular division process in biology, we simulate the combining of `chromosomes` through a `crossover` operation, where each parent shares a slice of its `gene` sequence and combines it with the other parents.

Figure 2.11 shows the `crossover` operation being applied using two parents. In `crossover`, a point is selected either randomly or using some strategy along the `gene` sequence. It is at this point the `gene` sequences of the parents are split and then recombined. In this simple example, we don't care about what percentage of the `gene` sequence is shared with each offspring.

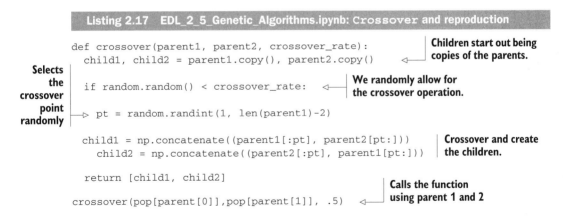
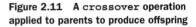

Figure 2.11 A crossover operation applied to parents to produce offspring

For more complex problems requiring thousands or millions of generations, we may prefer more balanced crossover strategies, rather than this random selection method. We further cover the strategies we can use to define this operation later in the chapter.

In code, the crossover operation first makes a copy of itself to create the raw children. Then we randomly determine if there is a crossover operation using the variable crossover_rate. If there is a crossover operation, then a random point along the gene sequence is generated as the crossover point. This point is used to split the gene sequence and then the children are generated by combining the gene sequences of both parents, as shown in the following listing.

Listing 2.17 EDL_2_5_Genetic_Algorithms.ipynb: Crossover and reproduction

```
def crossover(parent1, parent2, crossover_rate):
    child1, child2 = parent1.copy(), parent2.copy()      ◁─┐ Children start out being
                                                             copies of the parents.
    if random.random() < crossover_rate:       ◁─┐ We randomly allow for
                                                   the crossover operation.
      pt = random.randint(1, len(parent1)-2)

    child1 = np.concatenate((parent1[:pt], parent2[pt:]))    │ Crossover and create
      child2 = np.concatenate((parent2[:pt], parent1[pt:]))  │ the children.

    return [child1, child2]
                                        │ Calls the function
crossover(pop[parent[0]],pop[parent[1]], .5)   ◁─┘ using parent 1 and 2
```

Selects the crossover point randomly

There are several variations and ways in which crossover may be applied to the gene sequence. For this example, selecting a random crossover point and then simply combining the sequences at the split point works. However, in some cases, particular gene sequences may or may not make sense; in those cases, we may need other methods to preserve gene sequences.

2.5.7   *Applying mutation and variation*

In nature, we occasionally see offspring develop traits that neither parent possesses. In these cases, offspring develop mutations, causing traits not seen in their parents. Over time, these mutations can compound to create entirely new features or individual species. Mutation is a key operation through which we believe life evolved from the single-celled organism to humans.

In nature, GAs, and other similar evolutionary processes, mutation is generally unique and rare. With GA, we can control the amount and type of mutation we apply after the `crossover` operation. You can think of mutation, then, as the potential weird artifacts that may happen in the clumsy reproduction process.

Applying the `mutation` operation to our offspring in listing 2.18 is as simple as flipping a single bit or `gene` in the sequence. In the `mutation` function, each `gene` in the `individual` is tested for the possibility of `mutation`. For testing the function, we use a `mutation_rate` of .5, or 50%, though in general, `mutation` rates are much lower—less than 5%.

Listing 2.18   EDL_2_5_Genetic_Algorithms.ipynb: `Mutation`

```
def mutation(individual, mutation_rate):          We test for possible
  for i in range(len(individual)):        ◁——┘   mutation on all genes.

    if random.random() < mutation_rate:           If mutating, flip the
      individual[i] = 1 - individual[i]           gene 0 -> 1, 1 -> 0.
  return individual

mutation(pop[parent[0]], .5)
```

Again, as with the genetic operations of `selection` and `crossover`, `mutation` can also take a variety of forms. In some cases, you may prefer to keep the possibility of `mutation` low, while in others, a `population` may benefit from more random influences. `Mutation` is like the learning rate in DL, where a lower learning rate leads to more stable training that may get stuck, while higher rates yield good initial results but may never stabilize to a solution.

2.5.8   *Putting it all together*

Finally, when we put all the genetic operations together, we get the flowchart depicted in figure 2.12, which shows the entire GA process. In this figure, we start with initialization, which, in our case, is completely random. Then, the first operation is to calculate the `fitness` of all the `individuals`. From `fitness`, we can determine which `individuals` will reproduce offspring by using the `crossover` operation.

After the `crossover` operation is applied, `mutation` is applied, followed by the evaluation of `fitness`. Next, we check if the stopping criteria is met. In general, we define the stopping criteria by the number of `generations` the GA runs for, where each `generation` is counted as a full flow through the GA process. We may also use other stopping criteria, like achieving a maximum or minimum `fitness`.

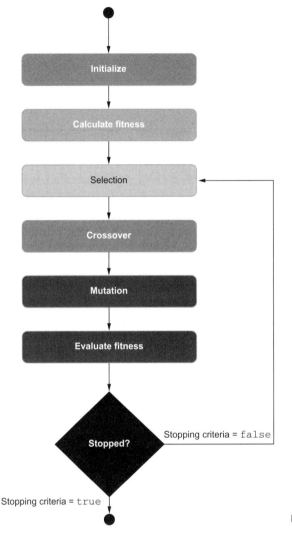

Figure 2.12 The GA process

We can put all the GA process code into a single function, as shown in the `simple_GA` function. In this function, we can see each genetic operation applied to the `population`, which results in a new `generation` of children. As shown in the following listing, this `population` of children is returned, to be `evaluated` further and passed as a new `generation` to `simple_GA`.

Listing 2.19   EDL_2_5_Genetic_Algorithms.ipynb: The full GA process

```
def simple_GA(pop, crossover_rate=.5, mutation_rate=.05):
    fitness = np.sum(pop,axis=1)        Calculates the fitness of the entire population

    parents = elite_selection(fitness)   Performs selection to select the parents
```

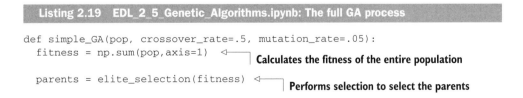

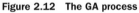

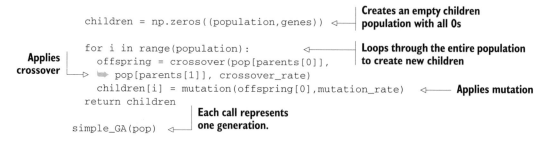

```
children = np.zeros((population,genes))   ⟵  Creates an empty children
                                              population with all 0s

for i in range(population):   ⟵           Loops through the entire population
  offspring = crossover(pop[parents[0]],  to create new children
⟶ ➡ pop[parents[1]], crossover_rate)
    children[i] = mutation(offspring[0],mutation_rate)   ⟵  Applies mutation
  return children
                        Each call represents
simple_GA(pop)  ⟵       one generation.
```
Applies crossover

This single function, `simple_ga`, represents one complete process of all genetic operations on a population or generation of individuals. We can evaluate consecutive generations using the code in the last code block of the notebook. If the notebook has completed training, run the last cell again, which allows you to see how the population evolves. The following code listing demonstrates the loop that simulates each generation of evolution.

Listing 2.20   EDL_2_5_Genetic_Algorithms.ipynb: Running the simulation

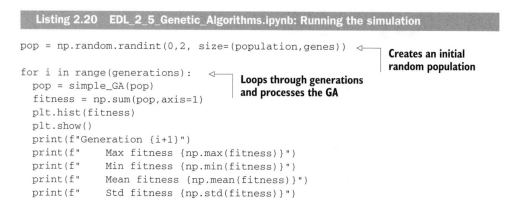

```
pop = np.random.randint(0,2, size=(population,genes))   ⟵  Creates an initial
                                                            random population
for i in range(generations):  ⟵
  pop = simple_GA(pop)              Loops through generations
  fitness = np.sum(pop,axis=1)      and processes the GA
  plt.hist(fitness)
  plt.show()
  print(f"Generation {i+1}")
  print(f"    Max fitness {np.max(fitness)}")
  print(f"    Min fitness {np.min(fitness)}")
  print(f"    Mean fitness {np.mean(fitness)}")
  print(f"    Std fitness {np.std(fitness)}")
```

Figure 2.13 shows the result of evolving the population through 100 generations. The figure shows a fitness of 98 was reached, with a minimum fitness of 88, an average of 93.21, and a standard deviation of 2. These are generally good results, and unlike in DL, in which the focus is a maximum or minimum loss or accuracy, in GA, we want to determine how well the entire population is progressing.

While the fitness of a single individual could solve a difficult problem, making sure to maintain a fit population overall allows for continued evolution. Unlike in DL, where training progress can slow over time, in GA there are often late breakthroughs in evolution that cause radical changes and advances to solutions. As a result, we generally want to consider the entire population's fitness when using evolving algorithms.

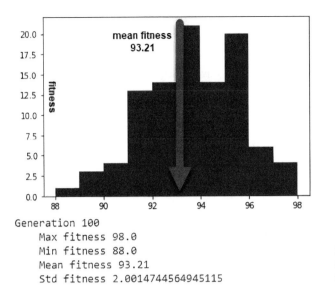

Generation 100
    Max fitness 98.0
    Min fitness 88.0
    Mean fitness 93.21
    Std fitness 2.0014744564945115

Figure 2.13   Results from evolving the `population` on the one max problem

---

Survival of the adaptable

Remember, our goal in training evolutionary algorithms is always to make sure the `population` is adaptive to change. This means we generally want to see a `population` of `individuals` score a normal distribution of `fitness`. We can control this adaptation to change with the type and form of `selection` and `mutation` operators.

2.5.9   *Understanding genetic algorithm hyperparameters*

As you may have already noticed, GA provides us with several hyperparameters and genetic operator options for optimizing the evolution of a solution. We explore the various operator options in this chapter, as these options are necessary for understanding what hyperparameters we can use to enhance evolution. The following is a list of the genetic hyperparameters we have explored thus far and how they work and can be used:

- *Population*—This represents the number of `individuals` simulated through each generation of evolution. The `population` value is closely related to the size of the chromosome or length of the `gene` sequence. Thus, `individuals` with more complex `gene` sequences require larger training `populations` to be effective.
- *Gene/chromosome length*—The number and length of `chromosomes` or the type of `genes` are often set by the problem. In the previous example exercise, we chose an arbitrary value for the number `genes` to demonstrate different `gene` sequence lengths.
- *Generations*—Like epochs in DL, the number of `generations` represents the number of iterations of evolution. The word *training* is reserved for `individual`

betterment, and in GA, we evolve an entire species or population of individuals. Like population, the number of generations is often dictated by the chromosome length and complexity. This may be balanced against the population size, where you could have a large population and small number of generations.

- *Crossover rate*—This may determine the possibility of crossover, or it may dictate the point or amount of crossover. In the last example, we used this rate to determine how frequently parents would share genes. However, in most cases, crossover is assumed, and the rate may then determine the crossover point.
- *Mutation rate*—This accounts for the possibility of something going wrong in the crossover mix. A high rate of mutation often causes lots of variation in the population, which may be beneficial for more complex problems. Except, high mutation may also prevent individuals from achieving optimum performance. Conversely, lower rates of mutation produce less population variety and more specialization.

At this point, a good way to understand how these hyperparameters work in practice is to go back to the last example and alter them and then rerun the notebook. Go ahead and try this, as it really is the best way to learn and understand how these basic values can alter the evolution of a population.

GAs lay the foundation for several EC methods we explore in the following chapters. Fundamentally, the concepts of evolution and survival of the fittest are the key components in any EC method. We use these general laws Darwin penned over 170 years ago throughout our journey toward finding better ways to optimize DL systems.

2.5.10 *Learning exercises*

We have covered a lot of foundational material in this section. Be sure to undertake at least one of the following exercises:

1 Modify the fitness calculation in listing 2.15. See what effect this has on evolution.
2 Modify the crossover and mutation rates in listing 2.19. Rerun the evolution, and see what effect changing each has on how quickly a solution is evolved.
3 Can you think of other ways parents may select mates? Write them down, and revisit this list later.

Summary

- Conway's Game of Life demonstrates one of the first basic forms of rule-based life simulation. Life simulation can assist us in optimizing computational and simulated real-world problems.
- Life simulation can be used to observe simple behaviors using functions to define reproduction and death.

- Evolution incorporated through basic life simulation can demonstrate the passing of successful traits to offspring. Traits passed through evolution can be used to optimize a particular problem.
- The evolutionary success of an optimization problem is measured using a `fitness` function. `Fitness` functions quantify the ability of a simulated `individual` to successfully solve a given problem.
- Python with NumPy can be used to demonstrate the basic concepts or operations of simulated genetic evolution. In genetic evolution (GAs), we use operators to mimic the base operations of biological meiosis or higher-organism reproduction. The base operations used in a genetic simulation are `selection`, `crossover`, `mutation`, and `evaluation/fitness`:
  - *Selection*—The stage or operation in which `individuals` are chosen to reproduce. There are a variety of `selection` methods used in GAs.
  - *Crossover*—The stage or operation in which two selected `individuals` mate and share a portion of genetic material.
  - *Mutation*—To simulate real-world biological processes, we apply some amount of randomization to the produced offspring from the previous `crossover` operation.
  - *Evaluation*—Newly produced `individuals` are `evaluated` through a function to produce a `fitness` score. This score determines how successful an `individual` will be at completing some problem or task.
- The base operators' inputs and configurations of genetic evolution can be tuned and modified. Typical configuration parameters we would modify include the following:
  - *Population size*—The number of `individuals` simulated in a `generation`.
  - *Number of generations*—How many iterations to simulate.
  - *Crossover rate*—The frequency with which `individuals` share genetic material during the `crossover` operation.
  - *Mutation rate*—The frequency a new `individual` will be subjected to randomized alteration of its genetic material.

Introducing genetic algorithms with DEAP

This chapter covers

- Creating genetic solvers using DEAP
- Applying GA to a complex design or placement problem
- Solving or estimating mathematically difficult problems with GA
- Determining which GA operators to employ when solving problems
- Constructing complex gene structures for design and drawing

In the last chapter, we explored the origins of life simulation and how evolution and natural selection can be used for optimization. We learned how genetic algorithms, a subset of evolutionary computation, could extend these concepts further into an elegant practical method of optimized search.

In this chapter, we directly extend what we learned in the last chapter to tackle larger and more complex problems using genetic algorithms. As part of this journey, we employ an EC toolkit called Distributed Evolutionary Algorithms in Python (DEAP) to make our lives easier. Like frameworks such as Keras or PyTorch, DEAP provides several tools and operators to make coding easier.

3.1   Genetic algorithms in DEAP

While we could continue writing all the GA code we need in straight Python, this book isn't about building an EC framework. Instead, in this chapter, we use the well-established DEAP EC framework. As its name suggests, this framework helps us review various EC methods, including GA.

DEAP, released in 2009, is a comprehensive and simplified framework for working with EC algorithms in various forms. Throughout this book, it is our main tool for building EDL solutions. The framework provides tool abstractions, which allows it to be cross-compatible with various evolutionary algorithms.

3.1.1   One max with DEAP

There is likely no better way to learn about DEAP than using it to solve a problem we already solved using straight Python and GA in the last chapter. This allows us to become familiar with the framework and toolbelt it uses. In the following exercise, we build a solver to the one max problem with DEAP.

Open EDL_3_1_OneMax_DEAP.ipynb in Colab and then run all the cells. Refer to the appendix if you need assistance.

In the first cell, we install DEAP using the following shell command. The ! prefix denotes this as a shell command, not Python code. We use pip to install DEAP, using the quiet option, --quiet, to suppress the noisy output:

```
!pip install deap --quiet
```

Move past the imports and then look at the next code cell showing the DEAP module creator setting up the fitness criteria and individual classes. The creator takes as input the name and base class for the first two parameters. As the following listing shows, this creates the template used to define, first, the maximum fitness and, second, the individual based upon the numpy.ndarray, much like in the last example.

> **Listing 3.1   Listing 3.1 EDL_3_1_OneMax_DEAP.ipynb: The `creator`**

```
creator.create("FitnessMax", base.Fitness,          Creates the max
➥  weights=(1.0,))                        ◁──────    fitness class

creator.create("Individual", numpy.ndarray,         Creates the individual
➥  fitness=creator.FitnessMax)            ◁──────    class, based on ndarray
```

In the next cell, we see a new module being used as the base to construct a toolbox. The toolbox is a container that holds the hyperparameters and options, like the genetic operators. In the code, a toolbox is constructed and then the basic gene type attr_bool is registered. Next, we register the individual based on the creator, using

the `attr_bool` gene type and size of n=100. On the final line, the `population` is registered as a `list` filled with the type of `toolbox.individual`. The pattern here is to construct and register the templates for `gene` type, followed by `individual`, and then
`population`, as shown in the following listing.

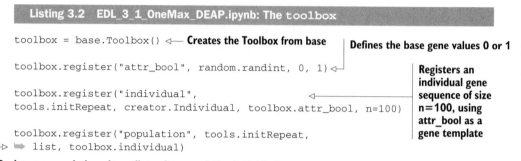

Listing 3.2 EDL_3_1_OneMax_DEAP.ipynb: The `toolbox`

```
toolbox = base.Toolbox()   ◁— Creates the Toolbox from base      │ Defines the base gene values 0 or 1

toolbox.register("attr_bool", random.randint, 0, 1)◁┘
                                                                   Registers an
                                                                   individual gene
toolbox.register("individual",                            ◁─────── sequence of size
tools.initRepeat, creator.Individual, toolbox.attr_bool, n=100)    n=100, using
                                                                   attr_bool as a
toolbox.register("population", tools.initRepeat,                   gene template
   ➡ list, toolbox.individual)

Registers a population of type list, using an existing individual
```

Next, we move on to registering the genetic operators used to process each `generation`.
We start with `evaluate` for evaluating `fitness` and populate that with a custom function,
called `evalOneMax`. After that, we add the genetic operation for `crossover`, calling it
`mate`, and employ another custom function called `cxTwoPointCopy`. The following line
sets the `mutate` operator, this time using a predefined DEAP tools function called
`mutFlipBit`. This, as before, flips the bit or logic of the `gene`. Finally, the `selection`
operator is registered as `select` this time, using a prebuilt `selTournament` operator,
which represents tournament `selection`. Tournament `selection` is a form of random
pairing that compares `fitness` to evaluate and selects the next `generation`'s parents,
as shown in the following listing.

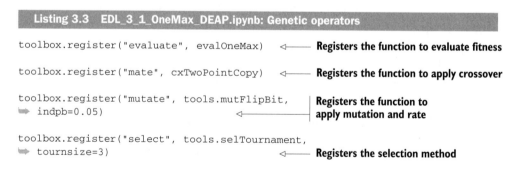

Listing 3.3 EDL_3_1_OneMax_DEAP.ipynb: Genetic operators

```
toolbox.register("evaluate", evalOneMax)   ◁─── Registers the function to evaluate fitness

toolbox.register("mate", cxTwoPointCopy)   ◁─── Registers the function to apply crossover

toolbox.register("mutate", tools.mutFlipBit,    │ Registers the function to
   ➡ indpb=0.05)                          ◁─────┤ apply mutation and rate

toolbox.register("select", tools.selTournament,
   ➡ tournsize=3)                          ◁─── Registers the selection method
```

In this exercise, we use two custom functions and two predefined functions for the
genetic operators. If you scroll up, you can see the two custom functions `evalOneMax`
and `cxTwoPointCopy`. The `evalOneMax` function is a single line of code returning the
sum of the `genes`, as shown previously.

We can scroll back down to the last cell to see how the evolution is run. First, we set
the `random.seed` to a known value, which allows for consistent runs. Then we use the

toolbox to create the population. Next, we create a HallOfFame object we can use to track the top number of performers. In this exercise, we are only interested in tracking the single top performer, and since the individuals are NumPy arrays, we need to override the similar or matching algorithm for sorting, as shown in the following listing.

Listing 3.4 EDL_3_1_OneMax_DEAP.ipynb: Setting up evolution

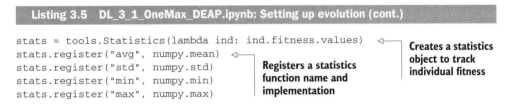

```
random.seed(64)                                    ⟵—— Sets the random see for consistency
pop = toolbox.population(n=300)                    ⟵┐
hof = tools.HallOfFame(1, similar=numpy.array_equal)│ Creates the population
```

Sets the number of top individuals to watch

The next lines of code create a new Statistics object, stat, we can use to track the progress of the population's fitness. We add the descriptive statistics using the register function passing in the corresponding NumPy function to evaluate the statistic, as shown in the following listing.

Listing 3.5 DL_3_1_OneMax_DEAP.ipynb: Setting up evolution (cont.)

```
stats = tools.Statistics(lambda ind: ind.fitness.values)  ⟵┐ Creates a statistics
stats.register("avg", numpy.mean)  ⟵┐                        │ object to track
stats.register("std", numpy.std)    │ Registers a statistics  │ individual fitness
stats.register("min", numpy.min)    │ function name and
stats.register("max", numpy.max)    │ implementation
```

Finally, the last line of code does the evolving using an out-of-the-box function called eaSimple from the algorithms module. This function takes as input the pop, toolbox, halloffame, and stats objects as well as sets hyperparameters for the probability of crossover (cxpb), mutation (mutpb), and the number of generations (ngen), as shown in the following listing.

Listing 3.6 EDL_3_1_OneMax_DEAP.ipynb: Evolving

```
algorithms.eaSimple(pop, toolbox, cxpb=0.5, mutpb=0.2, ngen=40, stats=stats,
                    halloffame=hof, verbose=None)
```

As the exercise runs, we see the statistics output showing the progress of evolution. Over 40 generations with a population of 300 this time, we should see the GA attain a maximum fitness of 100. The reason for this assured success over the first example was the choice in operators.

In the last scenario, almost everything was like the notebook we covered in the last section of chapter 2. So why did this population perform so well? Is DEAP that much better? DEAP isn't better, but it does provide a wide range of options for genetic operators and other settings. The key difference between the last notebook and the previous example was the use of tournament selection.

Tournament `selection` works by randomly selecting competition pairs of `individuals` and then passing them through several tournaments, where the winner is the one with the better `fitness`. At the end of the tournament, the winners are selected to be the parents of the next `generation`.

DEAP provides a useful library of genetic operators we can easily swap with, like tournament `selection`, out of the box. We take a close look at the wide range of options in a later section after we tackle some substantial problems beyond the scope of one max.

3.1.2 *Learning exercises*

Use the following exercises to help improve your understanding of the concepts we've discussed:

1 Increase the number of `genes` in a sequence by modifying the `creator` `.Individual` toolbox function from listing 3.2. Rerun the whole notebook to see the results.

2 Increase or decrease the size of the `population` in listing 3.4 and then rerun it to see the results.

3 Alter the `crossover` and `mutation` rates of the evolution in listing 3.6 and then rerun. What effect does this have on the evolution of the final solution?

Now that we have an understanding of the basics of DEAP, we can move on to solving more interesting examples in the next section.

3.2 *Solving the Queen's Gambit*

Evolutionary and genetic algorithms have been shown to successfully tackle many complex problems of design and placement. These forms of AI and ML methods excel at these types of problems due, in part, to the controlled random element of search they employ. This often allows systems designed with EA or GA to innovate beyond our understanding.

In the next notebook, we look at a classic design and placement problem: the Queen's Gambit. This problem uses typical chess or checkered style board of size *n*, with a classic chessboard having size 8, or 8 by 8. The goal is to place *n* number of queen chess pieces on the board such that no piece may capture another without moving.

Chess and the queen

In chess, the queen piece is the most powerful and can move in any direction and distance. Typically, each player has only one queen, but there is a special rule that allows players to crown more queens anytime a pawn makes it to the opponent's back row. The premise of the Queen's Gambit is that players have crowned several queens. However, this scenario would likely never happen in a real game because players lose when their king piece is captured.

Open the EDL_3_2_QueensGambit.ipynb and then run all the cells. If you need assistance opening the notebook, consult the appendix.

First, we want to look at the initial or random placement of the queens on a chessboard. Since the queen piece can move in any direction and at any distance, this hypothetical game is limited to a maximum number of queens equal to the size of the board. In this example, we use eight, and the block of code we look at in the following listing draws an initial placement of queens.

Listing 3.7 EDL_3_2_QueensGambit.ipynb: Plotting the board

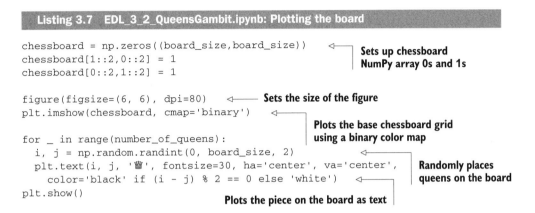

```
chessboard = np.zeros((board_size,board_size))          ⟵  Sets up chessboard
chessboard[1::2,0::2] = 1                                    NumPy array 0s and 1s
chessboard[0::2,1::2] = 1

figure(figsize=(6, 6), dpi=80)    ⟵──  Sets the size of the figure
plt.imshow(chessboard, cmap='binary')    ⟵
                                             Plots the base chessboard grid
                                             using a binary color map
for _ in range(number_of_queens):
  i, j = np.random.randint(0, board_size, 2)          ⟵
  plt.text(i, j, '♛', fontsize=30, ha='center', va='center',    Randomly places
    color='black' if (i - j) % 2 == 0 else 'white')   ⟵         queens on the board
plt.show()
                      Plots the piece on the board as text
```

Figure 3.1 shows the rendered board and a reminder of how the queen piece can move. Notice that the selected piece can immediately capture several other pieces. Remember the goal of this problem is to place the pieces such that no single piece may capture another.

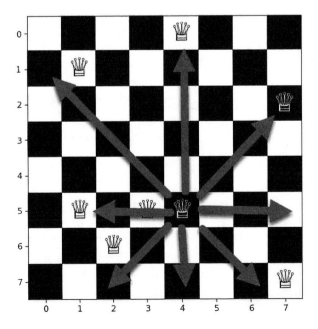

Figure 3.1 A random placement of queens on a chessboard

Again, much of the code in this notebook is like previous exercises. Next, we focus on how to fill the `toolbox`, as shown in listing 3.8. Notice that for this exercise, we use two new `toolbox` functions for `crossover` and `mutation`. We cover more examples of these `toolbox` genetic operators you can use at the end of the chapter. Another great resource for understanding these operators is the DEAP documentation at https://deap.readthedocs.io/en/master/api/tools.html.

Listing 3.8   EDL_3_2_QueensGambit.ipynb: Filling the `toolbox`

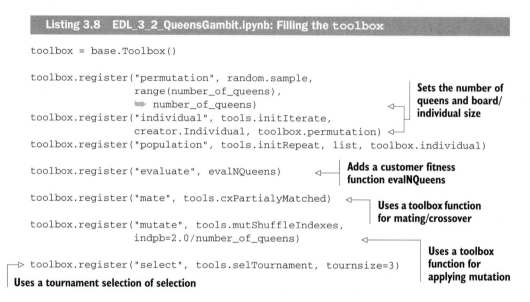

```
toolbox = base.Toolbox()

toolbox.register("permutation", random.sample,
                 range(number_of_queens),
              ➥ number_of_queens)                              ⟵  Sets the number of
toolbox.register("individual", tools.initIterate,                 queens and board/
                 creator.Individual, toolbox.permutation) ⟵      individual size
toolbox.register("population", tools.initRepeat, list, toolbox.individual)

toolbox.register("evaluate", evalNQueens)          ⟵   Adds a customer fitness
                                                       function evalNQueens

toolbox.register("mate", tools.cxPartialyMatched)  ⟵
                                                        Uses a toolbox function
toolbox.register("mutate", tools.mutShuffleIndexes,     for mating/crossover
                 indpb=2.0/number_of_queens)       ⟵
                                                        Uses a toolbox
toolbox.register("select", tools.selTournament, tournsize=3)  function for
                                                             applying mutation
Uses a tournament selection of selection
```

The queen's `fitness` evaluate function `evalNQueens` evaluates an `individual`'s `fitness` by taking a shortcut, and instead of running through every iteration of placement, the function assumes only a single queen can be placed on a row or column. Therefore, we just need to evaluate whether the queens are placed diagonally from one another, which simplifies the `fitness` function to the code in the following listing.

Listing 3.9   EDL_3_2_QueensGambit.ipynb: Evaluating the `fitness`

```
def evalNQueens(individual):                   Loops through the board and
  for i in range(size):         ⟵             evaluates diagonal placements
    left_diagonal[i+individual[i]] += 1
    right_diagonal[size-1-i+individual[i]] += 1

  sum_ = 0                              Loops over placements
  for i in range(2*size-1):    ⟵      and sums nonconflicts
    if left_diagonal[i] > 1:
      sum_ += left_diagonal[i] - 1
    if right_diagonal[i] > 1:
      sum_ += right_diagonal[i] - 1
  return sum_,                 ⟵     Returns the sum of nonconflicts
```

Following the `fitness` evaluation function, there is another function called `eaSimple`, which is just a copy of the standard `alogirthms.eaSimple` function from DEAP. This function is virtually identical to the one we used in the last exercise; however, it has much of the noisy logging removed, which allows us to custom output the top-performing `individual` as well as test for early stopping. Notice the test of the `individual`'s `fitness` against a maximum `fitness` in the following listing. This allows the evolution to stop early if the maximum `fitness` has been reached.

Listing 3.10 EDL_3_2_QueensGambit.ipynb: The evolution function

```
for ind, fit in zip(invalid_ind, fitnesses):       ←——  Loops through the individuals
    ind.fitness.values = fit                              and pairs to fitness with zip
    if fit[0] >= max:          If max fitness is reached, prints
        print("Solved")        solved and sets the exit flag
        done = True
Tests whether the individual's fitness has reached or exceeded max
```

At the end of the notebook, you can see how the `population` is evolved. We first create the `population` and a `HallOfFame` container for the top performer. After that, we register the various statistics and then, finally, call the `eaSimple` function to evolve the `population`. In the following listing, notice the use of the `max = number_of_queens` as an input to control early stopping or when an `individual` has reached maximum `fitness`.

Listing 3.11 EDL_3_2_QueensGambit.ipynb: Evolution

```
random.seed(seed)
                                    Creates the population and
pop = toolbox.population(n=100)     hall of fame for the best
hof = tools.HallOfFame(1)
stats = tools.Statistics(lambda ind: ind.fitness.values)   ←——  Registers the
stats.register("Avg", np.mean)                                  statistics functions
stats.register("Std", np.std)                                  for monitoring the
stats.register("Min", np.min)                                  population
stats.register("Max", np.max)

eaSimple(pop, toolbox, cxpb=0.5, mutpb=0.2, ngen=100, max = number_of_queens,
         stats=stats, halloffame=hof)
Calls the evolution function to evolve the population
```

Finally, we review the output of the evolution and see how well the algorithm evolved a solution. Figure 3.2 shows the solution for the given `seed` parameter we set earlier. You can see from the output that the evolution was able to stop early—67 `generations`—to create a viable solution.

Feel free to revisit the solution and confirm that each of the queens is unable to capture one another on your own. You can even go back and increase the `board_size` or `number_of_queens` to a larger value, like 16 or more. This likely requires you to also

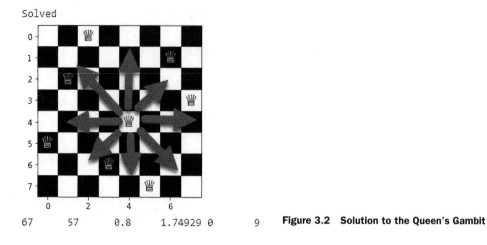

| 67 | 57 | 0.8 | 1.74929 0 | 9 | **Figure 3.2   Solution to the Queen's Gambit** |

increase the population size and the number of evolution generations. I recommend trying this now to gain some more experience working with GA.

3.2.1   *Learning exercises*

Improve your knowledge by exploring these fun exercises:

1   Change the population size to be evolved in listing 3.11 and then rerun. What effect does a larger population have on the evolution?
2   Alter the crossover and mutation rates in listing 3.11 and then rerun. Can you solve the solution in fewer generations?
3   Increase or decrease the selection tournament size in listing 3.8 and then rerun. What effect does the tournament size have on the evolution?

The Queen's Gambit is a fun problem to look at; we continue looking at other classic problems solved with EC in the next section.

3.3   *Helping a traveling salesman*

EA and GA have also been successful in optimizing difficult-to-solve mathematical problems, like the classic traveling salesman problem. You see, in the old days before the internet, the salesman would need to physically travel the country to sell their wares. The concept of this problem is to solve the route a salesman would need to take to never revisit the same location twice, while optimizing the length of their journey.

Figure 3.3 shows an example of the traveling salesman problem (TSP) depicted on a map grid of 100 units by 100 units. In the figure, the salesman has optimized their route, so they can visit each city just once and then return home at the end of the trip.

The TSP is considered an NP-hard problem in mathematics, which means it is not computationally solvable in linear time. Instead, the computational power to solve such a problem increases exponentially with the number of locations. In figure 3.3, the salesman has 22 destinations, including home.

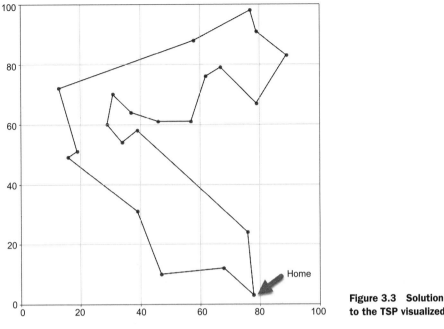

Figure 3.3   Solution to the TSP visualized

NP problems in computation and math

In mathematics and computation, algorithms are classified by their difficulty according to the amount of time or computational power required to solve them. We classify such problems as NP, where N stands for the number of elements needed to solve for and P is the time required to solve the problem. Problems are classified as NP easy if they can be solved in linear time—that is, N × P increases at a linear rate. Conversely, NP-hard problems are defined such that they cannot be solved in linear time and, instead, require exponential time. NP-hard solutions are defined with N2 × P or higher exponential, such that as the number of elements increases, the complexity of the problem increases exponentially.

Since the TSP problem is NP-hard, we have yet to find a mathematical solution that can solve the problem in linear time. Instead, many methods developed to solve the TSP are estimation methods that borrow from shortcuts in process and optimization. Such fine-tuned methods have been shown to work successfully over thousands of points.

Using big O notation, we can express the TSP problem as $O(n^2 2^n)$ for calculating the maximum time to calculate an answer. We get this for each new `destination` point; we need to recalculate the corresponding subpoints for each `destination`. In comparison, calculating 22 `destinations` would require a maximum of 2 billion calculations, while 23 `destinations` would require 4.5 billion calculations.

To put this amount of computation into perspective for 22 points, consider that if each calculation required 1 millisecond or $1/1000^{\text{th}}$ of a second to complete, then 2 billion calculations would take 23 days to complete. That number would grow exponentially with each additional `destination`, making typical programming solutions not practical. Instead, methods like EA/GA provide alternatives for finding solutions to such complex problems.

3.3.1 Building the TSP solver

In the next notebook, we use DEAP to construct a solution to solve the class of open-ended TSP problems. A closed form of the TSP is where the salesman is constrained to a certain driving distance or length. That means in the problem, the salesman may travel any distance to travel to all `destinations`.

Open the EDL_3_3_TSP.ipynb notebook in Colab and then run all the cells. If you need assistance, refer to the appendix.

We start by looking at the initialization and visualization of a random salesman path. The first thing we define is the base `map` of `destination` points that will hold all the locations for the traveling salesman's route. Next, we draw the `map` `destinations` using the `plt.scatter` function by passing in the 0 and 1 values from the map. After that, we grab the current plot using `plt.gca()` and add limits to the plot bounds, so we can clearly visualize the entire `map` of `destinations`, as shown in the following listing.

Listing 3.12   EDL_3_3_TSP.ipynb: Setting up the `map`

```
figure(num=None, figsize=(10, 10), dpi=80,        Sets the size and
  facecolor='w', edgecolor='k')          ◁────── resolution of the figure

map = np.random.randint(min_bounds,max_bounds,    Defines a random NumPy array of
  size=(destinations,2))                 ◁────── points with size = destinations

plt.scatter(map[:,0], map[:,1])   ◁────── Plots the points on the map
axes = plt.gca()
axes.set_xlim([min_bounds,max_bounds])
axes.set_ylim([min_bounds,max_bounds])            Sets the plot's limits
plt.grid()
```

When we apply GA, each `individual` in the `population` will represent a list of indexes on the `destination` map. That list also represents the `gene` sequence of the `individual`, where each index is a `gene`. Since our map represents a random set of points, we can assume starting `individuals` just visit each of those points in order. Doing that allows us to construct a simple path from an `individual`, using the code in the following listing.

Listing 3.13   EDL_3_3_TSP.ipynb: Creating a `path`

```
def linear_path(map):
  path = []
  for i,pt in enumerate(map):   ◁────── Enumerates the points on the map
```

```
    path.append(i)        ⟵—— Appends each destination to path
  return path

path = linear_path(map)   ⟵—— Creates a new path based on the map
```

Next, we want a way to visualize this path, so we can see what the route is and will be as the evolution progresses. The draw_path function operates by passing in the path constructed from the last step. Inside the function, the code loops through the indexes in the path and connects the points using the plt.arrow function passing in the point pairs, as shown in the following listing. After looping through the indexes in the path list, we draw a final path to the starting point. Figure 3.4 shows the output of calling the draw_path function with the starting path we constructed in the last step.

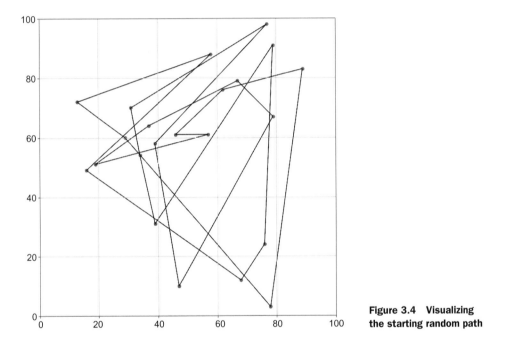

Figure 3.4 Visualizing the starting random path

Listing 3.14 EDL_3_3_TSP.ipynb: Visualizing the Path

```
def draw_path(path):
  figure(num=None, figsize=(10, 10), dpi=80, facecolor='w', edgecolor='k')
  prev_pt = None
  plt.scatter(map[:,0], map[:,1])   ⟵—— Plots the base map destinations
  for I in path:
    pt = map[i]
    if prev_pt is not None:
      plt.arrow(pt[0],pt[1], prev_pt[0]-pt[0],
      ➥ prev_pt[1]-pt[1])  ⟵┐
    else:                         ├ Draws arrows from point to point
      start_pt = pt          ⟵┘
    prev_pt = pt
```

```
plt.arrow(pt[0],pt[1], start_pt[0]-pt[0],
  start_pt[1]-pt[1])                              ⊲──── Plots an arrow back to the start
axes = plt.gca()
axes.set_xlim([min_bounds,max_bounds])
axes.set_ylim([min_bounds,max_bounds])
plt.grid()
plt.show()

draw_path(path)      ⊲──── Draws the entire path
```

Just below the draw_path function, we can see the evaluate_path function used to
determine the fitness of each path. This function in the following listing loops
through the point indexes in the path and calculates the L1, or Euclidean, distance. It
then sums up all these distances into the total path length, which also corresponds to
the individual's fitness.

Listing 3.15   EDL_3_3_TSP.ipynb: Evaluating the path

```
def evaluate_path(path):
  prev_pt = None
  distance = 0
  for i in path:    ⊲──── Loops through point indexes in the path
    pt = map[i]
    if prev_pt is not None:          ⊲─────┤ Calculates the L1 distance between points
      distance += math.sqrt((prev_pt[0]-pt[0]) ** 2 + (prev_pt[1]-pt[1]) ** 2)
    else:
      start_pt = pt
    prev_pt = pt
  distance += math.sqrt((start_pt[0]-pt[0]) ** 2 + (start_pt[1]-pt[1]) ** 2)
  return distance,      ⊲─────┤ Returns the distance as a set

evaluate_path(path)
```

From here, we pass the other familiar code and look at the toolbox setup as well as
how to construct the individuals. In this example, we construct a chromosome with
indices equal to the number of destinations to hold the indexes in the destination
map, as shown in the following listing. Each individual in this exercise represents a
path of indexes on the destination map.

Listing 3.16   EDL_3_3_TSP.ipynb: Filling the toolbox

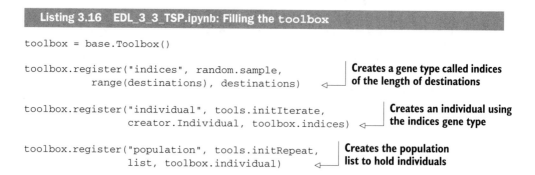

```
toolbox = base.Toolbox()

toolbox.register("indices", random.sample,                  Creates a gene type called indices
          range(destinations), destinations)   ⊲──┘         of the length of destinations

toolbox.register("individual", tools.initIterate,           Creates an individual using
          creator.Individual, toolbox.indices)  ⊲──┘        the indices gene type

toolbox.register("population", tools.initRepeat,            Creates the population
          list, toolbox.individual)   ⊲──┘                  list to hold individuals
```

Jump down to the bottom cell to review the code that performs the evolution. Again, this code is like the previous exercise, except this time we don't provide an early stopping parameter. That is because calculating the minimum path distance would be as or more expensive than the algorithm we are using to calculate the distance. Instead, we can use the evolutions output to confirm the evolution has reached a solution, as shown in the following listing.

Listing 3.17 EDL_3_3_TSP.ipynb: Evolution

```
pop = toolbox.population(n=300)

hof = tools.HallOfFame(1)

stats = tools.Statistics(lambda ind: ind.fitness.values)
stats.register("avg", np.mean)
stats.register("std", np.std)
stats.register("min", np.min)          Calls the evolution function with
stats.register("max", np.max)          hardcoded hyperparameters

eaSimple(pop, toolbox, 0.7, 0.3, 200, stats=stats, halloffame=hof)  ◄──────
```

Figure 3.5 shows the solution to a 22-point `destination` problem. A simple way to evaluate whether a solution is correct is to notice that all the connected points don't cross over each other and, essentially, form a loop, as shown in the figure.

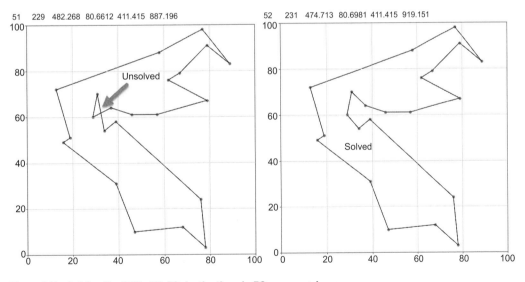

Figure 3.5 Solving the TSP with 22 destinations in 52 generations

In most cases, with a `destination` count of 22, this exercise should complete in under 200 `generations`. Even though we set the seed for the `random.seed`, we can still get diverse variations in the destination map as well as the final solution path. If you find the notebook is unable to solve the problem in under 200 generations, either reduce the number of destination points or increase the number of generations.

Try going back and increasing the number of destinations by 1 to 23 or up to 25 and then run the exercise again. Keep in mind that each additional point is an exponential increase in complexity, but in some cases, it is just as readily solvable. See if you can increase the number of destinations beyond 25 to find a solution. If you do, keep in mind that you also likely need to increase the number of generations and/or population.

3.3.2   *Learning exercises*

Use these exercises to explore the concepts in the notebook further:

1 Increase or decrease the number of destinations the salesman needs to visit and then rerun after each change. What is the maximum number of destinations you can create a solution for?
2 Tweak the population, crossover, and mutation rate and then rerun the notebook.
3 Alter the type or parameters of the selection function used for the evolution.

Now, with a couple of fun and interesting examples out of the way, we can dig into more details about selecting various genetic operators in the next section.

3.4   *Selecting genetic operators for improved evolution*

Evolutionary computation, not unlike other AI or ML disciplines, provides a wide variety of hyperparameters and options for tuning to problems. EA and GA are certainly no different and, as we have already seen, provide various hyperparameters and genetic operator options. In this section, we explore and attempt to understand more about these options.

DEAP provides several genetic operator options that, under the Evolutionary Tools documentation, can, in many cases, be easily swapped out. Other operators may require special circumstances with the gene or individual type, like the mutShuffleIndexes operator we used in the last two exercises; others may be custom-made according to your requirements and discretion, making the possibilities endless.

> **TIP**   DEAP has an excellent documentation resource that provides more details about the genetic operators we look at in this section and beyond. Documentation on evolutionary tools and genetic operators can be found on the following web page: https://deap.readthedocs.io/en/master/api/tools.html.

Of course, applying the right genetic operator to your evolver requires knowledge of what and how these tools do what they do. In the next exercise, we review a few of the most common operators and see how they modify the evolution of the target population. We use a simplified version of the TSP we explored in the last section to view the results of swapping out various genetic operators.

Open the EDL_3_4_TSP_Operators.ipynb in Colab and then run all the cells. Refer to the appendix if you need assistance. This exercise borrows most of its code from the previous exercise and annotates it with some additional visualizations.

This notebook heavily uses Colab forms to provide a UI to modify the various options and hyperparameters. Jump down to the cell titled Selecting the Genetic Operators, shown in figure 3.6.

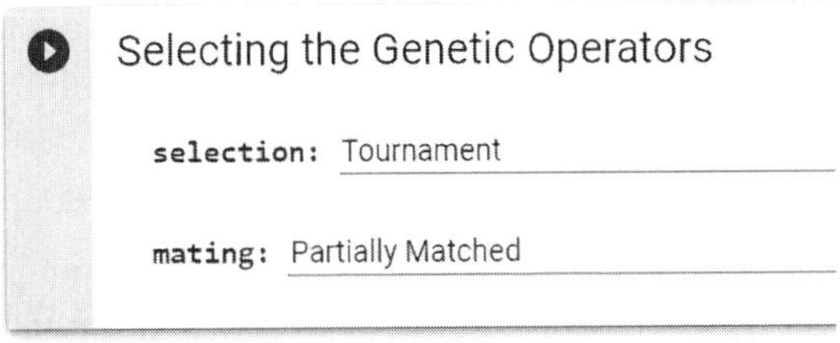

Figure 3.6 The Google Colab forms interface to select genetic operators

Let's start by testing variations to the `selection` genetic operators. This notebook provides several options for the type of `selection` operator we can choose and test for `crossover` and `selection`. Swapping out the `mutation` operator isn't an option, since we are using a specialized form of `mutation` that swaps indices. Choose one of the `selection` operators, and then from the menu, select Runtime > Run After to apply the changes and rerun the remaining cells in the notebook. The following list shows each of the operators and a brief description of the operation:

- *Tournament*—This operator selects by running tournament `selection` for *n* number of repetitions. Initial tournaments are selected randomly, and winners move to the next tournament. This operator works well, optimizing the best `individuals` while maintaining some amount of diversity.
- *Random*—This operator selects by randomly picking parents from the `population`. This is a good operator to employ if you find the `population` becomes specialized quickly or appears to get stuck at a local maximum/minimum. For problems like the TSP, this operator may be effective, depending on the chosen `crossover` and `mutation` operator.
- *Best*—This operator selects the best performers to use as parents. As seen in our first example, using elite `selection` or best `selection` works well to quickly find solutions, but it is much less effective long-term. This is because the `population` does not remain diverse enough to overcome sticking points.
- *Worst*—The opposite of the best operator, this operator selects the worst performers for parents. The benefit of using the worst as parents is the ability to entirely avoid specialization. This, in turn, works well when you find `populations` specialized and get stuck in incorrect solutions.
- *NSGA2*—This operator is based on the paper "A Fast Elitist Non-dominated Sorting Genetic Algorithm for Multi-objective Optimization: NSGA-II" by Deb

et al. (2002, Springer). It is an algorithm/operator that works well to maintain fitness optimization but still retains population diversity long-term. Using this algorithm results in the population tending to stay within a normal distribution. That makes this method useful for longer evolving problems.

- *SPEA2*—This operator originates from the paper "SPEA 2: Improving the Strength Pareto Evolutionary Algorithm" by Zitzler et al. (2001, ETH Zurich, Computer Engineering and Networks Laboratory). It attempts to maintain a Pareto front distribution of the population with a peak near the max/min fitness, resulting in an almost-U shape distribution. This is a good operator for problems requiring long-term evolution, since it maintains a balanced diversity, which avoids sticking points.

Be sure to set the population to 1000 and the number of generations to 15 to see the full effect of the selection operator. As you go through each of the selection operators, pay particular attention to the output generated from the last cell doing the evolution. The histogram output shown for various selection operators is depicted in figure 3.7. Notice how the tournament selection operator forms a Pareto distribution of fitness, while other methods tend to diversify the fitness. Remember that more diversity benefits longer evolution and generally adapts better around sticking points. However, at the same time, more diversity requires a higher number of generations to evolve an optimum fitness.

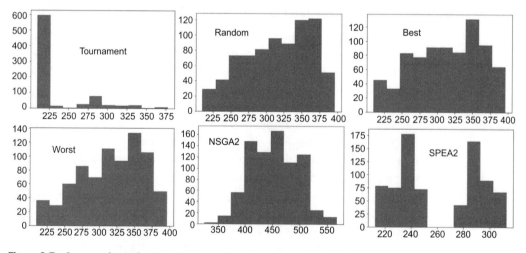

Figure 3.7   A comparison of selection operators on population diversity

Feel free to explore the various selection operators, and be sure to change the number of destinations and generations as well as the size of the populations. Take note of what effects larger and smaller populations have on selection. When you are done exploring selection, we can move on to change the crossover operator, as shown in figure 3.7. There are several types of crossover operators that can provide more efficient solution finding. When applying `crossover`, the resulting offspring often performs less effectively due to mismatching or misaligned sequences. `Genes` do not need to be aligned in sequences in all cases, but in this exercise, they do. The following is a list of the `crossover` operators used in this sample notebook and how they affect evolution:

- *Partially matched*—This method works by matching sequences of indices type `genes` and performing a `crossover` on sequences—it may not work well or as expected for other `gene` types. By preserving index sequences, this `crossover` operation is better at preserving the best parts of offspring, whereas other operators may disrupt the path or important evolved sequences.

- *Uniform partially matched*—This method is like the partially matched operator but differs in that it attempts to maintain a balanced and uniform trade of sequences between parents' `crossover`. The benefit of this method is a stronger adherence to persevering sequences over the long term, but it may make initial evolution difficult.

- *Ordered*—This `crossover` operator performs an ordered swap of index sequences. Doing so preserves the order but allows the sequence to be essentially rotated. This is a good operator to use for `populations` that may get stuck evolving sequence operations, like the TSP.

- *One point/two point*—Much like the first `crossover` operator earlier in this chapter, a one-point `crossover` selects a point at which to split the parent's `gene` sequences together. Extending this concept, the two-point `crossover` performs the same operation but uses two points to slice the `gene` sequences. These are good general methods but are not options when working with indexed sequences, like the TSP.

Genealogy plot

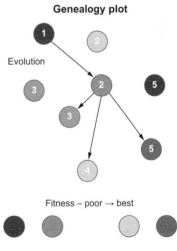

To understand the effects of changing `crossover`, we need to introduce a new type of plot called a *genealogy plot*, as shown in figure 3.8. In the figure, each circle represents a `generation`, and if that `generation` spawns a good offspring, then an arrow will be connected to the next `generation`. The genealogy plot is useful for confirming that your `crossover` operation is spawning viable, fit offspring. A good plot shows the flow from less fit to more fit offspring. Essentially, the more arrows and connections, the better; this indicates progress of the evolutionary process, where each arrow from one node to another represents a connected step, or *subspecies* in evolutionary nomenclature. Genealogy plots showing fewer connections, or no connections at all, indicate your `crossover` is not

Figure 3.8 A genealogy plot showing `individuals` evolving using `crossover`

producing viable offspring. Isolated points on this plot indicate random offspring that may have had good `fitness` but produced no viable offspring.

Increase the number of `destinations` to 10, and reduce the `population` and `generations` to 5. Generating a genealogy plot while evolving is very expensive and difficult to read for large `populations`, so this notebook limits rendering those plots to `populations` under 10. After you have done that, change the various `crossover` operators and then rerun the entire notebook with Run > Run All from the menu.

Figure 3.9 shows an example of the genealogy plots for the three different `crossover` operations this notebook supports. You can see in the figure that, apparently, the best `crossover` operation for this example is the partially matched option. As you can see in the figure, the first operator is able to successfully generate more fit offspring, whereas the uniform partially matched operator can produce viable offspring but with a less significant increase in `fitness`. To see the differences more clearly, be sure to run the notebook and visualize them yourself.

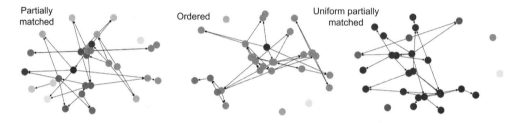

Figure 3.9   A comparison of genealogy plots of `crossover` operations

After completing this exercise, you should now have a sense of the differences between using the various genetic operators for `crossover` and `selection`. In future chapters, we look at various implementations of `mutation` operators when we get to applying EDL.

3.4.1   Learning exercises

Review the notebook by performing the following exercises:

1 Alter the `selection` or `crossover` operators from the Colab form in figure 3.6. Try each of the operators to see which works best for this problem.
2 See what effect altering the operators and hyperparameters (`population`, `crossover`, and `mutation` rate) has on the genealogy.
3 Revisit notebook EDL_3_2_QueensGambit.ipynb and change the `selection` or `crossover` operator to see what effect this has on evolution.

Building on the previous examples, we now look at another entertaining example in the final section of this chapter.

3.5 *Painting with the EvoLisa*

In 2008, Roger Johansson demonstrated the use of genetic algorithms to paint the Mona Lisa using a set of polygons. Figure 3.10 showcases the excellent results of that experiment during later stages of evolution. From the collection of images, you can see those results took almost a million `generations` to evolve.

Figure 3.10   Example of EvoLisa output from Roger Johansson's blog (https://rogerjohansson.blog/)

EvoLisa is an example of a form of generative modeling, where the goal of the algorithm is to model or replicate the output of some process. In recent years, GM has exploded, with the inception of generative deep learning (GDL) in the generative adversarial networks (GANs). Starting in chapter 8, we take a closer look at GM and GDL with GANs and how those techniques can be improved upon with EDL.

DEAP makes replicating the EvoLisa project quite easy, but it does require us to think of our simple `gene` sequences in a more complex and structured manner. Where previously, a `gene` was a single element in a list, we now need to think of a `gene` as a subset or group of elements in a list. Each of these subgroups of elements or `genes` defines one drawing polygon, with an `individual` having multiple `genes` of polygons used to draw on a canvas.

Let's get started on the next project: building the EvoLisa with DEAP and GA. As you can see from figure 3.10, getting good results could take a substantial amount of time. While we may not want to replicate those results, reviewing the process of creating complex genes is beneficial for later chapters and other projects you may work on. Open EDL_3_5_EvoLisa.ipynb in your browser, and let's begin. Consult the appendix if you need further assistance.

The first thing we need to understand is how a sequence of numbers can be converted to a gene that represents a drawing polygon or brush. Figure 3.11 outlines how we extract a set of attributes from a sequence and convert that into a drawing brush, where the first six elements represent three points on our simple polygon. After that, the next three denote color, and finally, the last element represents the alpha, or transparency. By introducing transparency, we allow each brush to overlay others, producing more complex features.

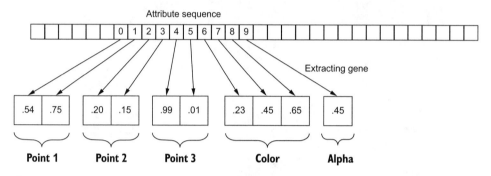

Figure 3.11   Extracting a gene from a sequence of attributes

In our previous scenarios, each attribute in a genetic sequence represented a single gene. Now, a subset of attributes comprises a single gene that represents a drawing brush. The following code listing takes a sequence of attributes (genes) and splits them by the gene length. This example is built to use a polygon as a drawing brush, but extra commented code demonstrates using other brushes, like a circle or rectangle.

Listing 3.18   EDL_3_5_EvoList.ipynb: Extracting genes

```
def extract_genes(genes, length):
    for i in range(0, len(genes), length):     │ Extracts and yields a single gene
        yield genes[i:i + length]    ◁─────────┘ from a sequence of attributes
```

In the same code block, we can see the render code that draws each of the genes. This is complex code, which we break into two listings. The first listing shows the construction of the drawing canvas and the extraction of the genes to loop through.

Listing 3.19   EDL_3_5_EvoList.ipynb: Rendering genes

```
def render_individual(individual):      Converts an individual to a NumPy array if list
    if isinstance(individual,list):
        individual = np.array(individual)   Creates a canvas based on image size
    canvas = np.zeros(SIZE+(3,))  ◁──────   and adds a third dimension for colors
```

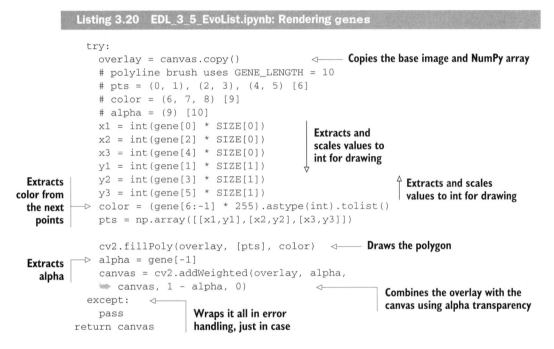

Listing 3.20 shows how each brush is defined from extracting the relevant gene attributes, where the first six values represent the three points or coordinates of the polygon to draw using the cv2.fillPoly function. Then, the extracted alpha is used to blend the brush (overlay) onto the canvas using the cv2.addWeighted function. Finally, after all the gene brushes have been drawn, the function returns the final canvas to be evaluated.

Figure 3.12 shows the result of a random individual being rendered using the render_individual function. You can generate this image by running all the notebook code via Runtime > Run All in the menu. Go ahead and do that now, as this notebook takes a substantial time to run completely.

For this demonstration, we use a classic image of the *Mona Lisa*. However, if you go to the top of the notebook, you can see other options to load various other images, from a stop sign to pictures of a celebrity, like Dwayne "the Rock" Johnson. If you want to use a different image, select from the Colab forms dropdown provided and then rerun the notebook.

We can evaluate the fitness of the function using a simple pixel-wise comparison of color values from one NumPy array to another, using mean-squared error. The

(100, 100, 3) Target image: Mona Lisa at 100x100   Sample rendered image: random individual

Figure 3.12   Target image and rendered image from a random `individual`

function in the following listing calculates the MSE between the rendered image and original image and then this error is returned as the `individual`'s `fitness` score. Keep in mind that the goal of EvoLisa is to minimize this error.

Listing 3.21   EDL_3_5_EvoList.ipynb: The `fitness` and `evaluate` functions

```
def fitness_mse(render):
    error = (np.square(render - target)).mean(axis=None)   ⊲──  Calculates MSE
    return error                                                 error from the
                                                                 render compared
                                                                 to the target
                                                       Renders
def evaluate(individual):                              the image
    render = render_individual(individual)   ⊲──┘
    print('.', end='')                       ⊲──
    return fitness_mse(render),                   Prints a point for each evaluation,
                                                  a simple progress bar
```

Returns MSE as the individual fitness

The last parts we need to look at are the setup of the genetic operators, as shown in listing 3.22. There are only a few new things going on here. We define a uniform function for generating float attributes from a uniform distribution defined by a lower and upper bound. This function is registers an `attr_float` operator and is used in the registration of the `creator.Individual` operator. Finally, we can see how the `evaluate` function is registered as the `evaluate` operator.

Listing 3.22   EDL_3_5_EvoList.ipynb: Setting up GA operators

```
def uniform(low, up, size=None):   ⊲──  A uniform function
    try:                                generates individual
```

```
    return [random.uniform(a, b) for a, b in zip(low, up)]
  except TypeError:
    return [random.uniform(a, b) for a, b in zip([low] * size, [up] * size)]

toolbox = base.Toolbox()
toolbox.register("attr_float", uniform, 0, 1, NUM_GENES)
toolbox.register("individual", tools.initIterate, creator.Individual,
     toolbox.attr_float)
toolbox.register("population", tools.initRepeat, list, toolbox.individual)

toolbox.register("mutate", tools.mutGaussian, mu=0.0, sigma=1, indpb=.05)
toolbox.register("evaluate", evaluate)
```

Registers an attr_float operator for individual creating

Registers an individual created with attr_float operator

Registers evaluate function

Figure 3.13 shows the results of running this example for around 5,000 generations using a rectangle brush and the polyline brush. The code to implement a circle or rectangle brush is commented out but shown as an option for interested readers.

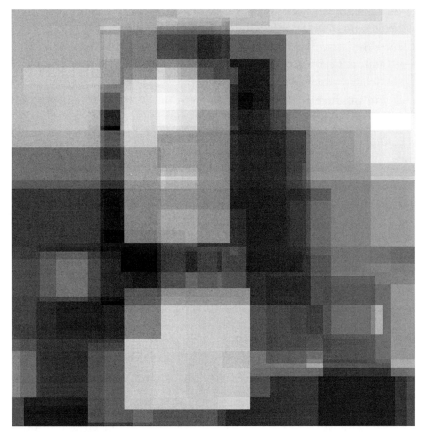

Gen (4828) : fitness = 972.099264861376   Rectangle brush

Figure 3.13   Example output of EvoLisa using different brush formats (rectangle and polyfill)

Be sure to go back and use the Colab forms options provided in this example to alter the settings and then rerun the EvoLisa. Are you able to improve on how quickly EvoLisa can replicate an image? Be sure to also try adjusting the number of polygons (brushes/genes) EvoLisa is using.

EvoLisa was a great demonstration of generative modeling with genetic algorithms just over a decade ago. Since that time, the advent of GDL has demonstrated far superior results using GANs. However, the EvoLisa demonstrates how we can encode and evolve sets of genes or instructions, which can define a much more complex process. While the applications appear similar, the underlying mechanism of the EvoLisa demonstrates a different form of optimization.

3.5.1   *Learning exercises*

Complete the following exercises to build on the concepts discussed in this section:

1   Switch to different images to see how well the evolution can copy the original. You may even want to add your own images.
2   Increase or decrease the number of genes and polygons used to render the image and then see what effect this has.
3   Alter the mutation, crossover, and population to see what effect they have on evolution. Can you reduce the number of generations to a better facsimile of the selected image?
4   Try to produce the best facsimile you can. Feel free to contact the author to show your impressive results.

After reading this chapter, we now know the basics of evolutionary computation and the inner workings of genetic algorithms.

Summary

- Distributed Evolutionary Algorithms in Python (DEAP) is an excellent tool that incorporate a variety of evolutionary algorithms, including genetic methods. Genetic algorithm hyperparameters of population size, number of generations, crossover rate, and mutation rate can be adjusted to fit individual solutions. DEAP can be quickly configured and set up to tackle a variety of problems using basic building blocks:
  - *The creator*—This holds the definition of the individual.
  - *The toolbox*—This defines a set of helper functions and a place to define the genetic operators and operations.
  - *The hall of fame*—This tracks the top successful individuals.
  - *Statistics*—These track basic metrics that can be used to evaluate the success of a population.
  - *Historical objects*—These provide the ability to track custom or other external operations.

- The Queen's Gambit is a simulated chess problem that can be solved using genetic algorithms with DEAP.
- The traveling salesman problem, a classic complex path organization problem, can be solved using genetic algorithms with DEAP.
- Visualizing the `population` diversity of `fitness` using a histogram can identify evolutionary `populations` that may stagnate.
- Genealogy plots can be read to determine how well the `crossover` operation is working during evolution. They provide insight into the evaluation and performance of various `selection` genetic operators on `population` evolution. The effectiveness of how well a particular `crossover` operation is performing can be evaluated with the use of a genealogy plot.
- An individual's simulated genetic code can represent a process or order of operations. They can even implement a complex genetic structure to represent an order of complex operations for replicating or copying images.

More evolutionary
computation with DEAP

This chapter covers

- Developing regression solvers with genetic programming in DEAP

- Applying particle swarm optimization to solve for unknowns in complex functions

- Breaking a problem into components and coevolving a solution

- Understanding and applying evolutionary strategies to approximating solutions

- Approximating continuous and discontinuous solutions with differentiable evolution

In chapter 3, we just started to scratch the surface of what evolutionary computation looks like by introducing GAs. Starting with GA helps us set several foundations we continue to develop in this chapter. We also continue our progression from GA by exploring other evolutionary search methods for solving more specialized and complex problems. In this chapter, we look at other forms of the evolutionary search for solving a wider variety of problems.

There are a wide variety and forms of evolutionary algorithms, each with different strengths and weaknesses. Understanding other available options strengthens our understanding of where to apply which algorithm. As seen in this chapter, there is more than one way to peel an orange.

4.1   Genetic programming with DEAP

We have already used DEAP extensively for developing GA solutions to a variety of problems. In the following notebook, we continue to use DEAP to explore a subset of EC/GA called *genetic programming* (GP). GP follows the same principles of GA and employs many of the same genetic operators. The key difference between GA and GP is the structure of the gene or chromosome and how fitness is evaluated. Genetic programming and gene expression programming (GEP) can be used to solve a diverse set of automation and control problems, as discussed later in this book.

The notebook we develop in this section demonstrates one application of genetic programming for solving regression. GEP could also be applied to a variety of other problems, from optimization to search. Demonstrating regression, however, is the most relevant for our purposes, since it is comparable to how we can solve the same problem with DL.

In this notebook, we are solving a problem of multivariable regression, using GEP to derive a solution equation. The goal is that this equation successfully regresses or predicts an output value, given several input values. This example only uses random inputs pre-fed into a target equation to validate the results. However, this method can and has been used to perform regression, in a similar manner that we would use in DL.

4.1.1   Solving regression with genetic programming

You can start the exercise by opening the EDL_4_1_GP_Regression.ipynb notebook in Google Colab. If you need assistance opening the file, consult the appendix. This exercise may feel similar to the DEAP exercises in chapter 3. For ease of use, go ahead and run all the cells in the notebook using the menu Runtime > Run All.

We can skip the first few code cells that do setup and imports to focus on the first piece of new code shown in listing 4.1. This code essentially defines a special set of genes we can represent in an individual. In this code, we can see the definition of three distinct types of genes: the operator, constant, and input or argument. To understand this code, let's take a step back and look at how GP works.

> **Listing 4.1   EDL_4_1_GP_Regression.ipynb: Setting up the expression**

```
pset = gp.PrimitiveSet("MAIN", 4)    ⟵── Starts by creating and naming the primitive set

pset.addPrimitive(np.add, 2, name="vadd")    ⟵── Adds the operators to the set
pset.addPrimitive(np.subtract, 2, name="vsub")
pset.addPrimitive(np.multiply, 2, name="vmul")
pset.addPrimitive(protectedDiv, 2)
pset.addPrimitive(np.negative, 1, name="vneg")
```

```
pset.addPrimitive(np.cos, 1, name="vcos")
pset.addPrimitive(np.sin, 1, name="vsin")

pset.addEphemeralConstant("rand101", lambda:
    random.randint(-1,1))                          ◁——— Adds ephemeral constants to the set

pset.renameArguments(ARG0='x1')    ◁——— Adds the variable inputs
pset.renameArguments(ARG1='x2')
pset.renameArguments(ARG2='x3')
pset.renameArguments(ARG3='x4')
```

Genetic programming (GP) allows us to be more specialized in the type of problems we solve and how we solve them. With GP, we don't just search for novel solutions but, rather, develop mathematical functions or programmatic code that can be used to derive such solutions. The benefit here is that these functions can be reused or investigated for a better understanding of specific problems.

In GEP, each gene represents either an operator, constant, or input, and the entire chromosome or gene sequence represents an expression tree, where an operator could represent something as simple as addition or subtraction or as complex as programmatic functions. Constants and inputs/arguments, then, represent single scalar values or more complex arrays and tensors.

Figure 4.1 demonstrates the gene sequence of an individual that may be consumed by GP. In the diagram, you can see how the order of operators and inputs/constants forms an expression tree that can be evaluated as an equation, which can then be evaluated using mathematical rules. The output of this equation

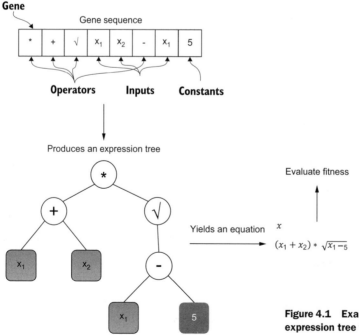

Figure 4.1   Example GP individual to expression tree to equation to fitness

can then be compared against some target value to determine the amount of error or `fitness` of the `individual`.

The `gene` sequence pictured in figure 4.1 shows how the order of the operators, inputs/arguments, and constants form an uneven leaf node expression tree. Looking at the `gene` sequence, we can see the first operator is *, which maps to the root of the tree. From those, the next two `genes` extend to first-level nodes, represented by the + and √ operators. The next two `genes` in the sequence map to the + node. Following that, the − operator is attached to the √ node, and finally, the last `genes` map to the bottom nodes.

The number of subnodes formed of each node depends on the order of the operator. Where the order of an operator could be unary, binary, ternary or *n*-nary in scope. For simplicity, in this example, we use binary operators *, −, and + and the unary operator √. Inputs and constants do not have an order and always represent leaf nodes in an expression tree.

From the expression tree, an equation can be evaluated with a result representing some target output. This targeted output is compared to the expected value in a form of supervised learning, with the difference representing the error or, in this case, `fitness`. The goal in this problem is to reduce the `fitness` or error to a minimum value.

We can scroll down from the last code block we looked at in the notebook and past the cells that create the `creator` to the start of the `toolbox` setup. After the `toolbox` is created, the next line sets up the expression tree evaluator. In this example, shown in the following listing, we use an out-of-the-box expression tree generator called `genHalfandHalf`, which has a 50% probability of using either of its two different forms of tree.

Listing 4.2   EDL_4_1_GP_Regression.ipynb: Setting up the `toolbox`

```
toolbox = base.Toolbox()
toolbox.register("expr", gp.genHalfAndHalf,           Defines the type of
     pset=pset, min_=1, max_=2)          ◁──────      expression generation

toolbox.register("individual", tools.initIterate, creator.Individual,
     toolbox.expr)
toolbox.register("population", tools.initRepeat, list, toolbox.individual)
toolbox.register("compile", gp.compile, pset=pset)
```
Creates a compile function using the primitive set definition

In expression tree generation, we can assume trees are generated using two basic rules. One rule assumes all leaf nodes in a tree are at the same level, or even. The other rule assumes leaf nodes can be uneven. The example shown in figure 4.1 is an example of an uneven leaf node expression tree. The code in listing 4.2 uses the `genHalfAndHalf` function to allow for the generation of both forms of tree.

Next, we look at how the sample input values are randomly generated using a couple of lines of code with the help of NumPy, as shown in the following listing. The x inputs are generated using NumPy's random `rand` function with a shape of 4, 10000, representing 4 inputs over 10,000 rows. Then, we calculate target y values using an ad hoc equation our solution should replicate later.

Listing 4.3   EDL_4_1_GP_Regression.ipynb: Generating data

```
x = np.random.rand(4, 10000)    ◁——— Creates a random tensor of 4, 10000
y = (x[3] + x[0]) / x[2] * x[1] ◁——┐
                                    │ Evaluates target values using the defined equation
```

The goal of our GP evolution is to recreate the equation we use in listing 4.3 to calculate the target values. We are using randomized data in this example, but you could certainly apply the same principles to structured data defined by input features *x* and target output *y* for solving other forms of regression problems.

Before we move on, let's jump back to one of the earlier code cells, as shown in listing 4.4. We can see the definition of a function, `protected_div`, which replaces the division operator we normally use. We need to do this to avoid division by zero errors we may encounter using NumPy. Refer to listing 4.1 to see how this function is used to define the division operator for the expression `primitive` set.

Listing 4.4   EDL_4_1_GP_Regression.ipynb: The `protected_div` function

```
def protectedDiv(left, right):                              ◁——┐ A wrapper to protect
  with np.errstate(divide='ignore',invalid='ignore'):          │ against division by zero
    x = np.divide(left, right)
    if isinstance(x, np.ndarray):
      x[np.isinf(x)] = 1
      x[np.isnan(x)] = 1
    elif np.isinf(x) or np.isnan(x):
      x = 1
  return x
```

From here, we move on to reviewing the `fitness` function, called `evalSymbReg` in this example, for evaluating the amount of difference in error between the compiled expression and the values by passing in each of the inputs. Notice in the following listing how NumPy allows us to process all 10,000 sample rows of data in one pass to output the total error or difference.

Listing 4.5   EDL_4_1_GP_Regression.ipynb: Evaluating the `fitness`

```
def evalSymbReg(individual):
  func = toolbox.compile(expr=individual)    ◁——┘ Compiles the expression into a tree
  diff = np.sum((func(x[0],x[1],x[2],x[3]) - y)**2)   ◁——┐
  return diff,   ◁——┐                                     │ Evaluates the difference from
                     │ Returns the difference or error    │ compiled expression func from
                     │ as the individual fitness          │ the values and square
```

The remainder of the code is quite like the previous chapter exercises, so we won't need to review it here. Figure 4.2 shows the output expression tree for an evolution that found a minimum amount of error or fitness below one. This expression tree graph is created with network, as defined in the plot_expression function shown in listing 4.6. When this expression tree is evaluated, we can see the produced equation and resulting code matches the original function to calculate y, as shown in listing 4.3. You may also notice that the expression tree introduced another protected division operator, which just resulted in the last term being flipped from the actual equation. Mathematically, the solved output expression tree matches the original equation used to produce y.

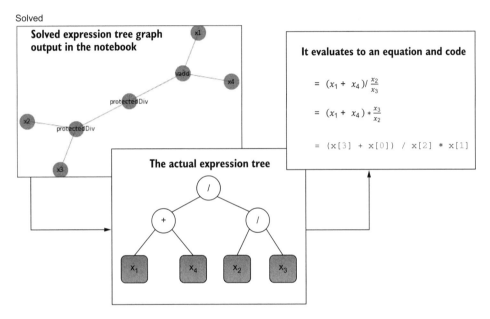

Solved

Solved expression tree graph output in the notebook

It evaluates to an equation and code

$$= (x_1 + x_4)/\frac{x_2}{x_3}$$

$$= (x_1 + x_4) * \frac{x_3}{x_2}$$

$$= (x[3] + x[0]) / x[2] * x[1]$$

The actual expression tree

Figure 4.2 Solved expression tree graph as it evaluates to equations and code

Listing 4.6 shows how the expression tree is plotted using the plot_expression function. As in the exercises in chapter 3, we continue to output the top or best individual by fitness. In this case, we want the fitness to minimize or approach a value of zero. The expression trees drawn with the plot_expression function uses a Fruchterman-Reingold force-directed algorithm to position the nodes. Networkx provides a variety of position algorithms or layouts, but spring works for most cases.

Listing 4.6 EDL_4_1_GP_Regression.ipynb: Plotting the expression tree

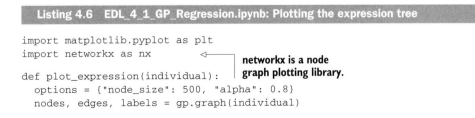

```
import matplotlib.pyplot as plt
import networkx as nx                    ◁─────┐  networkx is a node
                                                 graph plotting library.
def plot_expression(individual):
  options = {"node_size": 500, "alpha": 0.8}
  nodes, edges, labels = gp.graph(individual)
```

```
g = nx.Graph()
g.add_nodes_from(nodes)
g.add_edges_from(edges)

pos = nx.spring_layout(g)
nx.draw_networkx_nodes(g, pos, **options)
nx.draw_networkx_edges(g, pos, width=1.0, alpha=0.5)
nx.draw_networkx_labels(g, pos, labels, font_size=9, font_color='k')
plt.show()
```

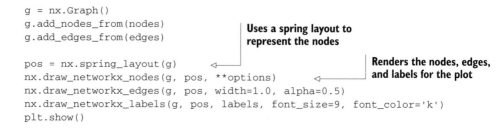

Uses a spring layout to represent the nodes

Renders the nodes, edges, and labels for the plot

In this example, we used randomized data to evolve a regression function that can generate our original equation. It is entirely possible to modify this example to consume CSV-structured data to produce regression equations that solve real-world problems.

GP provides the ability to generate equations or actual programmatic code using the same concept of expression tree generation. This is because, fundamentally, all programming code can be represented as an expression tree, where something like an `if` statement is a Boolean operator that takes binary inputs or complex functions, represented as *n*-nary operators with a single return value.

Gene expression programming

The form of genetic programming we use in this example is known more specifically as gene expression programming (GEP). GEP was developed in 2002 by Candida Ferreira, who is currently the director of Gepsoft, an AI/ML tools software organization that produces a tool called Gene Expression Programming Tools. This tool can be used to perform GEP over structured data that produces a variety of forms of output, from equations to actual programmatic code across several languages. If you want to explore using GEP for structured data, then you should certainly visit the Gepsoft website and download a trial version of the software (www.gepsoft.com).

The benefit of GEP is the generation of actual mathematical functions or programming code that can later be optimized and reused. However, GEP can also generate overly complex functions or code that may make the solution unusable. If you go back and run the last exercise with greater than four inputs, you can verify the increased complexity of the expression trees generated during evolution.

4.1.2   *Learning exercises*

Please complete the following exercises to help improve your knowledge of the concepts:

1 Change the target function in listing 4.3 and then rerun the notebook. What happens if you make the equation more complex?

2 Remove or comment on some of the operators in listing 4.1, and then rerun. What happens when there are fewer operators to evolve. Is it what you expect?

3 Alter the genetic operators and/or `crossover`, `selection`, or `mutation` parameters and then rerun.

After using evolution to construct gene sequences, we now want to move on to a more tangible implementation of survival of the fittest. In the next section, we go back to the roots of our life simulations in chapter 2 and introduce particle swarm optimization.

4.2 Particle swarm optimization with DEAP

Particle swarm optimization (PSO) is another EC method that borrows the concepts of survival of the fittest and swarming behaviors. In the next notebook, we use PSO to approximate the optimum parameters needed to solve a function using DEAP. This is a simple example that demonstrates the power of PSO for solving inputs to parametric functions.

A common use case for PSO is solving the required input parameters in a known equation or function. For example, if we wanted to shoot a cannon ball a specified distance, we would consider the equation from the physics shown in figure 4.3.

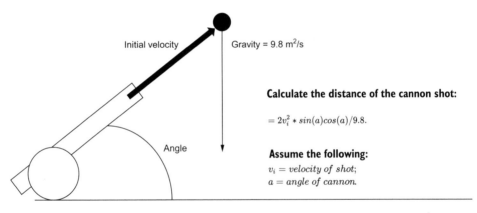

Figure 4.3 **Calculating distance of a cannon shot**

4.2.1 Solving equations with PSO

We could attempt to solve the equation in figure 4.3 using several mathematical and optimization methods. Of course, we are not going to do that but, instead, use PSO to find the desired optimum initial velocity of the shot and the angle at which it is shot. Open EDL_4_2_PSO.ipynb in Google Colab and start the following exercise.

The code in this exercise uses DEAP, so most of it should be familiar. Here, we focus on a few key cells of code that uniquely define PSO. Start by scrolling to the where the `toolbox` is set up, as shown in the following listing. The `toolbox` registers several key functions for generating, updating, and evaluating `particles`. It can be helpful to think of these as `particle` operators, making sure not to call them genetic operators.

> **Listing 4.7 EDL_4_2_PSO.ipynb: Setting up the `toolbox`**

```
toolbox = base.Toolbox()
toolbox.register("particle",
                 generate, size=2, pmin=-6,
                 pmax=6, smin=-3, smax=3)
```
Registers the generate function to create a new particle

```
toolbox.register("population",
                 tools.initRepeat, list,
         ➡ toolbox.particle)   ◁───┐ Registers the particle as
                                         individuals in the population
toolbox.register("update",
                 updateParticle, phi1=200, phi2=200)   ◁──┐
─▷ toolbox.register("evaluate", evaluate)                    Registers the updateParticle
                                                            function to update particles
  Registers the function to evaluate the fitness of individuals
```

We first look at the `generate` operator and the function of the same name. The generate function shown in listing 4.8 creates an array of `particles` with starting positions set by `pmin` and `pmax`. During a swarm optimization, each `particle` has a set speed or distance it can cover in an update. During an update, the `particles` are moved or swarmed to position using the evaluation of `fitness`.

Listing 4.8   EDL_4_2_PSO.ipynb: Generating a `particle`

```
def generate(size, pmin, pmax, smin, smax):
  part = creator.Particle(np.random.uniform(pmin,
  ➡ pmax, size))                              ◁─── Creates an array of particles

  part.speed = np.random.uniform(smin, smax, size)   ◁──┐
  part.smin = smin                                         Creates a random
  part.smax = smax                                         speed vector
 return part
```

Next, we look at the update operator function called `updateParticle`, shown in the following listing. This function is responsible for updating the position of the `particle` during each iteration of the swarm optimization. In PSO, the idea is to continually swarm the `particles` around the fittest `particles`. Within the update function, `particles` are swarmed by altering their speed and position.

Listing 4.9   EDL_4_2_PSO.ipynb: Updating the `particle`

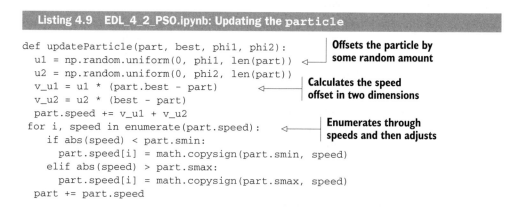

```
def updateParticle(part, best, phi1, phi2):          Offsets the particle by
  u1 = np.random.uniform(0, phi1, len(part))   ◁──┘ some random amount
  u2 = np.random.uniform(0, phi2, len(part))
  v_u1 = u1 * (part.best - part)        ◁──┐ Calculates the speed
  v_u2 = u2 * (best - part)                  offset in two dimensions
  part.speed += v_u1 + v_u2
 for i, speed in enumerate(part.speed):   ◁──┐ Enumerates through
    if abs(speed) < part.smin:                 speeds and then adjusts
      part.speed[i] = math.copysign(part.smin, speed)
    elif abs(speed) > part.smax:
      part.speed[i] = math.copysign(part.smax, speed)
  part += part.speed
```

Figure 4.4 demonstrates how PSO swarms the various `particles` around the target area of optimization. If we were to plot the angle and velocity on a graph, then we could think of each `particle` or point as a guess or attempt at shooting the cannon.

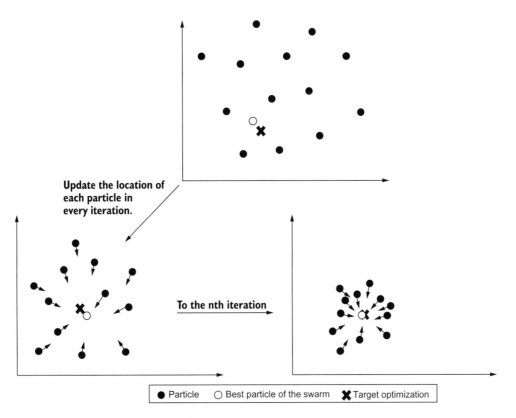

Figure 4.4   Particle swarm optimization

The goal of PSO, therefore, is to find the optimum parameters (velocity and angle) that shoot the cannon ball to a target distance.

We look at the evaluation function `evaluate` registered to the `toolbox` in listing 4.7 next. At the start of this block of code, we define the target distance, exposing it as a notebook slider input. Since the velocity term is squared in the equation from figure 4.3, we only want to allow positive values. This is the reason we guard against negative values. Similarly, we assume the angle is in degrees and then convert it into radians for use in the equation. Lastly, we use the equation to calculate the distance and subtract it from target distance. Then we return the squared value to return the sum of the squares' error term as a tuple from the function.

Listing 4.10   EDL_4_2_PSO.ipynb: Evaluating the `particle`

```
distance = 575 #@param {type:"slider", min:10,
⇒ max:1000, step:5}
def evaluate(individual):
    v = individual[0] if individual[0] > 0 else 0
    ⇒ #velocity
```

Allows the input distance to be exposed as a slider form control

Makes sure velocity is a positive value

```
      a = individual[1] * math.pi / 180  #angle to radians
      return ((2*v**2 * math.sin(a) * math.cos(a))/9.8 -
         distance)**2,
```

Converts the angle from degrees to radians

Returns the squared error from the distance to the calculated value

With the basic operations set up, we can move on to the swarming code. This block of code, shown in listing 4.11, is significantly simpler than our other GA or GP examples. Unlike GA or GP, in PSO, `particles` live for the entire simulation. Since the `particles` have long lives, we can track the best `fitness` value for each. Tracking the best `fitness` on each `particle` allows the current best `particle`, denoted by `best` in the code listing, to be swapped. The `toolbox.update` call on the last line is where the particles in the swarm are repositioned, based on the position of the best `particle`, using the `updateParticle` function from listing 4.9.

Listing 4.11   EDL_4_2_PSO.ipynb: Swarming

```
GEN = 100        Sets the number of swarming generations
best = None

for g in range(GEN):
    for part in pop:        Cycles through particles in the population
        part.fitness.values = tuple(np.subtract((0,), toolbox.evaluate(part)))

        if part.best is None or part.best.fitness <    Checks for the best
            part.fitness:                              fitness for the particle
            part.best = creator.Particle(part)
            part.best.fitness.values = part.fitness.values
        if best is None or best.fitness < part.fitness:
            best = creator.Particle(part)             Checks if it is better
            best.fitness.values = part.fitness.values  than the best particle
    for part in pop:
        toolbox.update(part, best)    Loops through the population
                                      and updates the toolbox
```

As the simulation runs, you will see how the `particles` begin to converge to the best or multiple best solutions, shown in figure 4.5. Notice there are two correct solutions for the angle and velocity in this problem. Also notice that the `particles` are still spread

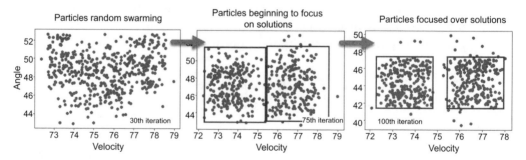

Figure 4.5   Particle swarm scatter by iteration

some distance across the solution. This is due to the selection of the hyperparameters pmin, pmax, smin, smax, phi1, and phi2, and you can change the amount of particle spread by adjusting those values. If you want to see a smaller spread of particles, adjust those hyperparameters to smaller values, and then run the notebook again.

Finally, the last block of code in the notebook allows us to evaluate the best particle's prescribed solution. Keep in mind, though, that since the problem has two solutions, there is a possibility we could evaluate multiple best solutions. From the output value, you can see that PSO can do a relatively quick approximation of the solution to firing a cannon a certain distance, as shown in the following listing.

Listing 4.12 EDL_4_2_PSO.ipynb: Outputting the best

```
v, a = best                        ◁——— Pulls out the velocity and angle from best
a = a * math.pi / 180  #angle to radians   ◁———
distance = (2*v**2 * math.sin(a) * math.cos(a))/9.8   Converts the angle from
print(distance)                                       degrees to radians
```
Calculates the distance of the shot

PSO can be applied to a variety of other problems with various effectiveness. Swarming optimization is a lightweight method to find unknown parameters. As seen in chapter 5, PSO can provide simple optimization of hyperparameters to DL systems.

4.2.2 Learning exercises

Improve your knowledge by exploring some or all the following exercises:

1 Alter the target distance in listing 4.10. What effect does this have on the PSO solution?
2 Modify the pmin, pmax, smin, and smax inputs in listing 4.7 and then rerun.
3 Modify the phi1 and phi2 parameters in listing 4.7 and then rerun. What effect does this have on finding the solution?

Now that we have covered optimizing particles, we move on in the next section to exploring more complex evolutionary processes, such as codependent or coevolving solutions.

4.3 Coevolving solutions with DEAP

Life on our planet exists in a symbiotic relationship, with millions of species dependent on one another for survival. Some terms to describe this relationship are *coevolution* and *codependent evolution*. We can, likewise, simulate coevolution using evolutionary methods when attempting to solve more complex problems.

In the next notebook, we revisit the regression problem we addressed with GP in the first example of this chapter. This time we move from a toy problem to something of a more real-world example, using a sample structured dataset called the Boston housing (BH) market.

The BH dataset encompasses 13 feature columns to help predict the value of a house in the Boston market. We could, of course, use GP alone to try to derive an equation, but the result would be overly complicated. Instead, in the following example, we look at pairing GP with GA using coevolution, in hopes of deriving a much simpler output.

4.3.1   Coevolving genetic programming with genetic algorithms

This exercise alternates between two notebooks. The first is an upgrade from our earlier GP example to EDL_4_GP_Regression.ipynb, which replaces the toy problem with the BH dataset. The second notebook, EDL_4_3_CoEV_Regression.ipynb, demonstrates using coevolution to solve the same problem—this time using both GP and GA.

Open the EDL_4_GP_Regression.ipynb notebook, and then run all cells with Runtime > Run All from the menu. The key difference between this notebook and EDL_4_3_COEV_Regression.ipynb is the use of the BH dataset that we can import, as shown in listing 4.13. The BH dataset is loaded from the sklearn.datasets, and we return the features, x, plus targets, y. Then the axes are swapped to accommodate the row, feature format, and number of inputs extracted. The number of inputs defines the number of arguments in the derived equation.

> **Listing 4.13   EDL_4_3_COEV_Regression.ipynb: Setting up data**

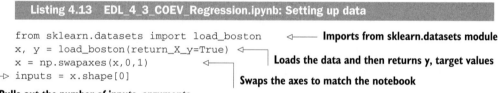

```
from sklearn.datasets import load_boston        ⟵── Imports from sklearn.datasets module
x, y = load_boston(return_X_y=True)  ⟵┐
x = np.swapaxes(x,0,1)               ⟵─┤   Loads the data and then returns y, target values
inputs = x.shape[0]                       └── Swaps the axes to match the notebook
```
┌─▷ inputs = x.shape[0]
│
Pulls out the number of inputs, arguments

Figure 4.6 shows the results of evolving the equation to a minimum fitness score less than 135, a value selected to simplify a solution. The resulting equation shows that not

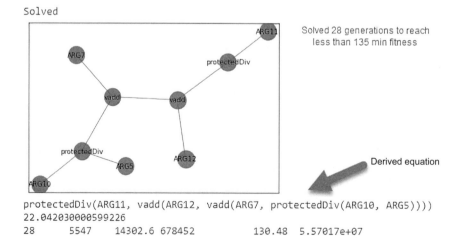

Solved

Solved 28 generations to reach less than 135 min fitness

Derived equation

```
protectedDiv(ARG11, vadd(ARG12, vadd(ARG7, protectedDiv(ARG10, ARG5))))
22.042030000599226
28      5547      14302.6 678452                  130.48   5.57017e+07
```

Figure 4.6   Output of GP_Regression notebook

all the features are used in the derived equation, with only ARG5, ARG7, ARG10, ARG11, and ARG12 being relevant. This also means the GP solution is automatically performing feature selection by ignoring less-relevant features.

Next, open the EDL_4_3_COEV_Regression.ipynb notebook in Colab, and then run all the cells. There is a lot of code in this notebook, but we have seen all of it before in various other examples. The primary difference in this example is we are simultaneously using both GP and GA methods to fine-tune a derived equation. That means there is double the code, but most of it we have seen before. The first thing to notice, as shown in the following listing, is that we construct two toolboxes—one for the GA population and the other for GP.

Listing 4.14 EDL_4_3_COEV_Regression.ipynb: Toolbox registration

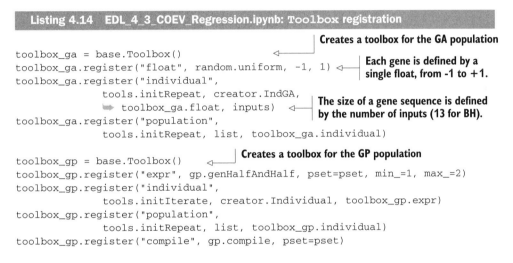

```
toolbox_ga = base.Toolbox()                          ←───┘ Creates a toolbox for the GA population
toolbox_ga.register("float", random.uniform, -1, 1) ←──┤ Each gene is defined by a
toolbox_ga.register("individual",                        single float, from -1 to +1.
          tools.initRepeat, creator.IndGA,
          ➡ toolbox_ga.float, inputs) ←──┤ The size of a gene sequence is defined
toolbox_ga.register("population",                    by the number of inputs (13 for BH).
          tools.initRepeat, list, toolbox_ga.individual)

toolbox_gp = base.Toolbox()   ←──┘ Creates a toolbox for the GP population
toolbox_gp.register("expr", gp.genHalfAndHalf, pset=pset, min_=1, max_=2)
toolbox_gp.register("individual",
          tools.initIterate, creator.Individual, toolbox_gp.expr)
toolbox_gp.register("population",
          tools.initRepeat, list, toolbox_gp.individual)
toolbox_gp.register("compile", gp.compile, pset=pset)
```

In this example, the GP solver is working to build a derived equation. The GA solver is, in tandem, coevolving a sequence of scaler genes with a size equal to the number of inputs/features. For the BH dataset, the number of inputs equals 13. Each GA scaler gene value is used to scale the features being input into the equations. We can see how this is applied in the evaluation function called evalSymbReg, shown in the following listing. When this function is used to evaluate fitness, we pass two individuals. The individual input represents a GP individual, and the points input represents a GA individual. Each evaluation of this function is done with two individuals from both the GA and GP populations.

Listing 4.15 EDL_4_3_COEV_Regression.ipynb: The fitness evaluation

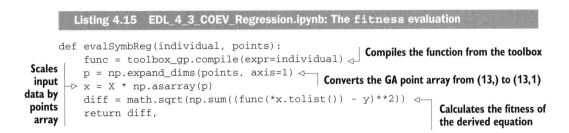

```
def evalSymbReg(individual, points):
    func = toolbox_gp.compile(expr=individual) ←┘ Compiles the function from the toolbox
    p = np.expand_dims(points, axis=1) ←──┐
    x = X * np.asarray(p)                   Converts the GA point array from (13,) to (13,1)
    diff = math.sqrt(np.sum((func(*x.tolist()) - y)**2)) ←──┐
    return diff,                                            Calculates the fitness of
                                                            the derived equation
```

Scales input data by points array

Often, in coevolution scenarios, you won't want both methods to evolve at the same rate. In this example, we, for instance, allow the GA population, the scalers, to evolve much more quickly than the GP population. This allows the GA method to fine-tune the scale or weight of parameters being used in the derived GP equation. Essentially, this allows the GA method to fine-tune the equation for a better fit. For this notebook, we set an evolution rate between the GA to GP at 10 to 1. These hyperparameters are set in the following code listing.

Listing 4.16 EDL_4_3_COEV_Regression.ipynb: Controlling the evolution step

```
GA_GEN, GP_GEN, BASE_POP = 1, 10, 10000          ◁────┐  Controls generation
pop_ga = toolbox_ga.population(n=BASE_POP*GA_GEN)      │  frequency hyperparameters
pop_gp = toolbox_gp.population(n=BASE_POP*GP_GEN)
```
Adjusts the population start by generation frequency

In the evolution code, we control how frequently each population evolves with the code from the following listing. This block of code shows the evolution for the GA population, but the same process is applied for GP as well. The hyperparameter GA_GEN controls the frequency of evolution.

Listing 4.17 EDL_4_3_COEV_Regression.ipynb: Evolving the population

```
if (g+1) % GA_GEN == 0:                          ◁────┐  If this is the evolution
  off_ga = toolbox_ga.select(pop_ga, len(pop_ga))      │  step, then evolve.
  off_ga = [toolbox_ga.clone(ind) for ind in off_ga]

  for ind1, ind2 in zip(off_ga[::2], off_ga[1::2]):    ◁──── Crossover
    if random.random() < CXPB:
      toolbox_ga.mate(ind1, ind2)
      del ind1.fitness.values
      del ind2.fitness.values

  for ind in off_ga:          ◁──── Mutation
    if random.random() < MUTPB:
      toolbox_ga.mutate(ind)
      del ind.fitness.values
                             ┐  Assigns offspring to
  pop_ga = off_ga     ◁──────┘  replace the population
```

Remember that when we evaluate fitness, the function requires individuals from both populations—GA and GP. That means the code for evaluating individuals is tied to each population. Notice that when we evaluate fitness for the GA or GP populations, we use the alternate population's best performer. This simplification approximates the top fitness for each population. An alternative method would be to loop through both populations and test each combination. This method would be computationally expensive, so we revert to the simplification shown in the following listing.

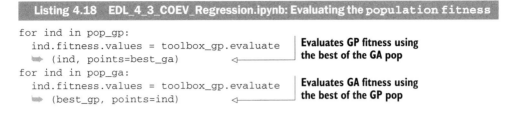

Listing 4.18   EDL_4_3_COEV_Regression.ipynb: Evaluating the population fitness

```
for ind in pop_gp:
    ind.fitness.values = toolbox_gp.evaluate          Evaluates GP fitness using
    ⇒ (ind, points=best_ga)                           the best of the GA pop
for ind in pop_ga:
    ind.fitness.values = toolbox_gp.evaluate          Evaluates GA fitness using
    ⇒ (best_gp, points=ind)                           the best of the GP pop
```

Figure 4.7 shows the final output of running this example to a solution, again assuming a `fitness` below 135. As you can see, the derived equation has been significantly simplified. The best GA `individual` assigns the scaler used to modify the equation inputs. In figure 4.7, you can see how the final equation applies the input scaling.

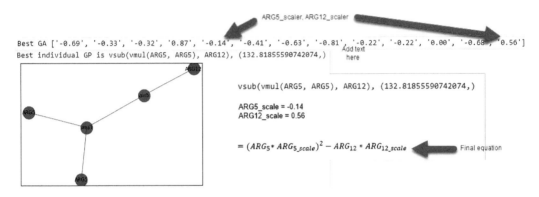

Figure 4.7   The best coevolved solution

The final derived equation shows a potential solution for predicting a BH market value. If we look at the resulting equation and consult the BH features, as displayed in the notebooks, we can see ARG5 is NOX (nitrous oxide concentration) and ARG12 is LSTAT (percentage of lower status `population`) are identified as the primary features used.

If you consult the GP regression notebook solved equation shown in figure 4.6, you will also notice that ARG5 and ARG12 are considered important features along with ARG7, ARG10, and ARG11. The coevolved solution was able to further reduce features weighting by the inputs passed into the equation. This resulted in a possibly oversimplified equation, but with it, we can identify a key correlation between the NOX and LSTAT features in the BH dataset.

GP regression results

As GP evolves, it often creates more complex or overly complex equations. Long-running evolutions may even break from the size of the expression tree. Introducing GA with GP allows equations to be fine-tuned. However, this may result in oversimplifications of problems. The size of the dataset can also be especially problematic, given the BH set is only 500+ rows. You will get better results with more data, in most cases.

Now, the coevolved solution we just evaluated is not without fault. It certainly addresses the complexity problem often found in GP. Obviously, though, the final answer may be too simple and missing other key features to infer good enough accuracy. Yet it is also simple enough to calculate with a basic calculator and on the fly.

We move on to using other coevolved solutions in later chapters to balance multiple forms of EC being applied to DL. As we have seen in the previous exercise, coevolution can bound multiple forms of EC to solve a common complex solution. Balancing coevolution is something we spend time mastering as we progress through later examples.

4.4   *Evolutionary strategies with DEAP*

Evolutionary strategies are an expansion of evolutionary and genetic methods that add controlling subgenes or phenotypes, called *strategies*. These strategies are nothing more than an additional vector that controls or influences the `mutation` operator. This provides ES for more efficient solving of various complex problems, including function approximation.

In the next notebook, we explore a function approximation problem we revisit later when we look at evolution with DL. To keep things simple, we look at approximating function parameters of a known continuous polynomial solution here. Then, we move on to more complex discontinuous solutions and see how well ES performs.

4.4.1   *Applying evolutionary strategies to function approximation*

ES differs from "vanilla" GAs in that an `individual` carries an additional `gene` sequence or vector, called a strategy. Over the course of the evolution, this strategy vector learns to adjust and apply better, fine-tuned `mutation` to `individual` evolution.

As we discovered in chapter 3, `mutation` and `mutation` rate are like the learning rate in DL. The `mutation` controls the variability of the `population` during evolution. The higher the `mutation` rate is, the more variable and diverse the `population` will be. The ability to control and learn this `mutation` rate over iterations allows us to determine solutions more efficiently.

In the following notebook, we set up an ES algorithm to approximate to known solutions. We also discuss how learning to optimize the `mutation` over time allows a `population` to better converge and approximate solutions. Let's start by opening notebook EDL_4_4_ES.ipynb in Google Colab and running the whole notebook.

Evolutionary strategies are an extension of GA, and as such, much of the code we need to use DEAP for is similar to what we have seen before. We look over the key differences here, focusing on how ES is implemented, starting with the hyperparameter definitions. The `IND_SIZE` value controls the dimensionality of the solved polynomial function or, effectively, the `gene` size. The `MAX_TIME` hyperparameter is for controlling the total amount of time to run the evolution. This is an effective way to control how long an evolution runs, instead of relying on number of `generations`. Lastly, the strategy allocation hyperparameters `MIN_VALUE`, `MAX_VALUE`, `MIN_STRATEGY`, and `MAX_STRATEGY` control the `mutation` vector and are examined further in the following listing.

Listing 4.19   EDL_4_4_ES.ipynb: Examining hyperparameters

```
IND_SIZE = 6      ⟵——— Dimensionality of the solved polynomial
NGEN = 1000       ⟵—┐
                     └ The number maximum evolution generations

MIN_VALUE = 4     ⟵—┐
MAX_VALUE = 5        │ Values for controlling
MIN_STRATEGY = 0.5   │ strategy allocation
MAX_STRATEGY = 3  ⟵—┘

CXPB = .6         ┐
                  │ Crossover and mutation rates
MUTPB = .3        ┘
GEN_OUTPUT = 25   ⟵——— The number of generations to produce output
MAX_TIME = 100    ⟵—┐
                     └ The maximum time evolution will run for
```

Continuing to the next cell, we can see how the initial target dataset is constructed. In this exercise, shown in listing 4.20, we provide three options or equations to evaluate against: a 5th-degree polynomial continuous function and two discontinuous functions, abs and step. The data is processed using the range parameters to generate the X and Y values, which are zipped into a list called data. At the bottom of the cell, we plot a scatter plot of the data to visualize the target function.

Listing 4.20   EDL_4_4_ES.ipynb: Prepping data

```
equation_form = "polynomial" #@param ["polynomial",
➡ "abs", "step"]⟵—┐
                    └ Exposes three options for target equations

X_START = -5      ┐
X_END = 5         │ The dataset range values for x
X_STEP = 0.5      ┘

                          The function to evaluate target equation
def equation(x):  ⟵——————┘
  if equation_form == "polynomial":
    return (2*x + 3*x**2 + 4*x**3 + 5*x**4 + 6*x**5 + 10)
  elif equation_form == "abs":
    return abs(x)
  else:
    return np.where(x>1, 1, 0)
                                                       ┌ Builds input
X = np.array([x for x in np.arange(X_START, X_END, X_STEP)])  ⟵┘ X values
Y = equation(X)   ⟵—┐
data = list(zip(X, Y))  └ Runs the equation and then generates Ys

plt.scatter(X,Y)  ⟵——— Plots the function in a scatterplot
```

Figure 4.8 shows the plot of the 5th-degree polynomial function along with the step and absolute functions. Let's start by targeting the continuous polynomial function to see how efficiently ES can approximate a solution. The other two functions represent discontinuous functions that are not differentiable and, thus, not typically solvable by DL networks.

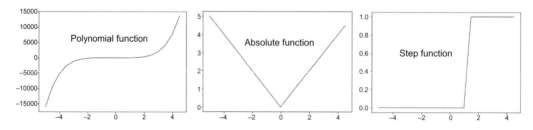

Figure 4.8   Function approximation options

Next, we look at the `creator` block of code, shown in listing 4.21, to understand how ES differs from typical GA. We can see `FitnessMin` and `Individual` being registered, as is normal with one difference. When the `individual` is registered, we add another attribute called `Strategy`, set to `None`. The `Strategy` is registered last with type double d array.

Listing 4.21   EDL_4_4_ES.ipynb: Creating `Individual` and `Strategy`

```
creator.create("FitnessMin", base.Fitness, weights=(-1.0,))
creator.create("Individual", array.array, typecode="d",
    fitness=creator.FitnessMin, strategy=None)
creator.create("Strategy", array.array, typecode="d")
```

> **Creates an individual of type array with strategy**

> **Creates a strategy of type array**

We now skip down to the cell that sets up the `toolbox`, as shown in listing 4.22. The first thing we notice is the `generatES` function being used to initialize an `individual` with inputs `creator.Individual`, `creator.Strategy`, `IND_SIZE`, `MIN_VALUE`, `MAX_VALUE`, `MIN_STRATEGY`, and `MAX_STRATEGY`. The crossover or `mate` operation uses a special ES blend operator for combining the parents, instead of a replacement operator found in normal crossover. Likewise, the `mutate` operator is using an ES log normal operation to control the `mutation` with the strategy. Then at the bottom of the code block, we can see a decorator being applied to the `mate` or `mutate` operators. Decorators provide a filter mechanism to the inputs, and in this case, we use the `checkStrategy` function shown shortly.

Listing 4.22   EDL_4_4_ES.ipynb: Setting up the `toolbox`

> **Registers the individual with a function that generates taking inputs**

```
toolbox = base.Toolbox()
toolbox.register("individual", generateES, creator.Individual,
    screator.Strategy,
    IND_SIZE, MIN_VALUE, MAX_VALUE, MIN_STRATEGY, MAX_STRATEGY)
toolbox.register("population", tools.initRepeat, list, toolbox.individual)
toolbox.register("mate", tools.cxESBlend, alpha=0.1)
```

> **The mate/crossover operator is cxESBlend.**

```
toolbox.register("mutate", tools.mutESLogNormal, c=1.0, indpb=0.03)    ◄┐
toolbox.register("select", tools.selTournament, tournsize=3)
                                                          The mutate operator
toolbox.decorate("mate", checkStrategy(MIN_STRATEGY))     is mutESLogNormal.
toolbox.decorate("mutate", checkStrategy(MIN_STRATEGY))
```
Decorates mate/mutate with checkStrategy

Jumping up a cell, we can see the definitions of the generateES and checkStrategy functions, as shown in listing 4.23. The first function creates the individual using the inputs passed into the function, where input icls represents the class used to construct an individual and scls represents the class to build a strategy. The second function checks the strategy using a decorator pattern to make sure the vector stays above some minimum. With the initialized individual setting, each random value in the gene sequence is set between the minimum and maximum values. Likewise, the initialization of the strategy follows the same pattern using different min/max values. This produces an individual with two vectors of size IND_SIZE or NDIM—one to define the primary gene sequence and the other as a learned mutation and blend rate applied to each gene during the mate and mutate operators.

Listing 4.23   EDL_4_4_ES.ipynb: Core functions

```
def generateES(icls, scls, size, imin, imax,        Creates the individual, based
    smin, smax):                          ◄         on input parameters
  ind = icls(random.uniform(imin, imax) for _ in range(size))
  ind.strategy = scls(random.uniform(smin, smax) for _ in range(size))
  return ind

def checkStrategy(minstrategy):      ◄┐
  def decorator(func):                │  The decorator to make sure the
    def wrappper(*args, **kargs):     │  strategy stays within the bounds
      children = func(*args, **kargs)
      for child in children:
        for i, s in enumerate(child.strategy):
          if s < minstrategy:
            child.strategy[i] = minstrategy
      return children
    return wrappper
  return decorator
```

The last toolbox registration we need to add is for evaluating fitness. Inside this block, shown in listing 4.24, there are two functions. The first, pred, is used to derive a value by looping through the individual genes and multiplying them by x to the factor i. The other, fitness, loops over the values x,y in data using the pred function to determine the mean squared error, where the final value returned is the average MSE. Notice in this example how we pass the dataset to the evaluate function by using it as a parameter in the register function.

Listing 4.24   EDL_4_4_ES.ipynb: Evaluating `fitness`

```
def pred(ind, x):                          Generates prediction
  y_ = 0.0                                  from the individual and x
  for i in range(1,IND_SIZE):
    y_ += ind[i-1]*x**I                     Calculates the polynomial factor i
  y_ += ind[IND_SIZE-1]
  return y_

def fitness(ind, data):        The function to calculate fitness
  mse = 0.0
  for x, y in data:
    y_ = pred(ind, x)
    mse += (y - y_)**2          Evaluates the total mean squared error
  return mse/len(data),

toolbox.register("evaluate", fitness, data=data)
```

As usual, the evolution code is in the last block, shown in listing 4.25, and should look familiar. We start by defining two hyperparameters, MU and LAMBDA, that represent the population of parents and the number of derived offspring. This means in selection, we take MU parents to generate LAMBDA offspring using the DEAP algorithm eaMuCommaLambda. For this exercise, we are not just limiting by generations total but also elapsed time. If the elapsed time, in seconds, passes the threshold MAX_TIME, then the evolution stops. Tracking elapsed time allows us to evaluate comparative EC methods, as we see in the next exercise.

Listing 4.25   DL_4_4_ES.ipynb: Evolution

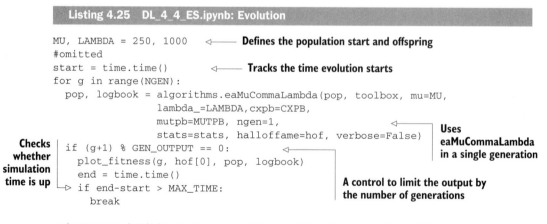

```
MU, LAMBDA = 250, 1000       Defines the population start and offspring
#omitted
start = time.time()          Tracks the time evolution starts
for g in range(NGEN):
  pop, logbook = algorithms.eaMuCommaLambda(pop, toolbox, mu=MU,
                    lambda_=LAMBDA,cxpb=CXPB,
                    mutpb=MUTPB, ngen=1,
                    stats=stats, halloffame=hof, verbose=False)   Uses
  if (g+1) % GEN_OUTPUT == 0:                                     eaMuCommaLambda
    plot_fitness(g, hof[0], pop, logbook)                         in a single generation
    end = time.time()
    if end-start > MAX_TIME:           A control to limit the output by
      break                            the number of generations
```

Checks whether simulation time is up

```
print("Best individual is ", hof[0], hof[0].fitness.values[0])
```

Figure 4.9 shows an example of the final output after running the evolution to a max time of 5 seconds, which is good. However, if we were to plot the input data into Excel, we could just as quickly generate an accurate function approximation using the Trendline feature, in shorter time. Excel is currently limited to 6-degree polynomial function, which is something we could quickly surpass using this example.

```
Generation 49, Best [2.9, 4.3, 4.1, 4.9, 6.0, 6.5]
gen     nevals  avg      std          min     max
0       0       9.60284  0.0577183    9.44144 9.72269
1       899     9.55136  0.0480563    9.35245 9.67632
```

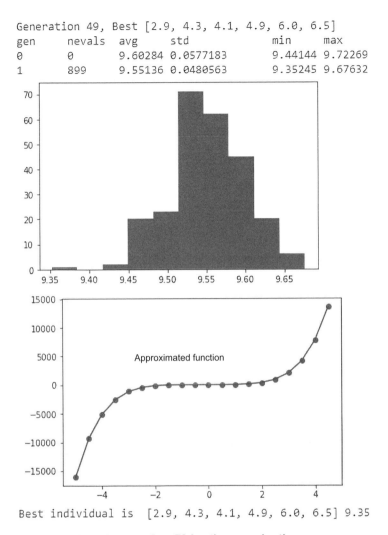

```
Best individual is  [2.9, 4.3, 4.1, 4.9, 6.0, 6.5] 9.35
```

Figure 4.9   Example output from ES function approximation

At this point, you can go back and alter the amount of time the evolution runs to see if you get better results or try the other functions abs and step. You will likely find that ES is not as effective at discontinuous solutions. The reason for this is mostly to do with the way the algorithm approximates the function.

However, if we were to compare ES to our previous exercises in chapter 3, we would see a quicker convergence for continuous problems. This is because ES manages the population diversity through learned mutation and mating strategies. You can see this if you compare the output histogram in figure 4.9 to previous example exercises.

4.4.2   *Revisiting the EvoLisa*

Function approximation is a good baseline problem, but to see the full power of ES, in this section, we revisit one of our most complex previous problems: the EvoLisa. Here we revise the problem, employing ES as our solution strategy. This is a very quick example that makes a useful comparison between ES and regular GA.

Open notebook EDL_4_4_EvoLisa.ipynb in Colab. If you need assistance, see the appendix. Go ahead and run all the cells of the notebook (Runtime > Run All from the menu).

We have already covered the main code elements in notebooks EDL_3_5_EvoLisa.ipynb and EDL_4_4_ES.ipynb. This notebook shows how a GA notebook may be upgraded to employ ES.

Let the notebook run for a few thousand `generations` to see the remarkable improvement shown in figure 4.10. Also shown in the figure is a comparison of the results generated with "vanilla" GA over double the number of `generations`—7,000 versus 3,000.

Best of generation   Target image   GA example from chapter 3

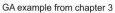

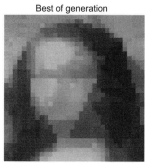

Output after 3,000+ generations   Output after 7,000+ generations
using ES   using GA

Figure 4.10   EvoLisa output employing ES compared to the previous GA solution

4.4.3   *Learning exercises*

The following exercises can help you further understand the concept of evolutionary strategy:

1   Alter the target function in listing 4.20 and then rerun to see what effect this has.
2   Modify several of the parameters in listing 4.19 to see what effect each change has on the resulting evolution. Try this with both the function approximation and EvoLisa notebook versions.
3   Compare results from this version of the EvoLisa to the GA example we covered in chapter 3. How much better does the `mutation` enhancement guided by ES improve the output?
4   Evolve the best facsimile of the Mona Lisa you can. You're encouraged to contact the author with your results.

Now, your takeaway from this last notebook may be to upgrade all our solutions to using ES. While ES is an excellent advancement we can keep in our toolkit, it still lacks the ability to converge discontinuous solutions quickly and efficiently. To do that, we need to understand what difficulty regular GA and modified ES have in solving more complex functions. This is something we explore further in the next exercise.

4.5 *Differential evolution with DEAP*

DL systems are often described simply as good function or convex approximators. By no means is function approximation limited to DL, but it currently ranks as the top favorite for most solutions.

Fortunately, EC encompasses several methods. It is not limited to continuous solutions but can solve discontinuous solutions as well. One such method focused on function approximation for continuous and discontinuous solutions is *differential evolution* (DE). DE is not calculus-based but, instead, relies on reducing the difference in optimized solutions.

In our next notebook, we employ DE to approximate a known continuous polynomial solution from our last exercise as well as basic examples of discontinuous and complex functions. This gives us another tool in our EC toolbelt when we look at building combined solutions with DL later.

4.5.1 *Approximating complex and discontinuous functions with DE*

Differential evolution has more in common with PSO than GAs or programming. In DE, we maintain a `population` of agents, each of some equal vector size. Like PSO, agents are long-running and don't produce offspring, but their component vector is modified using difference comparisons from other random agents to produce new and better agents.

Figure 4.11 shows the basic workflow for DE. At the start of this figure, three agents are randomly selected from a larger pool of agents. These three agents are then used to modify a target `Y` for each index value in the agent by taking the first agent, `a`, and adding its value to a scaled difference between agents `b` and `c`. The resulting `Y` agent is evaluated for `fitness`, and if that value is better, then that agent is replaced with the new agent `Y`.

The subtle enhancement in this method and why it works so effectively on discontinuous functions is the calculation of `individual` dimension difference. Unlike normal optimization functions, which often need to blend results, as in DL, or generalize results, as in genetic evolution, DE does a component-wise differentiation.

In DL, the gradient optimization method we use to backpropagate errors or differences during training is a global optimization problem. DE extracts the optimization into a component-wise differentiation of values and is, therefore, not limited by global methods. This means DE can be used to approximate discontinuous or difficult functions, as we will see.

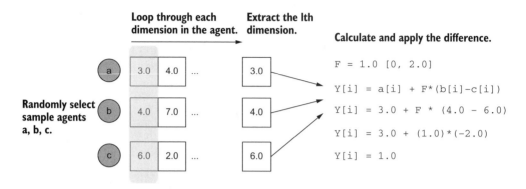

Figure 4.11   The DE workflow for producing new agents

For the next scenario, open notebook EDL_4_5_DE.ipynb in Colab and run all the cells. This example works on the same problem set from the last exercise. As such, we have three problems we can run this sample against: a polynomial, the absolute, and step functions. For comparison, we begin by running the example of the same polynomial function approximation problem we just looked at.

Running the whole example for a MAX_TIME of 5 seconds outputs a good, but not great, function approximation, compared to the ES example we just looked at. After doing that, we want to run this example on the absolute or step functions by changing the function type in the prepping data, shown in listing 4.20, using the Colab form dropdown to step a discontinuous function.

Before rerunning the notebook, we want to modify the max time hyperparameter, as shown in the following listing. Change the MAX_TIME value from 5 seconds to a value like 100. The absolute and step functions, being more complex, require more time.

Listing 4.26   EDL_4_5_DE.ipynb: The hyperparameters

```
NDIM = 6              ◁————————————  The number of dimensions in an agent
CR = 0.25            ◁
F = 1                ◁             Akin to crossover rate in genetic operations
MU = 300             ◁
NGEN = 1000                        The difference scaling factor [0.0, 2.0]
GEN_OUTPUT = 25
MAX_TIME = 100                     MU, or number of agents
```
The time to limit simulation for

After setting the function, reset the notebook's runtime from the menu, using Runtime > Factory Reset Runtime. Then, rerun all cells in the notebook with Runtime > Run All from the menu.

To get a good comparison, jump back to the EDL_4_ES.ipynb, and then change the MAX_TIME to 100 seconds, set the target function to step, restart the runtime, and rerun all the cells. Figure 4.12 shows the difference between running the DE and ES against the step function. It is interesting to note that the DE method performed

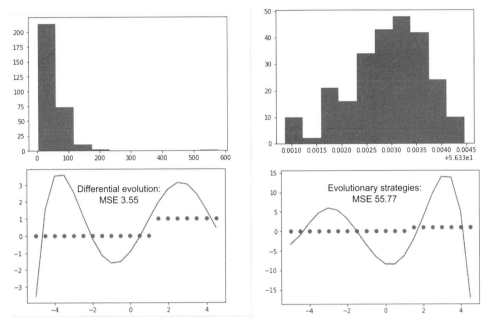

Figure 4.12 Comparison of DE and ES on a step function

more than 10 times better than ES, which has to do with the differential method. On the flip side, note how the ES histogram is normally distributed, whereas the DE chart distribution resembles a narrow Pareto or Cauchy distribution.

Next, we can look at both the `creator` and `toolbox` setup in a combined code listing. For the `toolbox`, we register an attribute of type `float` with initial values of -3 to +3 that is similar to a `gene` in genetic evolution. Then, we define the `individual` or agent of type `float` and of size `NDIM`, or number of dimensions. At the end of the following code listing, we can see a select function registered that uses and random method that picks three elements. Recall this from figure 4.11, where we select three agents (a, b, c) to apply the differentiation algorithm against.

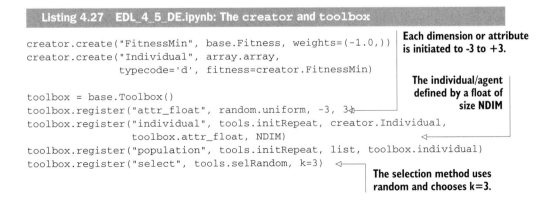

Listing 4.27 EDL_4_5_DE.ipynb: The creator and toolbox

```
creator.create("FitnessMin", base.Fitness, weights=(-1.0,))
creator.create("Individual", array.array,
               typecode='d', fitness=creator.FitnessMin)

toolbox = base.Toolbox()
toolbox.register("attr_float", random.uniform, -3, 3)
toolbox.register("individual", tools.initRepeat, creator.Individual,
                 toolbox.attr_float, NDIM)
toolbox.register("population", tools.initRepeat, list, toolbox.individual)
toolbox.register("select", tools.selRandom, k=3)
```

Each dimension or attribute is initiated to -3 to +3.

The individual/agent defined by a float of size NDIM

The selection method uses random and chooses k=3.

Much of the code in this example is shared with the previous ES exercise, since we are solving the same problem. Review the key differences between the two samples to understand what elements comprise each method.

Our simulation training code is at the bottom of the notebook, but we only need to focus on the section that makes DE unique, as shown in listing 4.28. There are two `for` loops in the code—the first iterates over the number of `generations`, and the second iterates through each agent. In the inner loop, we first sample three agents (a, b, c) and then clone the agent to be the target y. Then, we sample a random index into the agent's vector and use that with the CR value to determine whether a possible difference is calculated, as shown in figure 4.10. Finally, we check whether the new agent evaluates a better `fitness`, and if it does, we swap out the new agent with the old one.

Listing 4.28 EDL_4_5_DE.ipynb: Agent differentiable simulation

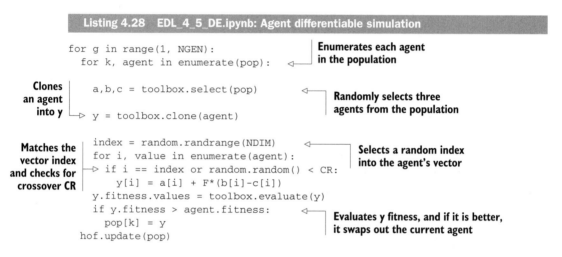

Feel free to go back and try a comparison of the absolute function between the ES and DE methods. You can also try tweaking the hyperparameters to see what effect they have for approximating a function with both ES and DE.

4.5.2 *Learning exercises*

Continue your exploration of the last notebook by completing the following exercises:

1 Alter various hyperparameters in listing 4.26, and then rerun. Are you able to improve the performance of discontinuous function approximation?

2 Compare the function approximation results from ES and DE for various functions. Which appears to perform better and worse for which types of functions?

Both DE and ES provide excellent function approximators for continuous problems. For discontinuous problems, it is generally better to apply DE, since it is not limited to gradual approximations across global space. As we discuss in later chapters, having both tools available makes our job easier when applying EDL. In this chapter, we extended our knowledge of EC and looked at more diverse and specialized methods that can address novel or difficult-to-solve problems.

Summary

- Genetic programming is the use of genetic sequences to define a process or program of steps.
- DEAP employs a genetic programming extension that makes it easy to convert a problem from GA to GP. One application of GP is to derive an equation for a known or unknown problem.
- DEAP also provides visualization tools that allow for the interpretation of an individual gene sequence as a gene expression tree and how it evaluates to a function.
- DEAP provides several secondary evolutionary algorithms. One such example is particle swarm optimization:
  - Particle swarm optimization uses a population of individuals to swarm over a solution space.
  - As the particles swarm, fitter individuals guide the swarm to focus on better solutions.
  - PSO can be used for finding solution parameters to functions or more-complex problems.
- DEAP supports coevolution scenarios. This is when two or more populations of individuals are identified to tackle unique tasks for specific problems. Coevolution can be used to find complex solutions by minimizing and scaling features in a derived equation.
- Evolutionary strategy is an extension of GAs that places emphasis on strategically updating the mutation function. This method works well for solving or guiding solutions that require individuals with large or complex genetic structures or sequences.
- Differential evolution is similar to PSO but only uses three agents to triangulate and narrow a solution-search space. DE works well on complex problems that use shorter genetic sequences. Employ differential evolution to solve continuous and discontinuous function approximation problems in DEAP.

Part 2

Optimizing deep learning

In this part of the book, we look at evolutionary and genetic algorithms that may be used to optimize and improve deep learning systems. We start in chapter 5 by solving a core problem in deep learning: hyperparameter optimization. This chapter demonstrates various methods, from random and grid search to genetic algorithms, particle swarm optimization, evolutionary strategies, and differential evolution.

In chapter 6, we move into neuroevolution with the optimization of deep learning architecture and parameters. We demonstrate how network parameters or weights can be optimized without the need to use backpropagation or deep learning optimizers.

Then in chapter 7, we continue demonstrating neuroevolution for the enhancement architecture and parameter enhancement of convolutional neural networks. We then look at developing an EvoCNN network model using custom architecture encodings with genetic algorithms.

Automating hyperparameter optimization

5

This chapter covers

- Developing a process to manually optimize hyperparameters for DL networks
- Building automatic hyperparameter optimization with random search
- Formalizing automatic HPO by employing a grid search algorithm
- Applying evolutionary computation to HPO using PSO
- Extending evolutionary HPO by using evolutionary strategies
- Applying DE to HPO

In the past few chapters, we have been exploring various forms of evolutionary computation, from genetic algorithms to particle swarm optimization and even advanced methods like evolutionary strategies and differential evolution. We continue to use all these EC methods through the rest of the book in some capacity to improve on DL. We combine these methods into a process we colloquially call *evolutionary deep learning* (EDL).

However, before building a set of EDL solutions to various DL problems, we would be remiss if we didn't understand the problems we are trying to solve and how they are solved without EC. After all, EC tools are just a few in a grand `toolbox` we can use to improve DL. Therefore, before we get into applying EC methods to HPO, we first look at the importance of hyperparameter optimization and some manual strategies. Second, when considering automated HPO we want to create a baseline by first reviewing other search methods, such as random and grid search.

5.1 Option selection and hyperparameter tuning

One of the most difficult problems practitioners of DL face is determining which options and "knobs" to dial in to improve their models. Most texts dedicated to teaching DL address the many options and hyperparameters but rarely detail the effects of changes. This is compounded by an AI/ML community showcasing state-of-the-art models that often omit the vast amount of work needed to attain them.

For most practitioners, learning how to use the many options and tuning hyperparameters comes from hours of experience building models. Without this tuning, many such models, as was demonstrated in the last section, could be seriously flawed. This becomes a problem not only for newcomers but the field of DL itself.

We start by looking at a base deep learning model that uses PyTorch to approximate a function. Later examples in this book use Keras and/or PyTorch to demonstrate how easily these techniques can be swapped between frameworks.

5.1.1 Tuning hyperparameter strategies

In this section, we look at some techniques and strategies to select options and tune hyperparameters for DL models. Some of these have been gleaned from years of experience, but realize such strategies will need to evolve. DL is constantly growing, and new model options are continually being enlisted.

> **Deep learning knowledge**
> This book assumes you understand basic DL principles of things like the perceptron, multi-layer perceptron, activation functions, and optimization methods. If you feel you need a refresher on DL in general, there are plenty of good resources online and published by Manning Publications.

A few key differences have been added to demonstrate working with hyperparameters and other options for the following exercise. Open the EDL_5_1_Hyperparameter_Tuning.ipynb notebook in your browser. Consult the appendix if you need assistance.

Start by running the whole notebook from the menu with Run > Run All. Confirm the output is like figure 5.1 for the initial function and predicted solution.

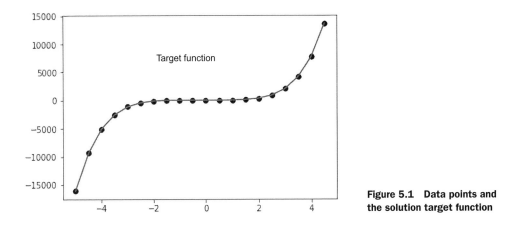

Figure 5.1   Data points and the solution target function

Next, scroll down, and look at the hyperparameters code block, as shown in listing 5.1. There are two new hyperparameters added here: `batch_size` and `data_step`. The first hyperparameter, `batch-size`, determines the number of inputs we feed into the network for each forward pass. Recall that in the last exercise, this was 1. The other hyperparameter, `data_step`, is not a typical hyperparameter but allows us to control the amount of data generated for training.

Listing 5.1   EDL_5_1_Hyperparameter_Tuning.ipynb: Hyperparameters

```
hp_test = "test 1" #@param {type:"string"}        Forms the parameter for
learning_rate = 3.5e-03                            setting the name of the test
epochs = 500
middle_layer = 25      The number of elements to
                       feed in a single forward pass
batch_size = 2
                       Controls the frequency of data
data_step = 1          samples for data generation
```

Change the test name `hp_test` to something like `test 2`. Then modify the `middle_layer` value to something like 25 or larger. Run the cell, and then run the remaining cells in the notebook with Run > Run After.

The predicted output is shown for both tests in figure 5.2, which also shows the output of `test 2` fitting much better. Notice the slight difference in time of training the model as well. This difference comes from larger models taking more time to train.

You can now go back and modify the other hyperparameters—`batch_size` and `data_step`. Be aware, though, that these values are linked, and if you dramatically increase the amount of data by decreasing `data_step` to .1, then you, likewise, need to increase the `batch_size`.

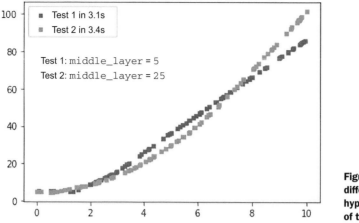

Figure 5.2 Comparing differences in the hyperparameter tuning of the middle layer

Figure 5.3 shows the results of altering and not altering the batch size when increasing the amount of data. The results comparison shown in figure 5.3 are quite dramatic with respect to the amount of training time for completing 500 epochs.

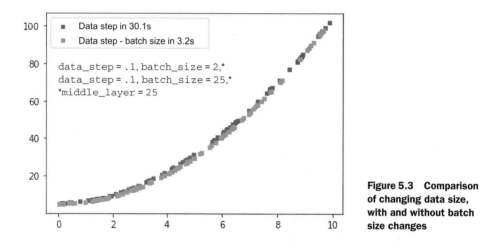

Figure 5.3 Comparison of changing data size, with and without batch size changes

Continue to change the test name, modify hyperparameters, and then run the remaining cells with Run > Run After. If you find the plots are getting too messy, you can reset the plot results by running Run > Run All from the menu. Figure 5.4 shows an example of modifying the `learning_rate` from `3.5e-06` to `3.5e-01`. Your overall goal when tuning hyperparameters is to create the smallest model that will train the fastest and produce the best results.

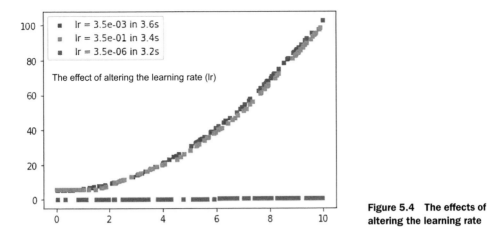

Figure 5.4 The effects of altering the learning rate

Even with our simple example of only five hyperparameters, you may struggle with where to start, so a good starting point is to follow these steps:

1 *Setting network size*—In our example, this was modifying the `middle_layer` value. Typically, you will want to start by adjusting the network size and/or number of layers. Be aware, though, that increasing the number of linear layers is less significant than increasing the number of network nodes in a layer.

> **Hyperparameter training rule #1: Network size**
>
> Increase the number of network layers to extract more features from data. Expand or decrease the model width (nodes) to tune the fit of the model.

2 *Understanding data variability*—There is an expectation that DL models need to consume vast amounts of data. While DL models may certainly benefit from more data, success depends more on how variable the source data is. In our example, we were able to control the variability of the data using the `data_step` value. However, that ability to control variability of data is often not an option. In turn, if your model is highly variable and, thus, requires more data, you will likely need to increase the size of the model in layers and/or width. Pictures of handwritten digits, like the MNIST dataset, have much less variance than the images of fashion depicted in the Fashion-MNIST dataset.

> **Hyperparameter training rule #2: Data variability**
>
> Understand the variability of your source data. More-varied data requires larger models to either extract more features or learn how to fit more complex solutions.

3 *Selecting batch size*—As we've seen in our example, tuning the batch size of a model can make it significantly more training-efficient. However, this hyperparameter

is not a silver bullet for fixing training performance, and increasing it may be detrimental to end results. Instead, batch size needs to be tuned based on the variability of the input data. More variable input data generally benefits from smaller batch sizes, in the range of 16–64, while less-varied data may benefit from large batch sizes, in the range 64–256—or even higher.

> **Hyperparameter training rule #3: Batch size**
> If input data is highly varied, then decrease the batch size. Increase the batch size for less varied and more uniform datasets.

4   *Adjusting learning rate*—The learning rate controls how quickly a model learns and is often the first hyperparameter abused by newcomers. Much like batch size, learning rate is dictated by the complexity of the model, driven by the variance of the input data. Higher data variance requires smaller learning rates, while more uniform data can support high rates of learning. This is pictured well in figure 2.6, where we can see the model benefit from higher learning rates as a result of having very uniform data. Adjusting the model size may also require a decrease in the learning rate, due to increased model complexity.

> **Hyperparameter training rule #4: Learning rate**
> Adjust the learning rate to match the variability of the input data. If you need to increase the size of a model, generally, decrease the learning rate as well.

5   *Tuning training iterations*—If you are working on smaller problems, you will often see the model quickly converge to some base solution. From that, you can then simply reduce the number of epochs (training iterations) of the model. However, if the model is more complex and takes much longer to train, determining total number of training iterations can be more problematic. Fortunately, most DL frameworks provide early stopping mechanisms that will watch for some arbitrary value of loss and, when that is achieved, will automatically stop training. As a general rule, then, you will often want to select the highest number of training iterations you think you need. Another option is to have the model save its weights periodically. Then, if needed, the same model may be reloaded and training continued.

> **Hyperparameter training rule #5: Training iterations**
> Always use the highest number of training iterations you think you will need. Use techniques like early stopping and/or model saving to reduce training iterations.

Use these five rules to guide you when training hyperparameters, but be aware that the techniques mentioned are only a general guide. There may be network configurations, datasets, and other factors that alter those general rules. In the next section, we advance to the various model options you may need to decide on when building robust models.

5.1.2   Selecting model options

Aside from hyperparameters, the biggest source of tuning the model comes in the various options you internally decide to use. DL models provide for numerous options, sometimes dictated by the problem or network architecture, but often, subtle variations radically alter the way a model fits.

Model options range from activation and optimizer functions to the addition of the number and size of layers. As mentioned in the last section, layer depth is often dictated by the number of features a model needs to extract and learn. The type of layer, be it convolutional or recurrent networks, is often determined by the type of features needed to be learned. For example, we use CNN layers to learn clusters of features and RNN to determine how features are aligned or in what order.

Therefore, most DL models' network size and layer types are driven by the variance of data and type of features needed to be learned. For image classification problems, CNN layers are used to extract visual features, like an eye or mouth. RNN layers, on the other hand, are used for processing language or time data, where the need is to understand how one feature relates to another in sequences.

That means that in most cases, the options a DL practitioner needs to concern themselves with are the base functions of activation, optimization, and loss. Activation functions are typically dictated by the type of problem and form of data. We typically avoid altering activation functions until the final steps of tuning.

Most often, the choice of optimizer and loss function dictates how well a model trains, if at all. Take, for example, figure 5.5, which shows the results of selecting three different optimizers to train our last exercise, using a `middle_layer` hyperparameter of 25. Notice in the figure that stochastic gradient descent (SGD) and Adagrad perform quite poorly in comparison to Adam and RMSprop.

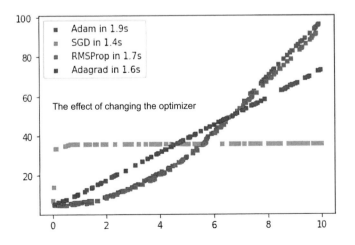

Figure 5.5   A comparison of optimizer functions

Likewise, the form of loss function used to critique the network's learning can have a substantial effect on model training. In our simple regression example, we have just two options: mean-squared error and mean absolute error, or L1 loss. Figure 5.6 shows a comparison between the two loss functions used in the last sample exercise. From the figure, it appears the better loss function for the last exercise may be L1 loss, or MAE.

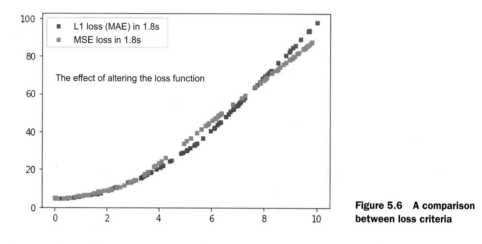

Figure 5.6   A comparison between loss criteria

Hyperparameter training rule #6: Changing the model

As a general rule, anytime the model architecture or critical model options, like the optimization and/or loss function, change you need to retune all hyperparameters.

By now, hopefully you realize that without a very keen eye and attention to detail, it is easy to miss finding the optimal model for your problem. In fact, you could spend countless hours tuning model hyperparameters, only to realize a better loss or optimization function may have performed far better.

Hyperparameter tuning and model option selection is prone to errors, even among the most seasoned deep learners. In chapter 4, we first introduced EDL by training model hyperparameters with evolutionary computation.

When it comes to building working DL models, you will typically define the model and select the options you feel most appropriate to your problem. You may then alter and tune the various hyperparameters, starting with the previously stated strategies. However, at some point, and unfortunately this happens often, you may decide to alter model options, like the optimizer or loss function. This, in turn, often requires you to loop back and retune hyperparameters based on the changed model.

5.2   Automating HPO with random search

We just looked at manual HPO of DL using a function approximation problem. In this scenario, we provided a set of tools by which the practitioners could run the notebook consecutively, using different hyperparameters to generate comparisons. As you likely discovered from working through that exercise, manual HPO is time-consuming and just downright boring.

Of course, there are now numerous tools for performing HPO automatically. These tools range from Python packages to full systems incorporated into cloud technologies as part of an AutoML solution. We could certainly use any of those tools to perform a baseline comparison against EC methods, but for our purposes, we want to understand the automation and search process deeper.

Random search HPO, as its name implies, is the process of sampling random values from a known set of hyperparameters within given ranges and then evaluating the effectiveness. The hope in random search is that you eventually find the best or desired solution. The process is comparable to someone throwing darts blindfolded, hoping to hit a bullseye. The blindfolded person likely won't hit a bullseye in a couple throws, but over many throws, we expect they might.

5.2.1   Applying random search to HPO

Notebook EDL_5_2_RS_HPO.ipynb is an upgraded version of our previous notebook that automates HPO using a simple random search algorithm. Open that notebook in Colab, and then run all the cells via Runtime > Run All from the menu. As a comparison, feel free to open the EDL_5_1_Hyperparameter_Tuning.ipynb notebook.

Let's start by exploring the problem function we want our DL network to approximate. The first cell of code revisits our polynomial function from chapter 4, as shown in figure 5.1. The following listing contains the code that generates the sample set of input and target data points we train the network on.

Listing 5.2   EDL_5_2_RS_HPO.ipynb: Defining the data

```
def function(x):
    return (2*x + 3*x**2 + 4*x**3 + 5*x**4 + 6*x**5 + 10)     ← Defines the polynomial target function

data_min = -5      ← Sets the bounds and step for the data
data_max = 5
data_step = .5
Xi = np.reshape(np.arange(data_min, data_max, data_step), (-1, 1))     ← Generates and reshapes input data
yi = function(Xi)     ← Generates target outputs
inputs = Xi.shape[1]
yi = yi.reshape(-1, 1)
plt.plot(Xi, yi, 'o', color='black')
```
Finds the number of inputs to the network

Next, we revisit the base model/class we are using as the network we want to learn to approximate this function, as defined in the following listing. This is the same base model we used to evaluate our simpler example from chapter 2.

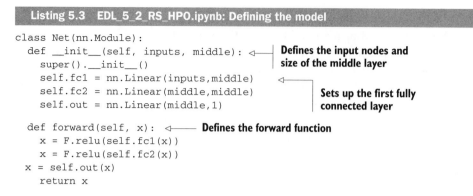

Listing 5.3   EDL_5_2_RS_HPO.ipynb: Defining the model

```
class Net(nn.Module):
  def __init__(self, inputs, middle):   ⟵── Defines the input nodes and
    super().__init__()                       size of the middle layer
    self.fc1 = nn.Linear(inputs,middle)   ⟵─┐
    self.fc2 = nn.Linear(middle,middle)      Sets up the first fully
    self.out = nn.Linear(middle,1)           connected layer

  def forward(self, x):   ⟵── Defines the forward function
    x = F.relu(self.fc1(x))
    x = F.relu(self.fc2(x))
  x = self.out(x)
    return x
```

Now, for the automation magic. Our process of automating HPO consists of using a new class to contain and manage the search. For random search, the version of this `Hyperparameters` class is shown in listing 5.4. This `init` function takes the input hyperparameters and converts them to class properties using `update`. When we use this class, we first set up the base properties as inputs, and then for each hyperparameter property, we define a generator that provides the next value. Calling the `next` function on this base `Hyperparameters` object generates a new generated object that is used in a single evaluation. Don't fret if this is not so obvious just yet; we are using some advanced functionality that is best explained in code to come.

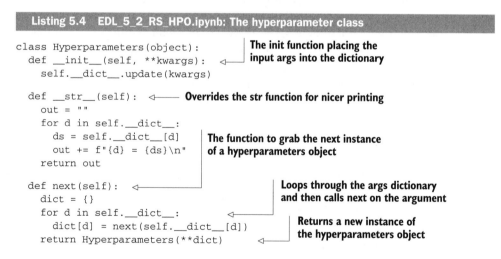

Listing 5.4   EDL_5_2_RS_HPO.ipynb: The hyperparameter class

```
class Hyperparameters(object):
  def __init__(self, **kwargs):   ⟵─┐ The init function placing the
    self.__dict__.update(kwargs)      input args into the dictionary

  def __str__(self):   ⟵── Overrides the str function for nicer printing
    out = ""
    for d in self.__dict__:
      ds = self.__dict__[d]        The function to grab the next instance
      out += f"{d} = {ds}\n"       of a hyperparameters object
    return out

  def next(self):   ⟵──────────┐
    dict = {}                   Loops through the args dictionary
    for d in self.__dict__:     and then calls next on the argument
      dict[d] = next(self.__dict__[d])
    return Hyperparameters(**dict)   ⟵─┐ Returns a new instance of
                                          the hyperparameters object
```

The `Hyperparameters` class internally uses the Python generator pattern to loop through all the properties to create a new instance. For our random search approach, we use a function generator called `sampler`, as shown in listing 5.5. The `sampler` function is meant to continuously sample from a given function within some range set by `min` and `max`. Python supports two forms of generators—the one we are using uses the `yield` keywork to interrupt the loop and return a value. To execute a generator, you need to wrap the function in `next`, as seen in the previous listing (listing 5.4).

```
def sampler(func, min, max):      ←—— The input is function and range, from min to max.
  while True:                 ←—
    yield func(min,max)           | The infinite generator set up with endless loop
```
Yields by calling the function with min,max range

We can put these pieces together when we initially set up the base or parent Hyper-parameters object, as shown in listing 5.6. In the parent object, we define each input equal to the sampler generator defined by various functions and min/max ranges. Notice how the sampling function we use changes from random.ranint to random.uniform, where both functions generate a random variable from a uniform distribution. Calling the next function generates a child hyperparameters object that can be used in an experiment evaluation.

```
hp = Hyperparameters(                              | Adds input for epochs to
  epochs = sampler(random.randint,20,400),  ←—     | the generator function
  middle_layer = sampler(random.randint, 8, 64),
  learning_rate = sampler(random.uniform,3.5e-01,
  ➡ 3.5e-03),                              ←—      | Additional input using
  batch_size = sampler(random.randint, 4, 64)      | random.input base function
)

print(hp.next())   ←—— Samples the next object and then prints
```

To understand how this works, jump down to the large block of code with the training function train_function, as shown in listing 5.7. Inside this function, we first call hp.next() to generate a child object. We can then use the values in our training algorithm by just using the name as a property on the object. Since we are using the sampler function with random evaluators anytime we call hp.next(), the output is a random set of hyperparameters.

```
def train_function(hp):
  hp = hp.next()    ←—— Generates a child hyperparameters object

  ...
    for i in range(hp.epochs):  ←—— Uses the hyperparameter by calling a property
```

Lastly, we can look at how all of this is brought together and automated to perform HPO, as shown in listing 5.8. Since we have encapsulated all our random sampling with the HP class, the rest of the code is quite simple. Since this is a minimization problem, we want to tune the hyperparameters to minimize the target network's loss, so we set the starting best value to max infinity. Then, in a loop defined by runs, we call the train_function using the parent hyperparameters object. Inside the training function, `HP` generates a new random instance of hyperparameters and uses those to evaluate network loss. We evaluate the overall `fitness` with a full prediction over all the points in the model.

Listing 5.8   EDL_5_2_RS_HPO.ipynb: Automatic HPO

```
runs = 10000
best = float("inf")      ◁——— Sets the initial max value for best
best_hp = None
run_history = []
for i in range(runs):
  span, history, model, hp_out = train_function(hp)    ◁—| Runs the training function
  y_ = model(torch.Tensor(Xi))
 fitness = loss_fn(y_, torch.Tensor(yi)).data.item()   ◁—| Evaluates fitness over all data
  run_history.append([fitness,*hp_out.__dict__.values()])
  if fitness < best:    ◁—| Checks if this is a new best
    best = fitness
    best_hp = hp_out
```

Figure 5.7 shows the output of performing automatic HPO using random search. At the top of the charts is the best `fitness` overall, with the hyperparameters listed. Below that are three plots showing the loss history for the network training, how well the model approximates the function, and, finally, a mapping of all the evaluations run so far. The evaluation plot shows a grayscale output of the best `fitness`, where the black hexagon represents the best overall evaluated `fitness` thus far. At the bottom of the figure, you can see the result after running for 10,000 runs, where the single black dot, which is hard to see, represents the minimum `fitness`.

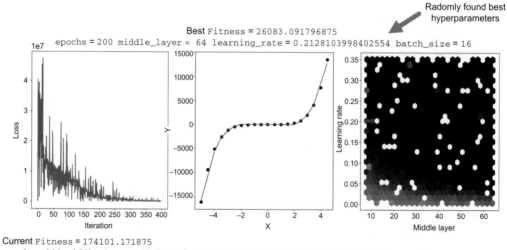

Current Fitness = 174101.171875
epochs = 200 middle_layer = 17 learning_rate = 0.24650877057924905 batch_size = 16

Figure 5.7   Results of running random hyperparameter search

Finally, we review the code that generates the output, as we use it for all the exercises in this chapter. This plotting output first draws the last run's loss history and function approximation, as shown in the following listing. The end plot is a hexbin map of the all the runs' history, plotted by learning rate and middle layer hyperparameters. As the automatic HPO is running, you will see this plot change over time.

Listing 5.9   EDL_5_2_RS_HPO.ipynb: Plotting the output

```
clear_output()

fig, (ax1, ax2, ax3) = plt.subplots(1, 3,          Sets up the combined figure
⮕ figsize=(18,6))                                   with three horizontal subplots
fig.suptitle(f"Best Fitness {best} \n{hp_out}")
ax1.plot(history)
ax1.set_xlabel("iteration")                         Plots the loss training history
ax1.set_ylabel("loss")

ax2.plot(Xi, yi, 'o', color='black')               Draws the function
ax2.plot(Xi,y_.detach().numpy(), 'r')              approximation
ax2.set_xlabel("X")
ax2.set_ylabel("Y")
                                                    Hexbins all run history
rh = np.array(run_history)
hexbins = ax3.hexbin(rh[:, 2], rh[:, 3], C=rh[:, 0],
                     bins=25, gridsize=25, cmap=cm.get_cmap('gray'))
ax3.set_xlabel("middle_layer")
ax3.set_ylabel("learning_rate")

plt.show()
time.sleep(1)
```

The results shown in figure 5.8 took several hours to generate, and you can clearly see where the optimum results land. In this scenario, we only use two hyperparameters for HPO, so we can clearly visualize the results in two dimensions. We could, of course, use all these techniques on more than two variables, but as expected, that would likely require more runs and time. In later scenarios, we introduce more advanced techniques to visualize and track multiple hyperparameters.

Random search is great for finding quick answers, but the problem with this approach is that random methods are just that: random. We have no way of knowing if we are getting closer to a solution or what a possible best solution may even look like. There are several statistical methods that could track progress and promote better solutions, but these still require hundreds—or thousands—of iterations.

In our simple example here, we are only managing two hyperparameters over relatively small ranges. That means that in a relatively short time, we could have a reasonably good guess. However, that guess provides us no insight on how close it is, other than it was the best over a certain number of random samplings. Random search works well for quick approximations, but there are far better methods, as discussed in upcoming sections.

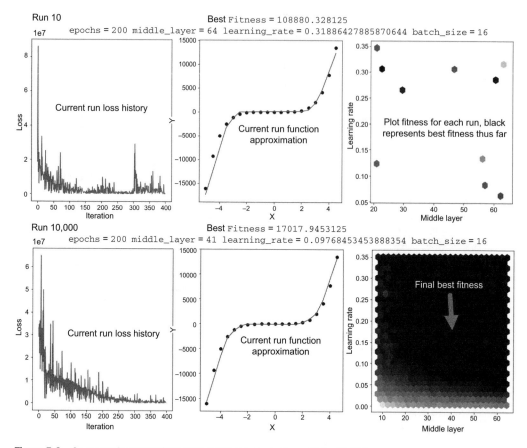

Figure 5.8 **An example output from HPO random search, from 10 to 10,000 runs**

5.3 *Grid search and HPO*

While random search can be an effective method to make better guesses quickly for finding accurate HPO, it is overly time-consuming. Generating the final output for figure 5.7 took over 8 hours, which is slow but can yield accurate results. Searching for fast and accurate automatic HPO requires more elevated techniques.

One such simple technique that works effectively for everything from archeological digs to search and rescue teams is *grid search*. Grid search works by laying out the search area or surface in a grid pattern and then methodically walking through every cell in the grid. Grid search is best visualized in two dimensions, but this technique is valid for any number of dimensional problems.

Figure 5.9 shows a comparison between a random search working over a hyperparameter space and grid search. The figure demonstrates one possible pattern for walking through the grid, and at each cell, it evaluates the `learning_rate` and `middle_layer` variables. Grid search is an effective method for evaluating a range of possible combinations in a methodical and efficient manner.

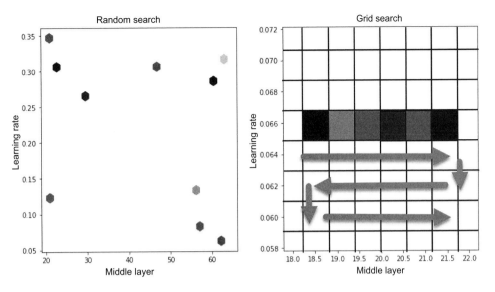

Figure 5.9   Comparison of random search and grid search

5.3.1 *Using grid search for automatic HPO*

In our next exercise, we upgrade our earlier random search attempt to use a more sophisticated grid search technique. While this technique is more robust and efficient, it is still bounded by the size of the grid. Using larger grid cells often limits results to local minimums or maximums. Finer and smaller cells can locate global minimums and maximums but at the cost of increased search space.

The code in the next exercise notebook, EDL_5_3_GS_HPO.ipynb, is derived from our earlier random search example. As such, much of the code is the same, and as usual, we focus on just the parts that make this sample unique. Open the EDL_5_3_GS_HPO.ipynb in Colab and run all the cells via Runtime > Run All.

The primary difference in the code for this example is the hyperparameter object now needs to track a parameter grid. We first look at the construction of a new HyperparametersGrid class and the init function. Inside this function, shown in listing 5.10, we extract the names of the input parameters into self.hparms and then test whether the first input points to a generator. If it does, then we generate a parameter grid with self.create_grid; otherwise, the instance will just be a child hyperparameter container.

Listing 5.10   EDL_5_3_GS_HPO.ipynb: The HyperparametersGrid init function

```
class HyperparametersGrid(object):
  def __init__(self, **kwargs):
    self.__dict__.update(kwargs)
    self.hparms = [d for d in self.__dict__]        ←  Extracts all the
    self.grid = {}                                      input arg names
    self.gidx = 0
```

Creates the parameter grid
```
if isinstance(self.__dict__[self.hparms[0]],
    types.GeneratorType):
    self.grid = self.create_grid()
    self.grid_size = len(self.grid)
```
Only creates a grid if it is a parent

Gets the size of the grid

Next, we look at how the parameter grid is constructed in the `self.create_grid` function. The function, shown in listing 5.11, starts by creating an empty `grid` dictionary and then loops through the list of hyperparameters. It calls the hyperparameter generator, using next to return, in this case, a value and the total number of values. Then we loop again through the generator to extract each unique value and append it to a `row` list. After this, we append the row to the grid and then finish by injecting the `grid` into the `ParameterGrid` class. `ParameterGrid` is a helper class from scikit-learn that takes as input a dictionary of inputs and list of values and then constructs a grid in which each cell represents the various hyperparameter combinations. While we are only running this example with two hyperparameters over a two-dimensional grid, `ParameterGrid` can manage any number of dimensions.

Listing 5.11   EDL_5_3_GS_HPO.ipynb: `create_grid` function

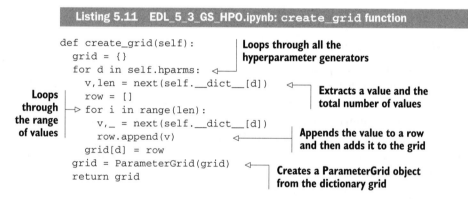

```
def create_grid(self):
    grid = {}
    for d in self.hparms:
        v,len = next(self.__dict__[d])
        row = []
        for i in range(len):
            v,_ = next(self.__dict__[d])
            row.append(v)
        grid[d] = row
    grid = ParameterGrid(grid)
    return grid
```

Loops through all the hyperparameter generators

Loops through the range of values

Extracts a value and the total number of values

Appends the value to a row and then adds it to the grid

Creates a ParameterGrid object from the dictionary grid

With the internal parameter grid holding all the combinations of hyperparameters, we can now look at how the updated next function works, as shown in listing 5.12. At the top, we have a reset function that works to reset an index into the parameter grid. Every call to next increases the index and, thus, extracts the next value from the parameter grid (`self.grid`). The last line of code unpacks the grid value with `**` as an input into a new instance of `HyperparametersGrid`.

Listing 5.12   EDL_5_3_GS_HPO.ipynb: The `HyperparametersGrid` next function

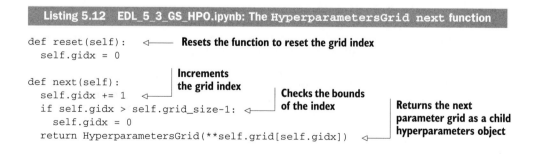

```
def reset(self):
    self.gidx = 0

def next(self):
    self.gidx += 1
    if self.gidx > self.grid_size-1:
        self.gidx = 0
    return HyperparametersGrid(**self.grid[self.gidx])
```

Resets the function to reset the grid index

Increments the grid index

Checks the bounds of the index

Returns the next parameter grid as a child hyperparameters object

Using the new grid hyperparameters class also requires us to upgrade the generators we use to control the hyperparameter creation. For simplicity, we define two functions: one for floats and the other integers. Inside each function, we create an array of values called `grid` from a minimum to maximum at a step interval. We iterate through this list of values, yielding a new value and the total list length, as shown in the following listing. Having the total list length allows us to iterate through the generator to create the parameter grid, as seen previously.

Listing 5.13 EDL_5_3_GS_HPO.ipynb: Generators

```
def grid(min, max, step):                    ◁——————  The float function accepts
    grid = cycle(np.arange(min, max, step))           the min/max and grid step.
    len = (max-min) / step
    for i in grid:                    Yields a value the
        yield i, int(len)   ◁——————  length of the grid cells

def grid_int(min, max, step):                ◁——————  The integer function accepts
    grid = cycle(range(min, max, step))               min/max and grid step.
    len = (max-min) / step
    for i in grid:                   Yields a value the
        yield i, int(len)   ◁——————  length of the grid cells
```

Cycles
through
the list
of values

Now, we can see how this new class and these generator functions are used to create the parent hp object, as shown in listing 5.14. Setting up the variables is the same as we saw earlier; however, this time we are using the `grid` generator functions. Internally, after the class is initialized, an internal parameter grid is created. We can query information about the grid, like getting the total number of combinations or values. Then we can also call `next` on the parent hp object to generate a couple of child objects. We can calculate the number of grid combinations by taking the number of values for each hyperparameter and multiplying them all together. In our example, there are 9 values for `middle_layer`, 10 for `learning_rate`, 1 for `epochs`, and 1 for `batch_size`, giving us a total of 90, or 10 x 9 x 1 x 1 = 90. Grid sizes can get large quickly, especially when working with multiple variables and smaller step sizes.

Listing 5.14 EDL_5_3_GS_HPO.ipynb: Creating a grid

```
hp = HyperparametersGrid(
    middle_layer = grid_int(8, 64, 6),
    learning_rate = grid(3.5e-02,3.5e-01, 3e-02),
    batch_size = grid_int(16, 20, 4),
    epochs = grid_int(200,225,25)
)
                                      Prints the number of
                                      grid combinations
print(hp.grid_size)    ◁—————
print(hp.grid.param_grid)    ◁——————  Prints the parameter grid inputs
print(hp.next())
print(hp.next())       Prints the next child
                       hyperparameters object
```

```
#OUTPUT#
90
[{'middle_layer': [14, 20, 26, 32, 38, 44, 50, 56, 62], 'learning_rate':
➥ [0.065, 0.095, 0.125, 0.155, 0.185, 0.215, 0.245, 0.275, 0.305…,
➥ 0.3349…], 'batch_size': [16], 'epochs': [200]}]
middle_layer = 20 learning_rate = 0.065 epochs = 200 batch_size = 16
middle_layer = 26 learning_rate = 0.065 epochs = 200 batch_size = 16
```

This example uses a GPU for training, but the code changes to implement are minor and won't be shown. Instead, we focus on some subtle changes in the automation setup. Runs is now defined by `hp.grid_size`, and we create a new variable called `grid_size`, defined by the number of runs, as shown in the following listing. The second variable is used to define the size of grid cells we draw on the `hexbins fitness` evaluation plot.

Listing 5.15   EDL_5_3_GS_HPO.ipynb: Creating a grid

```
runs = hp.grid_size                    ⟵──── runs now equals grid_size
grid_size = int(math.sqrt(runs))-1     ⟵──┐
hp.reset()                                 │   Defines plot grid_size
                                           │   based on the total runs
Resets the parent hp object before starting
```

Figure 5.10 shows the output of running this exercise to completion—all 90 runs in about 10 minutes. This is a far quicker result than the random search example but not as accurate. Notice that the final `fitness` in figure 5.3 (~17,000) is one-third that of the `fitness` shown in figure 5.5 (~55,000). Thus, our result with grid search is not as accurate, but it is certainly quicker and more efficient. We could always go back and narrow the search to a smaller one and reduce the step size to narrow in on accuracy.

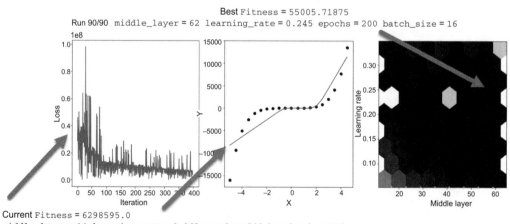

Best Fitness = 55005.71875
Run 90/90 middle_layer = 62 learning_rate = 0.245 epochs = 200 batch_size = 16

Current Fitness = 6298595.0
middle_layer = 14 learning_rate = 0.065 epochs = 200 batch_size = 16

Figure 5.10   The final output of the grid search

The last thing we want to look at is modifying the output evaluation plot to set the `grid_size` based on our previously calculated variable. We use a hexbin plot to automatically map the `fitness` values by color. Then, we set the `grid_size` based on the number of combinations. In this simple example, shown in the following listing, we assume a square grid of parameters, but that may not always be accurate.

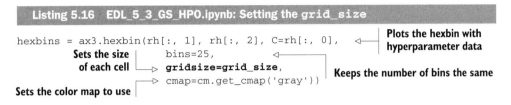

Listing 5.16   EDL_5_3_GS_HPO.ipynb: Setting the `grid_size`

Grid search is an excellent technique when you want a methodical view of various hyperparameter combinations. However, pay special attention, again, to the output in figure 5.10, and note how the best `fitness` (the dark area) is within two cells of the worst `fitness` (the light area). Yet we can see plenty of areas that have good `fitness` around this light-colored cell, indicating we are likely missing a global minimum and/or maximum. The fix for this would be to go back and narrow the grid to just cover this two- to three-cell area—something that would require manual intervention on our part to better isolate the optimum hyperparameters.

Given that we have some experience now using EC methods for various problems, it follows that we take our next steps employing them for HPO. In the rest of this chapter, we look at using EC to provide better search mechanisms when performing HPO.

5.4 Evolutionary computation for HPO

Now that we have established a good background on the problem of HPO, we can start to employ some EC methods to enhance both speed and accuracy. As we have seen in previous chapters, evolutionary methods provide an excellent toolset to optimize search on various problems. It only makes sense then that we evaluate the practical side of using EC to perform HPO.

5.4.1 Particle swarm optimization for HPO

We start out introducing EC to DL by using PSO for HPO. PSO, as discussed in chapter 4, uses a `population` of swarming `particles` to find an optimum solution. Not only is PSO simple enough to implement with DEAP, but it also showcases the power of EC for solving problems like HPO.

5.4.2 Adding EC and DEAP to automatic HPO

In the next exercise, we focus on two key aspects: adding EC/DEAP to perform automatic HPO and applying an EC method, like PSO, to the problem. We, again, continue to use the same base problem to compare results between methods. Not only does this make understanding the code easier, but it also provides us with a good base-line when comparing further methods.

Open the EDL_5_4_PSO_HPO_PCA.ipynb notebook in Colab, and run all the cells via Runtime > Run All. Scroll down to the cell with the `HyperparametersEC` class definition, as shown in the following listing. Again, much of the heavy lifting in combining EC with DL occurs in the `HyperparametersEC` class. This time, we create a specialized version of this class called `HyperparametersEC`. We start our focus by looking at the base functions.

Listing 5.17   EDL_5_4_PSO_HPO.ipynb: The `HyperparametersEC` base functions

```
class HyperparametersEC(object):
  def __init__(self, **kwargs):        ◄─── Initializes the class with input args
    self.__dict__.update(kwargs)
    self.hparms = [d for d in self.__dict__]

  def __str__(self):        ◄─── Overrides to a string function
    out = ""
    for d in self.hparms:
      ds = self.__dict__[d]
      out += f"{d} = {ds} "
    return out

  def values(self):        ◄─── Exposes the current values
    vals = []
    for d in self.hparms:
      vals.append(self.__dict__[d])
    return vals

  def size(self):        ◄─── Returns the size of hyperparameters
    return len(self.hparms)
```

After the base functions, look at the special `next` function used to call the parent `HyperparametersEC` object to derive a child. This is complex code that won't entirely make sense until we look at the new generator methods. Notice how this function, shown in listing 5.18, takes as input an `individual` or vector of values. In this example, an `individual` represents a `particle`, but it could also represent any form of `individual` we describe using a vector. Another important detail to focus on is the use of the `send` function on the generator. `send` is like the `next` function in Python, but it allows generators to be initialized or input with values.

Listing 5.18   EDL_5_4_PSO_HPO.ipynb: `HyperparametersEC` next function

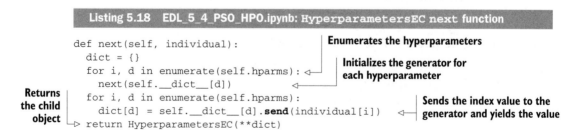

```
def next(self, individual):
  dict = {}
  for i, d in enumerate(self.hparms):        Initializes the generator for
    next(self.__dict__[d])                    each hyperparameter
  for i, d in enumerate(self.hparms):
    dict[d] = self.__dict__[d].send(individual[i])
  return HyperparametersEC(**dict)
```

Enumerates the hyperparameters

Sends the index value to the generator and yields the value

Returns the child object

Since the `send` function allows values to be passed into a generator, we can now rewrite the generator functions to accommodate. The two functions of interest are the `linespace` and `linespace_int` generators, as shown in listing 5.19. These generators allow inputs to be passed in using `i = yield`, where `yield` becomes the value input using the `send` function. The value `i` then becomes an index into the linear interpolated space between the values of `-1.0` and `1.0`, by applying the `clamp` function. As you may recall, the `send` function sent in the indexed value from the `individual`. Thus, each vector element in the `individual` becomes an index into the hyperparameter's linear space defined by the min/max values used when setting up the parent `hp`.

Listing 5.19   EDL_5_4_PSO_HPO.ipynb: Generator functions

```
def clamp(num, min_value, max_value):         ◁──────── Clamps the value between
    return max(min(num, max_value), min_value)           the min/max range

def linespace(min,max):
  rnge = max - min
  while True:                      Sets i to input the value yield
    i = yield       ◁────────┘
    i = (clamp(i, -1.0, 1.0) + 1.0) / 2.0    ◁──────── Linear interpolates the value
    yield i * rnge + min

def static(val):    ◁──────── Returns a static value
  while True:
    yield val
```

Now, we can look at how this works in the following cell, where we instantiate the class and create a child object. Again, the creation of the parent hyperparameter object is done by passing in generators for each hyperparameter we want to track. After that, a simple `individual` is defined using a list of values in the range of `-1.0` to `1.0`, where each value represents the index in the linear space defined by setting the min/max values to the generator. This time, when we call `next` on the hyperparameter parent object, we get back a child object that is defined by the indexed values from the input `individual`, as shown in the following listing.

Listing 5.20   EDL_5_4_PSO_HPO.ipynb: Creating a parent hyperparameter object

```
hp = HyperparametersEC(                         The linespace generator
  middle_layer = linespace_int(8, 64),  ◁─── defined with min/max values
  learning_rate = linespace(3.5e-02,3.5e-01),
  batch_size = static(16),    ◁──────┐
  epochs = static(200)                │ The static generators configured
)
                                    ┌── Creates a size 4 vector to
ind = [-.5, -.3, -.1, .8]   ◁──────┘   represent the individual
print(hp.next(ind))  ◁──────┐
## OUTPUT ##                │ Calls next to create a new hyperparameter child
middle_layer = 22 learning_rate = 0.14525 batch_size = 16 epochs = 200
```

The bulk of the PSO setup and operations code is borrowed from the EDL_4_PSO.ipynb notebook covered in chapter 4. Our focus here is on the configuration of the `toolbox` and `evaluate` function. In this code, we set the size of `particle` based on the `hp.size` or number of hyperparameters we want to track. Next, we reduce the `pmax/pmin` and `smin/smax` values to accommodate a smaller search space. Be sure to alter these values on your own to see what effect this has on HPO. At the end of the code in the following listing, we can see the registration of the `evaluate` function, where the `fitness` of each `particle` is evaluated.

Listing 5.21   EDL_5_4_PSO_HPO.ipynb: Creating a parent hyperparameters object

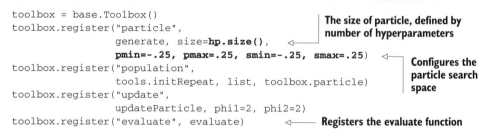

```
toolbox = base.Toolbox()
toolbox.register("particle",
              generate, size=hp.size(),        ◁──── The size of particle, defined by
              pmin=-.25, pmax=.25, smin=-.25, smax=.25)  ◁──  number of hyperparameters
toolbox.register("population",                              Configures the
              tools.initRepeat, list, toolbox.particle)    particle search
toolbox.register("update",                                 space
              updateParticle, phi1=2, phi2=2)
toolbox.register("evaluate", evaluate)   ◁────── Registers the evaluate function
```

The `evaluate` function now needs to call the `train_function` by passing in a child hyperparameter object. Notice how this is slightly different from the way we previously called the network training function. This time, we generate a child hyperparameter object by calling `next` on the parent by passing in the `individual`. Then, the child hyperparameter is input into the `train_function` to generate the output. To get a full evaluation, we check the model loss on the entire dataset and then return this as the `fitness`, as shown in the following listing.

Listing 5.22   EDL_5_4_PSO_HPO.ipynb: Creating a parent hyperparameter object

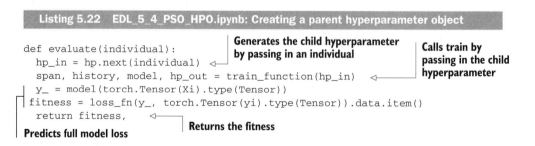

```
def evaluate(individual):
    hp_in = hp.next(individual)                          ◁── Generates the child hyperparameter
    span, history, model, hp_out = train_function(hp_in)     by passing in an individual
    y_ = model(torch.Tensor(Xi).type(Tensor))           ◁── Calls train by passing in the child hyperparameter
    fitness = loss_fn(y_, torch.Tensor(yi).type(Tensor)).data.item()
    return fitness,   ◁──── Returns the fitness
```
Predicts full model loss

We can now move on to the last code block, shown in listing 5.23, and examine how the particle swarming works with our changes. The changes have been marked in bold and are added to better track the `particle fitness` and associated hyperparameters. After `evaluate` is called on the part `particle`, we call `hp.next(part)` to create a child copy. This isn't required for PSO to function, but it helps us track `particle` history.

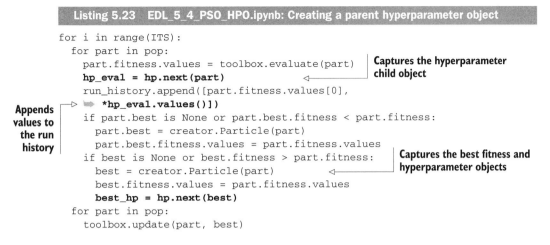

Listing 5.23   EDL_5_4_PSO_HPO.ipynb: Creating a parent hyperparameter object

```
for i in range(ITS):
  for part in pop:
    part.fitness.values = toolbox.evaluate(part)      Captures the hyperparameter
    hp_eval = hp.next(part)                            child object
    run_history.append([part.fitness.values[0],
      *hp_eval.values()])              Appends values to the run history
    if part.best is None or part.best.fitness < part.fitness:
      part.best = creator.Particle(part)
      part.best.fitness.values = part.fitness.values
    if best is None or best.fitness > part.fitness:    Captures the best fitness and
      best = creator.Particle(part)                    hyperparameter objects
      best.fitness.values = part.fitness.values
      best_hp = hp.next(best)
  for part in pop:
    toolbox.update(part, best)
```

Figure 5.6 is a capture of the final output from applying PSO to perform HPO over 10 iterations of swarming. You can clearly see in the far-left plot, the `fitness` evaluation plot, how the `particles` converged around a predicted best solution. Notice how the final best `fitness`, at around 34,000, was a better result than our grid search implementation. What's more, PSO was able to achieve this in a fraction of the time of grid search.

The results in figure 5.11 look quite impressive compared to our previous random and grid search examples. However, PSO is not without its own problems, and while it appears to be performing better than grid search, it may not always do so. Furthermore, PSO is tightly defined by the parameters `smin`/`smax` and `pmin`/`pmax`, and adjusting these values correctly often requires careful thought or trial and error.

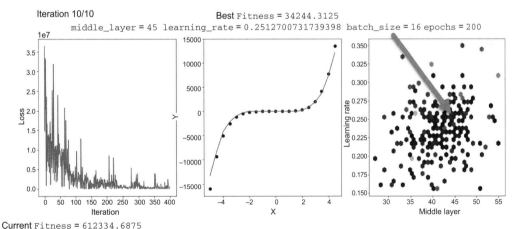

Current `Fitness` = 612334.6875
`middle_layer` = 45 `learning_rate` = 0.2512700731739398 `batch_size` = 16 `epochs` = 200

Figure 5.11   Output from using PSO for HPO

Reviewing the third subplot in figure 5.10, we can see how PSO converges to a region that it then swarms `particles` over to find better optimum solutions. The problem with this approach is that a swarm often gets stuck on a local minimum or maximum trying to find a global min/max value within the swarmed area. If no such global value is present in the area, then the swarm becomes stuck on a local min/max value.

Considering this potential dilemma with PSO, we can look to other EC methods that can perform HPO better and avoid or minimize this problem. As we saw in chapter 4, there are a few advanced EC methods that may help us overcome these concerns.

5.5   Genetic algorithms and evolutionary strategies for HPO

We spent some time understanding how GA works in chapter 3 and then expanded on these concepts when we employed ES in chapter 4. If you recall, ES is a specialized form of GA that applies a strategy to improve genetic operators, like mutation. We continue to use the same mutation strategy with GA and ES for the purposes of automatic HPO.

5.5.1   Applying evolutionary strategies to HPO

In chapter 4, we looked at how to apply evolutionary strategies as an additional vector that controls the rate and application of mutation. By controlling mutation in this manner, we can better focus a whole `population` to arrive at a solution more quickly. In our next project, we employ ES and a means to perform automatic HPO.

Open notebook EDL_5_5_ES_HPO.ipynb in Colab, and run all the cells via Runtime > Run All. This notebook is based on EDL_4_4_ES.ipynb and borrows much of the code from that example. We also borrow several pieces from the last exercise to build this sample, which means this code likely looks familiar.

We focus on the first difference by reviewing the ES hyperparameters. The first modification is setting the `IND_SIZE` variable to the number of hyperparameters. Then, we alter the `MAX_STRATEGY` to 5 to account for the larger search space, as shown in the following listing.

Listing 5.24   EDL_5_5_ES_HPO.ipynb: Setting ES hyperparameters

```
IND_SIZE = hp.size()        ◁──┐  Sets the individual size to the
NGEN = 10                        │  number of hyperparameters
MIN_VALUE = -1
MAX_VALUE = 1
MIN_STRATEGY = 0.5
MAX_STRATEGY = 5           ◁──┐  Increases the max strategy to
                               │  account for a wider search space
CXPB = .6
MUTPB = .3
```

Next, we jump down to the block of code that sets up the `toolbox`, as shown in listing 5.25. The only key changes we make here are modifying a couple of the hyperparameters, the alpha used in the `mate` operator, and the probability of mutation. Recall that alpha denotes the size of the blending that occurs between parents, rather than straight `crossover`.

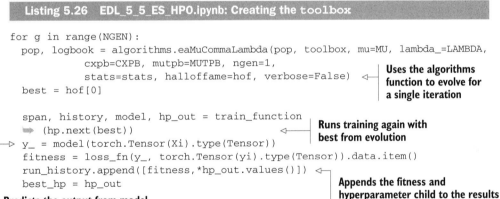

Listing 5.25 EDL_5_5_ES_HPO.ipynb: Creating the `toolbox`

```
toolbox = base.Toolbox()
toolbox.register("individual", generateES, creator.Individual, creator.Strategy,
    IND_SIZE, MIN_VALUE, MAX_VALUE, MIN_STRATEGY, MAX_STRATEGY)
toolbox.register("population", tools.initRepeat, list, toolbox.individual)
toolbox.register("mate", tools.cxESBlend, alpha=0.25)          ◁── Increases the
toolbox.register("mutate", tools.mutESLogNormal,                   alpha mask size
  ▶ c=1.0, indpb=0.06)
toolbox.register("select", tools.selTournament, tournsize=3)

toolbox.decorate("mate", checkStrategy(MIN_STRATEGY))
toolbox.decorate("mutate", checkStrategy(MIN_STRATEGY))
```
Increases the probability of mutation occurring

Lastly, we can look at the evolution code, shown in the following listing, to see how the `population` evolves to a solution.

Listing 5.26 EDL_5_5_ES_HPO.ipynb: Creating the `toolbox`

```
for g in range(NGEN):
  pop, logbook = algorithms.eaMuCommaLambda(pop, toolbox, mu=MU, lambda_=LAMBDA,
          cxpb=CXPB, mutpb=MUTPB, ngen=1,
          stats=stats, halloffame=hof, verbose=False)   ◁── Uses the algorithms
  best = hof[0]                                              function to evolve for
                                                            a single iteration
  span, history, model, hp_out = train_function
  ▶ (hp.next(best))                              ◁── Runs training again with
  y_ = model(torch.Tensor(Xi).type(Tensor))          best from evolution
  fitness = loss_fn(y_, torch.Tensor(yi).type(Tensor)).data.item()
  run_history.append([fitness,*hp_out.values()])  ◁┐
  best_hp = hp_out                                   Appends the fitness and
                                                     hyperparameter child to the results
```
Predicts the output from model

Figure 5.12 shows the final output of running ES to perform HPO. Notice how the third plot on the end, the `fitness` evaluation, shows a much tighter concentration. This concentration is tighter than the PSO, and ES suffers some of the same problems.

With PSO, we have seen a problem with a swarm of `particles` getting stuck on a local minima or maxima. While this appears to be a similar problem with ES, it is important to note that the convergence is quicker and more focused. Adding a larger `population` can reduce or help ES identify global minimums more regularly.

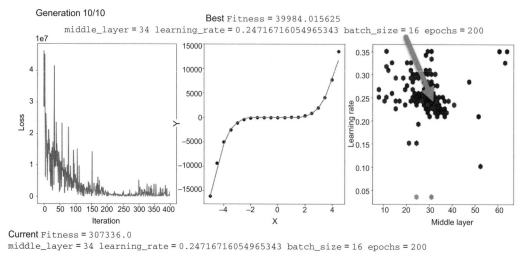

Generation 10/10

Best Fitness = 39984.015625

middle_layer = 34 learning_rate = 0.24716716054965343 batch_size = 16 epochs = 200

Current Fitness = 307336.0
middle_layer = 34 learning_rate = 0.24716716054965343 batch_size = 16 epochs = 200

Figure 5.12   Example output of ES on HPO

5.5.2   *Expanding dimensions with principal component analysis*

Up until now, we have been testing various methods across just two hyperparameters—the learning rate and batch size—to make visualizing results in two dimensions easier. If we want to visualize more hyperparameters in higher dimensions, we need to reduce the number of dimensions to two or three for visualization. Fortunately, there is a simple technique we can apply to visualize higher-dimensional output in two dimensions, called *principal component analysis* (PCA).

PCA is the process of reducing multi-dimensional vector data from higher to lower dimensions. In our example, we reduce four-dimensional outputs into two dimensions for visualization. You can think of the process as a projection from higher dimensions into lower dimensions. We show how this works and applies to visualizing HPO in the next exercise.

Open notebook EDL_5_5_ES_HPO_PCA.ipynb in Colab, and then run all the cells via Runtime > Run All. The variation of EDL_5_5_ES_HPO.ipynb adds PCA, so we can automate additional hyperparameters and still visualize results in 2D.

Most of the code is the same, but we focus on one cell that demonstrates setting up PCA and plotting some multidimensional output in 2D. scikit-learn provides a PCA class that can easily apply the transformation of data from higher dimensions into simpler component outputs. In the following code listing, we reduce example `individual` objects from four dimensions to two components.

Listing 5.27   EDL_5_5_ES_HPO_PCA.ipynb: Adding PCA

```
pop = np.array([[-.5,  .75,  -.1,  .8],
                [-.5,  -.3,  -.5,  .8],
                [-.5,  1,  -.5,  -.8],
                [ 1,  -.3,  -.5,  .8]])      Creates a sample pop of individuals
pca = PCA(n_components=2)                     Creates a PCA object
                                             with two dimensions
```

```
reduced = pca.fit_transform(pop)    ⊲────── Fits the data

t = reduced.transpose()    ⊲────── Transposes the results into a new vector

plt.scatter(t[0], t[1])    ⊲────── Plots the output in two dimensions
plt.show()
```

Figure 5.13 shows the example output from listing 5.27 and the application of PCA to the contrived `population` data. It is important to understand that each axis is a component that represents a distance between elements in the vector space. PCA output is calculated by measuring the variance, or differences, between elements and generates components or an axis, along which each element falls. It's important to understand that PCA plots are relative to the data being visualized. If you need or want to understand more about the PCA algorithm, be sure to check out the sklearn documentation or other online resources.

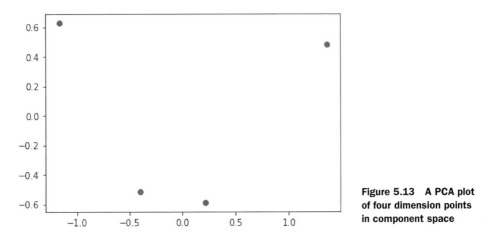

Figure 5.13   A PCA plot of four dimension points in component space

With the ability to visualize data points with more than two dimensions, we can also extend our `hyperparameter` object to vary additional inputs. We now add the `batch_size` and `epochs` as hyperparameters to vary, as shown in listing 5.28. Consider, for a moment, adding these two extra hyperparameters to a grid search problem. If we assume we want each hyperparameter to range across 10 cells or steps, then with 4 inputs, our search space would equal 10 x 10 x 10 x 10 = 10,000, or 10,000 cells. Think back to our random search example that was set up for 10,000 runs and took over 12 hours to complete. This is the same amount of time it would take to perform a grid search over this same four-dimensional space.

Listing 5.28   EDL_5_5_ES_HPO_PCA.ipynb: Adding hyperparameters

```
hp = HyperparametersEC(
  middle_layer = linspace_int(8, 64),
  learning_rate = linspace(3.5e-02,3.5e-01),
```

```
    batch_size = linespace_int(4,20),   ◁——— Varies the batch size
    epochs = linespace_int(50,400)      ◁—┐
)                                          └── Varies the number of epochs

ind = [-.5, .75, -.1, .8]
print(hp.next(ind))
```

The only other code change we need to apply is modifying the evaluation function output plot, as shown in listing 5.29. We can borrow from the code in listing 5.27 to apply the same process of reducing the hyperparameter outputs from the run history into two components. Then, we plot the transpose of these components into two-dimensional space using the `hexbins` function.

> **Listing 5.29** **EDL_5_5_ES_HPO_PCA.ipynb: Code to plot `fitness` evaluation**

```
rh = np.array(run_history)            ┐ Extracts the hyperparameters
  M = rh[:,1:IND_SIZE+1]   ◁——————————┘ from the run history
  reduced = pca.fit_transform(M)
  t = reduced.transpose()                            ┐ Outputs the PCA components
  hexbins = ax3.hexbin(t[0], t[1], C=rh[ :, 0],   ◁——┘
          bins=50, gridsize=50, cmap=cm.get_cmap('gray'))
```

Figure 5.14 shows the output of an ES being applied to HPO, with the third plot now composed of PCA components. This plot allows us to visualize the search for optimal hyperparameters across multiple dimensions. We can still see some clustering over the best solution, but it is also apparent that other points are now more spread out. Also notice how much the `fitness` has improved over our earlier examples, which can be attributed to the variation of the additional hyperparameters.

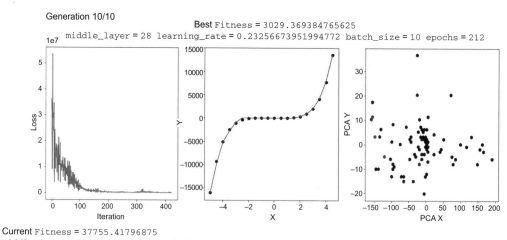

Figure 5.14   The output of ES HPO with PCA

The differences between our previous examples when only varying two hyperparameters are relatively minor. By adding additional hyperparameters, and thus dimensions, to the search space, we can see a clear increase in performance between ES and grid or random search. Remember, however, that ES is still susceptible to becoming stuck over local minima, suggesting we need to look at alternative methods.

5.6 Differential evolution for HPO

We saw the power of DE at the end of chapter 4 when we employed this method to solve discontinuous solutions over ES. Given the unique method DE uses to evolve solutions, it follows that it would make a good candidate to automate HPO. DE could also likely overcome the sticking condition we observed in both PSO and ES.

5.6.1 Differential search for evolving HPO

Differential evolution employs a simple iterative algorithm that samples three random individuals from a `population`. It then takes the difference between two of those individuals and adds a scaled value to the third one. The result produces a fourth point: the next search area to target.

Figure 5.15 depicts a single evaluation of the DE algorithm in two dimensions. In the figure, three points (A, B, C) have been randomly sampled from a `population`. A difference vector from A to B (A – B) is calculated and then passed through a scaling function F. In most cases, we keep things simple by multiplying by a scale value of 1.0. Then, we add the scaled difference vector to the third point to create a new target search point.

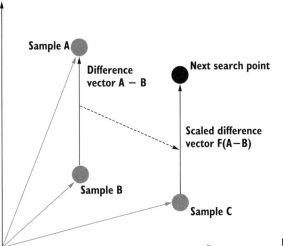

Figure 5.15   Differential evolution search

The search mechanism employed by DE is flexible enough to break free of the swarm or clustering problems we saw earlier with PSO and ES. Of course, we want to see DE in action to confirm for ourselves this is a better method for HPO. In the next exercise, we continue to solve the same problem using DE over optimization of four hyperparameters.

Open notebook EDL_5_ES_HPO_PCA.ipynb in Colab, and then run all the cells via Runtime > Run All. If you like, you can also review a non-PCA version of this notebook running on just two dimensions by exploring EDL_5_ES_HPO.ipynb. We have seen all the code in this exercise previously, so we just revisit the parts that make it unique here, starting with the hyperparameters in the following listing.

Listing 5.30   EDL_5_6_DE_HPO_PCA.ipynb: Set up the `creator` and `toolbox`

```
NDIM = hp.size()     ◁─────── The number of hyperparameter dimensions
CR = 0.25      ◁─────────── The crossover rate
F_ = 1    ◁
MU = 50      The scale factor/function
NGEN = 10

The total population
```

Next, we revisit the DEAP code that sets up the `creator` and `toolbox`—we have covered everything in this code previously. Notice the use of the `NDIM` value in the `individual` registration to set the size in the following listing. On the final line, we can select the registration to be set to a random `selection` operator that outputs three elements, k=3.

Listing 5.31   EDL_5_6_DE_HPO_PCA.ipynb: Setting up the `creator` and `toolbox`

```
creator.create("FitnessMin", base.Fitness, weights=(-1.0,))
creator.create("Individual",
               array.array, typecode='d', fitness=creator.FitnessMin)

toolbox = base.Toolbox()                                 Creates an individual with an
toolbox.register("attr_float", random.uniform, -1, 1)    equal size of hyperparameter
toolbox.register("individual", tools.initRepeat,                      dimensions
               creator.Individual, toolbox.attr_float, NDIM)    ◁───────────
toolbox.register("population", tools.initRepeat, list, toolbox.individual)
toolbox.register("select", tools.selRandom, k=3)

Registers a random select function of size 3
```

The only other code of interest is in the evolution section. This is code we already reviewed in chapter 4, but it is worth reviewing again. We call `individual` objects in DE, agents, since they have long lives like `particles` but evolve like agents. Notice the highlighted line, where the difference scaled vector is calculated and applied to single components of vector y. This calculation is guaranteed to only occur once for each randomly sampled index that matches the current vector component. However, the crossover rate does provide the opportunity to alter other component values to create a new y, as shown in the following listing.

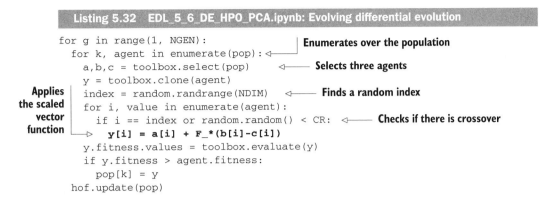

```
for g in range(1, NGEN):                    Enumerates over the population
    for k, agent in enumerate(pop):
        a,b,c = toolbox.select(pop)          Selects three agents
        y = toolbox.clone(agent)
        index = random.randrange(NDIM)       Finds a random index
        for i, value in enumerate(agent):
            if i == index or random.random() < CR:   Checks if there is crossover
                y[i] = a[i] + F_*(b[i]-c[i])
        y.fitness.values = toolbox.evaluate(y)
        if y.fitness > agent.fitness:
            pop[k] = y
    hof.update(pop)
```

Applies the scaled vector function

Figure 5.16 shows the final output of 10 `generations`, using DE to solve HPO for our target problem. Specifically, note the third evaluation plot and how the points are not clustered at all. Also notice that the best `fitness` generated from this method is around 81, a number that clearly exceeds any of our other previous attempts.

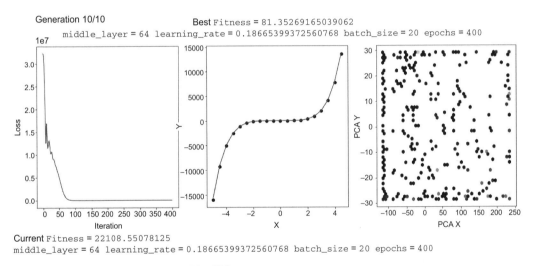

Figure 5.16   An example output of DE for HPO

As we can see, the application of DE to HPO appears to provide an excellent mechanism that avoids the local minima sticking problem observed with PSO and ES. We can make a comparison of the three techniques by upgrading the PSO example to use PCA, as demonstrated in the EDL_5_4_PSO_HPO_PCA.ipynb notebook. Feel free to run that notebook on your own to observe the differences between PSO, ES, and DE.

Figure 5.17 shows a comparison of the evaluation plots from PSO, ES, and DE. Notice how the PSO produces a wide swarm of `particles`, roughly centered on what it expects to be the best solution. Likewise, ES produces a much tighter cluster of attempts, but the distribution is more of a narrow band across the output. We can

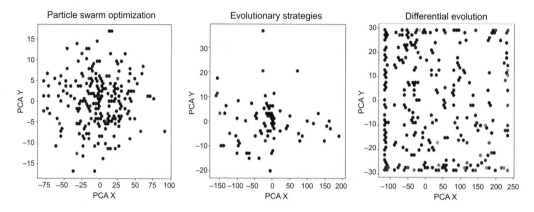

Figure 5.17   Comparison of EC methods for HPO

clearly see with the DE plot that this algorithm is well suited to explore boundaries and avoids getting stuck over local minima.

This has been our first chapter applying the principles of EDL through the integration of EC with DL for HPO. We started off exploring basic random search and then moved up to grid search to set a baseline for the other methods. From there, we expanded to applying EC with PSO, ES, and, finally, DE.

Through our exploration of techniques in this chapter, it should be obvious now that EC methods have definitive applications to DL. As we explore in the rest of this book, these and other techniques can be applied for the improvement of DL. For now, though, let's finish out the chapter with a summary of what we learned.

Summary

- This was the first chapter in which we combined EC methods with DL, in our first exposure to EDL. Along the way, we learned several new techniques we could apply to PyTorch and, likely, other frameworks.
- DL hyperparameter search (hyperparameter optimization HPO) requires extensive knowledge and experience to perform correctly:
  - Knowledge of strategies to perform manual hyperparameter searches for various problems can be developed using basic rules and templates.
  - Writing a basic hyperparameter search tool can be demonstrated quickly with Python.
- Random hyperparameter search is a search method that uses random sampling to generate results on a plot. By observing these random observations, a tuner can narrow the search down to specific areas of interest.
- Grid search is a method that maps hyperparameters to a grid of discrete values that are then evaluated in sequence. Visualizing the grid of results can assist the tuner in fine-tuning and selecting areas of specific interest for further tuning.

- DEAP can quickly provide a variety of evolutionary methods to employ for HPO:
  - From GAs to DE, evolutionary hyperparameter search is often more efficient than grid or random search.
  - For complex multidimensional hyperparameter optimizations, we can visualize the differences between various search forms by using dimensionality reduction techniques to produce 2D plots.
  - PCA is a good dimensionality reduction technique for visualization HPO.
- PSO is a great method to use on problems with relatively few hyperparameters.
- Differential evolution is ideal for more methodical and efficient searching of hyperparameters to avoid local minima clustering. Always evaluate the key differences between various search forms and understand when to employ which and when.

Neuroevolution optimization

This chapter covers

- How DL networks optimize or learn
- Replacing backpropagation training of neural networks with GAs
- Evolutionary optimization of neural networks
- Employing evolutionary optimization to a Keras DL model
- Scaling up neuroevolution to tackle image class recognition tasks

In the last chapter, we managed to get our feet wet by employing evolutionary algorithms for the purposes of optimizing DL network hyperparameters. We saw how using EA could improve the search for hyperparameters beyond simple random or grid search algorithms. Employing variations of EA, such as PSO, evolutionary strategy, and differential evolution, uncovered insights into methods used to search and for hyperparameter optimization (HPO).

Evolutionary DL is a term we use to encompass all evolutionary methods employed to improve DL. More specifically, the term *neuroevolution* has been used to define specific optimization patterns applied to DL. One such pattern we looked at in the last chapter was the application of evolutionary algorithms to HPO.

Neuroevolution encompasses techniques for HPO, parameter optimization (weight/ parameter search), and network optimization. In this chapter, we dive into how evolutionary methods can be applied to optimize network parameters directly, thus eliminating the need to backpropagate errors or loss through a network.

Neuroevolution is typically employed for the purpose of improving a single DL network model. There are other applications of evolution to DL that broaden search to more than one model. For now, though, let's look at how to build a simple multilayer perceptron (MLP) with NumPy as a basis for neuroevolution.

6.1 Multilayered perceptron in NumPy

Before we jump into neuroevolving a network's parameters, let's take a closer look at a basic DL system. The most basic of these is the multilayered perceptron written in NumPy. We don't use any frameworks like Keras or PyTorch, so we can clearly visualize the internal processes.

Figure 6.1 shows a simple MLP network. At the top of the figure, we can see how backpropagation works by pushing the calculated loss through the network. The

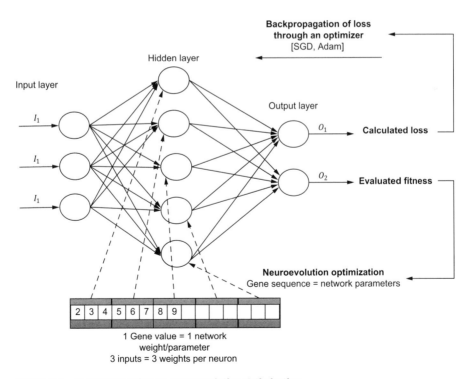

Figure 6.1 Backpropagation vs. neuroevolution optimization

bottom of the figure shows how neuroevolution optimization works by replacing each of the network's weights/parameters with a value from a gene sequence. Effectively, we are performing an evolutionary search similar to the one for hyperparameters in the last chapter.

Hopefully, if you have a solid background in DL, you already understand the MLP and its internal workings. However, to be complete, we review the structure of the MLP written with just NumPy. Then, we look at how this simple network trains across various sample classification problems.

Open the EDL_6_1_MLP_NumPy.ipynb notebook in Colab. If you need assistance, refer to the appendix. Run all the cells by selecting Runtime > Run All from the menu.

Figure 6.2 shows the second cell and options you can select. Select the options as shown in the figure and then run all cells in the notebook again by selecting Runtime > Run All.

[6]   Dataset Parameters

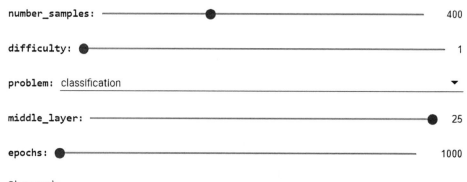

Show code

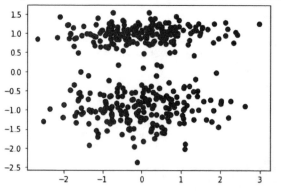

Figure 6.2   Selecting problem dataset generation parameters

Handling errors

Generally, if you encounter an error when running a notebook, it is the result of dupli-
cate code being run or code being run out of sync. The simplest fix is to factory reset
the notebook (Runtime > Factory Reset Runtime) and then run the cells again.

The code to generate the problem datasets is built using the sklearn `make datasets`
family of functions. We won't worry about the explicit code, instead focusing on the
parameter options (see figure 6.2) in table 6.1.

Table 6.1   Summary description of parameters and value ranges

Parameter	Description	Range
`number_samples`	The number of sample data points	100–1,000
`difficulty`	An arbitrary factor that increases problem difficulty	1–5
`problem`	Defines the problem dataset function used	classification = `make_classification` moons = `make_moons` circles = `make_circles` blobs = `make_blobs` Gaussian quantiles = `make_gaussian_quantiles`
`middle_layer`	Sets the number of nodes in the middle network layer	5–25
`epochs`	The number of training iterations to run on the MLP	1000–25000

Figure 6.3 shows examples from each of the dataset types at difficulty level 1. Go
ahead and change the problem type to see variations of each dataset. The most difficult dataset for the simple MLP network is circles, but be sure to explore all of them.

As a baseline, we compare a simple logistic regression (classification) model from
sklearn. Scroll down to the code shown in the following listing.

Listing 6.1   EDL_6_1_MLP_NumPy.ipynb: Sklearn logistics regression

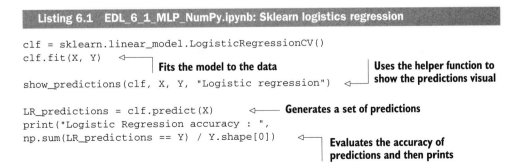

```
clf = sklearn.linear_model.LogisticRegressionCV()
clf.fit(X, Y)        ◁┐                                           Uses the helper function to
                      │  Fits the model to the data               show the predictions visual
show_predictions(clf, X, Y, "Logistic regression")   ◁┘

LR_predictions = clf.predict(X)        ◁─── Generates a set of predictions
print("Logistic Regression accuracy : ",
np.sum(LR_predictions == Y) / Y.shape[0])   ◁┐  Evaluates the accuracy of
                                               predictions and then prints
```

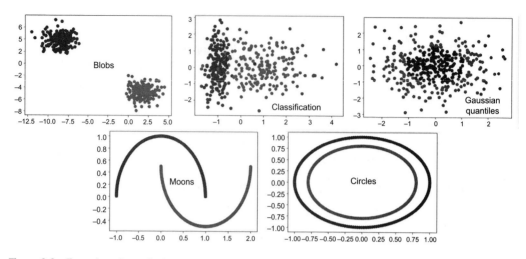

Figure 6.3   Examples of sample dataset types at difficulty level 1

Figure 6.4 shows the output of calling the helper `show_predictions` function. This function plots a nice visual of how the model classifies the data. As you can see in the figure, the results are less than stellar.

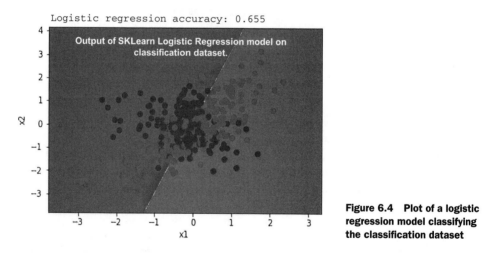

Figure 6.4   Plot of a logistic regression model classifying the classification dataset

Next, click on the Show Code link on the cell titled MLP in Python. Be sure to review the `init`, `forward`, `back_prop`, and `train` functions at your leisure. We don't spend time looking at the code here; we use this simple example to demonstrate the different functions. This code will be reused in future projects but without the `back_prop` and `training` functions. The last code block in the notebook, shown in the following listing, creates the MLP network, trains it, and outputs a visualization of the results.

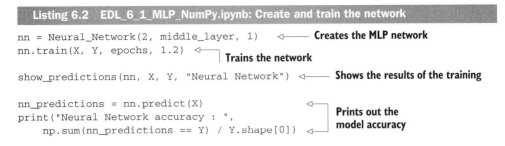

```
nn = Neural_Network(2, middle_layer, 1)     ◁──── Creates the MLP network
nn.train(X, Y, epochs, 1.2)   ◁──┐
                                 └ Trains the network

show_predictions(nn, X, Y, "Neural Network")  ◁──── Shows the results of the training

nn_predictions = nn.predict(X)                      ◁──┐
print("Neural Network accuracy : ",                    │ Prints out the
    np.sum(nn_predictions == Y) / Y.shape[0])  ◁──┘   model accuracy
```

Figure 6.5 shows the results of training the MLP network. As we can see in the rudimentary classification example, the results of using the MLP network are significantly better than the logistic regression model from sklearn. That is, in part, why neural networks and DL have become so successful. However, this simple network will still struggle to solve all the problem datasets.

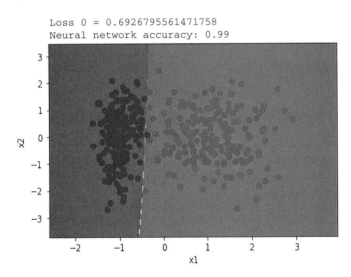

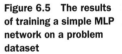

Figure 6.5 The results of training a simple MLP network on a problem dataset

Figure 6.6 shows the output of the MLP network trying to solve the circles and moons problem sets. As the figure shows, the accuracy peaks at 0.5, or 50%, for circles and 0.89, or 89%, for moons. We could, of course, look at more powerful optimizers, like Adam, but let's consider another way. What if we used GAs, for instance, to find the optimal network weights, like in many of our previous examples?

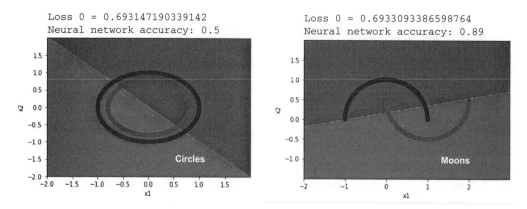

Loss 0 = 0.693147190339142
Neural network accuracy: 0.5

Loss 0 = 0.6933093386598764
Neural network accuracy: 0.89

Figure 6.6 Results of training MLP on circles and moons problem datasets

6.1.1 *Learning exercises*

Use the following exercises to improve your knowledge:

1 Increase or decrease the number of samples in figure 6.2 and then rerun the notebook.

2 Change the problem type and difficulty in figure 6.2 and then rerun the notebook after every change. Keep the size of the model consistent.

3 Change the model parameters and middle layer in figure 6.2 and then rerun.

Now that we have a perceptron MLP model, we can move on to optimizing it with genetic algorithms in the next section.

6.2 *Genetic algorithms as deep learning optimizers*

With the stage set from the previous project, we can now move on to replacing the DL optimization method used in our MLP, from backpropagation to neuroevolution optimization. So instead of using any form of backpropagation of loss through optimizers like gradient descent or Adam, we rely entirely on GAs.

The next project we look at uses the code from the last project as our base network model, and then we wrap the training optimization process with GAs from DEAP. A lot of this code should now feel quite familiar, so we only consider the highlights. If you need a refresher on setting up GA with DEAP, consider reviewing chapters 3–5.

Open notebook EDL_6_2_MLP_GA.ipynb in Colab. Refer to appendix A if you need assistance. Be sure to run all cells in the model by selecting Run > Run All from the menu.

We focus on the major changes by starting to look at the MLP network class block of code. This project uses the same MLP network model but replaces the `train` and `back_prop` functions with a new `set_parameters` function within the `Neural_Network` class, shown in listing 6.3.

This code loops through the list of parameters in the model, finds the size and shape, and then extracts a matching number of genes from the individual. Then, a new tensor is constructed and reshaped to match the original parameter/weight tensor. We subtract the original tensor from itself to zero it and maintain the reference and then add the new tensor. Effectively, we swap sections of the individual's gene sequence into tensors, which we then replace as new weights within the model.

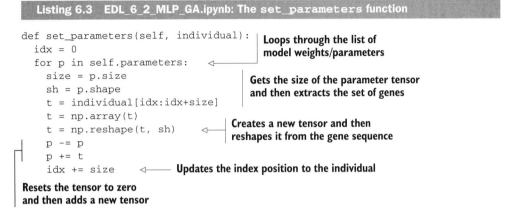

Listing 6.3 EDL_6_2_MLP_GA.ipynb: The `set_parameters` function

```
def set_parameters(self, individual):      Loops through the list of
    idx = 0                                 model weights/parameters
    for p in self.parameters:      ◁
        size = p.size                       Gets the size of the parameter tensor
        sh = p.shape                        and then extracts the set of genes
        t = individual[idx:idx+size]
        t = np.array(t)
        t = np.reshape(t, sh)      ◁        Creates a new tensor and then
        p -= p                              reshapes it from the gene sequence
        p += t
        idx += size      ◁──────── Updates the index position to the individual
```

Resets the tensor to zero
and then adds a new tensor

Be sure to note that the train and back_prop functions have been completely removed, thus preventing the network from performing any form of conventional backpropagation training. The set_parameters function sets the weights/parameters of the model and allows us to search for the values using GA. The next code listing we look at instantiates our network, sets all the parameters to 1.0, and then outputs the results shown in figure 6.7.

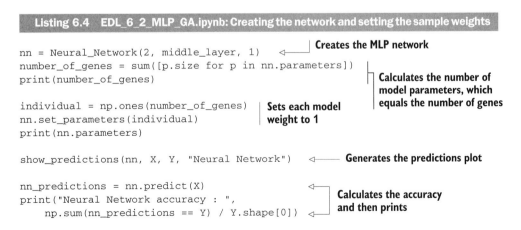

Listing 6.4 EDL_6_2_MLP_GA.ipynb: Creating the network and setting the sample weights

```
nn = Neural_Network(2, middle_layer, 1)      ◁──── Creates the MLP network
number_of_genes = sum([p.size for p in nn.parameters])
print(number_of_genes)                              Calculates the number of
                                                    model parameters, which
individual = np.ones(number_of_genes)   Sets each model    equals the number of genes
nn.set_parameters(individual)           weight to 1
print(nn.parameters)

show_predictions(nn, X, Y, "Neural Network")   ◁──── Generates the predictions plot

nn_predictions = nn.predict(X)                 ◁
print("Neural Network accuracy : ",                  Calculates the accuracy
    np.sum(nn_predictions == Y) / Y.shape[0])  ◁──── and then prints
```

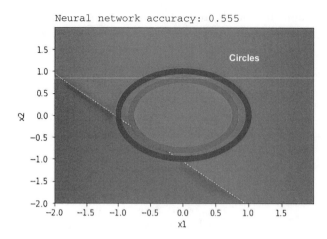

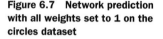

Figure 6.7   Network prediction with all weights set to 1 on the circles dataset

Figure 6.7 shows the output of the model predictions with all weights/parameters set to 1.0. The DEAP code to set up the GA is shown in the following listing, but it should already be familiar by now.

Listing 6.5   EDL_6_2_MLP_GA.ipynb: DEAP `toolbox` setup

```
toolbox = base.Toolbox()
toolbox.register("attr_float", uniform, -1, 1,     Creates a gene sequence of floats
    number_of_genes)                                of length number_of_genes
toolbox.register("individual", tools.initIterate, creator.Individual,
    toolbox.attr_float)
toolbox.register("population", tools.initRepeat, list, toolbox.individual)

toolbox.register("select", tools.selTournament,     Sets the selection to a
    tournsize=5)                                     tournament with a size of 5
toolbox.register("mate", tools.cxBlend, alpha=.5)
toolbox.register("mutate", tools.mutGaussian, mu=0.0,    Uses the Blend
    sigma=.1, indpb=.25)                                 function for crossover

Uses Gaussian mutation
```

Likewise, we can review the `evaluate` function, as shown in the following listing. Notice how we return the inverse of the accuracy. This allows us to minimize the `fitness` and, thus, maximize the accuracy of the `individual` during evolution.

Listing 6.6   EDL_6_2_MLP_GA.ipynb: The `evaluate` function

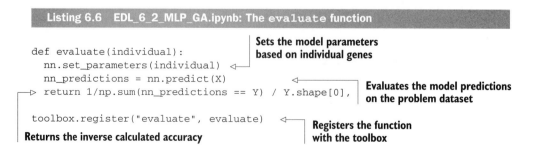

```
                                            Sets the model parameters
def evaluate(individual):                   based on individual genes
  nn.set_parameters(individual)
  nn_predictions = nn.predict(X)
  return 1/np.sum(nn_predictions == Y) / Y.shape[0],    Evaluates the model predictions
                                                        on the problem dataset
toolbox.register("evaluate", evaluate)
                                            Registers the function
Returns the inverse calculated accuracy     with the toolbox
```

Finally, we can jump down to the code that evolves the `population` to optimize the model, as shown in listing 6.7. As you might expect, we use the `eaSimple` function to train the `population` over a set of `generations`. Then, we output a sample `individual` from the last `generation`'s `population` and the current best `individual` as a comparison. At the end of the code, we check for an early stopping condition if the accuracy reaches some value. Checking for early stopping allows our code to break as soon as an acceptable solution is found.

Listing 6.7   EDL_6_2_MLP_GA.ipynb: Evolving the model

```
for g in range(NGEN):
    pop, logbook = algorithms.eaSimple(pop, toolbox,          Calls the evolution
            cxpb=CXPB, mutpb=MUTPB, ngen=RGEN,                 function to evolve
        ➥ stats=stats, halloffame=hof, verbose=False)  ◁──┘  the population
    best = hof[0]
    clear_output()
    print(f"Gen ({(g+1)*RGEN})")
    show_predictions(nn, X, Y, "Neural Network")  ◁─┐
    nn_predictions = nn.predict(X)                   Shows the results of the
    print("Current Neural Network accuracy : ",     last individual in the
    ➥ np.sum(nn_predictions == Y) / Y.shape[0])     last generation
    plt.show()

    nn.set_parameters(best)
    show_predictions(nn, X, Y, "Best Neural Network")
    plt.show()                                          Shows the results of
    nn_predictions = nn.predict(X)                      the best individual
    acc = np.sum(nn_predictions == Y) / Y.shape[0]
    print("Best Neural Network accuracy : ", acc)
    if acc > .99999: #stop condition  ◁──┐
        break                              Breaks if the early stopping
                                           condition is met
```

Figure 6.8 shows an example of evolving the `population` to an `individual` that can solve the circles problem with 100% accuracy. This is quite impressive when you

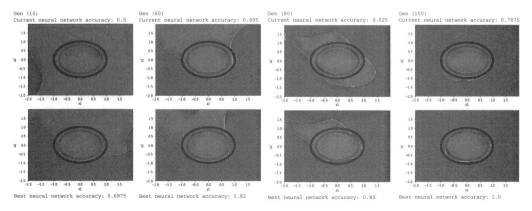

Figure 6.8   The evolution progression to solve the circle problem with GA

consider our MLP network using backpropagation could only attain 50% on this same problem.

Take some time to explore other problem datasets using GA and see how this method compares with simple backpropagation and gradient descent optimization. Again, there are more powerful optimizers, like Adam, we compare against later, but take the time to appreciate how well GA can optimize a simple MLP network.

6.2.1 *Learning exercises*

Use the following exercises to improve your neuroevolutionary knowledge:

1 Increase or decrease the number of samples and then rerun. Is it harder to converge the network parameters with fewer or greater samples?
2 Alter the `crossover` and `mutation` rates and the rerun. Can you improve the performance of the evolution for a given problem?
3 Increase or decrease the size of the middle layer and then rerun. What effect does the network size have on evolution?

Of course, we also have more powerful evolutionary methods, like evolutionary strategies and differential evolution, that may perform better. We take the time to look at both more advanced evolutionary methods in the next section.

6.3   *Other evolutionary methods for neurooptimization*

In chapter 5, when we tuned hyperparameters, we saw some great results using other evolutionary methods, like evolutionary strategies and differential evolution. Having seen good results like these, it only makes sense to apply both ES and DE to the set of problems worked on in the last section.

In this project, we apply ES and DE as neuroevolution optimizers. The two code examples are extensions of our last project and reside in separate notebooks. We jump back and forth between both notebooks and the last project to make comparisons.

Open up EDL_6_3_MLP_ES.ipynb and EDL_6_3_MLP_DE.ipynb in Colab in two separate browser tabs. You may also want to keep the last project notebook, EDL_6_2_MLP_GA.ipynb, open as well. If you need assistance, see the appendix.

Select the same problem, circles or moons, from the notebook's Dataset Parameters cell. If you are not sure which problem to choose, refer to figure 6.2 and the corresponding table that explains the options in greater detail.

Run all the cells of both notebooks via Runtime > Run All from the menu. Switch between both notebooks as they are running to see how each of the methods optimize the weights.

Figure 6.9 shows examples of running the ES and DE notebooks to completion (a maximum of 1,000 `generations`) on the circles and moons problems. It can be especially interesting to note how DE and ES evolve the weights for each problem. Notice how the ES notebook evolves and the 2D visualization produces several straight edges. Not only is ES solid at solving these more difficult datasets, but it also has the potential to solve more difficult problems.

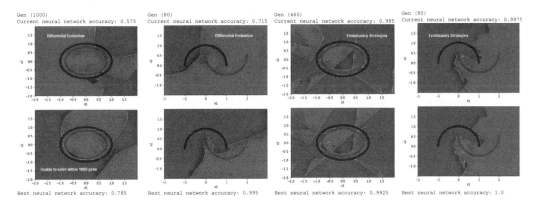

Figure 6.9 ES vs. DE on the circle and moons problem datasets

We have reviewed all the main code elements in both notebooks, so we won't revisit any code here. However, go ahead and look through the structure of the code on your own to see how easy it is to convert from using GA to ES and DE. You can also go back and try other problems or adjust other settings in the Dataset Parameters cell to see how either ES or DE performs.

For the sample datasets showcased in this suite of projects, the simpler GA approach generally performs the best. While this may vary slightly, DE is certainly the less optimal choice, but ES has some definite potential. In later chapters, we revisit this choice between methods again to dive deeper into which is the best option.

6.3.1 Learning exercises

Complete the following exercises to help improve your understanding:

1 Find a class of problems in which ES performs better than DE, and vice versa.
2 Tune the various hyperparameter options, and then see what effect they have on either DE or ES notebooks.
3 Play with the specific evolutionary methods hyperparameters—min and max strategy for ES, and pmin/pmax and smin/smax for DE.

In this section, we looked at how other evolutionary methods can be employed for a simple NumPy network weight optimization. In the next section, we apply the same principle but this time to a DL framework such as Keras.

6.4 Applying neuroevolution optimization to Keras

Admittedly, the MLP network we were making comparisons to in the previous projects was somewhat underpowered and limited. To make a valid comparison, we should "improve our game" and look at a more robust DL platform, like Keras. Keras, much like PyTorch and many other DL frameworks, provides a wide selection of advanced optimizers we can use out of the box.

In the following project, we set up a Keras multilayered DL network to solve for the classification datasets. Not only does this provide a great comparison between using a robust and established optimizer, like Adam, but it also showcases how we can incorporate *neuroevolution optimization* (NO) into a Keras network.

Open the EDL_6_4_Keras_GA.ipynb notebook in Colab. Refer to the appendix if you need assistance. Hold off on running all the cells in the notebook, as we take this step by step.

Locate and select the Keras model setup code cell, as shown in listing 6.8, and then run all the notebook's previous cells by selecting Runtime > Run Before from the menu. The code creates a simple Keras model with an input, hidden, and output layer. The output is a single binary node; we use binary cross entropy to calculate loss. We also determine the number of trainable parameters of the model, since this also relates to the number of genes later.

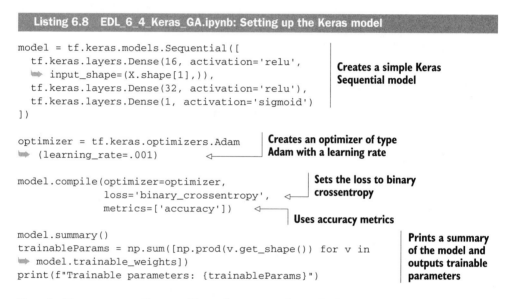

Listing 6.8   EDL_6_4_Keras_GA.ipynb: Setting up the Keras model

```
model = tf.keras.models.Sequential([
  tf.keras.layers.Dense(16, activation='relu',
⮕ input_shape=(X.shape[1],)),           Creates a simple Keras
  tf.keras.layers.Dense(32, activation='relu'),   Sequential model
  tf.keras.layers.Dense(1, activation='sigmoid')
])

optimizer = tf.keras.optimizers.Adam      Creates an optimizer of type
⮕ (learning_rate=.001)                    Adam with a learning rate

model.compile(optimizer=optimizer,            Sets the loss to binary
              loss='binary_crossentropy',     crossentropy
              metrics=['accuracy'])
                                          Uses accuracy metrics
model.summary()                                          Prints a summary
trainableParams = np.sum([np.prod(v.get_shape()) for v in   of the model and
⮕ model.trainable_weights])                                 outputs trainable
print(f"Trainable parameters: {trainableParams}")           parameters
```

Run the Keras set up cell; you will get the output shown in figure 6.10. The output shows the model summary and an output of the number of parameters/weights per layer. The total number of trainable parameters is also printed at the bottom of the output. This is important because it represents the number of genes in an individual.

Go back to the Dataset Parameters cell, as shown in figure 6.2, and select a difficult problem, like moons or circles. This reruns the cell and generates a view of the problem dataset.

```
Model: "sequential"
```

Layer (type)	Output Shape	Param #
dense (Dense)	(None, 16)	48
dense_1 (Dense)	(None, 32)	544
dense_2 (Dense)	(None, 1)	33

```
Total params: 625
Trainable params: 625
Non-trainable params: 0
```

Trainable parameters: 625 ⟵ This equates directly to the number of genes

Figure 6.10   Summary model output and count of parameters

Scroll down to the model training code cell, as shown in the following listing, and then run the cell. As part of this training code, we are using a helpful callback function: PlotLossesKeras from the LiveLossPlot module.

Listing 6.9   EDL_6_4_Keras_GA.ipynb: Fitting the model

```
model.fit(X, Y, epochs=epochs,        ⟵——     Trains the model on datasets
          callbacks=[PlotLossesKeras()], ⟵     for a number of epochs
       ⟶  verbose=0)
                                               Uses PlotLossesKeras to
    Turns off noisy output                     output progress plots
```

Run the training cell. You will get a similar output to that shown in figure 6.11.

Run the next couple of cells to evaluate the model's accuracy and output the results. Figure 6.12 shows the output from the show_predictions helper method. The rainbow pattern is representative of the model's output, which is a value from 0 to 1. The class separation is the middle at 0.5, shown by the yellow band.

Move to the next code cell, where there is a helper function that extracts an individual's genes and inserts them into the weights/parameters of the Keras model. This code is quite like how we set model weights in the simple MLP network. It loops over the model layers and model weights, extracting a tensor of weights. From this information, we rebuild a tensor from the next section of individual weights and add it to list of tensors.

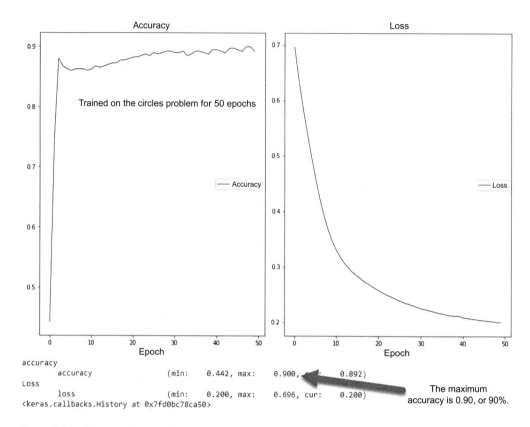

```
accuracy
        accuracy            (min:    0.442, max:   0.900,           0.892)
Loss
        loss                (min:    0.200, max:   0.696, cur:      0.200)
<keras.callbacks.History at 0x7fd0bc78ca50>
```

The maximum
accuracy is 0.90, or 90%.

Figure 6.11   An example output from training a Keras model with an Adam optimizer over 50 epochs

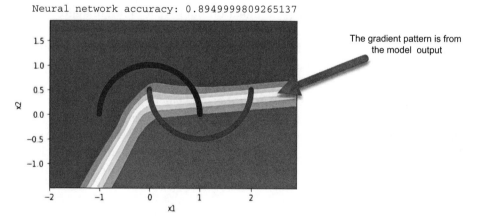

The gradient pattern is from
the model output

Figure 6.12   Output of model using `show_predictions`

Finally, the model weights are set using the `set_weights` function, as shown in the following listing.

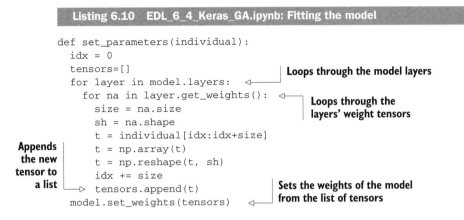

Listing 6.10 EDL_6_4_Keras_GA.ipynb: Fitting the model

```
def set_parameters(individual):
    idx = 0
    tensors=[]
    for layer in model.layers:                      Loops through the model layers
        for na in layer.get_weights():              Loops through the
            size = na.size                          layers' weight tensors
            sh = na.shape
            t = individual[idx:idx+size]
            t = np.array(t)                         Appends
            t = np.reshape(t, sh)                   the new
            idx += size                             tensor to
            tensors.append(t)                       a list      Sets the weights of the model
    model.set_weights(tensors)                                  from the list of tensors
```

The next cell sets all the model weights to 1 and outputs the results using `show_predictions`. Again, we follow the same procedure we used in the MLP project.

The rest of the code is identical to the previous GA example, so go ahead run the rest of the cells by selecting Runtime > Run After from the menu. Just be sure you have selected a cell in which the code and previous cells have already been fully run. If you are not sure which cell was last run, you can also just run all the cells.

Figure 6.13 shows the output of running GA optimization using a Keras network. Notice how well the model is optimizing without using any DL optimizers. If you are an experienced Keras user, go ahead and swap out various other optimizers to see if any can beat the evolutionary optimizer.

6.4.1 Learning exercises

The following exercises are intended to show the limits of neuroevolution in Keras:

1 Change the problem type to circles and then rerun the problem. Are the network-evolved weights able to solve the problem?

2 Alter the Keras model in listing 6.8 and then rerun the notebook. What happens when you remove or add new layers to the model?

3 Alter the network loss to use MSE rather than binary cross-entropy in listing 6.8. What effect does this have on the performance of the evolution and results?

We now have a powerful new tool in our toolbelt—something that should surely benefit all DL, it seems. Unfortunately, there are some limits to this method and evolutionary search in general. We look at an example of those limits in the next section.

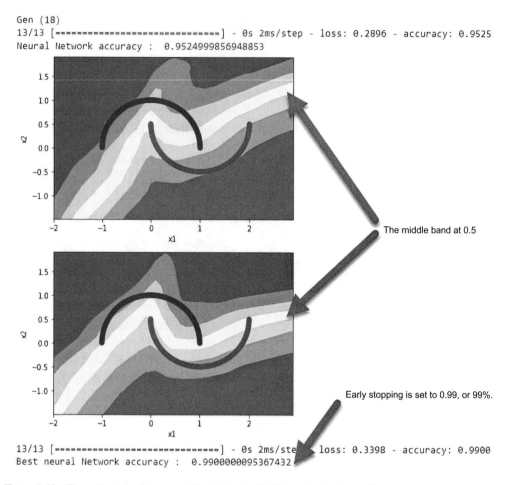

```
Gen (18)
13/13 [==============================] - 0s 2ms/step - loss: 0.2896 - accuracy: 0.9525
Neural Network accuracy :  0.9524999856948853
```

The middle band at 0.5

Early stopping is set to 0.99, or 99%.

```
13/13 [==============================] - 0s 2ms/ste    loss: 0.3398 - accuracy: 0.9900
Best neural Network accuracy :  0.9900000095367432
```

Figure 6.13   The output of a Keras model optimized with GA on the circles problem

6.5   *Understanding the limits of evolutionary optimization*

DL models have continuously exploded in size, from early models having hundreds of parameters to the latest transformers having billions. Optimizing or training these networks requires substantial computational resources, so trying to evaluate better ways will always be a priority. As such, we want to move away from toy datasets and look at more practical applications of evolutionary optimization.

In the next project, we move up slightly from toy datasets to a first-class example problem of classifying the Modified National Institute of Standards and Technology (MNIST) handwritten digits dataset. As part of your DL education, you have likely already used MNIST in some capacity. MNIST is often the first dataset we learn to build DL networks to classify.

Open the EDL_6_5_MNIST_GA.ipynb notebook in Colab. The appendix can help you if you need assistance in this task. Run the top two cells—the `pip install` and `import`—to set up the base of the notebook code. The next cell loads the MNIST dataset, normalizes the values, and puts them into training tenors x and y, as shown in the following listing.

Listing 6.11   EDL_6_5_MNIST_GA.ipynb: Loading the data

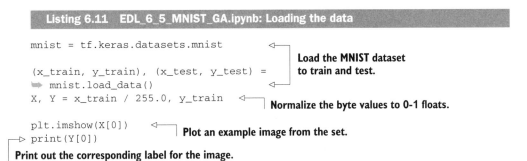

```
mnist = tf.keras.datasets.mnist

(x_train, y_train), (x_test, y_test) =
     mnist.load_data()
X, Y = x_train / 255.0, y_train

plt.imshow(X[0])
print(Y[0])
```

Load the MNIST dataset to train and test.

Normalize the byte values to 0-1 floats.

Plot an example image from the set.

Print out the corresponding label for the image.

Figure 6.14 shows a sample output of a single digit from the dataset. The next cell has the model building code, so run that cell and the training code shown in listing 6.12. This code trains the model and, again, uses module livelossplot's `PlotLossesKeras` function to show real-time results. After that, the model accuracy is displayed and a class classification report is generated.

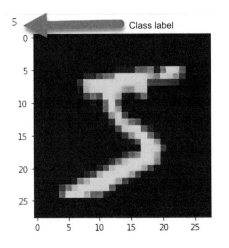

Class label

Figure 6.14   An example image from MNIST

Listing 6.12   EDL_6_5_MNIST_GA.ipynb: Training the model

```
model.fit(X, Y, epochs=epochs,
          validation_data=(x_test,y_test),
          callbacks=[PlotLossesKeras()],
          verbose=0)
```

Trains the model with data for epochs

Validates the model with test data

Plots accuracy and loss plots

```
print("Neural Network accuracy : ",
    model.evaluate(X,Y)[1])        ◁──── Performs a test prediction
y_pred = model.predict(x_test)
y_pred = np.argmax(y_pred, axis=1)  ◁────┐ Takes the highest prediction as a class
print(classification_report(y_test, y_pred))  ◁──── Prints the classification report
```

Figure 6.15 shows the class classification report generated by the sklearn module classification_report function based on the test prediction results. As you can see, our network is clearly excellent at classifying the digits from all classes.

```
Neural network accuracy: 0.9901166558265686
           precision   recall  fy-score  support
```

	precision	recall	fy-score	support
0	0.98	0.99	0.98	980
1	0.99	0.98	0.99	1135
2	0.98	0.96	0.97	1032
3	0.98	0.98	0.98	1010
4	0.98	0.97	0.98	982
5	0.98	0.98	0.98	892
6	0.98	0.99	0.98	958
7	0.99	0.96	0.97	1028
8	0.94	0.98	0.96	974
9	0.96	0.98	0.97	1009
accuracy			0.98	10000
macro avg	0.98	0.98	0.98	10000
weighted avg	0.98	0.98	0.98	10000

The class classification report, which shows accuracy for each digit class

Figure 6.15   Classification report of MNIST digits classification

Select Runtime > Run After from the menu to run all the remaining cells in the notebook. Again, most of the code in this notebook is identical to our previous projects, so we won't need to review it.

Figure 6.16 demonstrates sample output from the last cell performing the evolution. This figure shows the accuracy progression over time as well as the classification report. As you can see from this quick example, evolutionary optimization has critical limitations when it approaches larger models.

As seen in the last project, using evolutionary optimization/search for finding optimal network weights/parameters produces poor results, while the network yields up to 60% accuracy over a couple of hours of training, which is far better than random. However, accuracy results for each class are subpar and not acceptable.

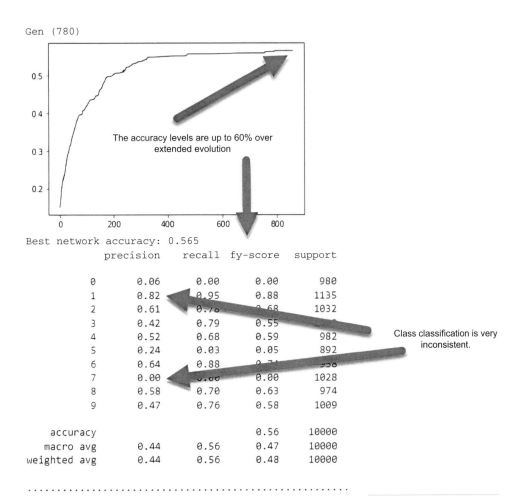

```
Best network accuracy: 0.565
                precision      recall   fy-score    support

        0          0.06         0.00      0.00         980
        1          0.82         0.95      0.88        1135
        2          0.61         0.70      0.68        1032
        3          0.42         0.79      0.55
        4          0.52         0.68      0.59         982
        5          0.24         0.03      0.05         892
        6          0.64         0.88                
        7          0.00                   0.00        1028
        8          0.58         0.70      0.63         974
        9          0.47         0.76      0.58        1009

 accuracy                                 0.56       10000
 macro avg         0.44         0.56      0.47       10000
weighted avg       0.44         0.56      0.48       10000
```

Class classification is very
inconsistent.

Figure 6.16   Example output from GA EO, showing poor results

6.5.1   *Learning exercises*

These exercises are intended for advanced readers wanting to test the limits of neuro-evolutionary weight/parameter optimization:

1   Change the base Keras model by altering the network size and shape. Do you get better results with a smaller network?
2   Add convolutional layers and max pooling to the model. This can help reduce the total number of model parameters to evolve.
3   Adapt the notebook code to wrap another model you have used or worked with in the past.

Obviously, the results of the last project demonstrate that using evolutionary search for DL optimization won't work on larger parameter models. That doesn't mean this technique is totally without merit, as we discuss in later chapters.

Summary

- A simple multilayer perceptron network can be developed using the NumPy library. Sklearn can be used to generate a variety of single-label classification datasets that demonstrate binary model classifications with a simple NumPy MLP network.

- DEAP and genetic algorithms can be used to find the weights/parameters of a simple DL network.

- DEAP with evolutionary strategies and differential evolution can be used to optimize weight/parameter search on a simple MLP network. Comparing both methods can be useful to evaluate the tool to use for various evolutionary optimization methods and various sample classifications on problem datasets.

- A Keras DL model can be adapted to use an evolutionary search for weight optimization instead of the traditional method of differential backpropagation.

- Evolutionary weight optimization can be successful in solving complex and undifferentiable problems.

- DL problems that use automatic differentiation and backpropagation are limited to solving continuous problems.

- Evolutionary optimization can be used to solve discontinuous problems previously unsolvable with DL networks.

- Evolutionary optimization becomes much less successful as the problem scales. Applying EO to more complex problems, such as image classification, is not typically successful.

7

Evolutionary convolutional neural networks

This chapter covers

- Convolutional neural networks with a Keras primer
- Defining a neural network architecture with a gene sequence
- Building a custom crossover operator
- Applying a custom mutation operator
- Evolving the best convolutional network architecture for a given dataset

The last chapter showed us the limits of evolutionary algorithms when applied to a complex problem like parameter search. As we have seen, genetic algorithms can provide excellent results on a certain class of problems. However, they fail to deliver when employed for larger image classification networks.

In this chapter, we continue looking at larger networks for image classification. However, this time instead of optimizing parameter weights or model hyperparameters, we look at improving network architecture. More specifically, we cover the network architecture of convolutional neural networks (CNNs).

CNNs were instrumental to the adoption of DL for image classification and other tasks. They are a fantastic tool in the DL practitioner's toolbelt but are often misunderstood and under-utilized. In the next section, we review CNN models and how they are built in TensorFlow and Keras.

7.1   *Reviewing convolutional neural networks in Keras*

This section's project is a review of constructing CNN models for image classification with Keras. While we cover some of the basics of CNN, our focus is more on the details of what makes building these types of networks difficult.

> ### The future of CNN
> CNN layers are quickly being replaced with more advanced technologies, like residual networks and attention mechanisms (aka transformers). The same principles we learn in this chapter could be applied to optimizing these other architectures.

In this project, we perform image classification over the Fashion-MNIST dataset, shown in figure 7.1. This is a good basic test dataset that can be trimmed down, without compromising results too drastically. Trimming the amount of data we use for training or inference reduces the running time of our later evolutions.

> ### GPU training
> The notebook projects used in this chapter are ready to use GPU, due to the heavy processing. However, Colab may put limitations on or restrict your access to a GPU instance. If you find this problematic and you have access to a machine with a GPU, you can always run Colab connected to a local instance.

Open the EDL_7_1_Keras_CNN.ipynb notebook in Colab. Check the appendix if you need help opening the notebook. As always, the first few cells are installs, imports, and set up. We can ignore those and go ahead and run the entire notebook via Runtime > Run All from the menu.

The first cell we want to look at is the data loading, shown in listing 7.1. Where we load the Fashion dataset, normalize and reshape the data into 28, 28, 1 tensors, where the ,1 at the end represents the channel. We do this because the dataset comes in as a 2D array without channels defined. At the end of the code block, we extract the first 1,000 samples of the original for training and 100 for testing.

Figure 7.1 Fashion-MNIST dataset

Reducing the dataset this much is not ideal but will save us minutes or hours later when we try to optimize tens or hundreds of `individuals` or numerous `generations`.

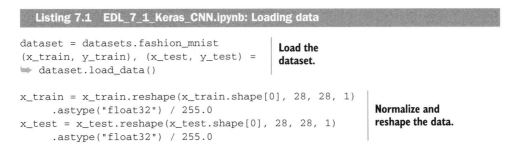

```
Listing 7.1   EDL_7_1_Keras_CNN.ipynb: Loading data
```

```
dataset = datasets.fashion_mnist                  Load the
(x_train, y_train), (x_test, y_test) =            dataset.
➥ dataset.load_data()

x_train = x_train.reshape(x_train.shape[0], 28, 28, 1)
      .astype("float32") / 255.0                        Normalize and
x_test = x_test.reshape(x_test.shape[0], 28, 28, 1)     reshape the data.
      .astype("float32") / 255.0
```

```
x_train = x_train[:1000]
y_train= y_train[:1000]        Extract a smaller
x_test = x_test[:100]          subset of data.
y_test= y_test[:100]
```

The next couple of cells construct the output shown in figure 7.1. We don't review them further here.

Figure 7.2 demonstrates how a single layer is defined, from code to visual implementation. Each CNN layer defines a set of filters or neurons that describe a patch or kernel. A single kernel is passed over an image using a stride, typically of 1 pixel by one pixel. For simplicity, we keep the stride fixed at 1, 1.

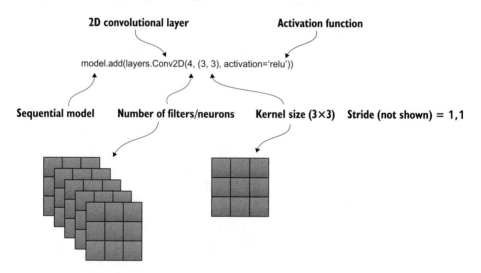

Figure 7.2   How a CNN layer is defined in Keras

Code for building the convolutional layers of the model is shown in listing 7.2. Each Conv2D layer defines a convolutional operation applied to the input. At each successive layer, the number of filters or channels expands from the last layer. For example, the first Conv2D layer expands the input channels from 1 to 64. Then, successive layers reduce this to 32 and then 16, where each convolution layer is following by a MaxPooling layer that collects or summarizes the features.

Listing 7.2   EDL_7_1_Keras_CNN.ipynb: Building CNN layers

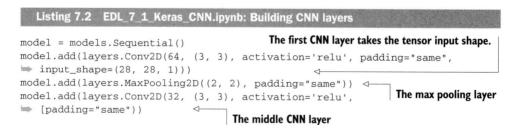

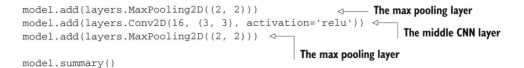

```
model.add(layers.MaxPooling2D((2, 2)))           ←——— The max pooling layer
model.add(layers.Conv2D(16, (3, 3), activation='relu'))  ←┐
model.add(layers.MaxPooling2D((2, 2)))  ←┐         │ The middle CNN layer
                                          │
model.summary()                           │
                                      The max pooling layer
```

Figure 7.3 shows how a single filter or kernel operation is applied to a single image patch and the way it extracts a value corresponding to the output. The corresponding output is produced by sliding the filter patch across the image, where each kernel operation represents a single output value. Note that the kernel values or weights/parameters in the filter are learned.

Application of a single convolutional filter operation

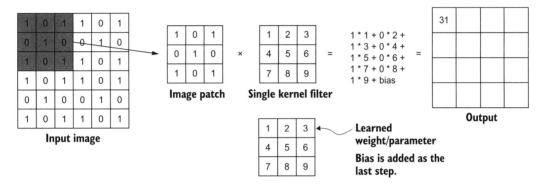

Figure 7.3   Demonstration of the convolutional filter operation

Typically, the output of such convolutional operations is quite large and noisy. Keep in mind that each kernel/filter produces an output patch resembling the image. A useful operation to reduce the amount of data is to use another layer type called *pooling*. Figure 7.4 demonstrates how a max pooling layer reduces the output from the previous operation. Maximum pooling is one option; you can also use other variations to take the minimum or average of the collated features.

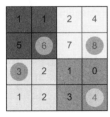

The result of applying max pooling over the output patch at stride 2,2

The output of a single filter or kernel

Figure 7.4   Max pooling operation

After setting up the convolution and max pooling layers of the model, a summary is printed using `model.summary()`, as shown in the following listing. Keep in mind this is just the top, or feature extractor, portion of the full model.

Listing 7.3   EDL_7_1_Keras_CNN.ipynb: CNN model summary

```
Model: "sequential_4"

_____
 Layer (type)                Output Shape              Param #
=================================================================
 conv2d_8 (Conv2D)           (None, 28, 28, 64)        640

 max_pooling2d_7 (MaxPooling  (None, 14, 14, 64)        0
 2D)

 conv2d_9 (Conv2D)           (None, 14, 14, 32)        18464

 max_pooling2d_8 (MaxPooling  (None, 7, 7, 32)          0
 2D)

 conv2d_10 (Conv2D)          (None, 5, 5, 16)          4624

 max_pooling2d_9 (MaxPooling  (None, 2, 2, 16)          0
 2D)

=================================================================
Total params: 23,728
Trainable params: 23,728
Non-trainable params: 0
_____
```

A 3×3 kernel plus bias gives 10 parameters per filter— 10×64 = 640.

Pooling layers are not trainable and have no parameters.

The total number of parameters

In the next cell, the output from the CNN layers is flattened and input into a single dense layer, which outputs to 10 classes, as shown in the following listing.

Listing 7.4   EDL_7_1_Keras_CNN.ipynb: Finishing the model

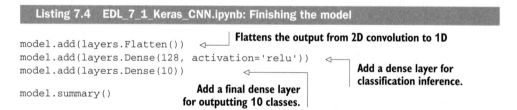

```
model.add(layers.Flatten())
model.add(layers.Dense(128, activation='relu'))
model.add(layers.Dense(10))

model.summary()
```

Flattens the output from 2D convolution to 1D

Add a dense layer for classification inference.

Add a final dense layer for outputting 10 classes.

Figure 7.5 shows the output of the model being trained over the much-reduced dataset. Typically, this dataset is optimized to perform at an accuracy around 98%. However, for reasons mentioned earlier, training on the full dataset is time-consuming and not practical when we apply evolution. Instead, focus on the accuracy we see with this reduced dataset; we don't review the model compile and training code, since we discussed it in chapter 6.

Your results may vary somewhat, but you should see consistent values max out around 81% for the training or validation data. If you do decide to use other datasets

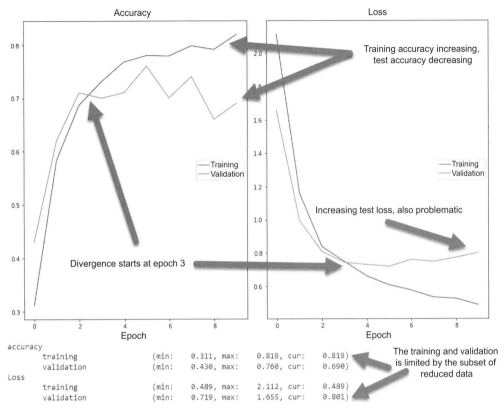

Figure 7.5   Model training on a reduced dataset

for this project, be aware that your results may vary dramatically. The Fashion-MNIST works well for this application because there is little class variability. This certainly wouldn't be the case for a dataset like CIFAR-10 or CIFAR-100, for instance.

Refer to figure 7.5; look at the problematic differences in training, and test both loss and accuracy. We can see the model falls apart around epoch 3 for performing any good inference on blind test data. This is likely related to the reduced size of our data but also, in part, the construction of the model. In the next section, we cover a couple obvious CNN layer architectures and see what problems they introduce.

7.1.1   Understanding CNN layer problems

In this section, we explore a couple further CNN layer architecture examples and understand the problems they introduce. CNN is a great tool when used properly but can quickly become a disaster if used ineffectively. Understanding when problems arise can be beneficial to our later attempts at evolutionary optimization.

Reopen the EDL_7_1_Keras_CNN.ipynb notebook, and then navigate to the section labeled SECTION 7.1.1. Be sure to run all the cells using Runtime > Run All from the menu.

The first cell contains the code of a new model, this time with only one CNN layer. As you can see, we have a single layer defined with 64 filters/neurons and a 3×3 kernel. Figure 7.6 shows the output of running this cell; note the extreme difference between the total parameters in this model (over 6 million), shown in the following listing, and those in the previous model (23 thousand), shown in listing 7.3.

Listing 7.5   EDL_7_1_Keras_CNN.ipynb: Single CNN layer

```
model = models.Sequential()
model.add(layers.Conv2D(64, (3, 3), activation='relu',      A single 2D
    padding="same", input_shape=(28, 28, 1)))      ◁————    convolutional layer
model.add(layers.Flatten())
model.add(layers.Dense(128, activation='relu'))    ◁————    A single dense layer
model.add(layers.Dense(10))    ◁—
                                    Outputs to 10 classes
model.summary())
```

```
Model: "sequential_1"
_____
 Layer (type)              Output Shape            Param #
=================================================================
 conv2d_3 (Conv2D)         (None, 28, 28, 64)      640

 flatten_1 (Flatten)       (None, 50176)           0

 dense_2 (Dense)           (None, 128)             6422656    = 50176 * 128 + 128 (bias)

 dense_3 (Dense)           (None, 10)              1290

=================================================================
Total params: 6,424,586                There is explosive growth
Trainable params: 6,424,586            in the number of parameters.
Non-trainable params: 0
```

Figure 7.6   The summary of a single CNN layer model

Figure 7.7 shows the training output of the model from running the next cell. Notice how well the model performs on the training data but how poorly it performs on the validation/test data. This is because the model with over 6 million parameters memorizes the reduced dataset. As a result, you can see that the accuracy of the training set moves to almost 100%, which is fantastic. However, the test/validation set begins to decrease.

Model memorization/specialization vs. generalization

We often want to build models that generalize, and therefore, we break our data into training and test sets to validate this generalization. There are some other techniques we can apply to help generalize, like batch normalization and dropout, that we look at later. However, in some cases, generalization may not be your end goal, and instead, you may want to identify very specific sets of data. If that is the case, then a model that memorizes data is ideal.

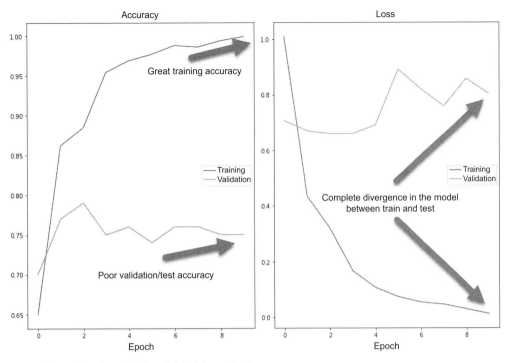

Figure 7.7 A single-layer CNN model training output

Now, we move on to a discussion of the effect of pooling on convolutional output. Listing 7.6 shows the change in the model and a summary of the total trained parameters. It is worth noting that this model is about a quarter of the size of the previous model from the addition of pooling. We also added a batch normalization layer between the pooling layer to better generalize the model.

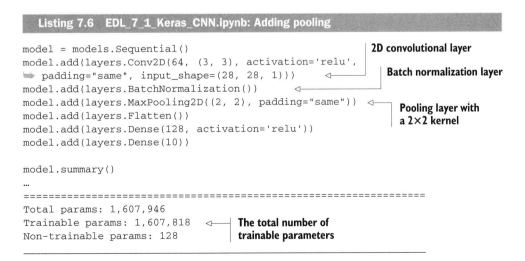

Listing 7.6 EDL_7_1_Keras_CNN.ipynb: Adding pooling

```
model = models.Sequential()                                    2D convolutional layer
model.add(layers.Conv2D(64, (3, 3), activation='relu',
    padding="same", input_shape=(28, 28, 1)))                  Batch normalization layer
model.add(layers.BatchNormalization())
model.add(layers.MaxPooling2D((2, 2), padding="same"))         Pooling layer with
model.add(layers.Flatten())                                    a 2×2 kernel
model.add(layers.Dense(128, activation='relu'))
model.add(layers.Dense(10))

model.summary()
…
================================================================
Total params: 1,607,946
Trainable params: 1,607,818          The total number of
Non-trainable params: 128            trainable parameters
```

Figure 7.8 shows the output of training the model over 10 epochs. While this model is still showing signs of memorization, the model is also better at generalizing. We can see indications of this by looking at the increasing validation accuracy and corresponding decreasing loss.

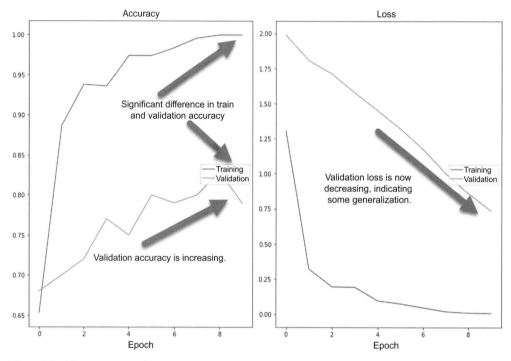

Figure 7.8   The output of training a more advanced CNN model

We could, of course, continue going through numerous variations of the model, adding in more CNN layers or layers like batch normalization, dropout, or pooling. Then, we would go through and tweak the various hyperparameters, like kernel sizes and the number of neurons and filters, but that would obviously be time-consuming.

7.1.2   *Learning exercises*

Use the following learning exercise to help improve your understanding of convolution, if required:

1   Increase or decrease the kernel size in listing 7.6, and then see what effect this has on the results.

2   Increase or decrease the size of the pooling from (2,2) in listing 7.6, and then rerun.

3   Add an additional convolutional layer to the model in listing 7.6, and then rerun.

Ultimately, understanding how and where to use CNN layers requires some trial and error—not unlike hyperparameter optimization. Even if you deeply understand the convolutional process, defining the right CNN architecture can be difficult. This, of course, makes this an ideal candidate for employing some evolutionary process for optimizing CNN network architecture.

7.2   Encoding a network architecture in genes

In this section's project, we look at the details of encoding the network architecture of a CNN model into `genes`. This is a precursor to evolving these `individual gene` sequences to produce the optimum model for a given dataset.

There have been several papers and a few tools published for evolving network architectures. The code in this project was partly derived from a paper titled "Evolving Deep Convolutional Neural Networks for Image Classification" by Yanan Sun et al. In this paper, the authors develop a process called EvoCNN for building CNN model architectures.

EvoCNN defined a process for encoding a convolutional network into a variable length `gene` sequence, as shown in figure 7.9. When building our `gene` sequence, we want to define a base rule that all will start with a convolutional layer and finish with a dense layer that will feed into another dense output layer. To simplify things, we don't worry about encoding the last output layer here.

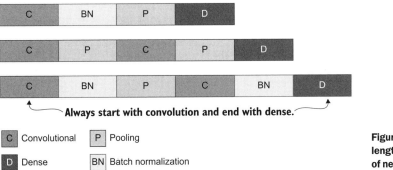

Figure 7.9   Variable length gene encodings of network architecture

Inside each main component layer, we also want to define corresponding hyperparameter options, such as the number of filters/neurons and kernel sizes. To encode such varied data, we use a negation trick to separate the main layer components and related hyperparameters. The code in this next notebook project only looks at building the encoding sequence; we work through the remaining bits later.

Open the EDL_7_2_Encoding_CNN.ipynb notebook in Colab. Don't worry if you can't use a GPU for this project; we are only looking at the architecture encoding and not performing evolutionary training just yet.

The first block of code we look at (listing 7.7) is the constants we set up to help us define the layer types and lengths to encapsulate the various relevant hyperparameters.

We start with constants that define the total maximum number of layers and other ranges for various layer hyperparameters. After that, we can see the block identifiers for each type and their corresponding size. This size value denotes the length of each layer definition, inclusive of hyperparameters.

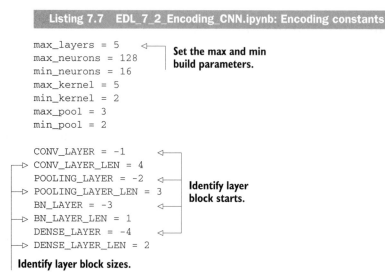

Listing 7.7   EDL_7_2_Encoding_CNN.ipynb: Encoding constants

```
max_layers = 5          ◁──┐  Set the max and min
max_neurons = 128          │  build parameters.
min_neurons = 16
max_kernel = 5
min_kernel = 2
max_pool = 3
min_pool = 2

      CONV_LAYER = -1       ◁──┐
  ──▷ CONV_LAYER_LEN = 4       │
      POOLING_LAYER = -2   ◁   │  Identify layer
  ──▷ POOLING_LAYER_LEN = 3    │  block starts.
      BN_LAYER = -3        ◁   │
  ──▷ BN_LAYER_LEN = 1         │
      DENSE_LAYER = -4     ◁───┘
  ──▷ DENSE_LAYER_LEN = 2
```

Identify layer block sizes.

Figure 7.10 demonstrates how a gene sequence looks with encoding layer blocks and their corresponding hyperparameters. Notice how the negated values -1, -2, -3, and -4 represent the start of a layer component. Then, depending on the layer type, additional hyperparameters are further defined for the number of filters/neurons and kernel size.

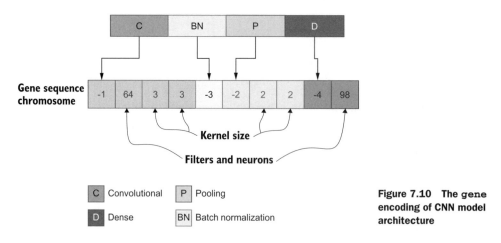

C Convolutional   P Pooling

D Dense   BN Batch normalization

Figure 7.10   The gene encoding of CNN model architecture

We can now go over the code that constructs a gene sequence (chromosome) of an individual, shown in listing 7.8. First, we look at the function create_offspring, which is the base for how the sequence is built. This code loops over the maximum layer count and checks, with a 50% chance of adding a convolution layer. If so, it further checks, with a 50% chance of adding a batch normalization and/or pooling layer.

Listing 7.8 EDL_7_2_Encoding_CNN.ipynb: Creating offspring (gene sequences)

```
def create_offspring():
  ind = []
  for i in range(max_layers):
    if random.uniform(0,1)<.5:
      ind.extend(generate_conv_layer())      ◁──── Add a convolutional layer.
      if random.uniform(0,1)<.5:
        ind.extend(generate_bn_layer())      ◁──── Add a batch normalization layer.
      if random.uniform(0,1)<.5:
        ind.extend(generate_pooling_layer())  ◁──── Add a pooling layer.
  ind.extend(generate_dense_layer())
  return ind
```

For completeness, we can also review the various layer-building functions. Not all the code is shown in the following listing, but what is shown should give you an idea of how the helper functions work.

Listing 7.9 EDL_7_2_Encoding_CNN.ipynb: Layer component helper functions

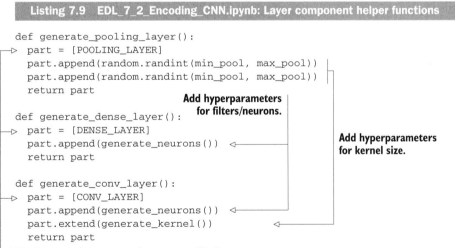

```
def generate_pooling_layer():
  part = [POOLING_LAYER]
  part.append(random.randint(min_pool, max_pool))
  part.append(random.randint(min_pool, max_pool))
  return part
                        Add hyperparameters
                        for filters/neurons.
def generate_dense_layer():
  part = [DENSE_LAYER]
  part.append(generate_neurons())   ◁
  return part
                                              Add hyperparameters
                                              for kernel size.
def generate_conv_layer():
  part = [CONV_LAYER]
  part.append(generate_neurons())   ◁
  part.extend(generate_kernel())    ◁
  return part
```
Add a layer marker to start the sequence block.

Calling create_offspring generates a gene sequence, as shown in the output of running the last cell. Go ahead and run the cell a few times to see the variation of the gene sequences created, as shown in the following listing.

Listing 7.10   EDL_7_2_Encoding_CNN.ipynb: Examining the generated gene sequence

```
individual = create_offspring()          Create an offspring
print(individual)                         individual.
```

```
[-1, 37, 5, 2, -3, -1, 112, 4, 2, -4, 25]
```
Example output of a random gene sequence

With a gene sequence, we can now go on to build the model, essentially parsing the gene sequence and creating a Keras model. As you can see from the code, the input to build_model is a single gene sequence that produces a Keras model. Otherwise, the code is a standard token parser that looks for layer component tokens -1, -2, -3, or -4. After defining the layer, it adds the additional hyperparameters based on the layer type, as shown in the following listing.

Listing 7.11   EDL_7_2_Encoding_CNN.ipynb: Building the model

```
def build_model(individual):
  model = models.Sequential()
  il = len(individual)
  i = 0
  while i < il:
    if individual[i] == CONV_LAYER:          Add a convolution layer.
      n = individual[i+1]
      k = (individual[i+2], individual[i+3])
      i += CONV_LAYER_LEN
      if i == 0:
        model.add(layers.Conv2D(n, k, activation='relu', padding="same",
          input_shape=(28, 28, 1)))
      else:
        model.add(layers.Conv2D(n, k, activation='relu', padding="same"))
    elif individual[i] == POOLING_LAYER:
      k = k = (individual[i+1], individual[i+2])      Add a pooling layer.
      i += POOLING_LAYER_LEN
      model.add(layers.MaxPooling2D(k, padding="same"))
    elif individual[i] == BN_LAYER:
      model.add(layers.BatchNormalization())      Add a batch normalization layer.
      i += 1
    elif individual[i] == DENSE_LAYER:          Add a dense layer.
      model.add(layers.Flatten())
      model.add(layers.Dense(individual[i+1], activation='relu'))
      i += 2
  model.add(layers.Dense(10))
  return model
```

Add an input shape to the first convolution layer.

The next block of code creates a new individual gene sequence, builds a model from the sequence, and then trains the model, outputting the training/validation plots, as we have already looked at.

Your results may be quite poor or relatively good, depending on the random initial sequence. Go ahead and run this last cell a few times to see the differences between different initial randomized individuals.

7.2.1 *Learning exercises*

Use the following exercises to improve your understanding:

1 Create a list of new gene encoded sequences from listing 7.8 by calling create_offspring in a loop. Print, and then compare the individuals.

2 Alter the max/min range hyperparameters from listing 7.6, and then produce a list of new offspring (see exercise 1).

3 Add a new input to create_offspring that changes the static probability from 0.5 to the new value. Then, produce a list of offspring (see exercise 1) to compare.

Now that we have a way to define a gene sequence that represents a model architecture, we can move on to building the genetic operators that support such a sequence. Unfortunately, we can't just use a built-in operator from DEAP but must create our own for mating (crossover) and mutation.

7.3 *Creating the mating crossover operation*

The standard genetic operators available in the DEAP toolbox are insufficient for our custom network architecture gene sequences. This is because any standard mating operator would likely corrupt the format of our gene sequence. Instead, we need to build our own custom operators for both mating (crossover) and mutation.

Figure 7.11 shows what this custom crossover operation look like when applied to two mating parents. The operation works by taking the two parents and extracting the various layer collections into lists—one for convolution, one for pooling, and so on. From each list, a random selection of pairs of layers are swapped between gene sequences. The resulting sequences of genes become the produced offspring.

The code to perform this custom crossover operation is in our next notebook, but really, it is an extension of the last notebook we looked at. Keep in mind while reviewing this code that this is just one option for performing crossover, and you may likely consider others. What is important is maintaining a correctly formatted gene sequence after the crossover operation.

Open the EDL_7_3_Crossover_CNN.ipynb notebook in Colab. Run all the cells (Runtime > Run All), and then scroll to near the bottom of the notebook. Again, this notebook just builds on our last exercises, and we don't need to review that previous code here.

Scroll down the cell titled Custom Crossover Operator. There is a bit of code here, so we break it down into sections to review starting with the main crossover function,

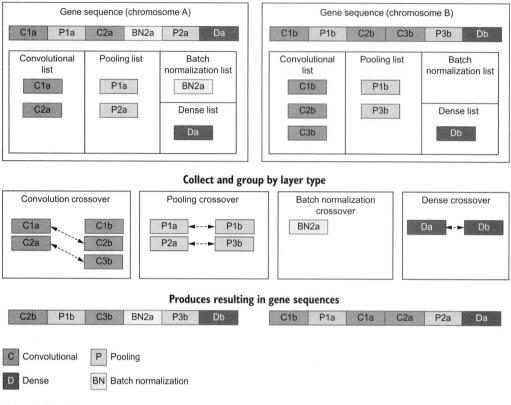

Figure 7.11 The `crossover` operation visualized

shown in the following listing. This main function calls the `swap_layers` function for each set of layers.

Listing 7.12 EDL_7_3_Crossover_CNN.ipynb: A custom `crossover` function

```
def crossover(ind1, ind2):        ◁─────┐ The function takes two individuals as input.
    ind1, ind2 = swap_layers(ind1, ind2, CONV_LAYER,
    ⮩ CONV_LAYER_LEN)
    ind1, ind2 = swap_layers(ind1, ind2, POOLING_LAYER,          Swap
    ⮩ POOLING_LAYER_LEN)                                         various
    ind1, ind2 = swap_layers(ind1, ind2, BN_LAYER, BN_LAYER_LEN) groups
    ind1, ind2 = swap_layers(ind1, ind2, DENSE_LAYER, DENSE_LAYER_LEN) of layers.
    return ind1, ind2     ◁─────┐
                                 │ return results in two new offspring.
```

The `swap_layers` function is where each layer type is extracted from the sequence and then randomly swapped. We start by getting the list of layers by type from each sequence. `c1` and `c2` are both index lists we loop through to determine the swap points. From these lists, we randomly grab a value to swap for each sequence and then perform the swap with the `swap` function, as shown in the following listing.

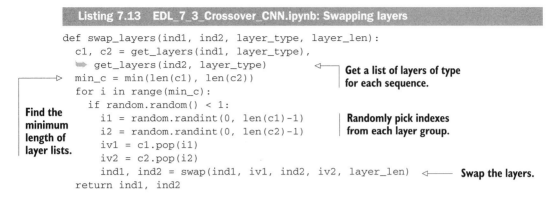

Listing 7.13 EDL_7_3_Crossover_CNN.ipynb: Swapping layers

```
def swap_layers(ind1, ind2, layer_type, layer_len):
    c1, c2 = get_layers(ind1, layer_type),
      get_layers(ind2, layer_type)           Get a list of layers of type
    min_c = min(len(c1), len(c2))            for each sequence.
    for i in range(min_c):
      if random.random() < 1:
        i1 = random.randint(0, len(c1)-1)    Randomly pick indexes
        i2 = random.randint(0, len(c2)-1)    from each layer group.
        iv1 = c1.pop(i1)
        iv2 = c2.pop(i2)
        ind1, ind2 = swap(ind1, iv1, ind2, iv2, layer_len)    Swap the layers.
    return ind1, ind2
```

Find the minimum length of layer lists.

The `get_layers` function is where we extract the layer indexes from each `gene` sequence. This can be done rather succinctly with a list comprehension by checking each value in the sequence and extracting the matching positions in a list, as shown in the following listing.

Listing 7.14 EDL_7_3_Crossover_CNN.ipynb: Finding the layer indexes

```
def get_layers(ind, layer_type):                    Inputs a sequence and the
    return [a for a in range(len(ind)) if ind[a]    type of layer to extract
      == layer_type]
```
Returns a list of indexes of layer type in sequence

The last function we look at here is the `swap` function, shown in the following listing, which is responsible for swapping the layer block of each `individual`. `swap` works by extracting each layer block from the sequence from the given index. Since the layer types are always the same length, a simple index replace is appropriate. Keep in mind that if our layer blocks were variable in length, we would have to develop a more advanced solution.

Listing 7.15 EDL_7_3_Crossover_CNN.ipynb: The swap function

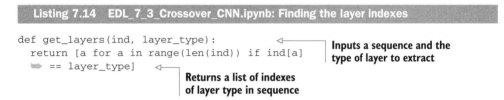

```
def swap(ind1, iv1, ind2, iv2, ll):
    ch1 = ind1[iv1:iv1+ll]              Extracts the chunk from the sequence
    ch2 = ind2[iv2:iv2+ll]
    print(ll, iv1, ch1, iv2, ch2)       Prints the output of the layer swap
    ind1[iv1:iv1+ll] = ch2
    ind2[iv2:iv2+ll] = ch1              Swaps the sequence of chunks
    return ind1, ind2
```

Figure 7.12 shows the results of performing the `crossover` function on two initial offspring. Notice from the figure how we are swapping three convolutional, one pooling, one batch normalization, and one dense layer group. The resulting output sequences are shown in figure 7.12.

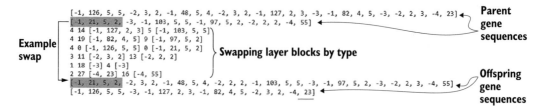

Figure 7.12 Examining `crossover` output

The rest of the notebook builds, compiles, and trains the resulting `individuals` and outputs the results. Be sure to review those last cells to confirm the `crossover` operation is not corrupting the `gene` sequence format. Now that we have a `crossover` operation for mating and producing offspring, we can move on to developing the last operation: `mutation`.

7.4   *Developing a custom mutation operator*

Again, the standard `mutation` operators available in DEAP are of no use for our custom `gene` sequences. As such, we need to develop a custom `mutation` operator to simulate the type of `mutations` we would like to apply to our `gene` sequences. For the purposes of this project, we keep the `mutation` rather simple and only alter the current layer blocks. In more advanced applications, a `mutation` could add or remove new layer blocks, but we leave that up to you to implement.

Open notebook EDL_7_4_Mutation_CNN.ipynb in Colab. Run all the cells (Runtime > Run All). Scroll down to near the bottom of the notebook to the section titled Custom Mutation Operator.

We start by examining the main `mutation` function, as shown in the following listing. The function starts by checking if the `individual` is not empty. If it isn't, we move on to mutating each of the layer groups using the `mutate_layers` function. Finally, we return the result in a tuple, per DEAP convention.

Listing 7.16   EDL_7_4_Mutation_CNN.ipynb: A custom `mutation` operator

```
def mutation(ind):
    if len(ind) > CONV_LAYER_LEN:        Only mutate convolution networks.
        ind = mutate_layers(ind, CONV_LAYER,
        ➥ CONV_LAYER_LEN)
        ind = mutate_layers(ind, DENSE_LAYER,          Mutate layers
        ➥ DENSE_LAYER_LEN)                             by type.
        ind = mutate_layers(ind, POOLING_LAYER,
        ➥ POOLING_LAYER_LEN)
    return ind,        Return tuple, per DEAP convention.
```

The `mutate_layers` function loops through the layer groups of a particular type and `mutates` just the corresponding hyperparameters. Start by extracting the layer group indexes for the given type using `get_layers`, as seen in the last section. Then, wrapped in a `try/except` block, we apply `mutation` by calling the `mutate` function to replace the given indexed layer block, as shown in the following listing.

Listing 7.17   EDL_7_4_Mutation_CNN.ipynb: The `mutate_layers` function

```
def mutate_layers(ind, layer_type, layer_len):
  layers = get_layers(ind1, layer_type)     ◁──────── Use get_layers to extract
  for layer in layers:  ◁────────                      layer indexes by type.
    if random.random() < 1:   │ Loop through indexes.
      try:
        ind[layer:layer+layer_len] = mutate(          Call the mutate function to
            ind[layer:layer+layer_len], layer_type) ◁─ replace the layer chunk.
      except:
        print(layers)    ◁──── Print out layers that cause errors.
  return ind
```

The `mutate` function is where all the work happens. We start by checking that the extracted part has the correct length, as shown in listing 7.18. This is done to prevent any potential formatting corruption issues that may happen to an `individual`. Next, depending on the layer type, we may alter the number of filters/neurons and kernel sizes. Notice how we limit the kernel sizes to a value within the original min/max ranges but leave the number of filters/neurons to grow or shrink. At this point, we also check whether the `individual` gene sequence has any corrupt blocks—blocks that don't match the required length. If we do find that a `gene` sequence is corrupt during `mutate`, then we throw an exception. This exception will be caught in the `mutation` function.

Listing 7.18   EDL_7_4_Mutation_CNN.ipynb: The `mutate` function

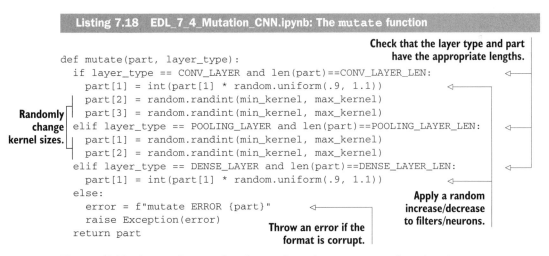

```
                                                   Check that the layer type and part
def mutate(part, layer_type):                      have the appropriate lengths.
  if layer_type == CONV_LAYER and len(part)==CONV_LAYER_LEN:     ◁───
    part[1] = int(part[1] * random.uniform(.9, 1.1))    ◁───
    part[2] = random.randint(min_kernel, max_kernel)
Randomly  part[3] = random.randint(min_kernel, max_kernel)
change  elif layer_type == POOLING_LAYER and len(part)==POOLING_LAYER_LEN:  ◁─
kernel sizes.  part[1] = random.randint(min_kernel, max_kernel)
    part[2] = random.randint(min_kernel, max_kernel)
  elif layer_type == DENSE_LAYER and len(part)==DENSE_LAYER_LEN:    ◁─
    part[1] = int(part[1] * random.uniform(.9, 1.1))    ◁───
  else:                                                Apply a random
    error = f"mutate ERROR {part}"   ◁───             increase/decrease
    raise Exception(error)                            to filters/neurons.
  return part          Throw an error if the
                       format is corrupt.
```

Figure 7.13 shows the result of running the `mutation` function/operator on an `individual` gene sequence. Notice how the hyperparameters defining the layer groups number of neurons/filters or kernel sizes are the only things modified. You will likely see different results when you run the notebook, but you should still observe the changes highlighted in figure 7.13.

```
35    print(ind1)
36    ind1 = mutation(ind1)[0]
37    print(ind1)
```

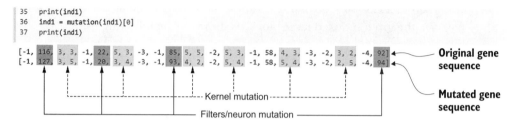

Figure 7.13 **Example of a** mutation **operator applied**

Again, the rest of the notebook builds, compiles, and trains the mutated gene sequence to confirm we can still produce a valid Keras model. Go ahead and run the mutation code block a few times to confirm the output gene sequences are valid. With the custom operators built to handle the crossover and mutation operations, we can now move on to applying evolution in the next section.

> ### Advantages of using Keras
>
> Keras model compilation is robust and forgiving, which is useful when it is likely some of the models we randomly build will be problematic and not produce good results. In comparison, a framework like PyTorch is much less forgiving and would likely complain about several build issues, producing blocking errors. With Keras, we can get away with minimal error handling, as most of the models will run; however, they likely won't run well. If we were to apply this same evolution on PyTorch, we would likely encounter more build issues over minor concerns producing fewer surviving offspring. Conversely, Keras would produce more viable offspring that could develop into a more fit solution. This doesn't necessarily mean PyTorch lacks as a DL framework; instead, it points more to the rigidity of both frameworks.

7.5 *Evolving convolutional network architecture*

Evolving the convolutional network architecture is now just a matter of adding DEAP to employ genetic algorithms. A lot of what we cover in this section is review from previous chapters, but it should be useful for understanding how the custom operators work. In this section, we continue working off the previous notebooks and extending them to perform evolving architecture search.

Open the EDL_7_5_Evo_CNN.ipynb notebook in Colab. Go ahead and run all the cells (Runtime > Run All). Notice that at the top of this notebook, we install DEAP with pip and import the standard modules we have used in previous chapters.

Scroll down to the section titled Evolutionary CNN, and examine the DEAP toolbox set up code, as shown in the following listing. Notice how we reuse the create_ offspring function from listing 7.8 and register with the toolbox using the name network. This function is responsible for creating new first-generation offspring. Then, a list is used to hold the individual gene sequence. The benefit of using a list here is that a set of individuals can vary in length.

Listing 7.19   EDL_7_5_Evo_CNN.ipynb: DEAP `toolbox` setup

```
toolbox = base.Toolbox()
toolbox.register("network", create_offspring)          Add the custom create_offspring
                                                        function called network.
toolbox.register("individual", tools.initIterate,
    creator.Individual, toolbox.network)               Register the new network
                                                        initialization function.
toolbox.register("population", tools.initRepeat,
    list, toolbox.individual)                           Use a list to contain
                                                        individuals in population.
toolbox.register("select", tools.selTournament,
    tournsize=5)                                        Use a standard tournament selection operator.
```

Scroll down a little to see how to register the custom `crossover` (listing 7.12) and `mutation` (listing 7.16) functions we created earlier, as shown in the following listing.

Listing 7.20   EDL_7_5_Evo_CNN.ipynb: Register custom functions

```
toolbox.register("mate", crossover)      Register a custom mate function.
toolbox.register("mutate", mutation)     Register a custom mutate function.
```

The next cell, shown in listing 7.21, contains the code for building, compiling, training, and evaluating the model. We start by looking at the `evaluate` function. This function first builds the model using the `build_model` function (listing 7.11), and then it compiles and trains the model with a new function, `compile_train`. After that, it returns the `1/accuracy` clamped to a range between almost 0 and 1. We do this because we want to minimize the `fitness` by `1/accuracy`. Notice that we wrap the code in `try/except` to be sure that if anything fails, we gracefully recover. Our code still has the potential to build nonsensical models, and this is a way of protecting against failures. If the code does fail, we return `1/.5` or, 50% accuracy—not 0 or close to 0. By doing this, we allow these failures to remain within the `population` and hopefully `mutate` into something better later.

Listing 7.21   EDL_7_5_Evo_CNN.ipynb: The `evaluate` function

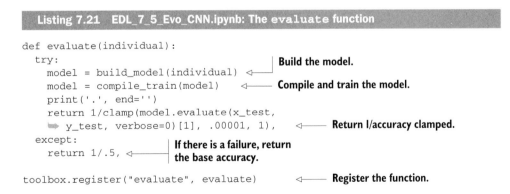

```
def evaluate(individual):
  try:
    model = build_model(individual)       Build the model.
    model = compile_train(model)          Compile and train the model.
    print('.', end='')
    return 1/clamp(model.evaluate(x_test,
      y_test, verbose=0)[1], .00001, 1),   Return 1/accuracy clamped.
  except:                                 If there is a failure, return
    return 1/.5,                          the base accuracy.

toolbox.register("evaluate", evaluate)    Register the function.
```

> ### Survival of the fittest
>
> By allowing the failed `individuals` some base `fitness`, we are encouraging those gene sequences to potentially remain in the `population` pool. In nature, `individuals` with severe `mutations` almost certainly quickly fail. Cooperative species, like humans, are better at caring for weaker `individuals` with potential. This, most certainly, is the reason human babies can be born so weak and frail yet grow and survive to become contributing `individuals`.

The `compile_train` function is very similar to our earlier training code, but it's worth a quick look in the following listing. Not much is different here, but notice we have fixed training at 3 epochs, for brevity. Again, you may want to alter this and see what effect it has on the result.

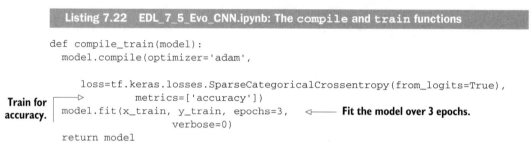

Listing 7.22   EDL_7_5_Evo_CNN.ipynb: The `compile` and `train` functions

```
def compile_train(model):
  model.compile(optimizer='adam',

      loss=tf.keras.losses.SparseCategoricalCrossentropy(from_logits=True),
                metrics=['accuracy'])
  model.fit(x_train, y_train, epochs=3,      ⊲─── Fit the model over 3 epochs.
                  verbose=0)
  return model
```

Train for accuracy.

Scroll down to the evolution set up code we have reviewed in previous chapters, and look at the output of evolving the `population` over 5 generations, shown in figure 7.14. Since our gene sequences are relatively small, we should generally expect a quick convergence. Your results may vary, but in most cases, your accuracy should maximize at around 0.81, or 81%. Go ahead and try to increase the size of the `population` or number of `generations` to see what effects this has.

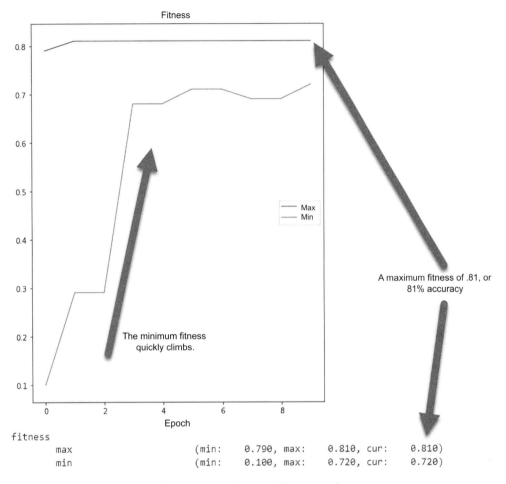

fitness
```
        max                 (min:    0.790, max:    0.810, cur:    0.810)
        min                 (min:    0.100, max:    0.720, cur:    0.720)
```

Figure 7.14 The results of evolving a population over 5 generations

After evolution is done, we build, compile, and train the best `individual` to see the results in figure 7.15. We can still see a divergence after 3 epochs, suggesting that if we want a more durable model, we likely need to increase the training epochs in evolution. This can be easily achieved, but it increases evolution time substantially.

Finally, we can look at the summary of the evolved model architecture in figure 7.16. It is quite likely your results will vary a little, but you should see a similar layer structure to what is shown in the figure. In fact, if you have worked with Fashion-MNIST dataset previously, this is likely an architecture you have seen applied.

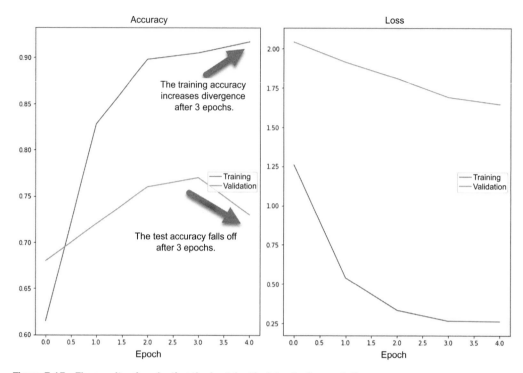

Figure 7.15   The results of evaluating the best `individual` after evolution

Model: "sequential_192"

Layer (type)	Output Shape	Param #	
conv2d_503 (Conv2D)	(None, 28, 28, 36)	468	Single convolution layer to start
conv2d_504 (Conv2D)	(None, 28, 28, 127)	41275	
batch_normalization_184 (BatchNormalization)	(None, 28, 28, 127)	508	
max_pooling2d_195 (MaxPooling2D)	(None, 10, 10, 127)	0	Conv2D > batch normalization > max pooling
flatten_179 (Flatten)	(None, 12700)	0	
dense_366 (Dense)	(None, 37)	469937	
dense_367 (Dense)	(None, 10)	380	

Total params: 512,568
Trainable params: 512,314
Non-trainable params: 254

Figure 7.16   Model summary results produced from evolution

You are welcome, of course, to modify this notebook as you see fit and add several customizations we discussed throughout the chapter. The following are summaries of the modifications you may want to make to this notebook:

- *Dataset size*—We reduced the size of the original dataset drastically to reduce runtime. Expect that if you increase the dataset size, you will also see an increase in simulation runtime.
- *Training epochs*—During our earlier evaluation, we decided to use 3 epochs as our training limit. Depending on your data, you may want to increase or decrease this value.
- *Layer types*—For this simple demonstration, we kept to standard layer types, like convolutional, pooling, batch normalization, and dense. You may want to add different layer types, like dropout, and/or increase the number of dense layers or other variations.
- *Crossover/mutation*—The custom operators we built for mating and `mutation` are just one implementation. As mentioned, when building the `mutation` function, there is a lot of room for further customization, perhaps by letting `mutation` add or remove layer blocks.
- *Fitness/evaluation function*—We based our `individual fitness` on a straight accuracy score. If we wanted to minimize the number of trainable parameters or layers, we could have added that as logic into our `evaluate` function.

7.5.1 Learning exercises

Use the following exercises to improve your understanding of EvoCNN:

1 Modify the dataset size or type. Explore different datasets, taking note of the differences in evolved CNN models.
2 Add a new layer type of `Dropout` to the `gene` sequence. This will require some work but could provide a basis for enhanced CNN model building.
3 Think about how other forms of evolution could be applied from hyperparameter optimization to neuroevolving the weights/parameters.

Hopefully, as the concept of evolutionary optimization for automated ML models evolves, we can expect frameworks to package all this up for us. However, the amount of code to perform such powerful optimizations isn't too difficult to produce, as you've seen in this chapter. In the end, even if an encompassing framework comes about, you would likely need to customize functions like `mate` and `crossover`.

Summary

- Convolutional neural networks are layer extensions to DL models that provide localized feature extraction:
  - Typically used for 2D image processing, CNN can be very successful in enhancing classification or other tasks.

- CNN layers are complex to set up and define for various image recognition tasks, given the amount of hyperparameters, configuration, and placement.
- *Neuroevolution* is another term used to describe evolutionary methods for DL optimization, specifically those related to architecture and parameter optimization:
  - The CNN architecture of a DL network can be optimized with genetic algorithms and DEAP.
  - The complex architecture of the CNN layers includes the type, size, and placement of layers that can be encoded in a custom genetic sequence.
  - This genetic encoding takes the number, kernel size, stride, normalization, and activation function of the various CNN layers.
- Custom `crossover` (mating) and `mutation` genetic operators need to be developed to support custom genetic encoding structures.
- Evolve a `population` of `individuals` with genetic algorithms to optimize CNN model architecture on a particular dataset.
- The EvoCNN custom encoding architecture has limitations to the number of layers used in a model. However, the use of neuroevolution can quickly assist with the complex task of defining complex CNN architectures.

Part 3

Advanced applications

As we enter the final part of the book, our focus moves to more complex examples in the areas of generative modeling, neuroevolution of augmenting topological networks, reinforcement learning, and instinctual learning. We introduce each of these advanced topics before adding these evolutionary methods.

Chapters 8 and 9 introduce and explore the areas of generative modeling, or generative deep learning. Chapter 8 demonstrates the basic autoencoder and how it can be enhanced into an evolutionary autoencoder. Then, in chapter 9, we introduce the basics of the generative adversarial network. As generative adversarial networks are notorious for being difficult to train, we demonstrate how evolutionary methods can better optimize training.

Neuroevolution for augmenting topologies is showcased in chapters 10 and 11. We first introduce the basics of NEAT in chapter 10, with various examples of how to configure this powerful algorithm to enhance speciation. Then, in chapter 11, we apply NEAT to solve deep reinforcement learning problems found in the OpenAI Gym.

The part and book finish off in chapter 12, where we explore the future of evolutionary methods in machine learning as well as introduce instinctual learning. Instinctual learning is a broader concept concerning the search for reusable functional components or instincts. In this chapter, we cover a few examples that apply instinctual learning to solving reinforcement learning problems found in the OpenAI Gym using gene expression programming and genetic algorithms. The outcomes of these problems demonstrate how common reusable functions/ components can be isolated within deep learning systems.

Evolving autoencoders

8

This chapter covers

- Introducing convolutional autoencoders
- Discussing genetic encoding in a convolutional autoencoder network
- Applying mutation and mating to develop an evolutionary autoencoder
- Building and evolving autoencoder architecture
- Introducing a convolutional variational autoencoder

In the last chapter, we covered how convolutional neural network (CNN) architecture could be adapted using evolutionary algorithms. We used genetic algorithms to encode a gene sequence defining a CNN model for image classification. The outcome was successfully building more optimized networks for image recognition tasks.

In this chapter, we continue to extend the fundamentals and explore evolving autoencoders (AEs). We take some of our experience from building evolving CNN architecture in the last chapter and apply it to convolutional AEs. Then, we move on to more advanced variational AEs and explore novel ways of evolving model loss.

AEs are a foundation to DL that introduces unsupervised and representation learning. Chances are if you have spent any time studying DL, you have encountered AEs and variational AEs. From the perspective of EDL, they introduce some novel applications we explore in this chapter.

AEs come in several variations, from under complete or standard to deep and convolutional. The deep convolutional AE is a great one to begin with, since it extends many ideas from previous chapters, and it's where we start this chapter.

8.1   *The convolution autoencoder*

In this section, we explore and review a convolutional AE written in Keras. This is the same code we use for building an evolutionary, or evo, AE later in the chapter. For those new to AEs, the next section reviews the main principles of training, building, and retraining.

8.1.1   *Introducing autoencoders*

AEs are often used to introduce the concepts of unsupervised and representative learning. *Unsupervised learning* is the process of training models using no labels. *Representative learning* is when we train models to understand the differences between input features.

Figure 8.1 shows a simple convolutional AE that is comprised of convolutional, `MaxPool`, and `UpSampling` layers. Aside from the addition of convolution, this model architecture is standard for an AE.

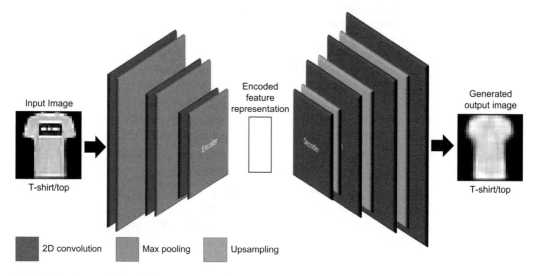

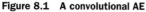

Figure 8.1   A convolutional AE

An AE works by funneling the input through a narrow channel called the *latent* or *feature representation view*—the middle part. This middle part is also known as the *latent* or *hidden encoding* of the image.

The latent encoding of an image is learned through iterations of passing images into the encoder and then measuring the difference in the output. Typically, we measure this difference or loss using mean squared error or pixel-wise loss of the input and output images. Through iterating, the middle part learns to encapsulate the features of the input image.

Figure 8.2 shows an example of plotting the learned encoding from an AE trained on the MNIST Handwritten Digits dataset. In the figure, the encoding/latent space is converted to two dimensions using *t*-distributed stochastic neighbor embedding (*t*-SNE). By visualizing this plot, you can clearly see how the model learns to differentiate between the various classes of digits.

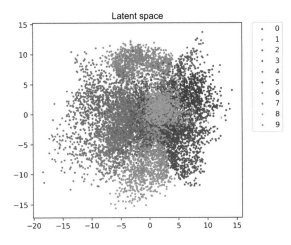

Figure 8.2   A mapping of AE latent space, showing a clustering of classes

An AE uses unsupervised learning to train, which means none of the data fed into the model needs to be labeled. Essentially, the model learns through self-training by comparing how well the input and generated output can represent the encoded features. This simplifies the training of the model and, at the same time, creates a powerful feature encoding extractor.

Representation learning, or what may also be referred to as *generative deep learning*, is a relatively new field. We take a close look at GDL in the next chapter, but for now, let's jump back into the code and see how an AE works.

8.1.2   *Building a convolutional autoencoder*

The AE we look at in the next notebook incorporates convolutional layers to better extract features in images. Applying convolution to an AE model introduces additional complexity in the network architecture. In future sections, this example also demonstrates how applying evolution to optimize these networks is advantageous.

Open the EDL_8_1_Autoencoders.ipynb notebook in Colab. Refer to the appendix if you need a review of opening notebooks in Colab.

Scroll down, and then select the Stage 1: AEs cell. From the menu, select Runtime > Run Before. This runs the notebook, loading the data and displaying an example plot, as shown in Figure 8.3. Several sections of code have been covered in past chapters and won't be reviewed again here.

Figure 8.3   Fashion-MNIST standard training dataset

Next, we come to the first block of code of interest, shown in listing 8.1: building the AE. The first layer set up is the input layer, defined by image shape (28×28 and 1 channel). Next, a convolutional layer is added with 64 filters, using a kernel size of 3×3. Then, after each CNN layer, a MaxPool layer reduces/aggregates the input into the next layer. The final layer added is a MaxPool layer that represents the latent or hidden view of the input.

Listing 8.1   EDL_8_1_AE.ipynb: The encoder

```
input_layer = Input(shape=(28, 28, 1))   ◁──── Defines the input layer

encoded_layer1 = layers.Conv2D(64, (3, 3),
➥ activation='relu', padding='same')(input_layer)      ◁─┐
encoded_layer1 = layers.MaxPool2D( (2, 2),
➥ padding='same')(encoded_layer1)
encoded_layer2 = layers.Conv2D(32, (3, 3),
➥ activation='relu', padding='same')(encoded_layer1)  ◁─┤  The 2D
encoded_layer2 = layers.MaxPool2D( (2, 2),                     convolution layer
➥ padding='same')(encoded_layer2)
encoded_layer3 = layers.Conv2D(16, (3, 3),
➥ activation='relu', padding='same')(encoded_layer2)  ◁─┘
latent_view    = layers.MaxPool2D( (2, 2),
➥ padding='same')(encoded_layer3)          ◁──── The MaxPool layer
```

Now that we have built the encoder model to output the latent or encoded view, we need to rebuild the image using further convolutional layers and a special layer called UpSampling. UpSampling layers can be thought of as the opposite of pooling layers. Their effect is converting the latent view generated by the encoder back into a full image. This is done by successively convolving the input and UpSampling to successive layers. At the end of this output chain, we add a final CNN layer that converts the convolved output to a single channel. If we were using color images, we would instead convert the output to three channels, as shown in the following listing.

Listing 8.2   EDL_8_1_AE.ipynb: The decoder

```
decoded_layer1 = layers.Conv2D(16, (3, 3), activation='relu',
➥ padding='same')(latent_view)                   ◁─┐
decoded_layer1 = layers.UpSampling2D((2, 2))               The 2D
➤➥ (decoded_layer1)                                          convolutional layer
decoded_layer2 = layers.Conv2D(32, (3, 3),
➥ activation='relu', padding='same')(decoded_layer1)  ◁─┤
decoded_layer2 = layers.UpSampling2D((2, 2))
➤➥ (decoded_layer2)
decoded_layer3 = layers.Conv2D(64, (3, 3), activation='relu')(decoded_layer2) ◁─┘
decoded_layer3 = layers.UpSampling2D((2, 2))
➤➥ (decoded_layer3)

output_layer   = layers.Conv2D(1, (3, 3),        The final CNN layer for
➥ padding='same')(decoded_layer3)   ◁──────     output to 1 channel
```
The 2D UpSampling layer

We combine the models by feeding the corresponding input and output layers into a Keras model. Then, we compile the model using an Adam optimizer and MSE for loss.

After that, we plot a model summary and use `plot_model` to output a nice visual of the completed model, as shown in the following listing.

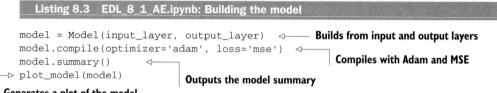

Listing 8.3 EDL_8_1_AE.ipynb: Building the model

```
model = Model(input_layer, output_layer)    ⟵── Builds from input and output layers
model.compile(optimizer='adam', loss='mse')  ⟵┐
model.summary()    ⟵─────────────────────────┘  Compiles with Adam and MSE
plot_model(model)            Outputs the model summary
```
Generates a plot of the model

Run the cells that build the encoder and decoder and build the model. Figure 8.4 shows the summary output of building the model. By looking at each successive layer, you can visualize how the model shrinks the input space in the latent encoding and then rebuilds it. It is important to note the size of the respective CNN layers and how they reduce and then increase in size.

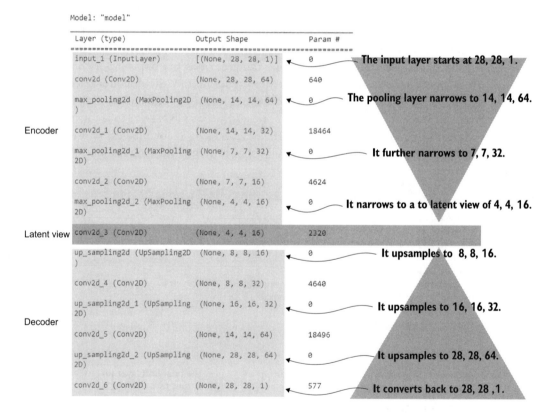

Figure 8.4   AE model summary explained

The next couple of cells set up output code for training the model. Go ahead and run those cells, including the training code. Having reviewed this code previously, we won't revisit it here, other than to look at example output after 10 epochs of training shown in figure 8.5.

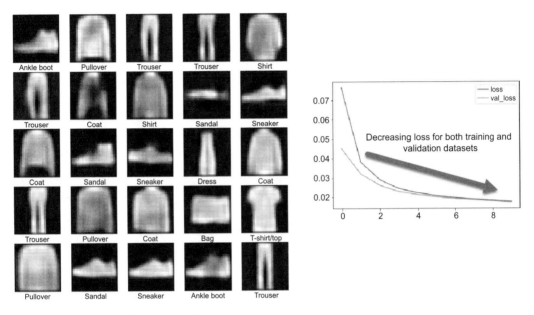

Figure 8.5 Training an AE example cell output

As the model trains, the output, as shown in figure 8.5, goes from showing fuzzy representations to clear features. AEs can require extensive training, and this simple example will likely never be able to accurately depict finer-grained features. However, it does do a good job differentiating between the various classes effectively. A good indicator of how well the model is training is to compare sandal class images to the original or against sneakers.

8.1.3 Learning exercises

Use the following exercises to improve your understanding of AEs:

1. Try using a different dataset, like the MNIST Handwritten Digits dataset.
2. Alter the model hyperparameters, like learning rate and batch size, to see what effect this has on training.
3. Add or remove convolutional layers from both the encoder and decoder. Be sure to keep both sides of the AE balanced.

While this simple AE works reasonably well, we want to improve on the model's ability to generalize the learning of the representations. In the next section, we advance to add generalization features, like dropout and batch normalization layers.

8.1.4 Generalizing a convolutional AE

In chapter 7, we covered, in some depth, how convolutional layers function by extracting features. We also learned that CNN models can do *too good* of a job of identifying features. To compensate for this, we often add a layer called Dropout, which can help generalize feature extraction.

Figure 8.6 shows how dropout layers work by randomly disabling network nodes for each training iteration, not each epoch. Disabling random neurons through each training iteration causes the model to better generalize and reduce memorization. This results in training loss and validation loss remaining consistent.

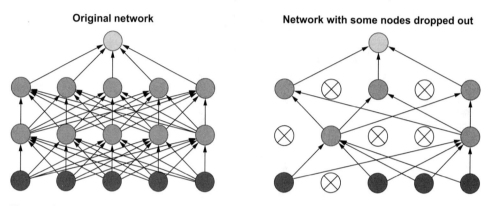

Figure 8.6   A demonstration of Dropout

Vanishing and exploding gradients are other factors that come into play when training CNN and, in particular, networks with several layers. This happens because the weights/parameters in the network may need to become very large or small because of inputs passing through multiple layers. To compensate for this, we introduce a normalization step between layers, called BatchNormalization.

Figure 8.7 shows how BatchNormalization is calculated over a convolutional feature map. In the figure, the mean and variance are calculated for each feature map, and this is used to normalize the values of the feature map as inputs to the next layer. This results in data being kept centered at about 0, also significantly reducing problems with vanishing or exploding gradients.

Normalization occurs using the following equation. Each input value is subtracted from the mean and then divided by the square root of the variance, or standard deviation, σ.

$$X_{new} = \frac{x - \mu}{\sigma}$$

Now that we understand how we create more generalized models and avoid exploding and vanishing gradients, we can move on to incorporating these features into the AE.

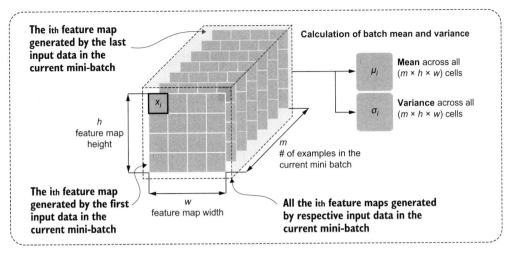

Figure 8.7   The `BatchNormalization` process

8.1.5   *Improving the autoencoder*

By adding `BatchNormalization` and `Dropout` layers, we can improve the simple AE we looked at previously. We continue with the same notebook but now look at adding these new layer types in the following walkthrough.

Reopen the EDL_8_1_Autoencoder.ipynb notebook in Colab. Refer to the appendix if you need assistance. Go ahead and run all the cells in the notebook via Runtime > Run All from the menu. Scroll down to the section starting with Improving the Autoencoder.

We start by looking at the updated encoder section of the model in listing 8.4. Most of the code is the same as the code we last looked at, but notice the inclusion of the batch normalization and dropout layers. The parameter passed into the dropout layers is the amount or percentage of neurons that will be disabled over each training iteration.

Listing 8.4   EDL_8_1_AE.ipynb: An improved encoder

```
inputs = layers.Input(shape=(28, 28 ,1))

x = layers.Conv2D(32, 3, activation='relu', padding='same')(inputs)
x = layers.BatchNormalization()(x)
x = layers.MaxPool2D()(x)
x = layers.Dropout(0.5)(x)
x = layers.BatchNormalization()(x)
x = layers.MaxPool2D()(x)
x = layers.Dropout(0.5)(x)
x = layers.Conv2D(64, 3, activation='relu', padding='same')(x)
x = layers.BatchNormalization()(x)
encoded = layers.MaxPool2D()(x)
```

The BatchNormalization layer

The Dropout layer

Following this, we, of course, look at the improved decoder section, as shown in the following listing. Again, the only difference is the inclusion of `BatchNormalization` and `Dropout` layers in the decoder section.

Listing 8.5   EDL_8_1_AE.ipynb: An improved decoder

```
x = layers.Conv2DTranspose(64, 3,activation='relu',strides=(2,2))(encoded)
x = layers.BatchNormalization()(x)
x = layers.Dropout(0.5)(x)                        The BatchNormalization layer
x = layers.Conv2DTranspose(32, 3, activation='relu',strides=(2,2),
  padding='same')(x)
x = layers.BatchNormalization()(x)
x = layers.Dropout(0.5)(x)
x = layers.Conv2DTranspose(32, 3, padding='same')(x)
x = layers.LeakyReLU()(x)
x = layers.BatchNormalization()(x)
decoded = layers.Conv2DTranspose(1, 3, activation='sigmoid',strides=(2,2),
  padding='same')(x)
```

The Dropout layer

Figure 8.8 shows the output of training this "improved" model over 10 epochs. If you compare this figure to figure 8.5, you can clearly see these "improvements" are not as effective as the original model.

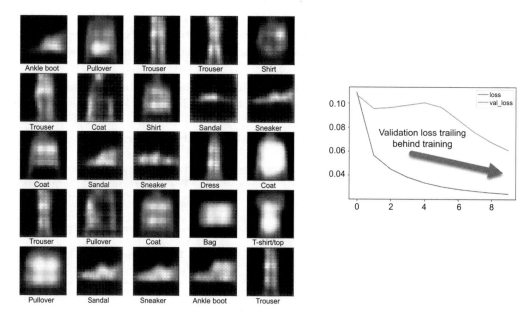

Figure 8.8   Training the improved AE example cell output

So if these layer types are about improving model performance, why are we getting such poor results? The answer, in this case, is simple: we are overusing the features of

`BatchNormalization` and `Dropout`. This generally means we need to tune the network architecture in a manual fashion to improve model performance. Instead, we look at how to optimize AE model development with EC next.

8.2   *Evolutionary AE optimization*

We have already seen how we can automatically optimize a CNN model using GAs called EvoCNN. In the following walkthrough, we take the same approach as we did previously but introduce the added complexity of AEs. This means our model architecture needs to adhere to stricter guidelines.

8.2.1   *Building the AE gene sequence*

Our first step in building a GA AE optimizer is to build a pattern to encode the architecture into a `gene` sequence. We build off previous examples but this time introduce the constraints of an AE. Likewise, this model also improves on the EvoCNN project by allowing `BatchNormalization` and `Dropout` to be added.

Open the EDL_8_2_Evo_Autoencoder_Encoding.ipynb notebook in Colab. Please refer to the appendix for instructions if needed. Go ahead and run all the cells in the notebook via Runtime > Run All. Scroll down to the section titled Encoding the Autoencoder. We reviewed most of the following code in chapter 7, so we only review the highlights here.

Start by looking at the `create_offspring` function. If you recall, this was the main function for creating the entire `gene` sequence, but this version differs. This time, the function is broken into two loops: one for the encoder section and the other for the decoder section. The encoder section loops over the layers and randomly checks if another convolution layer should be added. If a layer is added, then it continues to randomly check if a BN and/or dropout layer should also be added. Notice in this example, we automatically add a `MaxPool` layer to account for the funnel or reduction architecture of the AE.

The second loop for the decoder is set up to mirror the architecture of the encoder. It, therefore, loops through the same number of iterations as the encoder. This time, it adds up convolutional layer codes to represent the combination of `UpSampling` and convolution layers. After that, a chance check is applied to add `BatchNormalization` and/or `Dropout` layers, as shown in the following listing.

Listing 8.6   EDL_8_2_Evo_AE_Encoding.ipynb: Creating the gene sequence

```
def create_offspring():
    ind = []
    layers = 0
    for i in range(max_layers):          The first layer is
        if i==0:                         always convolution.
            ind.extend(generate_conv_layer())
            layers += 1                   Chance to add another
        elif random.uniform(0,1)<.5:      convolution layer
```

```
      ind.extend(generate_conv_layer())
      layers += 1
      if random.uniform(0,1)<.5:          ⟵┐  Chance to add a
        ind.extend(generate_bn_layer())   └── BatchNormalization layer
      if random.uniform(0,1) < .5:        ⟵── Chance to add a Dropout layer
        ind.extend(generate_dropout_layer())
   for i in range(layers):                ⟵┐
     ind.extend(generate_upconv_layer())   │  Loop through encoder
     if random.uniform(0,1)<.5:            │  layers to create a decoder.
       ind.extend(generate_bn_layer())
     if random.uniform(0,1) < .5:
       ind.extend(generate_dropout_layer())
   return ind
```

Notice that we change the encoding pattern of the gene sequence to account for convolutional/MaxPool layers and UpSampling/convolutional layers. You can see this minor change in the tokens we have set in the code cell. Now, the encoding tokens representing the encoder convolutional layers are defined as CONV_LAYER, and the decoder UpSampling or convolution layers are UPCONV_LAYER, as shown in the following listing.

Listing 8.7   EDL_8_2_Evo_AE_Encoding.ipynb: The gene sequence tokens

```
CONV_LAYER = -1        ⟵┐  The encoder
CONV_LAYER_LEN = 4      │  convolution/pooling layer
BN_LAYER = -3
BN_LAYER_LEN = 1
DROPOUT_LAYER = -4
DROPOUT_LAYER_LEN = 2    ┐  The decoder
UPCONV_LAYER = -2      ⟵─┘  UpSampling/convolution layer
UPCONV_LAYER_LEN = 4
```

Likewise, the functions to generate the encoder layers (CONV_LAYER) and decoder layers (UPCONV_LAYER) become simplified, as shown in the following listing.

Listing 8.8   EDL_8_2_Evo_AE_Encoding.ipynb: Generating layers

```
def generate_conv_layer():     ⟵┐
  part = [CONV_LAYER]           │  The encoder
  part.append(generate_neurons())  convolution/pooling layer
  part.extend(generate_kernel())
  return part
                                ┐  The decoder
def generate_upconv_layer():  ⟵─┘  UpSampling/convolution
  part = [UPCONV_LAYER]
  part.append(generate_neurons())
  part.extend(generate_kernel())
  return part
```

Similarly, the functions to add the BN and dropout layers are simplified, as shown in the following listing.

Listing 8.9   EDL_8_2_Evo_AE_Encoding.ipynb: Generating special layers

```
def generate_bn_layer():     ◁─── Generates the BN layer
  part = [BN_LAYER]
  return part

def generate_dropout_layer():  ◁─── Generates the Dropout layer
  part = [DROPOUT_LAYER]
  part.append(random.uniform(0,.5))
  return part
```

Next, we look at building the model by parsing the gene sequence. This code is quite long, so we break it into the relevant sections, starting with the initial parsing in listing 8.10. We start by looping over each gene and checking if it matches a layer token. If it does, we add the respective layer and options to the model. In the case of the encoder convolutional layers (CONV_LAYER), if the input shape is greater than (7, 7), we add a MaxPool layer. This ensures our model maintains a fixed latent view.

Listing 8.10   EDL_8_2_Evo_AE_Encoding.ipynb: Building the model—Parsing

```
def build_model(individual):               The input_layer is
  input_layer = Input(shape=(28, 28, 1))  ◁─ always the same.
  il = len(individual)
  i = 0
  x = input_layer        Loops over genes
  while i < il: ◁───                The encoder
    if individual[i] == CONV_LAYER: ◁── convolutional layer
      pad="same"
      n = individual[i+1]
      k = (individual[i+2], individual[i+3])
      i += CONV_LAYER_LEN
      x = layers.Conv2D(n, k, activation='relu', padding=pad)(x)
    ↳ if x.shape[1] > 7:
        x = layers.MaxPool2D( (2, 2), padding='same')(x)
```

If the shape is greater than 7, 7, add pooling.

Moving down a little, we can see the continuation of adding layers from inspecting the tokens, as shown in the following listing. This time, though, for the UPCONV_LAYER decoder layers, we check if the model is the same as the input size. After all, we don't want the resulting images to be too big or too small.

Listing 8.11   EDL_8_2_Evo_AE_Encoding.ipynb: Building the model—Layers

```
elif individual[i] == BN_LAYER:      ◁─── Adds a BN layer
  x = layers.BatchNormalization()(x)
  i += BN_LAYER_LEN
elif individual[i] == DROPOUT_LAYER:  ◁─── Adds a Dropout layer
```

```
    x = layers.Dropout(individual[i+1])(x)
    i += DROPOUT_LAYER_LEN                       ┐   Adds a decoder
elif individual[i] == UPCONV_LAYER:      ◁───────┘   UpSampling/convolution layer
    pad="same"
    n = individual[i+1]
    k = (individual[i+2], individual[i+3])
    x = layers.Conv2D(n, k, activation='relu', padding=pad)(x)
    x = layers.UpSampling2D((2, 2))(x)
    i += CONV_LAYER_LEN
    if x.shape[1] == (28):     ◁──────── Checks if the model is complete
        break #model is complete
else:
  break
```

The function completes by building the model, compiling it, and returning it. Before doing that, though, we confirm the model is not too small by checking the shape of the last decoder layer, as shown in the following listing. If the output is too small, we add another UpSampling layer to double the size from 14, 14 to 28, 28.

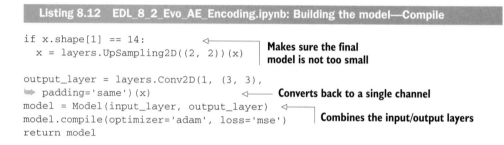

Listing 8.12 EDL_8_2_Evo_AE_Encoding.ipynb: Building the model—Compile

```
if x.shape[1] == 14:                 ◁─────────┐   Makes sure the final
  x = layers.UpSampling2D((2, 2))(x)           │   model is not too small

output_layer = layers.Conv2D(1, (3, 3),
↪ padding='same')(x)              ◁──────── Converts back to a single channel
model = Model(input_layer, output_layer)  ◁─┐
model.compile(optimizer='adam', loss='mse')  │  Combines the input/output layers
return model
```

To test the build_model function, the next block of code, shown in listing 8.13, creates 100 random offspring and evaluates the size of the models. This code generates random individual gene sequences and then builds corresponding models from those sequences. Along the way, the code tracks the minimum and maximum models generated.

Listing 8.13 EDL_8_2_Evo_AE_Encoding.ipynb: Evaluating build_model

```
max_model = None
min_model = None
maxp = 0
minp = 10000000

for i in range(100):                            ┐  Creates a random gene sequence
  individual = create_offspring()    ◁──────────┘
  model = build_model(individual)    ◁──────── Builds the model from the sequence
  p = model.count_params()           ◁─────────┐
  if p > maxp:                                  │  Counts the model parameters
    maxp = p
    max_model = model
  if p < minp:
```

```
    minp = p
    min_model = model

max_model.summary()
min_model.summary()
```

Scrolling down further shows the output, as summarized in figure 8.9. In the figure, a minimum size parameter model is used to train the model over 10 epochs.

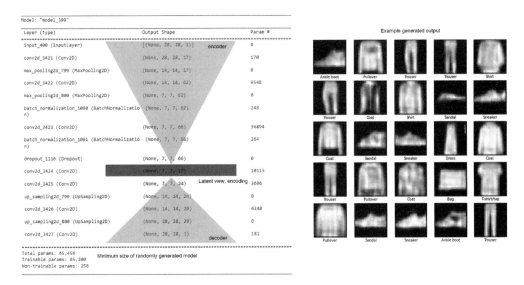

Figure 8.9   The output of the minimum size model built from randomly generated offspring

This randomly generated model using `create_offspring` and `build_model` appears to be better than our last "improved" AE, which is promising, since it is also an approximate minimum size model. Be sure to check the code and test the training for a maximum size model as well. Keep in mind that the sample size in this example only uses 100 variations.

8.2.2   Learning exercises

Use the following exercises to improve your understanding:

1   Create a list of `individuals` by calling `create_offspring` in a loop and then print and compare the various models.
2   Change the base probability from 0.5 in listing 8.6 to another value. See what effect this has on the generated models using exercise 1.

We now have a way to create a `gene` sequence that, in turn, can be used to build an AE model. As we learned in chapter 6, our next stage is to build the custom functions to `mate` and `mutate` these `gene` sequences. This is where we continue this project in the next section.

8.3   *Mating and mutating the autoencoder gene sequence*

Just like we did for the EvoCNN project in chapter 7, we also need to create custom `mutation` and `mating/crossover` operators. These custom operators are quite like what we used previously, so again, we only review some highlights here. After adding the genetic operators, we test the EvoAE.

Open the EDL_8_3_EvoAutoencoder.ipynb notebook in Colab. Refer to the appendix if you need assistance. Scroll down to the Creating Mating/Mutation Operators section, and then select the next code cell. From the menu, select Runtime > Run Before to execute all the previous cells in the notebook. Be patient, and wait for the sample training to finish.

Figure 8.10 demonstrates the `crossover` process—this time with the modified gene sequences that represent the AE architecture. Notice that the number of encoder convolutional layers and decoder convolutional layers are always equal. This is required to achieve the funnel effect of AE.

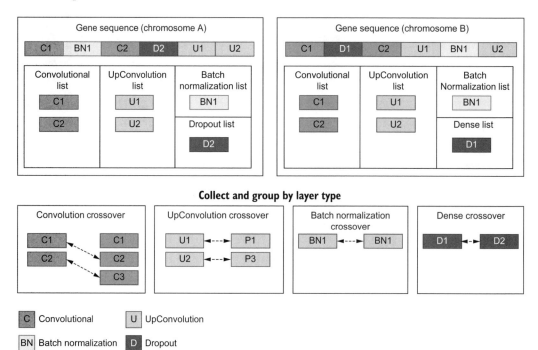

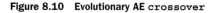

Figure 8.10   Evolutionary AE `crossover`

Fortunately, most of the `crossover/mating` code written in chapter 7 works on our updated `gene` sequence, and we won't need to revisit it here. DEAP calls the `crossover` function/operator, passing in the two parent `individuals` during evolution. Inside this function, the core of the work happens in the `swap_layers` function we covered previously. As shown in the following listing, the only difference in this function is the modification of the main layer structures we wanted to support: `Convolution` (encoder), `UpConvolution` (decoder), `BatchNormalization`, and `Dropout`.

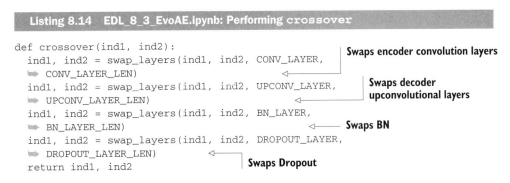

Listing 8.14 EDL_8_3_EvoAE.ipynb: Performing `crossover`

```
def crossover(ind1, ind2):
  ind1, ind2 = swap_layers(ind1, ind2, CONV_LAYER,      ◁──────  Swaps encoder convolution layers
  ➥ CONV_LAYER_LEN)
  ind1, ind2 = swap_layers(ind1, ind2, UPCONV_LAYER,    ◁──────  Swaps decoder
  ➥ UPCONV_LAYER_LEN)                                            upconvolutional layers
  ind1, ind2 = swap_layers(ind1, ind2, BN_LAYER,
  ➥ BN_LAYER_LEN)                                       ◁──────  Swaps BN
  ind1, ind2 = swap_layers(ind1, ind2, DROPOUT_LAYER,
  ➥ DROPOUT_LAYER_LEN)                                  ◁──────  Swaps Dropout
  return ind1, ind2
```

Performing `mutation` requires a bit more attention to perform modifications to the various layer types in the architecture. We start by looking at the main `mutation` function, which is called by DEAP evolution and takes a single `individual`. This function heavily uses the `mutate_layers` function and applies it to only layers that can be modified. Notice we omit BN layers, since they don't require additional parameters, as shown in the following listing.

Listing 8.15 EDL_8_3_EvoAE.ipynb: The `mutation` function

```
def mutation(ind):
  ind = mutate_layers(ind, CONV_LAYER,        ◁──────  Mutates encoder
  ➥ CONV_LAYER_LEN)                                    convolution layers
  ind = mutate_layers(ind, DROPOUT_LAYER,
  ➥ DROPOUT_LAYER_LEN)                        ◁──────  Mutates dropout layers
  ind = mutate_layers(ind, UPCONV_LAYER,
  ➥ UPCONV_LAYER_LEN)                         ◁──────  Mutates decoder upconvolution layers
  return ind,
```

The `mutate_layers` function highlights how each layer is selected for `mutation`. The layers are gathered by type and checked for a chance of `mutation`. Notice that, currently, the chance is always 100%. If a layer is chosen for `mutation`, its sequence is passed into the `mutate` function to be `mutated`, as shown in the following listing.

Listing 8.16 EDL_8_3_EvoAE.ipynb: The `mutate_layers` function

```
def mutate_layers(ind, layer_type, layer_len):
  layers = get_layers(ind1, layer_type)     ◁──────  Gets layers of type
  for layer in layers:
    if random.random() < 1:                 ◁──────  Checks for chance mutation
      try:
        ind[layer:layer+layer_len] = mutate(◁──────  Mutates the layer
              ind[layer:layer+layer_len], layer_type)
      except:
        print(layers)
  return ind
```

Catches exceptions

The `mutate` function performs the specific `mutation` of the respective layer types, as shown in listing 8.17. Each layer type has a slightly different form of `mutation` applied relevant to the layer type. If an unknown layer type is passed into `mutate`, an error is thrown, meaning the `gene` sequence is likely corrupt or broken. This, as in nature, results in an unviable offspring that is terminated from further execution.

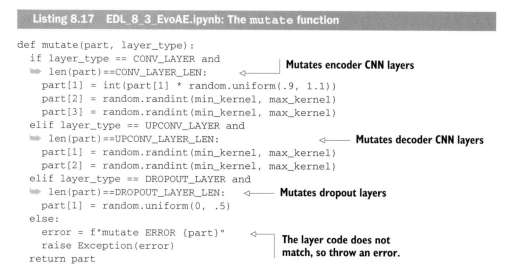

Listing 8.17   EDL_8_3_EvoAE.ipynb: The `mutate` function

```
def mutate(part, layer_type):
  if layer_type == CONV_LAYER and
     len(part)==CONV_LAYER_LEN:                    Mutates encoder CNN layers
    part[1] = int(part[1] * random.uniform(.9, 1.1))
    part[2] = random.randint(min_kernel, max_kernel)
    part[3] = random.randint(min_kernel, max_kernel)
  elif layer_type == UPCONV_LAYER and
     len(part)==UPCONV_LAYER_LEN:                   Mutates decoder CNN layers
    part[1] = random.randint(min_kernel, max_kernel)
    part[2] = random.randint(min_kernel, max_kernel)
  elif layer_type == DROPOUT_LAYER and
     len(part)==DROPOUT_LAYER_LEN:    Mutates dropout layers
    part[1] = random.uniform(0, .5)
  else:
    error = f"mutate ERROR {part}"       The layer code does not
    raise Exception(error)               match, so throw an error.
  return part
```

At the end of the `mating/mutation` cells, there is code to test the respective operators by creating new offspring and passing them through the `crossover` or `mutation` functions. With the `mating/mutation` operators constructed, we can move on to evolving an AE architecture in the next section.

8.4   *Evolving an autoencoder*

Evolving the AE is now a relatively simple matter of just adding DEAP. Again, a lot of the code here is the same as in previous examples. This means we refer here to just the highlights, changes, and points of interest.

Open the EDL_8_4_EvoAutoencoder.ipynb notebook in Colab. Run the whole notebook via Runtime > Run All from the menu. This notebook can take a long time to run, so it's best to start as soon as possible.

The AE architecture can take a considerable amount of time to evolve. As such, we use a previously covered data reduction trick to make evolving less time-consuming. Referring to the data loading cell, notice how we reduce the size of the training and validation sets by simply taking slices of the original dataset, as shown in the following listing. This is just for the purposes of demonstrating how the code runs and operates. Obviously, if the goal was to create an optimized model, we would be better off using the full dataset.

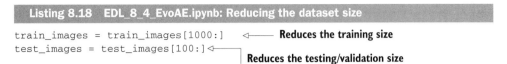

Listing 8.18 EDL_8_4_EvoAE.ipynb: Reducing the dataset size

```
train_images = train_images[1000:]    ◁——— Reduces the training size
test_images = test_images[100:]◁———
                                      ┐ Reduces the testing/validation size
```

Next, we review all the base DEAP set up code to create the GA solver for performing the architecture optimization, shown in listing 8.19. We register the main `fitness` function as `FunctionMin`, since our goal is to minimize `fitness`. Next, the `create_ offspring` function is registered for creating new `individuals`. Then, the code completes with the registration of the custom `crossover` and `mutation` functions.

Listing 8.19   EDL_8_4_EvoAE.ipynb: Setting up DEAP

```
creator.create("FitnessMin", base.Fitness, weights=(-1.0,))
creator.create("Individual", list,
➡  fitness=creator.FitnessMin)      ◁——┐ Registers the target function
                                        │ and minimum fitness
toolbox = base.Toolbox()                                Registers the initial AE function
toolbox.register("AE", create_offspring)  ◁——┘
toolbox.register("individual", tools.initIterate, creator.Individual,
➡  toolbox.AE)
toolbox.register("population", tools.initRepeat, list, toolbox.individual)

toolbox.register("select", tools.selTournament, tournsize=5)
                                            ┐ Registers the custom crossover
toolbox.register("mate", crossover)   ◁———
toolbox.register("mutate", mutation)  ◁——— Registers the custom mutate
```

As shown in listing 8.20, the `evaluate` function is up next. This is where each network model architecture is evaluated. Previously, we registered a list called `fitness` to hold all the evaluated `fitness`. We did this to better track the maximum observed `fitness`. Inside the function, we first call `build_model` to create a model based on the `individual` gene sequence. After this, we call the `train` function to train the model and return the model plus `history`. From the `history` function, we extract the last validation history value and observe that as the model's `fitness`. If no errors occur generating the model and training, then the `fitness` is returned, clamped between 0 and maximum `fitness`. We use the `np.nanman` function to avoid returning nan values. If an error is encountered, we return the maximum observed `fitness`.

Listing 8.20   EDL_8_4_EvoAE.ipynb: The `evaluate` function

```
fits = []   ◁——— The global variable to track fitness

def evaluate(individual):
  global fits
  try:                                   ┐ The build_model from
    model = build_model(individual)  ◁——┘ the gene sequence
    model, history = train(model)    ◁——— Trains the model
    fitness = history.history["val_loss"]
    fits.append(fitness)
    print(".", end='')
```

```
    return clamp(fitness, 0, np.nanmax(fits)),  ⟵——— Returns the clamped fitness value
except:
    return np.nanmax(fits),  ⟵—┤ If there is an error, return the
                                │ maximum observed fitness.
toolbox.register("evaluate", evaluate)
```

Figure 8.11 shows the results of evolving the architecture with an initial `population` of 100 `individuals` run over 3 `generations`. From these initial results, you can see this presents an interesting approach to self-optimizing model architectures.

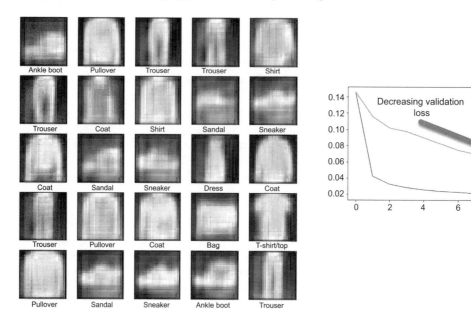

Figure 8.11   The results of evolving AE architecture

It is quite likely your results may vary, and this sample runs better with greater initial `populations`, which, again, can be time-consuming to run. Compare figure 8.11 to figures 8.5 and 8.8. Are the results better or worse than you expected?

Training AEs and other RL networks can be time-consuming, and we often need more than 3 epochs, as in the last notebook. The evolutionary output from this notebook demonstrates the possibilities stemming from evolving architecture for AEs.

8.4.1   Learning exercises

Continue exploring the evolutionary AE by working through these exercises:

1 Increase or decrease the number of training samples in listing 8.18.
2 Change the target dataset. A good option is the MNIST Handwritten Digits dataset.
3 Try tuning the hyperparameters of learning rate and batch size to see what effect this has on evolving a model.

To wrap this chapter up, we continue looking at AEs—but with a twist. Instead of straight mapping of the encoding to decoding, we try adding a sampling layer to implement a variational AE in the next section.

8.5   Building variational autoencoders

Variational AEs are an extension to AEs that learn by understanding the differences in learned representations by understanding sampling loss. This is an important concept we need to cover before jumping into the next chapter on evolutionary generative DL.

For the next notebook project, we look at building a variational AE to perform the same analysis as the previous notebooks. Experienced practitioners of DL are likely familiar with this pattern, but we review it further in the next section, just in case.

8.5.1   Variational autoencoders: A review

Architecturally, variational autoencoders (VAEs) are nearly identical, except for one key difference within the middle encoding layer: in a VAE, the middle layer becomes a sampling layer that learns to represent the encoding input and translate that learned representation back to an original image. By learning the representation of inputs, the VAE is then able to generate new outputs based on this understanding.

Figure 8.12 shows how a VAE differs from the traditional AE architecture shown in figure 8.1. We can see in the figure the latent encoding vector is replaced by two learned parameters: mean (μ) and variance (σ). These learned parameters are then used to sample or generate a new latent encoding vector, called Z, that is then pushed into the decoder.

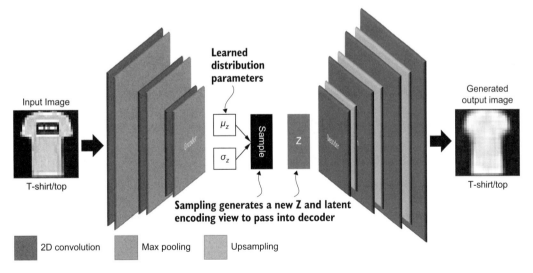

Figure 8.12   Variational AE

Instead of learning to compress and extract relevant features, as is done in the AE, the VAE learns how an input is represented by training the network to output the mean and variance of the input. Then based on this learned representation, a sampling layer generates a new latent encoding vector, called Z, that is fed back through the decoder.

Since the VAE learns representations across a known space, we can generate values from this space by walking over the range of mean and variance learned by the model. Figure 8.13 demonstrates the results of a VAE by iterating over the range of mean and variance to output what the model is learning. Now that we have an overview of a VAE, we can move on to building it in the next section.

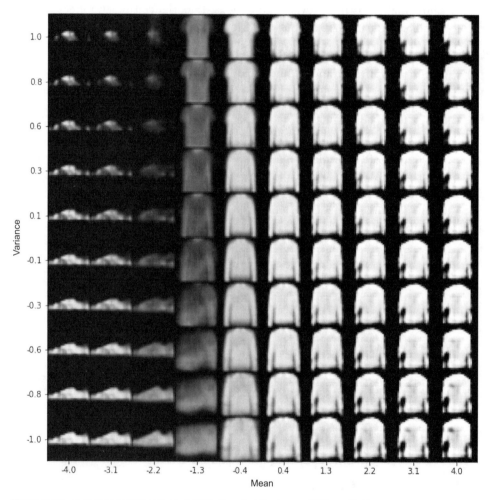

Figure 8.13   Sample learned output of VAE, showing the learned 2D manifold

8.5.2   *Implementing a VAE*

A VAE is simply an AE that swaps out the middle encoding for a sampling mechanism. Structurally, a VAE and AE are identical, but in this notebook, we introduce another pattern for implementing this architecture. Not only does this simplify the architecture, but it sets the stage for other innovations in later chapters.

Open the EDL_8_5_VAE.ipynb notebook in Colab. Refer to the appendix if you need assistance. Go ahead and run all the cells of the notebook by selecting Runtime > Run All from the menu.

Scroll down to the cell labeled Network Hyperparameters. We start by looking at the notebook's hyperparameters in detail, shown in listing 8.21, since a couple of new inputs are introduced. The code starts by setting the `input_shape` using the extracted `image_size` from the dataset loaded in the previous cell. Then, a base kernel size and the number of filters are set; we see later how these are used. After that, `latent_dim` is set to 2, representing the number of middle dimensions the encoder outputs. In this case, the latent dimensions, 2, are representative of the input mean and variance.

Listing 8.21 EDL_8_5_VAE.ipynb: VAE hyperparameters

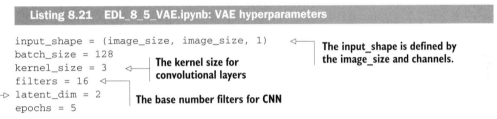

```
input_shape = (image_size, image_size, 1)    ◁──┐  The input_shape is defined by
batch_size = 128                                    the image_size and channels.
kernel_size = 3    ◁──┐  The kernel size for
filters = 16    ◁──┐     convolutional layers
latent_dim = 2         The base number filters for CNN
epochs = 5
```
The size of the latent/middle dimension

The next cell showing the construction of the convolutional layers of the encoder is quite different from the AE, as shown in listing 8.22. The VAE is constructed in a loop that adds successive CNN layers. At each iteration, the next layer doubles the number of filters. One thing to note is the omission of pooling layers to create the reduction of the funnel effect of an AE. Instead, we increase the `strides` from 1 to 2, which reduces the output dimensions by two. Thus, an image of 28×28 would reduce to 14×14 in the output.

Listing 8.22 EDL_8_5_VAE.ipynb: Building an encoder CNN

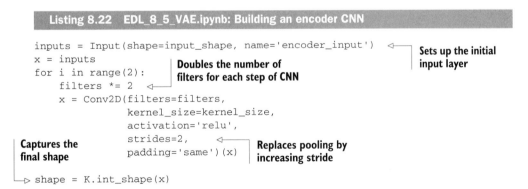

```
inputs = Input(shape=input_shape, name='encoder_input')    ◁──┐  Sets up the initial
x = inputs                          Doubles the number of         input layer
for i in range(2):                  filters for each step of CNN
    filters *= 2    ◁──┘
    x = Conv2D(filters=filters,
               kernel_size=kernel_size,
               activation='relu',
               strides=2,           ◁──┐  Replaces pooling by
               padding='same')(x)         increasing stride
Captures the
final shape
shape = K.int_shape(x)
```

Moving down to the next cell, we can see how the output from the encoder CNN layers reduces to the latent dimension and outputs the mean and variance, as shown in listing 8.23. To do this, a `Flatten` layer is added to squash the output of the encoder to a `Dense` layer. After that, two more `Dense` layers are added that produce the sample mean `z_mean` and variance `z_log_var`. These values are then passed into the sampling layer `z`, a custom layer constructed using lambda that takes as input the `sampling` function, the desired output shape, and the mean and variance as inputs. Pay special attention to how the `latent_space` hyperparameter is used to define the input and output shapes of the sampling layer.

Listing 8.23 EDL_8_5_VAE.ipynb: Building latent sampling

```
x = Flatten()(x)                                         ◁── Flattens the output from the encoder
x = Dense(16, activation='relu')(x)
z_mean = Dense(latent_dim, name='z_mean')(x)
z_log_var = Dense(latent_dim, name='z_log_var')(x)       Reduces to latent_dim to
                                                         produce the mean and variance
z = Lambda(
    sampling,
    output_shape=(latent_dim,),
    name='z')([z_mean, z_log_var])                       ◁── Generates the sampling layer

encoder = Model(inputs, [z_mean, z_log_var, z],
➥ name='encoder')                                       ◁── Instantiates the encoder model
encoder.summary()
```

Figure 8.14 shows the `model.summary` of the encoder model, annotated with the layer structure on the side. Notice how the model flattens the convolutional layers of the encoder and then pushes the input into a `Dense` layer of size `16`. This is further broken apart into two parallel layers—one for mean and the other for variance. That is later combined in the sampling layer that then outputs a vector of a size of latent dimensions to be consumed by the decoder.

```
Model: "encoder"
__________________________________________________________________________________________
Layer (type)                   Output Shape          Param #     Connected to
==========================================================================================
encoder_input (InputLayer)     [(None, 28, 28, 1)]   0           []

conv2d (Conv2D)                (None, 14, 14, 32)    320         ['encoder_input[0][0]']

conv2d_1 (Conv2D)              (None, 7, 7, 64)      18496       ['conv2d[0][0]']

flatten (Flatten)              (None, 3136)          0           ['conv2d_1[0][0]']

dense (Dense)                  (None, 16)            50192       ['flatten[0][0]']

z_mean (Dense)                 (None, 2)             34          ['dense[0][0]']

z_log_var (Dense)              (None, 2)             34          ['dense[0][0]']

z (Lambda)                     (None, 2)             0           ['z_mean[0][0]',
                                                                  'z_log_var[0][0]']

==========================================================================================
Total params: 69,076
Trainable params: 69,076
Non-trainable params: 0
__________________________________________________________________________________________
```

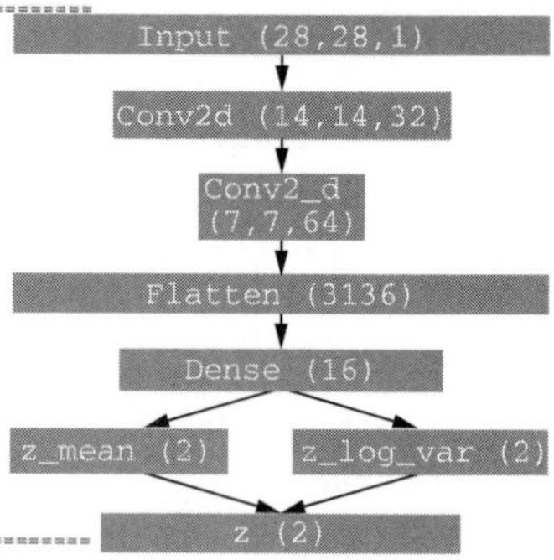

Figure 8.14 An annotated summary of the encoder model

Before we get to the decoder, let's review the `sampling` function, shown in the code cell at the top of the file and listing 8.24, that takes as input the mean and variance. Inside the function, the values for mean and variance are unpacked from `args`. Then, we extract two shape values from the mean input, first using `K.shape` to return the tensor shape and the second `K.int_shape` to return a tuple. Simply put, this sets up the size of output of the sampled vector. We then create a random sample tensor of size `(batch, dim)` called `epsilon`, which becomes the base randomized vector. After this, we scale the vector by applying the mean and variance to determine a final output, vector z.

Listing 8.24   EDL_8_5_VAE.ipynb: The `sampling` function

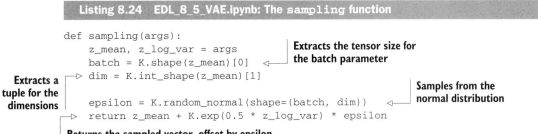

```
def sampling(args):
    z_mean, z_log_var = args
    batch = K.shape(z_mean)[0]          Extracts the tensor size for
                                        the batch parameter
    dim = K.int_shape(z_mean)[1]

    epsilon = K.random_normal(shape=(batch, dim))    Samples from the
                                                     normal distribution
    return z_mean + K.exp(0.5 * z_log_var) * epsilon
```

Extracts a tuple for the dimensions

Samples from the normal distribution

Returns the sampled vector, offset by epsilon

The architecture of the decoder model has also been simplified, but we still need to handle the z sampling layer output from the encoder. This time, we construct an `Input` layer of size `latent_dim` that matches the final sampling output from the encoder, z, as shown in listing 8.25. Next, a new `Dense` layer is expanded to match the size of the final decoder output, which is then reshaped with a `Reshape` layer to match the original encoder output. A simple way to think about this is the new middle sampling function is just swapping the middle latent encoding we built with an AE. However, we still need to keep the dimensions of the data consistent.

Listing 8.25   EDL_8_5_VAE.ipynb: Unpacking the decoder inputs

```
latent_inputs = Input(shape=(latent_dim,),      The input layer constructed
    name='z_sampling')

x = Dense(shape[1] * shape[2] * shape[3],        Adds a dense layer to
    activation='relu')(latent_inputs)            rebuild the shape

x = Reshape((shape[1], shape[2], shape[3]))(x)
```

Reshapes the output to match the decoder input

After that, we can see the remainder of the decoder being constructed, as shown in listing 8.26. The first thing to note is the use of `Conv2DTranspose` layers instead of `Conv2D` and `UpSampling`, as used previously. Put simply, this layer type is a more explicit reverse of the convolution process. Again, the layers are added in a loop, but this time, the number of `filters` is reduced after each iteration, with the remaining `filters` left after building the encoder. After that, a single `Conv2DTranspose` layer is used to reduce the output to a single channel.

208   CHAPTER 8   *Evolving autoencoders*

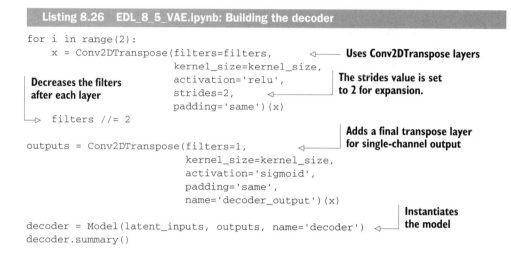

```
for i in range(2):
    x = Conv2DTranspose(filters=filters,          ◁——— Uses Conv2DTranspose layers
                        kernel_size=kernel_size,
Decreases the filters   activation='relu',        The strides value is set
after each layer        strides=2,           ◁    to 2 for expansion.
                        padding='same')(x)
  └▷  filters //= 2
                                                  Adds a final transpose layer
                                                  for single-channel output
outputs = Conv2DTranspose(filters=1,         ◁——┘
                          kernel_size=kernel_size,
                          activation='sigmoid',
                          padding='same',
                          name='decoder_output')(x)
                                                       Instantiates
                                                       the model
decoder = Model(latent_inputs, outputs, name='decoder')  ◁——┘
decoder.summary()
```

Listing 8.26 EDL_8_5_VAE.ipynb: Building the decoder

Figure 8.15 shows an annotated view of the decoder model summary. As you can see, this part is simpler and more modular than an AE. Notice how the input in the model is now just two inputs generated from the encoder `sampling` layer. This, however, allows us to walk or sample through the space that the decoder learns to generate from.

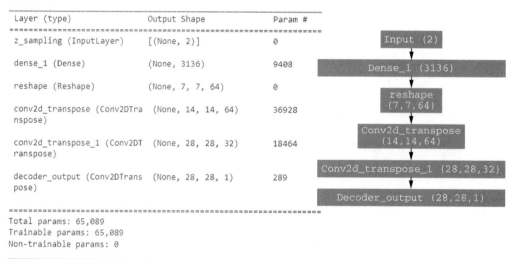

Figure 8.15   Annotated view of the decoder model

The other major difference between a VAE and AE is the way loss is calculated. Recall in an AE, we calculated loss using pixel-wise loss calculated with MSE. This was simple and worked well. However, if we calculated loss in this manner for a VAE, we would miss the nuance of learning the input distribution. Instead, with a VAE, we measure the distributional loss between the input and output using a measure of divergence.

This requires us to add a specialized loss determination to the Keras model. We start by first calculating the base reconstruction loss—the loss calculated by comparing the input image against the output image. After that, we calculate the `kl_loss`, or Kullback-Leibler divergence, which is the statistical distance between two probability distributions. The calculation to determine this amount of divergence from the input and learned representation is shown in the following listing. We cover statistical distance and loss calculations like this in greater depth in chapter 9. Finally, the mean of the `kl_loss` and `reconstruction_loss` is added as a new loss metric to the model with the `add_loss` function.

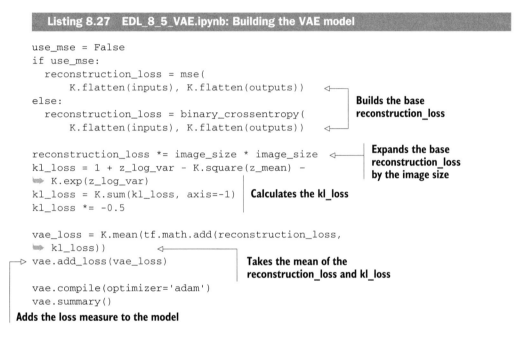

Listing 8.27 EDL_8_5_VAE.ipynb: Building the VAE model

```
use_mse = False
if use_mse:
  reconstruction_loss = mse(
      K.flatten(inputs), K.flatten(outputs))      ◁
else:                                                         Builds the base
  reconstruction_loss = binary_crossentropy(                  reconstruction_loss
      K.flatten(inputs), K.flatten(outputs))      ◁

reconstruction_loss *= image_size * image_size    ◁          Expands the base
kl_loss = 1 + z_log_var - K.square(z_mean) -                 reconstruction_loss
⇒ K.exp(z_log_var)                                           by the image size
kl_loss = K.sum(kl_loss, axis=-1)    Calculates the kl_loss
kl_loss *= -0.5

vae_loss = K.mean(tf.math.add(reconstruction_loss,
⇒ kl_loss))                      ◁
▷ vae.add_loss(vae_loss)                  Takes the mean of the
                                          reconstruction_loss and kl_loss
vae.compile(optimizer='adam')
vae.summary()
Adds the loss measure to the model
```

Scroll down a little further to examine the training output shown in figure 8.16. In this example, we use a normalized loss metric, the loss divided by maximum observed loss, to track the training of the model. By tracking a normalized loss, we can switch between other forms of reconstruction and statistical distance/divergence measures. Go ahead and try switching the flag on the reconstruction loss from MSE to binary cross entropy to observe training differences. Both these measures generate output on different scales, but by normalizing the loss, we can compare measures.

Finally, we can observe output like figure 8.13, which shows the `generation` of sampled images by cycling through sample mean and variance parameters. This code creates a large grid image of size 10×10, which is just a NumPy array. Then, linear spaces or lists of values are generated for a range of values of mean and variance, as shown in listing 8.28. After that, the code loops through these values, mean/variance, and uses them as inputs into the decoder model. The decoder model then uses the `predict`

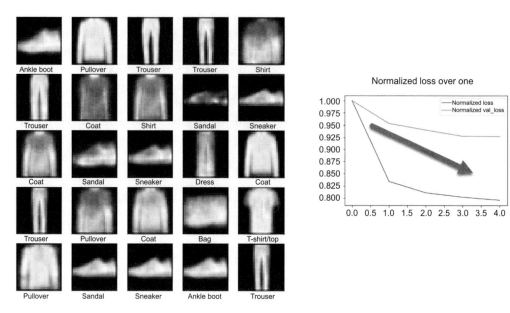

Figure 8.16   An example VAE output

function to generate an image based on the mean/variance values. This predicted or generated image is then plotted into the grid, as shown in the results of figure 8.13.

Listing 8.28   EDL_8_5_VAE.ipynb: Generating manifold images

```
n = 10
digit_size = 28
figure = np.zeros((digit_size * n, digit_size * n))
grid_x = np.linspace(-4, 4, n)
grid_y = np.linspace(-1, 1, n)[::-1]        Creates linear space values

                                             Loops through values
        for i, yi in enumerate(grid_y):
  Creates a │ for j, xi in enumerate(grid_x):
    sample  └─▷  z_sample = np.array([[xi, yi]])
 parameters      x_decoded = decoder.predict(z_sample)   ◁─── The decoder generates
    tensor       digit = x_decoded[0].reshape                  an output image.
           ┌─▷ ➡ (digit_size, digit_size)
   Plots the     figure[i * digit_size: (i + 1) * digit_size,
figure into the            j * digit_size: (j + 1) * digit_size] = digit
 image grid
```

The results produced by a VAE can be quite good in a short time. On top of that, we have more control over the model and can easily identify what the model is learning. This, in turn, makes it easier to optimize the model, given several options.

8.5.3 *Learning exercises*

Use the following exercises to help improve your understanding of VAE:

1 Alter various hyperparameters in listing 8.21 and then rerun the notebook. See what effect each of the hyperparameters has on the generated results.
2 Increase or decrease the number encoder and decoder model layers in listings 8.22 and 8.26 and then rerun the notebook.
3 Adjust and tune the VAE model, so it produces the best version of figure 8.13.

Reviewing and understanding how a VAE works is essential background for chapter 9. Take an opportunity to understand the basics of what we just covered, especially understanding how images can be generated from the learned representation space. This information is fundamental to the next chapter's journey into evolutionary generative DL.

Summary

- AEs are the foundation of generative modeling/learning and use unsupervised learning to train the model.
- AEs function by encoding data down to a latent/middle representation and then rebuilding or decoding the data back to its original form.
- The internal middle/latent representation requires a middle bottleneck to reduce or compress the data. The process of compression allows the model to learn a latent representation of data.
- Complex AEs that use convolutional (CNN) layers can be complicated to build. Neuroevolution can be used to build a layered architecture that defines encoder and decoder sections. The use of convolutional layers in the encoder and decoder requires additional `UpSampling` layers and matching layer configurations. These specialized configurations can be encoded into custom genetic sequences.
- Custom `mutation` and `crossover` operators can be developed to handle the custom genetic encoding needed for building an evolutionary AE.
- Training an evolutionary AE that builds an evolved architecture may take some time to explore multiple architectures.
- The learned latent representation in a variational AE can be used to visualize what the internal representation looks like. Variational AEs are an extension to AE that uses a middle sampling layer to disconnect the encoder from the decoder. Disconnecting the encoder or decoder provides for better performance.

Generative deep
learning and evolution

9

This chapter covers

- Overviewing generative adversarial networks
- Understanding problems in generative adversarial network optimization
- Fixing generative adversarial network problems by applying Wasserstein loss
- Creating a generative adversarial network encoder for evolutionary optimization
- Evolving a deep convolutional generative adversarial network with genetic algorithms

In the last chapter, we were introduced to autoencoders (AEs) and learned how features could be extracted. We learned how to apply evolution to the network architecture optimization of an AE, and then we covered the variational AE that introduced the concept of generative deep learning, or representative learning.

In this chapter, we continue exploring representation learning, this time by looking at generative adversarial networks (GANs). GANs are a fascinating topic worthy of several books, but for our purposes, we only need to explore the basics.

So in this chapter, we look at the fundamentals of the GAN and how it may be optimized with evolution.

GANs are notoriously difficult to train, so being able to optimize this process with evolution will be beneficial. We start by introducing the basic, or what is often referred to as the "vanilla," GAN in the next section.

9.1 Generative adversarial networks

The GAN is the artist of DL, and while it can create beautiful representations, it also has nefarious uses. While we don't explore those extremes in this section, we do look at how the basic GAN works. Before we jump into the code though, we'll quickly introduce or review how a GAN works.

9.1.1 Introducing GANs

We often romanticize the explanation of GANs using the analogy of the art forger and art discriminator, detective, or critic. Art forgery being a lucrative business, the art forger tries to generate fakes that can fool the art critic or detective. Likewise, the detective uses their knowledge base to determine the validity of the generated art and prevent fakes from being sold.

Figure 9.1 is a classic representation of this adversarial battle between the art generator and the art discriminator or detective. The discriminator learns by evaluating real art and generated fakes from the forger. The generator or forger is blind to the real art and only learns from feedback from the detective or discriminator.

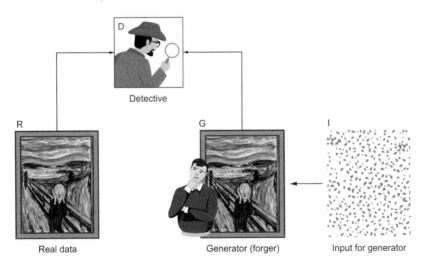

Figure 9.1 Classic explanation of a GAN

Figure 9.2 depicts the process from figure 9.1 as a DL system. The generator (G) receives as input a randomized latent space with a little noise added. This represents the random thoughts an art forger takes as input (I) from figure 9.1. From these random

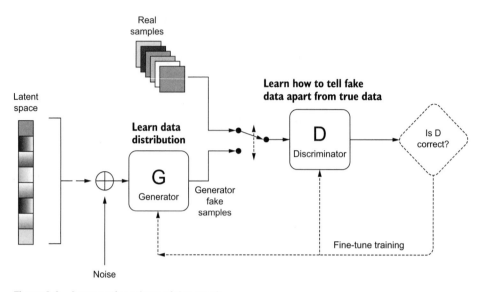

Figure 9.2   A generative adversarial network

thoughts, generated images are sent to the discriminator (D) to verify the art's validity—whether it is real or fake.

Likewise, D takes as input samples of real images and the fake generated images from G. D learns to detect real versus fakes by getting feedback on its predictions—negative feedback if D predicts a real as fake and positive feedback for successfully detecting real images.

Conversely, G learns from feedback from D. Again, this feedback is positive if the generator can fool D and negative if it fails. D, in turn, receives negative feedback if it authenticates a fake as real and positive if it detects a fake as fake.

On the surface, the simple elegance of the adversarial training process is overshadowed by the difficulty of its training. GANs work best when G and D learn at the same rate. If either learns more quickly or slowly, then the system breaks down and neither benefit from this symbiotic relationship.

GAN training and optimization, as discussed in this chapter, makes an excellent candidate to apply evolutionary optimization against. However, before we get to there, it is helpful to review the technical implementation of how a GAN works and how it is built in the next section.

9.1.2   *Building a convolutional generative adversarial network in Keras*

In this section, we look at the basic, "vanilla" GAN that uses convolution and which we typically refer to as a dual convolution GAN of DCGAN. The addition of the DC simply signifies the GAN is more specialized with the addition of convolution. A lot of what we cover here is a review of previous chapters on convolution and autoencoders. As such, we don't cover those details here but simply investigate how to build and train a GAN.

Open the EDL_9_1_GAN.ipynb notebook in Google Colab. Refer to the appendix if you need assistance. Run all the cells in the notebook by selecting Runtime > Run All form the menu.

We use the MNIST Handwritten Digits and Fashion-MNIST datasets in this chapter. However, to reduce training times, we extract a single class of images from the dataset with the extract function, as shown in listing 9.1. The extract function takes as input the batch of images and labels and the class number to extract. The first line extracts the indexes that match the labels equal to the class number. Then, the list of indexes is used to isolate the subset of images from the original dataset that match the class. The result is a dataset with just one class of images: train_images. We can see from the call to the extract function, using a class of 5 represents the digit 5 in the dataset, as shown in the plot output.

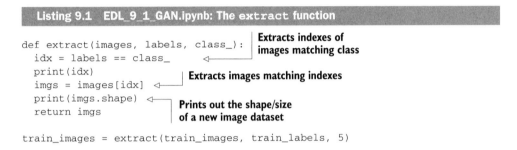

```
def extract(images, labels, class_):          Extracts indexes of
  idx = labels == class_          ◁           images matching class
  print(idx)
  imgs = images[idx]  ◁           Extracts images matching indexes
  print(imgs.shape)  ◁
  return imgs                     Prints out the shape/size
                                  of a new image dataset

train_images = extract(train_images, train_labels, 5)
```

Next, we look at setting some base hyperparameters and optimizers for the generator and discriminator. The first parameter is a hyperparameter that defines the size of the latent space or random thoughts that are input into the generator. Next, we create a different optimizer for G and D to attempt to balance the training, as shown in listing 9.2. After that, we calculate a convolutional constant we will use to build the networks as well as extract the number of channels and image shape. This notebook was developed to support various other sample datasets, including CIFAR.

Listing 9.2 EDL_9_1_GAN.ipynb: Optimizers and hyperparameters

```
latent_dim = 100     ◁——— Defines the latent space input size

g_optimizer = Adam(0.0002, 0.5)          Creates optimizers
d_optimizer = RMSprop(.00001)            for G and D

cs = int(train_images.shape[1] / 4)   ◁——— Calculates the convolution space constant
print(train_images.shape)
channels = train_images.shape[3]
img_shape = (train_images.shape[1],          Extracts image
➥  train_images.shape[2], channels), 5)      channels and size
```

As shown in listing 9.3, a GAN is built by breaking up the discriminator and generator into separate models and combining them, not unlike building an AE. The generator architecture resembles a decoder in an AE, where the `build_generator` function creates a convolutional network to generate images from a random and noisy latent space.

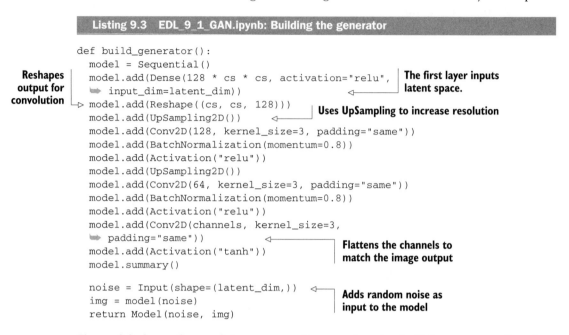

Listing 9.3   EDL_9_1_GAN.ipynb: Building the generator

```
def build_generator():
  model = Sequential()
  model.add(Dense(128 * cs * cs, activation="relu",
➥ input_dim=latent_dim))
  model.add(Reshape((cs, cs, 128)))
  model.add(UpSampling2D())
  model.add(Conv2D(128, kernel_size=3, padding="same"))
  model.add(BatchNormalization(momentum=0.8))
  model.add(Activation("relu"))
  model.add(UpSampling2D())
  model.add(Conv2D(64, kernel_size=3, padding="same"))
  model.add(BatchNormalization(momentum=0.8))
  model.add(Activation("relu"))
  model.add(Conv2D(channels, kernel_size=3,
➥ padding="same"))
  model.add(Activation("tanh"))
  model.summary()

  noise = Input(shape=(latent_dim,))
  img = model(noise)
  return Model(noise, img)
```

Reshapes output for convolution

The first layer inputs latent space.

Uses UpSampling to increase resolution

Flattens the channels to match the image output

Adds random noise as input to the model

Figure 9.3 shows the model summary after running the `build_generator` function. Notice that this is only the summary of the internal model and that we add another model wrapper around the base generator to add the noise inputs.

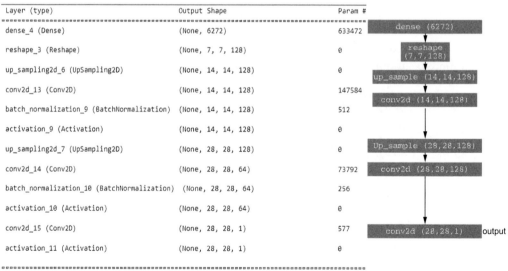

Figure 9.3   Summary of the output of the generator model

The discriminator is constructed in a similar fashion, but this time, we add a validation input, as shown in listing 9.4. The model starts with a convolutional layer taking the image as input, using a stride of size 2 to reduce or pool the image for the next layer. Increasing the strides here works similarly at reducing image size as pooling. The output from the discriminator is a single value that classifies the input image as fake or real.

Listing 9.4 EDL_9_1_GAN.ipynb: Building the discriminator

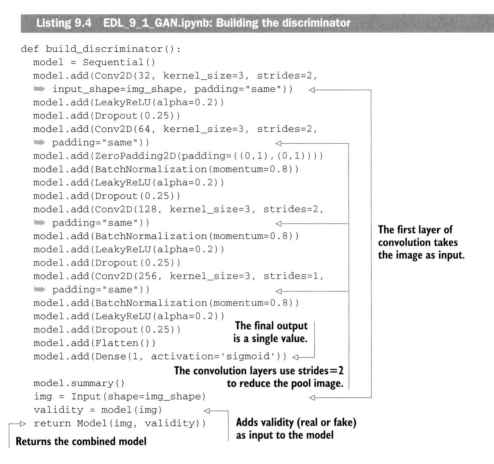

```
def build_discriminator():
  model = Sequential()
  model.add(Conv2D(32, kernel_size=3, strides=2,
➥   input_shape=img_shape, padding="same"))        ◁──────
  model.add(LeakyReLU(alpha=0.2))
  model.add(Dropout(0.25))
  model.add(Conv2D(64, kernel_size=3, strides=2,
➥   padding="same"))                               ◁──
  model.add(ZeroPadding2D(padding=((0,1),(0,1))))
  model.add(BatchNormalization(momentum=0.8))
  model.add(LeakyReLU(alpha=0.2))
  model.add(Dropout(0.25))
  model.add(Conv2D(128, kernel_size=3, strides=2,
➥   padding="same"))                               ◁──
  model.add(BatchNormalization(momentum=0.8))
  model.add(LeakyReLU(alpha=0.2))
  model.add(Dropout(0.25))
  model.add(Conv2D(256, kernel_size=3, strides=1,
➥   padding="same"))                               ◁──
  model.add(BatchNormalization(momentum=0.8))
  model.add(LeakyReLU(alpha=0.2))
  model.add(Dropout(0.25))
  model.add(Flatten())
  model.add(Dense(1, activation='sigmoid'))  ◁──
  model.summary()
  img = Input(shape=img_shape)
  validity = model(img)                    ◁──
➥ return Model(img, validity))
```

The first layer of convolution takes the image as input.

The final output is a single value.

The convolution layers use strides=2 to reduce the pool image.

Adds validity (real or fake) as input to the model

Returns the combined model

Since we train the discriminator separately from the generator, we also compile the created model with `d_optimizer`, a loss of binary cross entropy, and accuracy for metrics, as shown in the following listing.

Listing 9.5 EDL_9_1_GAN.ipynb: Compiling the discriminator

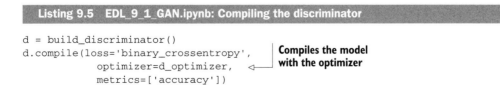

```
d = build_discriminator()
d.compile(loss='binary_crossentropy',
          optimizer=d_optimizer,     ◁──
          metrics=['accuracy'])
```

Compiles the model with the optimizer

Now, we can construct the combined GAN model with the D and G models we built earlier. Inside the cell, we create an input representing the latent space input for the generator, as shown in listing 9.6. Then, we create an output from G, called `img`, for the generated image. After that, we turn off training for the discriminator model that will be used in the combined GAN. We don't train the discriminator within the combined GAN. Rather, the generator is trained separately, within the combined GAN, using a separate optimizer: the `g_optimizer`. The validity of an image output from the discriminator, `d`, is used to train the generator in the combined model.

Listing 9.6   EDL_9_1_GAN.ipynb: Compiling the discriminator

```
z = Input(shape=(latent_dim,))
img = g(z)                       ⟵—— Generates an image from latent space

d.trainable = False   ⟵—— Turns off discriminator training in the GAN

valid = d(img)   ⟵—— Introduces adversarial ground truths

gan = Model(z, valid)                    ⟵—— Builds a combined model
gan.compile(loss='binary_crossentropy',
➥ optimizer=g_optimizer)])              ⟵—— Compiles with loss and optimizer
```

Since we have separate training flows, we can't simply use the Keras `model.fit` function. Instead, we must train the discriminator and generator separately. The code, shown in listing 9.7, starts by creating the adversarial ground truths for real and fake image sets, making a tensor of `1`s for valid images and `0`s for fake images. Training is done within two loops: the outer, controlled by the number of epochs, and the inner, the calculated number of batches. Inside the loop, we sample a random set of real images, `imgs`, and then generate a fake set of images, `gen_images`, using random noise. Then, we train and calculate the loss of the real and fake images on the discriminator. Notice for each set of training how we pass the respective ground truths. A final combined discriminator loss is calculated by taking the average of the real and fake loss. Finally, we train the combined GAN or just the generator by passing in the valid ground truth against the generated fake images.

Listing 9.7   EDL_9_1_GAN.ipynb: Training the GAN

```
batches = int(train_images.shape[0] / BATCH_SIZE)

# Adversarial ground truths
valid = np.ones((BATCH_SIZE, 1))     | Generates adversarial
fake = np.zeros((BATCH_SIZE, 1))     | ground truths

for e in range(EPOCHS):
  for i in tqdm(range(batches)):
    idx = np.random.randint(0, train_images.shape[0],
    ➥ BATCH_SIZE)                                        | A sample random batch
    imgs = train_images[idx]                             | of real images
```

```
                noise = np.random.normal(0, 1, (BATCH_SIZE,
                    latent_dim))
                gen_imgs = g.predict(noise)
```

| Creates noise and
| generates fake images

Trains the
generator
using a
valid
ground
truth

```
                d_loss_real = d.train_on_batch(imgs, valid)
                d_loss_fake = d.train_on_batch(gen_imgs, fake)
                d_loss = 0.5 * np.add(d_loss_real, d_loss_fake)

                g_loss = gan.train_on_batch(noise, valid)
```

| **Trains the discriminator**
| **and calculates loss on**
| **real and fake images**

Figure 9.4 shows the results of training the GAN on 10 epochs over one class of data: the digit 5. You can just start to see the generator creating images that resemble a hand-drawn 5. Combined with the generated images, we also see results of the loss training for the discriminator broken out by real and fake as well as the generator. Without getting deep into the mathematics, the goal of training a "vanilla" GAN is to maximize the loss of the fake images and minimize the loss of the real images. In essence, D needs to become better at identifying real images but also needs to get

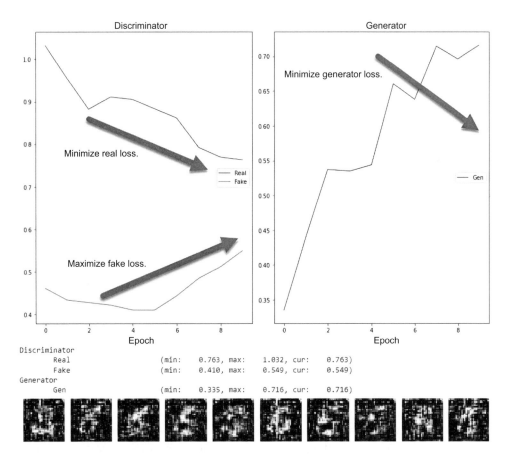

Figure 9.4 Training a GAN for 10 epochs

worse at identifying the fakes. Reciprocal to this, the generator must minimize the loss of creating fake images. In the figure, it appears to be the opposite, but this is because it is still in the early stages of training.

Go ahead and increase the number of EPOCHS for training the GAN, and then run the notebook again via Runtime > Run All from the menu. You will see how the various real and fake losses maximize and minimize, respectively.

9.1.3 *Learning exercises*

Use the following exercises to help improve your understanding of the basic GAN:

1 Increase or decrease the BATCH_SIZE and then rerun the notebook. What effect does changing this hyperparameter have on GAN training?
2 Increase or decrease the learning rate for the g_optimizer and d_optimizer in listing 9.2. What effect does changing either optimizer have on GAN training?
3 Don't use the extract function to limit the dataset to one class in listing 9.1. How does that affect training the GAN?

Now, we have a working GAN that can learn to generate realistic and accurate digits of a given class. While the concept is simple, hopefully you can also appreciate, at this point, the subtle complexity and nuances of the code we just quickly covered. We explore those technical nuances and attempt to understand the difficulty of training a GAN in the next section.

9.2   *The challenges of training a GAN*

A GAN can best be described as a balancing act between the discriminator and generator, where if either model surpasses the other, then the whole system fails. Since the discriminator is trained separately, it may still produce valid models, but this is rarely useful in broader applications.

> **Discriminator repurposing**
>
> While the goal of building and training a GAN is being able to generate realistic fakes, another benefit is a robust discriminator that can distinguish between real images and fakes. Discriminators essentially become classifiers that can identify the difference between real or fake images for a given dataset, allowing the model to be reused as a simple classifier of the entire dataset. For example, if you trained a GAN on faces, the resulting discriminator could be used to classify any image as being a face or not a face.

Building and training a GAN that can perform this balancing act and produce excellent results is notoriously difficult. In this section, we explore some obvious and not so obvious points of failure when training GANs. Then, of course, as we progress through the chapter, we look at various strategies to resolve these problems manually and with evolution. Before we do that, however, let's review why GAN optimization is a problem.

9.2.1 The GAN optimization problem

Often, the main problem of GAN training is getting the generator and discriminator to converge at a solution effectively and in tandem. Fortunately, when these problems manifest themselves, they often become obvious in the form of various artifacts. The following is a summary of some of the most common and identifiable problems you may face training a GAN:

- *Vanishing gradients*—If the discriminator becomes strong at identifying fakes, this often reduces the amount of loss fed back to the generator. In turn, that reduced loss diminishes the training gradients applied to the generator and results in vanishing gradients.
- *Mode collapse or overfitting*—A generator can get stuck continually generating the same output with little variation. This happens because the model becomes too specialized and essentially overfits the generated output.
- *Failure to converge*—If the generator improves too quickly during training, the discriminator becomes overwhelmed and confused. This causes the discriminator to break down and, essentially, make random 50/50 guesses between observed real or fake images.

Observing each of these problems and being able to identify when they occur is useful for understanding and training GANs. In the next few subsections, we look at modifying the original notebook to replicate and observe these artifacts.

9.2.2 Observing vanishing gradients

To replicate vanishing gradients in the generator, we often just need to adjust the optimizer used for the discriminator. Network architecture may also play into the vanishing gradient problem, but we showcase a couple elements we already put in place to address that. Open your browser, and let's jump into the next notebook.

Open the EDL_9_2_GAN_Optimization.ipynb notebook in Colab. Hold off on running the entire notebook until we review some sections of the code. Scroll down a couple cells to where the optimizer setup is, and then look for the comment `vanishing gradients`, as shown in the following listing. Uncomment the following line that sets the discriminator optimizer, `disc_optimizer`. Comment out the original discriminator optimizer, and then uncomment the optimizer labelled `vanishing gradients`.

> **Listing 9.8 EDL_9_2_GAN_Optimization.ipynb: Setting the optimizer**

```
gen_optimizer = Adam(0.0002, 0.5)
#disc_optimizer = RMSprop(.00001)    ◁─── Comments out the original optimizer

# vanishing gradients
disc_optimizer = Adam(.00000001, .5)    ◁─── Uncomments the Adam optimizer
```

The result of swapping out the optimizer for the discriminator is, effectively, making it better or very good at identifying fakes and real images. Consequently, we should see loss for the generator minimize as training progresses, with no appreciable improvement in output.

After you make the change, run all the cells in the notebook by selecting Runtime > Run All from the menu. Scroll down to the training output; you should see similar output to that shown in figure 9.5. The results show the classic indication that the generator is in trouble because of vanishing gradients. The two strong indicators a GAN may be undergoing this problem are generator loss and discriminator loss on the fakes. As we can see in the figure, the discriminator fake loss remains fixed within a small range for the entire training session. For the generator, this results in smaller observed changes in loss over time, producing vanishing gradients.

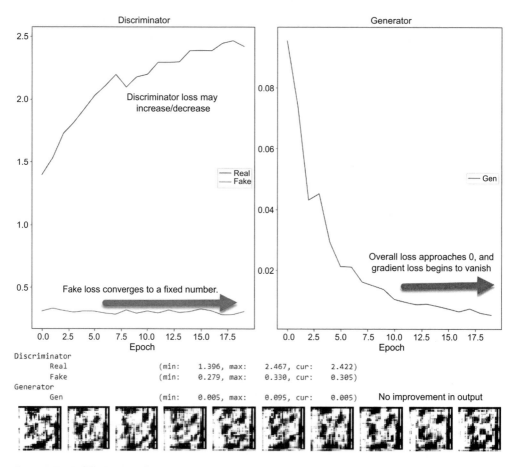

Figure 9.5   GAN training output showing vanishing gradients

Normally, when we observe vanishing gradients in a DL model, we review the model architecture and look for areas that may result in VG. If you refer to where the generator model is built, you may notice we are using ReLU activation functions. We can change this by swapping out the comments on the code, as shown in the following listing.

Listing 9.9   EDL_9_2_GAN_Optimization.ipynb: Trying `LeakyReLU`

```
model.add(Dense(128 * cs * cs, activation="relu", input_dim=latent_dim))
model.add(Reshape((cs, cs, 128)))
model.add(UpSampling2D())
model.add(Conv2D(128, kernel_size=3, padding="same"))
model.add(BatchNormalization(momentum=0.8))
#model.add(Activation("relu"))
model.add(LeakyReLU(alpha=0.2))
model.add(UpSampling2D())
model.add(Conv2D(64, kernel_size=3, padding="same"))
model.add(BatchNormalization(momentum=0.8))
#model.add(Activation("relu"))
model.add(LeakyReLU(alpha=0.2))
model.add(Conv2D(channels, kernel_size=3, padding="same"))
model.add(Activation("tanh"))
```

Uncomments the LeakyReLU activation function

Comments out the original activation function

Run all the cells in the notebook Runtime > Run All from the menu. Unfortunately, we observe very little improvement. This is because swapping the activation function of the generator has little effect, since the problem is the discriminator. If you want to observe how this GAN should work, go ahead and swap the code back by commenting and uncommenting and then rerunning the notebook.

The typical way to address vanishing gradients in a GAN is to either adjust the optimizer or resolve the manner of loss calculation. We attempt to understand and improve the loss calculation later in this chapter, but before that, let's jump back to observing other forms of GAN failure in the next section.

9.2.3 Observing mode collapse in GANs

Mode collapse occurs when a GAN struggles to produce variation in its output. This happens when the generator finds only a single or small set of outputs that can fool the critic. Then, as the critic improves, the generator becomes stuck producing a small range of variation in output.

Open the EDL_9_2_GAN_Optimization.ipynb notebook in Colab. Make sure to load a fresh copy from the repository if you made any modifications in the last section. Scroll down again to the optimizer set up section, and then uncomment the code below the comment `mode collapse`, as shown in the following listing.

Listing 9.10   EDL_9_2_GAN_Optimization.ipynb: Setting the optimizer again

```
gen_optimizer = Adam(0.0002, 0.5)
#disc_optimizer = RMSprop(.00001)        ◁──── Comments out the original optimizer

# mode collapse
disc_optimizer = Adam(.002, .9)))        ◁──── Uncomments the Adam optimizer
```

After you make the changes, run all the cells in the notebook via Runtime > Run All from the menu. Figure 9.6 shows the output of training the GAN over 25 epochs. Your results may vary slightly, but you should observe mode collapse of the output images, as shown in the figure.

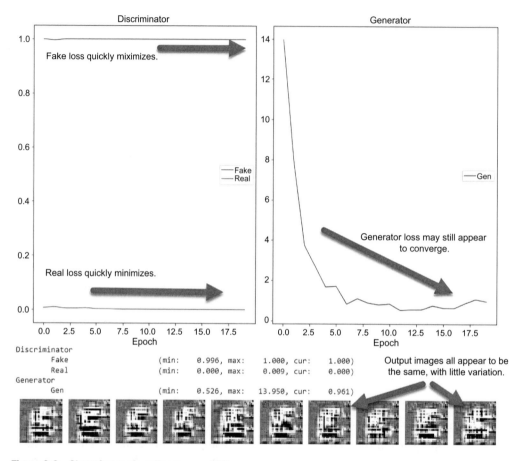

Figure 9.6   Observing mode collapse on a GAN

The simple fix to overcome mode collapse is, of course, to find the right optimizer. There are other approaches that also can help minimize this problem, including adjusting the loss function and unrolling the GAN.

Unrolling GANs

The idea behind unrolling GANs is to train the generator on current and future states of the discriminator. This allows the generator to look ahead and account for future incarnations of the discriminator in a form of time travel. While the concept is not complex, the code to implement this management of current and future states is.

We cover swapping the GAN loss function later, and unrolling the GAN is too complex for our simple needs. Instead, we choose a very simple method to alleviate mode collapse: using noise.

Scroll down to the training function; notice the addition of a new `ADD_NOISE` Boolean form constant, as shown in the following listing. You can use the Colab form to switch this variable between `True` and `False`. Switch it to `True`, and then run all the cells in the notebook via Runtime > Run All.

> **Listing 9.11   EDL_9_2_GAN_Optimization.ipynb: Adding noise to adversarial ground truths**

```
if ADD_NOISE:
  fake_d = np.random.sample(BATCH_SIZE) * 0.2        ◁──┐ The fake ground truth is
  valid_d = np.random.sample(BATCH_SIZE) * 0.2 + 0.8 ◁──  now between 0 and 0.2.
  valid_g = np.ones((BATCH_SIZE, 1))   ◁──┐ The valid ground truth is
else:                                        now between 0.8 and 1.0.
  valid_d = np.ones((BATCH_SIZE, 1))
  fake_d = np.zeros((BATCH_SIZE, 1))   Keeps the same valid ground
  valid_g = np.ones((BATCH_SIZE, 1))   truth for the generator
```

Figure 9.7 shows the result of training the GAN over 25 epochs with the addition of noise. While the results are still not exceptional due to the discrepancy in optimizers, we can see an improvement in output variation.

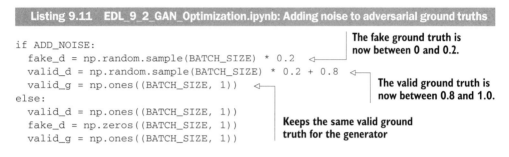

Generated images increase in variation.

Figure 9.7   An example output showing increased variation in model outpu

As you can see from the changes in the last notebook, we were able to correct the mode collapse problem by simply adding noise to the adversarial ground truths. In the next section, we address one more problem area of GANs.

9.2.4   Observing convergence failures in GANs

Convergence is an underlying problem in GANs and can be a consequence of mode collapse, vanishing gradients, or badly balanced optimization. Thus, we can replicate convergence failures relatively easily. However, in this observation, we want to look at an example in which just the generator or discriminator fails to converge.

Open the EDL_9_2_GAN_Optimization.ipynb notebook in Colab. Be sure to start with a new copy from the repository if you modified it. Scroll down to the optimizers set up cell and uncomment/comment the appropriate lines marked `convergence`, as shown in the following listing.

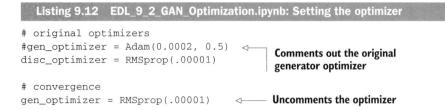

```
# original optimizers
#gen_optimizer = Adam(0.0002, 0.5)        Comments out the original
disc_optimizer = RMSprop(.00001)          generator optimizer

# convergence
gen_optimizer = RMSprop(.00001)           Uncomments the optimizer
```

Run all the cells in the notebook via Runtime > Run All from the menu. Figure 9.8 shows the convergence failure of the GAN generator. While the discriminator looks to be converging well, we can see the increasing loss of the generator has resulted in an inability to converge.

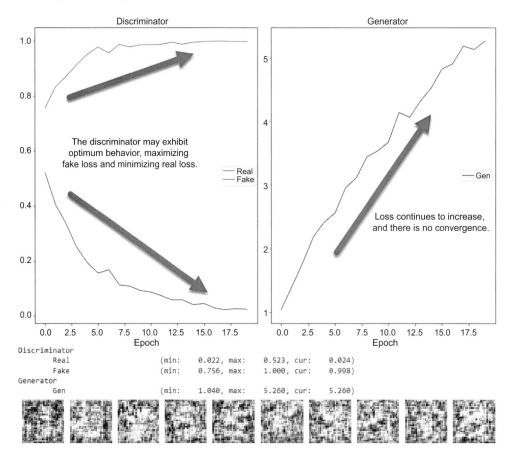

Figure 9.8 GAN failure to converge on the generator

As in our previous examples, there is a relatively simple fix to correct convergence problems. One solution is to break the tight loop between the generator and discriminator training. We can do this by allowing the D and G training to cycle independently of one another.

To support this independent iteration scheme, we have added more code and additional inputs to control it, as shown in listing 9.13. The code in the listing only shows the essential parts of the training loop, during which we add two inner loops— one to train the discriminator and the other the generator. How often these respective loops run can be controlled from Colab using the variables `CRITIC_ITS`, to control discriminator iterations, and `GEN_ITS`, to control generator iterations.

> **Listing 9.13 EDL_9_2_GAN_Optimization.ipynb: Breaking the training loop**

```
CRITIC_ITS = 5 #@param {type:"slider", min:1,          The variable to control the
➥ max:10, step:1}                                      number of iterations on the
GEN_ITS = 10 #@param {type:"slider", min:1,            discriminator/generator
➥ max:10, step:1}

for e in range(EPOCHS):
  for i in tqdm(range(batches)):        The loop for the discriminator
    for _ in range(CRITIC_ITS):    ◁──┘
      idx = np.random.randint(0, train_images.shape[0], BATCH_SIZE)
      imgs = train_images[idx]
      noise = np.random.normal(0, 1, (BATCH_SIZE, latent_dim))
      gen_imgs = g.predict(noise)

      d_loss_real = d.train_on_batch(imgs, valid_d)
      d_loss_fake = d.train_on_batch(gen_imgs, fake_d)
      d_loss = 0.5 * np.add(d_loss_real, d_loss_fake)

    for _ in range(GEN_ITS):    ◁──┘  The loop for the generator
      g_loss = gan.train_on_batch(noise, valid_g)
```

Set the `CRITIC_ITS` value to 5 and the `GEN_ITS` to 10, and then rerun all the notebook cells. via Runtime > Run All. Figure 9.9 shows the results of breaking the tight dependency between generator and discriminator as well as the GAN converging.

9.2.5 Learning exercises

Use the following exercises to improve your understanding of GAN training:

1 How can you reduce the possibility of mode collapse while training the generator in a GAN?
2 What is the primary cause of convergence failure in generators?
3 How can you reduce the vanishing gradient problem in GANs (generators)?

Getting the right number of iterations between the generator and discriminator becomes a matter of rerunning the model with different values. This, of course, can be done manually or, you guessed it, with some form of evolutionary optimization. While this GAN is working better, we can add another improvement by updating the loss function we use in the next section.

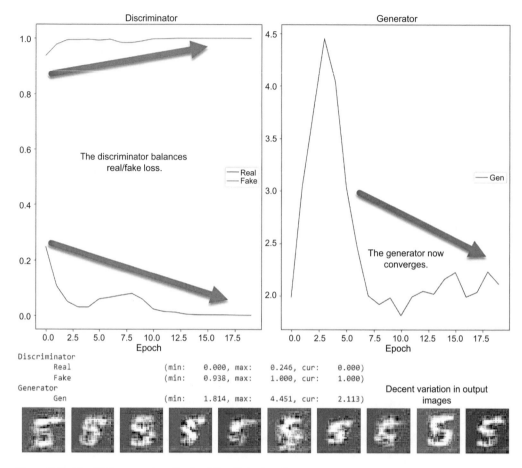

Figure 9.9   **The GAN converges after breaking tight coupling**

9.3   *Fixing GAN problems with Wasserstein loss*

In the next notebook, we look at improving the GAN performance and fixing problems by reducing or eliminating convergence failures, vanishing gradients, and mode collapse. We do this by introducing an alternate method of measuring loss or distance, called *Wasserstein loss*, within a GAN. Before jumping into the notebook, let's review what Wasserstein loss is in the next section.

9.3.1   *Understanding Wasserstein loss*

One of the key problems we face when training GANs is resolving and balancing the loss between the generator and discriminator. In a standard GAN, the discriminator measures loss in terms of probability, or the probability an image is fake or real. Mathematically measuring the difference in probabilities, a measure of uncertainty, becomes less accurate over consecutive iterations of training.

In 2017, Martin Arjovsky et al. proposed a revised method of loss in their paper titled "Wasserstein GAN": swapping out the discriminator for a critic. In their method, the critic, instead of measuring probabilities, predicts a value representing how real or fake an image is. Thus, a generated image could be measured on a scale of real to fake.

Fundamentally, when we train a GAN, our goal is to narrow or optimize the distance between what is real and fake. When we measure this distance in terms of probabilities, we are fixed to using a measure of uncertainty. By introducing a scaled distance for loss, we introduce an alternate measure of distance optimization.

Figure 9.10 shows a comparison between measuring variational, or probabilistic, distance and Wasserstein distance. Wasserstein distance is nicknamed *earthmover distance*, as it better describes how the two distributions are measured. Where Kullback-Lieber and Jensen Shannon distance measure the horizontal distance, earthmover distance accounts for vertical differences as well.

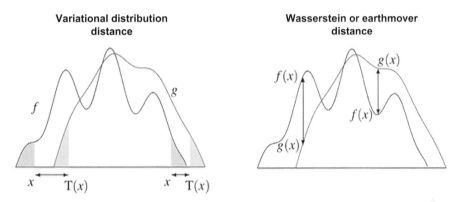

Figure 9.10   The difference between variational distance and Wasserstein distance

The benefit of using earthmover distance is that the loss or measure of distance between a real or fake image is better quantified and results in a more robust and less sensitive model. Using Wasserstein distance also eliminates or reduces the possibility of the GAN encountering mode collapse, failure to converge, and vanishing gradients, as we see in the next section, when we implement Wasserstein loss in a GAN.

9.3.2   *Improving the DCGAN with Wasserstein loss*

Now, we can jump in and review how to implement Wasserstein, or earthmover, loss within a GAN. This notebook is the same as the DCGAN we just built with the extension of Wasserstein loss.

Open the EDL_9_3_WGAN.ipynb notebook in Colab. Go ahead and run all the cells in the notebook via Runtime > Run All from the menu.

Scroll down to where the optimizers are instantiated. The first thing you may notice is that we switch the name of the discriminator model to critic, as shown in the following listing. This is because the critic predicts the measure of realness or fakeness rather than the probability of it being real or fake. Also, notice how we are now using the same optimizer for the `generator` and `critic`. We can also do this because the scale of real versus fake normalizes the differences between the measures.

Listing 9.14   EDL_9_3_WGAN.ipynb: Optimizer set up

```
gen_optimizer = RMSprop(lr=0.00005)      ⟵——— The generator optimizer
critic_optimizer = RMSprop(lr=0.00005)   ⟵
                                              The discriminator
                                              swapped to the critic
```

Move down to the next cell, shown in listing 9.15; we can see the calculation of Wasserstein loss in a function called `wasserstein_loss`. From the single line of code, you can see how the average of the true or real inputs is multiplied across the predictions. The output of this is the earthmover distance between both distributions.

Listing 9.15   EDL_9_3_WGAN.ipynb: The Wasserstein loss function

```
def wasserstein_loss(y_true, y_pred):      | Computes the average
  return K.mean(y_true * y_pred)   ⟵——————| across real and predicted
```

We can then see how the `wasserstein_loss` function is used by looking at the `critic` construction code, shown in the following listing. Notice again how we updated the name of the `discriminator` to `critic` and employed the `wasserstein_loss` function when compiling the model.

Listing 9.16   EDL_9_3_WGAN.ipynb: Building the critic

```
critic = build_critic()
critic.compile(loss=wasserstein_loss,      ⟵——— Use Wasserstein loss.
          optimizer=critic_optimizer,      ⟵
          metrics=['accuracy'])                 Uses the selected optimizer
```

The last major change we need to look at is updating the critic training code. Calculating loss with the `critic` is the same as the `discriminator`—nothing changes aside from the naming. Implementing Wasserstein loss introduces a possibility of exploding gradients; to overcome this, we add a clipping step, shown in listing 9.17. For every training iteration of the `critic`, we now make sure to clip each of the model weights to within the `clip_value` hyperparameter. This clipping of weights eliminates any possibility of exploding gradients and reduces the convergence model space.

Listing 9.17   EDL_9_3_WGAN.ipynb: Training the critic

```
c_loss_real = critic.train_on_batch(imgs, valid)
c_loss_fake = critic.train_on_batch(gen_imgs, fake)
c_loss = 0.5 * np.add(c_loss_real, c_loss_fake)   ⟵——— The average of real and fake loss
```

```
for l in critic.layers:      ⟵── Loops through the critic layers
  weights = l.get_weights()
  weights = [np.clip(w, -clip_value, clip_value)
  ⟿ for w in weights]        ⟵
  l.set_weights(weights))        │ The clip layer weights with range
```

Figure 9.11 shows the results of training this GAN over 80 epochs on a single extracted class of the MNIST Handwritten Digits dataset. If you want to see how this dataset performs on the Fashion-MNIST dataset, rerun the entire notebook with the code change in listing 9.18. You can also remove the call to the extract function to see how well the model works across all classes in the datasets.

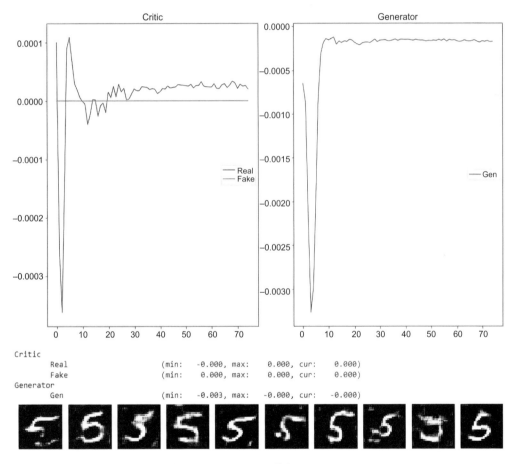

Figure 9.11   Training a Wasserstein GAN on extracted digits

Listing 9.18   EDL_9_3_WGAN.ipynb: Switching to the Fashion-MNIST dataset

```
from tensorflow.keras.datasets import mnist as data    ⟵── Comments out the line
#from tensorflow.keras.datasets import fashion_mnist
⟿ as data                                              ⟵── Uncomments the line
```

Introducing Wasserstein loss to the DCGAN, making it a WGAN or WDCGAN, alleviates several shortcomings of the standard GAN. Reducing these additional complica-
tions makes it easier for us to build an evolutionary optimizer to find our best possible
GAN. Before we do that, we need to wrap our WDCGAN up, so it can become an
encoded model usable in evolutionary optimization in the next section.

9.4   *Encoding the Wasserstein DCGAN for evolution*

We have already undergone the process of encoding the hyperparameters or architecture of various models in previous chapters. For our next notebook, we look to do the
same thing but limit the encoding to just hyperparameters. This allows for a more
concise optimization space for the evolutionary optimizer to explore.

> **Evolutionary optimizing complex models**
>
> As the models we attempt to optimize become more complex, we are faced with iter-
> ating through more intense training operations. We can no longer rely on a model just
> being trained for 3 epochs to give us reasonable results; instead, some models may
> require training for hundreds of epochs. GAN optimization is one of those problem sets
> that can be expensive to train. Because of this, if you want to see interesting or good
> results, expect to train some of these optimizations for hours or even days.

The next notebook is an extension and consolidation of the GAN code we have been
developing in this chapter into a single class. This class is instantiated by passing an
`individual` gene sequence to populate the various model hyperparameters. The gene
sequence is a simple array of floats we have seen many times before when employing
genetic algorithms.

Open the EDL_9_4_WDCGAN_encoder.ipynb notebook in Colab. Go ahead and
run all the cells by selecting Runtime > Run All from the menu.

In this notebook, a single class encapsulates the entire model and variation of each
class is controlled by an input gene sequence: an array of floats, where each element
in the array has a corresponding controlled hyperparameter defined by the index to
the sequence. The code to define these indexes and min/max limits of the hyperparameter values is shown in the following listing.

Listing 9.19   EDL_9_4_WDCGAN_encoder.ipynb: `gene` encoding parameters

```
FILTERS = 0          ◁—— Base number of filters used in convolution
MIN_FILTERS = 16
MAX_FILTERS = 128
ALPHA = 1            ◁—— Alpha parameter used in LeakyReLU
MIN_ALPHA = .05
MAX_ALPHA = .5
CRITICS = 2          ◁—— Number of critic iterations per generator
MIN_CRITICS = 1
MAX_CRITICS = 10
```

```
CLIP = 3              ◁——— The clipping range to clip critic weights
MIN_CLIP = .005
MAX_CLIP = .1
LR = 4                ◁——— The optimizer learning rate
MIN_LR = .00000001
MAX_LR = .0001
```

We can next look at the __init__ function of the DCGAN class to see how the gene sequence i defines each of the hyperparameters used in the model, as shown in listing 9.20. First, we make sure the image_shape is divisible by four and can fit within the model's convolutional architecture. Next, each of the hyperparameter values is generated by mapping the float to the corresponding space. The code also initiates the weights around the value zero to better align the weights with the clipping function. Finally, the code creates a single optimizer and then constructs the various models.

Listing 9.20 EDL_9_4_DCGAN_encoder.ipynb: Initializing the model

```
class DCGAN:
  def __init__(self, i):
    assert image_shape[0] % 4 == 0, "Image shape must
    ➥ be divisible by 4."        ◁
                                   | Confirms the image size is divisible by 4
    self.image_shape = image_shape
    self.z_size = (1, 1, latent_dim)

    self.n_filters = linespace_int(i[FILTERS],
    ➥ MIN_FILTERS, MAX_FILTERS)
    self.alpha = linespace_int(i[ALPHA], MIN_ALPHA,
    ➥ MAX_ALPHA)
    self.lr = linespace(i[LR], MIN_LR, MAX_LR)
    self.clip_lower = -linespace(i[CLIP], MIN_CLIP,     Converts float to a
    ➥ MAX_CLIP)                                        hyperparameter
    self.clip_upper = linespace(i[CLIP], MIN_CLIP,
    ➥ MAX_CLIP)
    self.critic_iters = linespace_int(i[CRITICS],
    ➥ MAX_CRITICS, MIN_CRITICS)
    self.weight_init = RandomNormal(mean=0.,
    ➥ stddev=0.02)
    self.optimizer = RMSprop(self.lr)    ◁——— Creates a single optimizer

    self.critic = self.build_critic()    Builds the
    self.g = self.build_generator()      models
    self.gan = self.build_gan()
```

Initializes the starting weights → (points to `self.weight_init = RandomNormal(mean=0., stddev=0.02)`)

Much of the remaining code we have seen before, but we should highlight an updated section in the training function, shown in listing 9.21. Comparing loss between models in GANs is complicated by variations in loss functions and model performance. To compare losses between one GAN and another, we normalize the loss. We do this by tracking the min and max losses for the critic and generator, and then we output this value on a linear space between 0 and 1, using the reverse_space function.

Listing 9.21   EDL_9_4_DCGAN_encoder.ipynb: Normalizing the output loss

```
min_g_loss = min(min_g_loss, g_loss)                    Tracks the
min_fake_loss = min(min_fake_loss, c_loss[1])           minimum loss
min_real_loss = min(min_real_loss, c_loss[0])

max_g_loss = max(max_g_loss, g_loss)                    Tracks the
max_fake_loss = max(max_fake_loss, c_loss[1])           maximum loss
max_real_loss = max(max_real_loss, c_loss[0])

loss = dict(
  Real = reverse_space(c_loss[0],min_real_loss,
  ➥ max_real_loss),
  Fake = reverse_space(c_loss[1],min_fake_loss,         Normalizes the
  ➥ max_fake_loss),                                     values to 0–1
  Gen = reverse_space(g_loss, min_g_loss, max_g_loss) )
```

By encapsulating everything into a class, including the training function, we can quickly instantiate a GAN with a known `gene` sequence to test the results. To do this, as shown in listing 9.22, we use the `reverse_space` function to convert known hyperparameter values to the appropriate float values embedded in the sequence, called an `individual`. This `individual` is then passed into the `DCGAN` construction to create the model. After that, the class's `train` function is called, using the `verbose=1` option to display the training results.

Listing 9.22   EDL_9_4_DCGAN_encoder.ipynb: Testing the encoding and GAN training

```
                                         Creates a random individual
individual = np.random.random((5))    ◄
individual[FILTERS] = reverse_space(128, MIN_FILTERS, MAX_FILTERS)
individual[ALPHA] = reverse_space(.2, MIN_ALPHA, MAX_ALPHA)
individual[CLIP] = reverse_space(.01, MIN_CLIP, MAX_CLIP)          Converts values
individual[CRITICS] = reverse_space(5, MIN_CRITICS, MAX_CRITICS)   to 0–1 space
individual[LR] = reverse_space(.00005, MIN_LR, MAX_LR)
print(individual)
                                 Creates the model
                                 with the individual
dcgan = DCGAN(individual)    ◄                      Trains the model, and
history = dcgan.train(train_images, verbose=1)  ◄   shows the results
```

Figure 9.12 shows the results of training the model over 10 epochs on an extracted class from the MNIST Handwritten Digits dataset. By normalizing the loss, we can clearly see what the model is working to optimize. If you compare these results to figure 9.11, you can clearly see how easy it is to identify the target of optimization within a known range. This is a critical piece to optimizing the model when using genetic algorithms, as discussed later in this chapter.

Go ahead and try other hyperparameter values to see how these affect model training. You may want to try using completely random `gene` sequences to see what the model generates as well.

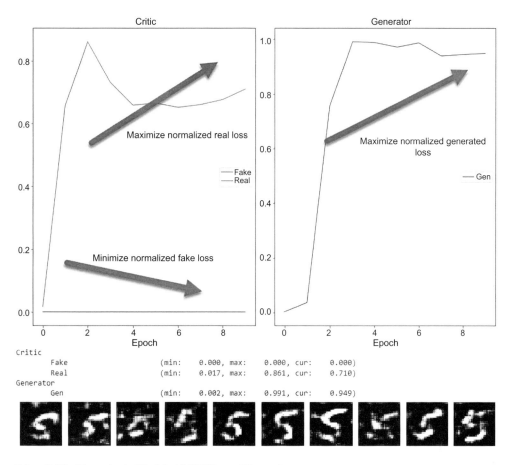

Figure 9.12   The output of training DCGAN over 10 epochs

9.4.1   Learning exercises

Use the following exercise to improve your understanding of the WGAN:

1 Increase or decrease the `gene` encoding hyperparameters in listing 9.19 and then rerun the notebook.
2 Don't use the `extract` function to limit the dataset to a single class and then rerun the notebook with all the data.
3 Use a different dataset, like Fashion-MNIST and then rerun the notebook.

Now that we have an encapsulated class that represents the GAN and the ability to pass a representative `gene` sequence to initialize the model, we can move on to optimization. In the next section, we add the genetic algorithm code to optimize this DCGAN model.

9.5   *Optimizing the DCGAN with genetic algorithms*

Now that we have the genetic encoder built for replicating a DCGAN, we can pull everything together. At this point, optimizing the encapsulated DCGAN class is a matter of simply adding DEAP and defining the GA parameters we require for evolution. Again, adding evolutionary search provides us the ability to self-optimize GAN networks—which is exactly what we do in the next notebook.

Open the EDL_9_5_EVO_DCGAN.ipynb notebook in Colab. Run the entire notebook by selecting Runtime > Run All from the menu.

As you may notice, this notebook installs DEAP and adds the required tools and operators for performing GA evolution. Code cells that are not relevant are hidden, but if you want to review their contents, just click the Show Code link or double-click on the cell. We have seen most of this code before, and as always, we just refer to the relevant code sections here.

We first look at the evaluate function, shown in listing 9.23, where we evaluate the fitness of the model. At the start of the function, we convert the individual to a string for use as an index in the trained dictionary. Notice how we are rounding the values to a single decimal point. Thus, a starting value of [.2345868] becomes [.2], which simplifies or discretizes the number of entries in the dictionary. This is done to simplify the training from an infinite exploration space to a finite one. To be precise, by rounding off the values to a single digit and knowing the gene sequence length is 5, we can determine that there are $10 \times 10 \times 10 \times 10 \times 10 = 100,000$ possible models to test. The real benefit of doing this is that it allows greater populations to be evolved, without having to reevaluate similar individuals. As shown in this section, evaluating each model takes a significant amount of time.

Listing 9.23   EDL_9_5_EVO_DCGAN_encoder.ipynb: The evaluate function

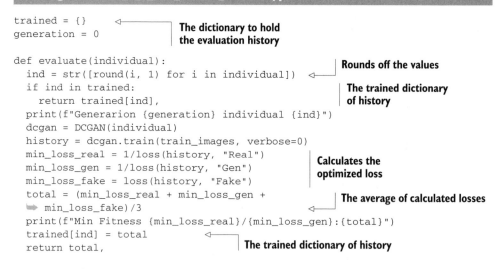

```
trained = {}              ◁──────────     The dictionary to hold
generation = 0                            the evaluation history

def evaluate(individual):
  ind = str([round(i, 1) for i in individual])    ◁──     Rounds off the values
  if ind in trained:                                      The trained dictionary
    return trained[ind],                                  of history
  print(f"Generarion {generation} individual {ind}")
  dcgan = DCGAN(individual)
  history = dcgan.train(train_images, verbose=0)
  min_loss_real = 1/loss(history, "Real")
  min_loss_gen = 1/loss(history, "Gen")               Calculates the
  min_loss_fake = loss(history, "Fake")               optimized loss
  total = (min_loss_real + min_loss_gen +
➥   min_loss_fake)/3          ◁──────     The average of calculated losses
  print(f"Min Fitness {min_loss_real}/{min_loss_gen}:{total}")
  trained[ind] = total        ◁──
  return total,                         The trained dictionary of history

toolbox.register("evaluate", evaluate)
```

Optimizing a DCGAN is not a simple matter of comparing accuracy. We need to account for three output values or losses from the model: the real, fake, and generated losses. Each of these losses need to be optimized—in this case, minimized—in different ways. If you refer to listing 9.23, you can see how each loss is extracted and, in the case of the real and generated losses, which are inverted to produce a partial `fitness`. The total `fitness` is calculated as an average of the three derived loss or `fitness` values.

The output in the notebook shows the partial results of evolving an optimal solution for the DCGAN. We leave it up to you to run this example further and explore the best potential GAN you can produce.

The last notebook can take a significant amount of time to evolve, but it is automated and will eventually produce good results. As AutoML solutions go, GANs, or other complex models, are not typically high on the list of those requiring automated optimization. Over time and as the field of AI/ML evolves, methods like the one we introduced here will likely become more mainstream.

9.5.1 *Learning exercises*

Use the following exercises to continue exploring this version of an Evo DCGAN:

1 Take the time to evolve a GAN model. Then, use this model to continue training on a dataset to see how well you can generate new output.
2 Take an evolved model developed on one dataset and reuse it to train a GAN on a new dataset. This works best on datasets with similar sizes, like the Fashion-MNIST and MNIST Handwritten Digits datasets.
3 Adapt this notebook to use evolutionary strategies and/or differential evolution. Evaluate how well this may or may not improve the evolution of the GAN training hyperparameters.

Summary

- Generative adversarial networks are a form of generative modeling that employs dual networks—one for data discrimination and the other for data generation:
  - GANs work by feeding real samples to the discriminator while, at the same time, allowing the generator to generate fake samples.
  - The generator learns to generate better output by getting feedback from the discriminator, which is also learning to better classify data as real or fake.
  - Building a GAN can be done simply with Python and Keras.
- GANs are notoriously difficult to train effectively:
  - The core problem in training GANs is attaining a balance between how quickly the discriminator and generator learn.
  - Both networks need to learn at the same rate to balance their adversarial relationship.

- When GANs fall out of balance, many common problems can occur, such as the inability to converge, mode collapse, and vanishing gradients.
  - Solving this problem of training can be tackled by using evolutionary algorithms.
- Wasserstein loss, or earthmover distance, is a measure of loss that can help a GAN resolve or minimize common training problems.
- Balancing the training hyperparameters of a GAN can be assisted by encapsulating a GAN (DCGAN) into a class that accepts a genetic encoded genome representation for evolutionary optimization.
- Genetic algorithms can be used to balance the training of a discriminator and generator within a GAN.

NEAT: NeuroEvolution of Augmenting Topologies

This chapter covers

- Building evolving augmenting topological networks
- Visualizing a NeuroEvolution of Augmenting Topologies network
- Exercising the capabilities of NeuroEvolution of Augmenting Topologies
- Exercising NeuroEvolution of Augmenting Topologies to classify images
- Uncovering the role of speciation in neuroevolution

Over the course of the last couple of chapters, we explored the evolutionary optimization of generative adversarial and autoencoder networks. Much like our previous chapters, in those exercises, we layered or wrapped evolutionary optimization around DL networks. In this chapter, we break from distributed evolutionary algorithms in Python (DEAP) and Keras to explore a neuroevolutionary framework called *NeuroEvolution of Augmenting Topologies* (NEAT).

NEAT was developed by Ken Stanley in 2002 while at the University of Texas at Austin. At the time, GAs (evolutionary computation) and DL (advanced neural networks) were equals, and both were considered the next big things in AI. Stanley's NEAT framework captured the attention of many because it combined neural networks with evolution to not just optimize hyperparameters, weight parameters, and architecture but the actual neural connections themselves.

Figure 10.1 shows a comparison between a regular DL network and an evolved NEAT network. In the figure, new connections have been added and removed, and the position of a node has been removed and/or altered in the evolved NEAT network. Notice how this differs from our previous efforts of simply altering the number of nodes in a DL-connected layer.

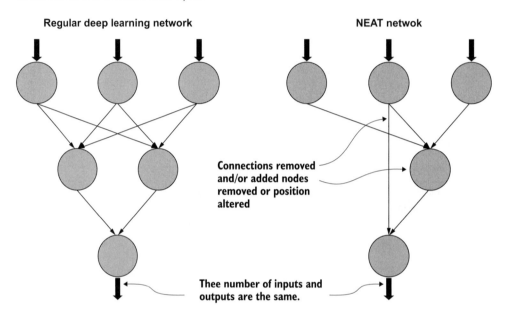

Figure 10.1   A comparison between DL and NEAT networks

NEAT takes the concept of evolving a DL network to the limit by allowing the network's neural connections and number of nodes to evolve. Since NEAT also internally evolves the network weights of each node, the complexities of calculating backpropagation of errors using calculus are eliminated. This allows NEAT networks to evolve to some complex interwoven and interconnected graphs. It can even allow networks to evolve recurrent connections, as we see in the next chapter when we explore NEAT in greater depth.

In this chapter, we explore the basics of NEAT and dig into a Python implementation called NEAT-Python. This framework does a good job of abstracting the finer details of setting up evolution and DL systems. The following list identifies each component of NEAT that encompasses many of the other methods used throughout this book:

- *Neuroevolution of parameters*—Weights and parameters in NEAT evolve as part of the system. In chapter 6, we used evolution to alter the weights of a neural network.
- *Neuroevolution of architecture*—NEAT evolves network layers, and the structure itself adapts through evolution. See chapter 7, in which we covered neuroevolving architectures using genetic algorithms, for more on the topic.
- *Hyperparameter optimization*—NEAT doesn't use learning rates, optimizers, or other standard DL assisters. As such, it doesn't need to optimize those parameters. However, NEAT, as we will see, introduces several hyperparameters to control network evolution.

In the next section, we start our exploration of NEAT by starting with the basics.

10.1   *Exploring NEAT with NEAT-Python*

The first notebook we look at in this chapter sets up a NEAT network to solve the classic first-order XOR problem. NEAT exposes several configuration options, and this first exercise showcases some of the most important ones. Open your web browser, and let's start looking at some code.

Open the EDL_10_1_NEAT_XOR.ipynb notebook in Google Colab. Refer to the appendix if you need assistance. Run all the cells in the notebook by selecting Runtime > Run All from the menu.

NEAT-Python is still in active development, and at the time of writing, the best practice is to install it directly from the GitHub repository rather than the PyPi package. The first code cell in the notebook does this using `pip` on the first line, as shown in the following listing. Then, the next line imports the package with `import neat`.

> **Listing 10.1   EDL_10_1_NEAT_XOR.ipynb: Install NEAT-Python**

```
!pip install
➥ git+https://github.com/CodeReclaimers/neat-python.git    ⟵┐  Installs from the
                                                             │  GitHub repository
#then import
import neat   ⟵——— Imports the package
```

Scrolling down, the next cell shows the setup of the data, divided into the `xor_inputs` (X) and the `xor_outputs` (Y), as shown in the following listing.

> **Listing 10.2   EDL_10_1_NEAT_XOR.ipynb: The data setup**

```
xor_inputs = [(0.0, 0.0), (0.0, 1.0), (1.0, 0.0),
➥ (1.0, 1.0)]                                       ⟵——— Inputs: X
xor_outputs = [    (0.0,),      (1.0,),      (1.0,),
➥ (0.0,)]                                            ⟵——— Outputs: Y
```

Next, as we have done several times before, we build an evaluation function to calculate the `fitness` of an evolved NEAT network. The concept here should be quite familiar now, and the code is similar to that in previous exercises. Unlike with DEAP, the evaluation function takes a set of gene sequences called genomes. The function loops through the genomes and calculates the fitness for each, starting by assigning some maximum fitness, as shown in listing 10.3. Then, it creates a new version of a classic feed-forward network using the FeedForwardNetwork.create function passing in the genome and a config. The constructed network is then exercised on all the data by using the net.activate function, passing in one of the X or xi values and producing the Y output. After each input is activated, the output is compared with the expected output, xo, and the mean squared error (MSE) is subtracted from the genome.fitness. Finally, the result of the eval_genomes function updates the current fitness of each evolved genome.

Listing 10.3   EDL_10_1_NEAT_XOR.ipynb: Creating the evaluation function

```
def eval_genomes(genomes, config):          Loops through genomes
    for genome_id, genome in genomes:   ←┘
        genome.fitness = 4.0            ←──── Assigns the maximum fitness
        net = neat.nn.FeedForwardNetwork.create
              (genome, config)          ←──── Creates a NEAT network
        for xi, xo in zip(xor_inputs, xor_outputs):   from the genome
            output = net.activate(xi)
            genome.fitness -= (output[0] - xo[0]) ** 2   ←── Calculates the MSE and then
                                                             subtracts from the fitness
```

Loops through the data (annotation pointing to the `for genome_id` and `for xi, xo` lines)

The next cell sets up the configuration file we use to configure and run the NEAT code. NEAT-Python (NP) is primarily configuration driven, and there are several options you can alter or tweak. To keep things simple, we just review the primary options in listing 10.4: the first two sections. The config starts by setting the fitness criterion, a fitness threshold, population size, and reset option. After that, the default genome configuration is set, first with the option for activation, which, in this case, is simply the sigmoid function. NEAT allows you to choose from a number of activation functions as options used for both internal interconnected nodes and outputs.

Listing 10.4   EDL_10_1_NEAT_XOR.ipynb: Configuration setup

```
%%writefile config      ←──── Writes the contents of a cell to a file called config

[NEAT]                   ←──── The general configuration parameters
fitness_criterion     = max
fitness_threshold     = 3.99
pop_size              = 150  ←──── Sets the number of individuals to evolve
reset_on_extinction   = False

[DefaultGenome]         ←──── The genome configuration parameters
# node activation options
activation_default    = sigmoid
activation_mutate_rate = 0.0
activation_options    = sigmoid   ←──── The default activation function
```

The last code cell in the notebook contains all the code we need to evolve a NEAT network. We start by reviewing the first few lines in listing 10.5. The code starts by loading the configuration and setting the base assumptions for the type of `genome`, `reproduction`, `speciation`, and `stagnation`. We cover each of those defaults later in this and the next chapter. After that, the `genome` population is created from the `config`. Then, a reporter, the `StdOutReporter`, is added to the `population` object to track the evolutionary process. Notice how the `population` object p becomes the focus for evolution and is how it differs from DEAP.

Listing 10.5   EDL_10_1_NEAT_XOR.ipynb: Setting up NEAT evolution

```
config = neat.Config(neat.DefaultGenome, neat.DefaultReproduction,
                     neat.DefaultSpeciesSet, neat.DefaultStagnation,
                     'config')

p = neat.Population(config)

p.add_reporter(neat.StdOutReporter(False))
```

Creates the population

Loads the configuration from the config file

Adds a reporter to see results while evolving

Running or performing the evolution of the `population` is simply done by calling the `run` function on the `population` object, as shown in the following listing. After evolution is complete, the code prints out the winner, or `genome` with the best `fitness`, and outputs the prediction over the XOR inputs.

Listing 10.6   EDL_10_1_NEAT_XOR.ipynb: Evolving the `population`

```
winner = p.run(eval_genomes)

print('\nBest genome:\n{!s}'.format(winner))

print('\nOutput:')
winner_net = neat.nn.FeedForwardNetwork.create(winner, config)
for xi, xo in zip(xor_inputs, xor_outputs):
    output = winner_net.activate(xi)
    print(" input {!r}, expected output {!r}, got {!r}".format(xi, xo,
    ⟶ output))
```

Performs evolution on the population

Prints out the best genome

Uses the genome to predict XOR and display

The output of running this example is shown in figure 10.2. Unlike DEAP, NP uses the concept of `fitness` thresholds to control evolution iterations. If you recall, in the `config` setup, we set the `fitness_threshold` to `3.99` (see listing 10.4). The figure also shows the textual output of the network configuration and weights. Of course, this is not something easily visualized, but we cover that in a future section. At the bottom of the figure, you can see how well the XOR inputs are being correctly predicted.

This exercise demonstrated how we can quickly set up a NEAT evolution to create a network capable of predicting the XOR function. As you can see, there are plenty of details abstracted through the code, but hopefully, at this stage, you understand some of the inner workings of how evolution is being applied. Aside from the augmenting

```
****** Running generation 53 ******

Population's average fitness: 2.43254 stdev: 0.50393
Best fitness: 3.99818 - size: (2, 5) - species 6 - id 7700          Maximum fitness of 3.99 exceeded

Best individual in generation 53 meets fitness threshold - complexity: (2, 5)

Best genome:
Key: 7700
Fitness: 3.99817583108197
Nodes:
        0 DefaultNodeGene(key=0, bias=-1.4205106523656705, response=1.0, activation=sigmoid, aggregation=sum)
        321 DefaultNodeGene(key=321, bias=-1.897319643633109, response=1.0, activation=sigmoid, aggregation=sum)
Connections:
        DefaultConnectionGene(key=(-2, 0), weight=-1.421129174816354, enabled=True)
        DefaultConnectionGene(key=(-2, 321), weight=2.255678382048443, enabled=True)  Summary of network architecture
        DefaultConnectionGene(key=(-1, 0), weight=2.07042241033656, enabled=True)           and weights
        DefaultConnectionGene(key=(-1, 321), weight=-3.888509740443919, enabled=True)
        DefaultConnectionGene(key=(321, 0), weight=6.231066342700942, enabled=True)

Output:
  input (0.0, 0.0), expected output (0.0,), got [0.0008242682360126595]
  input (0.0, 1.0), expected output (1.0,), got [0.9999962603001374]     Network prediction outputs of XOR
  input (1.0, 0.0), expected output (1.0,), got [0.9626572551545072]                  inputs
  input (1.0, 1.0), expected output (0.0,), got [0.020712529862966646]
```

Figure 10.2   The final output of evolving a NEAT network on XOR

node topologies, we have performed everything being done internally previously with DEAP.

10.1.1 *Learning exercises*

Use the following learning exercises to understand more about NEAT:

1 Alter the `population` size (`pop_size`) in listing 10.4 and then rerun the notebook. How does `population` size affect evolution?

2 Decrease the `fitness_threshold` in listing 10.4 and then see what effect this has on the results after rerunning the notebook.

3 Change the inputs or outputs to match another function or write a function to create the outputs in listing 10.2. Then, rerun the notebook to see the results of approximating the new function.

From this basic introduction, we move on to explore visualizing what an evolved NEAT network looks like in the next section.

10.2 *Visualizing an evolved NEAT network*

Now that we have the basics of setting up NEAT-Python out of the way, we can look at adding some useful tools to our tool belt. Visualizing a NEAT network can be useful for understanding how the network architecture is forming. It also highlights how well the network is overfitting or underfitting a problem.

   In this section, we take the previous notebook example and add the ability to visualize the evolved best `genome` network. We also take a close look at how the evaluation `fitness` function is developed.

Open the EDL_10_2_NEAT_XOR_Visualized.ipynb notebook in Google Colab. Refer to the appendix if you need assistance. Run all the cells in the notebook by selecting Runtime > Run All from the menu.

Jump down to the code cell after the `config` is loaded to start. All this code is normally handled within the `population` class, but we extracted this small section, shown in listing 10.7, to highlight building an evaluation function. In NP, all `genomes` need a key or unique identifier, and here we arbitrarily use `fred`. Then, a `genome` is created from `config` based on the default type—in this case, a `DefaultGenome`. After that, the `genome` is configured with `genome.configure_new` passing in the `genome_config`. Finally, a new `fred` 1.0 random network is created, with `FeedForwardNetwork.create` passing in the `genome` and `config`.

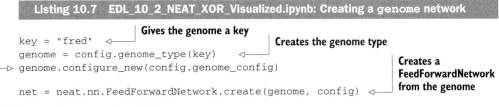

Listing 10.7   EDL_10_2_NEAT_XOR_Visualized.ipynb: Creating a genome network

```
key = "fred"                                      ← Gives the genome a key
genome = config.genome_type(key)                  ← Creates the genome type
genome.configure_new(config.genome_config)        → Configures the genome from config
                                                    Creates a FeedForwardNetwork from the genome
net = neat.nn.FeedForwardNetwork.create(genome, config) ←
```

Next, the network `net` is `evaluated`, using a `for` loop to iterate over the data to accumulate the MSE subtracted from a max `fitness`, as shown in listing 10.8. Recall that within the actual evaluation function in listing 10.4, the code also looped through the full `population` of `genomes`. For simplicity, we just `evaluate` the genome `fred` here. The output of this code block shows the input and output from the network as well as the total `fitness`.

Listing 10.8   EDL_10_2_NEAT_XOR_Visualized.ipynb: Evaluating the genome

```
fitness = 4                          ← Assigns a maximum value for fitness
for x, y in zip(X, Y):               ← Loops through the x and y values
  output = net.activate(x)           ← Activates the network on the input
  print(output, y)
  fitness -= (output[0]-y[0])**2     ← Calculates the MSE and then subtracts
print(fitness)
```

Following the setup of `fred`, we move on to the `draw_net` function. This function has been directly extracted from the NEAT examples and uses Graphviz to draw an evolved network. Go ahead and review the code on your own, but we won't focus on the specifics here. Rather, we want to look at how to call the function and what it generates.

Calling the `draw_net` function is shown next; it starts with naming the input and output nodes in a dictionary. After that, the `draw_net` function is called by passing in the `config`, a `genome`, and the names of the primary nodes (input and output). We pass in the value `True` to visualize the output, as shown in the following listing.

Listing 10.9   EDL_10_2_NEAT_XOR_Visualized.ipynb: Calling the `draw_net` function

```
node_names = {-1: 'X1', -2: 'X2', 0: 'Output'}    ◄──── Name the input
draw_net(config, genome, True, node_names=node_names)        and output nodes.
```
Call the function with True to view.

Figure 10.3 shows the output of the base and unevolved `genome` we have called `fred`. As you can see, the network is a very simple one-node network with two inputs, labeled X1 and X2.

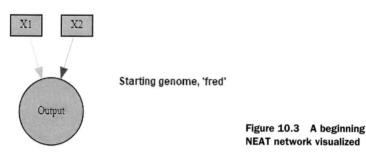

Starting genome, 'fred'

Figure 10.3   A beginning NEAT network visualized

At this point, the NEAT `population` should have evolved, and we can again call the `draw_net` function, this time passing in the winning `genome` winner. Calling `run` on `population` outputs the winner, or best `genome`. Then, the network is created from the winner to demonstrate activations. Next, `draw_net` is called with the winner's `genome` to visualize the network, as shown in the following listing.

Listing 10.10   EDL_10_2_NEAT_XOR_Visualized.ipynb: Visualizing the winning genome

```
winner = p.run(eval_genomes)    ◄──── Evolves the winner genome

print('\nBest genome:\n{!s}'.format(winner))    ◄──── Outputs the winner score

print('\nOutput:')
winner_net = neat.nn.FeedForwardNetwork.create(winner, config)
for xi, xo in zip(X, Y):    ◄───┐
  output = winner_net.activate(xi)    │ Loops through and shows activations
  print("  input {!r}, expected output {!r}, got {!r}".format(xi, xo,
➥ output))
                                              ┌── Draws the evolved
draw_net(config, winner, True, node_names=node_names)    ◄──┘ winning genome
```

Figure 10.4 shows the output of the winning `genome` network. This certainly doesn't resemble the classic DL network with regular layers. Instead, what we see here is an optimized network capable of efficiently processing the XOR problem.

Being able to visualize the resulting evolved network is helpful for understanding how NEAT works. It can also be helpful to visualize an evolving network to see and understand if the configuration parameters are adequate. As we see in the next section, NEAT has many knobs and dials we need to understand to develop solutions to more complex problems.

```
1   draw_net(config, winner, True, node_names=node_names)
```

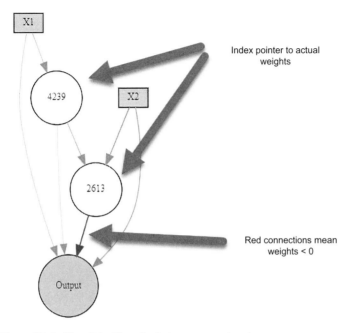

Figure 10.4   Visualizing the winning genome network

10.3   *Exercising the capabilities of NEAT*

NEAT and its implementation in NEAT-Python are tools that encapsulate many of the optimization patterns we have practiced in this book. NEAT incorporates network hyperparameter, architecture, and parameter optimization as well as augmenting topologies. But does it do it well?

In this section, we revisit one of our fun visual classification examples that used the sklearn package to make example datasets. If you recall, we demonstrated parameter weight optimization with EC in chapter 6. Not only does this provide an excellent baseline, but it also demonstrates several other configuration options of NEAT.

Open the EDL_10_3_NEAT_Circles.ipynb notebook in Google Colab. Refer to the appendix if you need assistance. Run all the cells in the notebook by selecting Runtime > Run All from the menu.

We start with the Dataset Parameters form and output shown in figure 10.5. This is the same form we used in earlier chapters to generate various forms of classification problem datasets. To start, we use the moons problem to generate a simple dataset. The generated output shows a dataset that should be relatively easy to classify with a simple network.

Since we are handling more complex problems than XOR now, we want to alter the configuration options in the NEAT config file. Listing 10.11 is still only a partial view of all the `config` options, and we again highlight the critical ones, starting with

Dataset Parameters

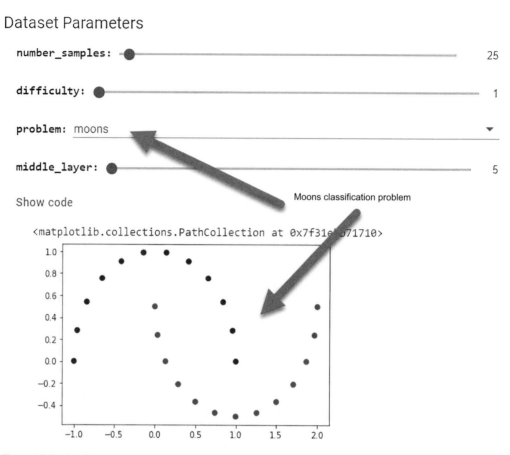

Figure 10.5   Configuring parameters for dataset generation

reducing the maximum `fitness_threshold` to `3.0` out of `4.0`, or 75%. Then, we increase or add a middle or in-between node layer. With NEAT, we don't think of nodes in layers; rather, we only concern ourselves with the number of input/output and middle, or in-between, nodes. If those middle nodes happen to align in layers, that is a happy accident but not something to be expected. Next, we are presented with a couple of options, starting with compatibility. These options are for `speciation` and will be covered later. The last thing to note is that we've updated the activation options by adding two other possible functions (`identity` and `relu`).

Listing 10.11   EDL_10_3_NEAT_Circles.ipynb: Checking the configuration options

```
[NEAT]
fitness_criterion    = max
fitness_threshold    = 3.0      ◁┐  The fitness_threshold
pop_size             = 250       │  is reduced to 3.0.
reset_on_extinction  = 0
```

```
[DefaultGenome]
num_inputs                          = 2
num_hidden                          = 10
num_outputs                         = 1
initial_connection       = partial_direct 0.5
feed_forward             = True
compatibility_disjoint_coefficient     = 1.0
compatibility_weight_coefficient       = 0.6
conn_add_prob            = 0.2
conn_delete_prob         = 0.2
node_add_prob            = 0.2
node_delete_prob         = 0.2
activation_default       = sigmoid
activation_options       = sigmoid identity relu
activation_mutate_rate   = 0.1
```

Increases the number of hidden middle nodes

Used for speciation

The activation options are expanded.

Figure 10.6 shows the output of a starting genome network, with the new configuration options applied. It is interesting to note that not all nodes are connected to the output and node 10 is not connected to inputs or outputs. This allows the network to eliminate unneeded nodes, which prevents problems of over- or underfitting.

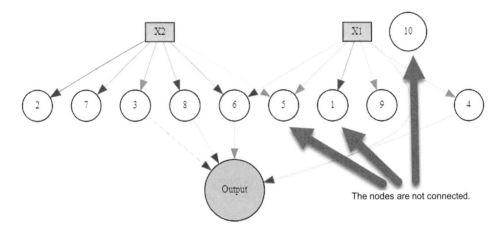

The nodes are not connected.

Figure 10.6   The output of an unevolved random network

At this point, jump down to the bottom of the notebook and review the evolution code, as shown in the following listing. Most of this code has been covered, but notice the addition of the CustomReporter = to the population, p, with the add_reporter function call. The addition of this custom report allows us to fine-tune the evolution output and allows us to add visuals.

Listing 10.12   EDL_10_3_NEAT_Circles.ipynb: Evolving the network

```
p = neat.Population(config)        ◁──── Creates the population

p.add_reporter(CustomReporter(False))    ◁──── Adds CustomReporter for visuals
```

```
winner = p.run(eval_genomes)    ◄─── Evaluates a winner

print('\nBest genome:\n{!s}'.format(winner))           ◄─┐

print('\nOutput:')                                     ◄─┤   Outputs
winner_net = neat.nn.FeedForwardNetwork.create(winner, config)   results
show_predictions(winner_net, X, Y)
draw_net(config, winner, True, node_names=node_names)  ◄─┘
```

Scroll up to the `CustomReporter` class definition, shown in listing 10.13. NEAT-Python allows for various customizations, and this implementation is just a copy of the standard reporter, with a small addition for visualizing fitting progress. Inside this new reporter class, we add custom code to the `post_evaluate` function, which is called after the `genomes` are `evaluated`. We don't want this code to render for every iteration, so we add a modulo check that is controlled with a new `self.gen_display` parameter set in the `init` function. If the `generation` is equal to the display gen, then the code creates a network from the `genome` and `evaluates` it in an update `show_predictions` function.

Listing 10.13   EDL_10_3_NEAT_Circles.ipynb: The `CustomReporter` class definition

```
from neat.math_util import mean, stdev           The class definition extends
                                                 from BaseReporter.
class CustomReporter(neat.reporting.BaseReporter):   ◄─┘
    "Uses 'print' to output information about the run; an example
reporter class."

    def __init__(self, show_species_detail,      The init function,
    ➡ gen_display=100):              ◄──────      shown for reference
        #omitted

    def post_evaluate(self, config, population, species,
    ➡ best_genome):                        ◄─┐                  The start of the
        #omitted                              Adds to post_evaluate    custom code
        if (self.generation) % self.gen_display == 0 :   ◄─┘
            net = neat.nn.FeedForwardNetwork.create(best_genome, config)
            show_predictions(net, X, Y)
            time.sleep(5)
```

Recall from chapter 6 how we first used the `show_predictions` function on Keras networks. Using this function on NEAT has been updated, which we can see in the following listing. The main change from the previous code is using the `net.activate` function instead of `model.predict` from Keras.

Listing 10.14   EDL_10_3_NEAT_Circles.ipynb: The updated `show_predictions` function

```
def show_predictions(net, X, Y, name=""):
    x_min, x_max = X[:, 0].min() - 1, X[:, 0].max() + 1     Creates a grid of
    y_min, y_max = X[:, 1].min() - 1, X[:, 1].max() + 1     inputs and outputs
```

```
xx, yy = np.meshgrid(np.arange(x_min, x_max, 0.01),
    np.arange(y_min, y_max, 0.01))
X_temp = np.c_[xx.flatten(), yy.flatten()]
Z = []

for x in X_temp:
  Z.append(net.activate(x))
Z = np.array(Z)
plt.figure("Predictions " + name)
plt.contourf(xx, yy, Z.reshape(xx.shape),
    cmap=plt.cm.Spectral)
plt.ylabel('x2')
plt.xlabel('x1')
plt.scatter(X[:, 0], X[:, 1],c=Y, s=40, cmap=plt.cm.Spectral)
plt.show()
```

Creates a grid of inputs and outputs

Activates the network and output results

Plots the results with a spectral map

Shows the output

Figure 10.7 shows the results of evolving a NEAT network over the moons problem dataset. Notice how most of the network nodes don't output to the output node. Your results and network may vary, but in the figure, you can see only two nodes are relevant and connect to the output.

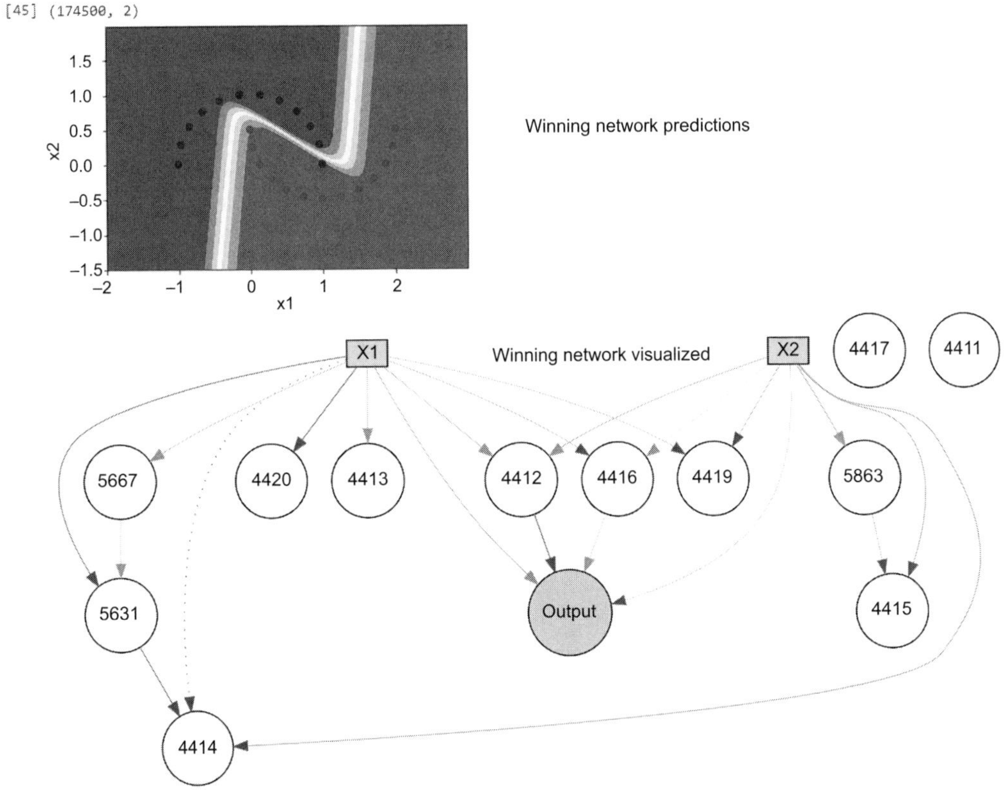

Figure 10.7 The output of evolving a NEAT network on the moons problem

If you recall, in chapter 6, our most difficult problem was the circles problem. Go ahead and switch the problem to circles and then run the notebook again. From experience, we know this problem is solvable using a standard Keras network. However, given our current configuration options, it is unlikely a solution will be found.

10.3.1 Learning exercises

Use the following exercises to explore the capabilities of NEAT:

1 Alter the number of data samples in figure 10.5. Observe what effect this has on NEAT approximation.
2 Change the problem type in figure 10.5 and then rerun the notebook. Does NEAT handle certain problems better than others?
3 Increase or decrease the number of hidden nodes (num_hidden) in listing 10.11. Then, try solving various problem types. What effect does the number of hidden nodes have on building solutions?

Before we get into properly solving the circles problem, we dive into a more practical example using NEAT in the next section.

10.4   Exercising NEAT to classify images

To really understand the limitations and capabilities of NEAT, we offer a practical comparison in this section. A well-established one comes to mind: image classification with the MNIST Handwritten Digits dataset. For our next exercise, we use NEAT to classify the MNIST dataset.

Open the EDL_10_4_NEAT_Images.ipynb notebook in Google Colab. Refer to the appendix if you need assistance. Run all the cells in the notebook by selecting Runtime > Run All from the menu.

This notebook loads the MNIST dataset, as shown in figure 10.8. We only use the training data portion of the dataset to evaluate the genome fitness over a batch sample. After the data is loaded, it is normalized, and then a sample digit is displayed. Note that we are using all 10 classes from the full dataset.

Next, we look at the various changes to the NEAT configuration options, shown in listing 10.15. The first change is the fitness threshold is now set to .25, or 25%. We will be updating the fitness function to score the evolving networks on accuracy rather than errors. Then, notice how the inputs have been increased to 784 to match the input images' 28×28 pixels, which are no different from a Keras model. In this exercise, we set the number of hidden nodes to 10 for demonstration. After that, we change the initial_connection option to full_direct. This essentially means we are starting with a fully connected network, not unlike a Keras sequential model. Near the bottom of the shown configuration options, we can see options set for the activation function, identity, and relu. Finally, we see a new aggregation option being employed. Aggregation is the operation that occurs inside the node or perceptron, and by default,

```
1   #@title Dataset Parameters  { run: "auto" }
2   mnist = tf.keras.datasets.mnist
3
4   (x_train, y_train), (x_test, y_test) = mnist.load_data()
5   X, Y = x_train / 255.0, y_train
6
7   plt.imshow(X[0])
8   print(Y[0])
```

Load the training dataset and normalize.

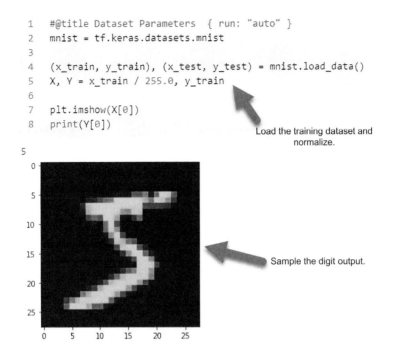

Sample the digit output.

Figure 10.8   Loading the MNIST training dataset

we always assume it to be summation. With NEAT, we can alter the aggregation function a node uses, as we do here.

Listing 10.15   EDL_10_4_NEAT_Images.ipynb: Updated configuration options

```
[NEAT]
fitness_criterion     = max
fitness_threshold     = .25      ◁──── Fitness is now accuracy.
pop_size              = 100
reset_on_extinction   = 1

[DefaultGenome]                          Flattened image inputs
num_inputs            = 784      ◁────
num_hidden            = 10       ◁──── The maximum number of middle nodes
num_outputs           = 10
initial_connection    = full_direct   ◁──── Always starts fully connected
feed_forward          = True
compatibility_disjoint_coefficient   = 1.0
compatibility_weight_coefficient     = 0.6
conn_add_prob         = 0.2
conn_delete_prob      = 0.2
node_add_prob         = 0.2
node_delete_prob      = 0.2
activation_default    = relu
activation_options    = identity relu   ◁──── The choice of activation functions
```

```
activation_mutate_rate  = 0.0
aggregation_default     = sum
aggregation_options     = sum mean product min max
  median                          ◁──────┐
aggregation_mutate_rate = 0.2            │  Alters the node aggregation function
┌─▷                                      
```
Always starts fully connected

From configuration, we jump down to updating the evaluation function, shown in
listing 10.16. Recall that we want to use accuracy for scoring fitness now, since our
networks will be classifying images. That means we want to score the network on a set
of images—typically, the training set. However, scoring the entire set of training
images is not practical, so instead, we take random batches of images to evaluate a
genome. In this notebook, we use a value of 256 to speed up performance. This batch
size is used to generate a random set of indexes that will be used to pull data from the
training sets X and Y.

Listing 10.16   EDL_10_4_NEAT_Images.ipynb: Random batching images

```
BATCH_SIZE = 256    ◁──┐  Sets the constant
idx = np.random.randint(0, X.shape[0], BATCH_SIZE)    ◁──── Samples random indexes
xs, ys = X[idx], Y[idx]    ◁────┐
                                │  Extracts the batch from the original data
```

After the evaluation batch of images and labels are extracted, we can evaluate a
genome network for accuracy, as shown in listing 10.17. As the code loops through
each image and label in the batch, it first flattens the 2D 28×28 image into 784 inputs.
From there, it activates the network and applies SoftMax and np.argmax functions to
get the predicted class. The class predictions are collected in a yis variable and later
used to extract a balanced accuracy score with the balanced_accuracy_score function. A detailed explanation of balanced accuracy can be found on the excellent
SciKit Learn documentation page covering the types of loss and metrics: http://mng
.bz/Q8G4. In summary, balanced accuracy balances predictions from unbalanced
datasets. Since the batch data we are using for evaluation is random, we can't assume
predictions will be balanced. Using balanced accuracy allows the evaluation to overcome any bias.

Listing 10.17   EDL_10_4_NEAT_Images.ipynb: Evaluating a genome fitness

```
from sklearn.metrics import balanced_accuracy_score
yis = []                                ┌  Loops through batch data
for x, y in zip(xs,ys):    ◁────────────┘
  x = np.reshape(x, (784,))    ◁──── Flattens the image
  output = net.activate(x)            ┌ Activates and scores
  class_ = softmax(output)            │ the output by class
  yis.append(np.argmax(class_))       
print(ys, yis)                                    ┌ Evaluates the genome
fitness = balanced_accuracy_score(ys, yis)   ◁────┘ balanced accuracy
print(fitness)
```

Scrolling down to the next cell, shown in the following listing, we can see the finished evaluation function the NEAT evolution will use. The code is the same as what we just reviewed, but it showcases it in the genome set evaluation function.

Listing 10.18   EDL_10_4_NEAT_Images.ipynb: The evaluate fitness function

```
def eval_genomes(genomes, config):
  for genome_id, genome in genomes:
    idx = np.random.randint(0, X.shape[0], BATCH_SIZE)      Extracts a random
    xs, ys = X[idx], Y[idx]                                 batch of data
    net = neat.nn.FeedForwardNetwork.create(genome, config)
    score = 0
    yis = []
    for x, y in zip(xs,ys):
      x = np.reshape(x, (784,))      ◁──── Flattens the image
      output = net.activate(x)
      output = softmax(output)
      class_ = np.argmax(output)      ◁──── Gets the predicted class
      yis.append(class_)                                              Evaluates all
    genome.fitness = fitness = balanced_accuracy_score(ys, yis)  ◁──┘ predictions
```

The code to run the evolution is the same as the code previously shown. Running this code to achieve just 25% accuracy will take some time, even with a few of the performance tweaks we added (e.g., setting the batch size). This is an unfortunate consequence of the current NEAT-Python implementation. DEAP, the framework we wrapped around Keras/PyTorch in previous examples, provides options for distributed computation. NEAT, being a much older framework, does not have this option.

Figure 10.9 demonstrates the predictive accuracy of a network trained to 25% accuracy. This figure was generated from the plot_classify function shown in previous notebooks. As you can see, the results are OK, given the evaluation is on the training set. Your results may be less accurate and will depend greatly on the batch size you set. Larger batch sizes increase accuracy but also extend evolution time to several minutes, or even hours.

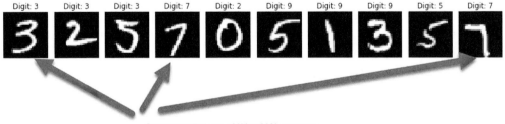

Correct predictions = 3/10 = 30% accuracy

Figure 10.9   The winning network prediction results

Finally, the last block of code in this notebook draws the winning genomes network using the draw_net function we have used previously. Unfortunately, the output of this network is unreadable, due to the plethora of connections. In most cases, evolved networks with the chosen configuration options have 10,000 or more connections—yes, you read that right.

So given the poor performance of this image classification notebook, what are the benefits of using a framework like NEAT? Well, much like several of the evolutionary examples of the previous chapters, NEAT works best on closed-form, smaller dataset optimization problems. As discussed later, that doesn't mean evolving topologies isn't a viable application of EDL but one that requires more fine-tuning.

10.4.1 Learning exercises

Use the following exercises to test the limits of NEAT further:

1 Swap the target dataset from MNIST Handwritten Digits to Fashion-MNIST. Does the model perform any better?

2 Increase or decrease the number of hidden nodes (num_hidden) in listing 10.15 and then rerun the notebook.

3 Play with the hyperparameters in listing 10.15 to attempt to improve the results. How well can you get the evolved network to classify digits or fashion?

We explore another evolving topology framework in the final chapter of the book. For now, though, we look at an interesting feature of NEAT that improves evolution, called speciation, in the next section.

10.5 Uncovering the role of speciation in evolving topologies

In the next notebook, we look at how NEAT employs a feature called speciation to track population diversity. *Speciation*, originating in biology, is a way of describing how similar organisms evolve unique traits to become different species. The concept of *species*, first developed by Darwin, is a way of describing or breaking down how life evolved on Earth.

Figure 10.10 shows how a biologist would identify the species and subspecies of a dog in a taxonomy chart. *Taxonomy* is a tool biologists use to show or classify the evolution of life on Earth. At the top of the figure, a dog subspecies is identified, showing how a biologist would define the common household dog.

NEAT uses the same concept of grouping genomes into species for optimization and diversification. Grouping genomes into species highlights how a diverse population of networks may evolve. If you recall from previous chapters, we often want to keep a population diverse to avoid falling into the trap of some local maxima or minima.

Not encouraging diversity often causes an evolving population to become too specialized or fixed to some local minima/maxima. In the real world, organisms that become overly specialized and unable to adapt go extinct, due to constant changes.

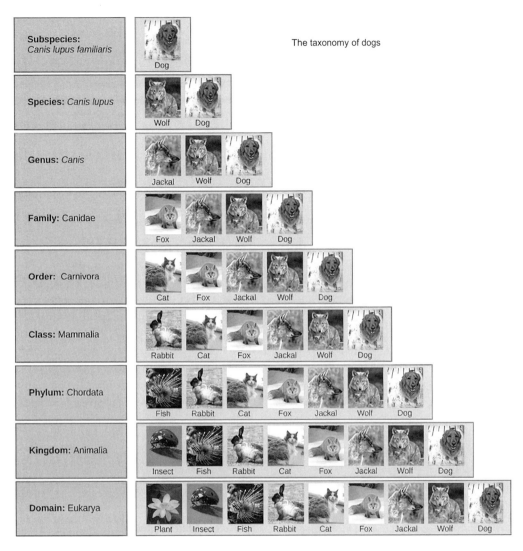

Figure 10.10 The taxonomy of a dog breed

Extinction bias

In our world, we often view species extinction purely as a bad event. This is certainly because we, as humans, are now able to identify the role of our own actions in the ongoing extinction of thousands of species worldwide. Without human intervention, though, extinction is a natural process that life has undergone for billions of years on Earth. Within evolutionary computation, extinction can also be a good thing, as it encourages diversity and better individual performance.

NEAT also uses the concept of extinction to force species to constantly evolve or become extinct. Doing so promotes species from becoming stagnant or overly specialized and encourages population diversity. In the next section, we look at how using speciation can help NEAT solve complex problems.

10.5.1 *Tuning NEAT speciation*

The next notebook revisits the circles set of problems we looked at in the previous notebook. This time, we look at making a few minor improvements to the notebook and how the NEAT speciation feature can help. We also explore some more of the NEAT configuration options, of which there are several.

Open the EDL_10_5_NEAT_Speciation.ipynb notebook in Google Colab. Refer to the appendix if you need assistance. Run all the cells in the notebook by selecting Runtime > Run All from the menu.

NEAT-Python is heavily driven by configuration options that can control every aspect of the genome's evolution, including the node connections, nodes, activation/aggregation functions, and weights. All those options give a lot of power to NEAT, but they also make it more difficult to evolve networks over complex problems. To solve the circles problem, we need to better understand how those configuration options play with each other.

Scroll down to the NEAT configuration options section, shown in listing 10.19. For this notebook, we have updated the fitness function to produce a maximum fitness of 1.0. Because of that, we have also updated the fitness_threshold. The number of middle nodes has also been increased to 25 to allow the network topology room to grow. From experience, we know the circles problem is solvable, given a simple few-layer architecture. To reduce the number of topological changes within a network, we have greatly reduced the connection and node's chances of addition or deletion.

Listing 10.19   EDL_10_5_NEAT_Speciation.ipynb: NEAT configuration options

```
[NEAT]
fitness_criterion      = max
fitness_threshold      = .85      ◁── The revised fitness function
pop_size               = 100           replaces the threshold.
reset_on_extinction    = 1


[DefaultGenome]
num_inputs                = 2
num_hidden                = 25    ◁─── Increases the middle layer
num_outputs               = 1
initial_connection        = partial_direct 0.5
feed_forward              = True
compatibility_disjoint_coefficient   = 1.0
compatibility_weight_coefficient     = 0.6
conn_add_prob          = 0.02        Reduces the rate of
conn_delete_prob       = 0.02        connection changes
node_add_prob          = 0.02
node_delete_prob       = 0.02      Reduces the rate of node changes
```

Since we know the circles problem can be solved with just weight alteration, we focus on minimizing weight changes here. The idea here is to allow a `genome` to gradually adapt and slowly adjust weights. This is similar to the way we would reduce the learning rate when training a DL network. At the bottom of the file, we also updated two options to better control `speciation`, as shown in listing 10.20. The first option, `compatibility_threshold`, controls the distance between species—we will see what that means in a minute. The second is `max_stagnation`, which controls the number of `generations` to wait before checking for species extinction.

Listing 10.20   EDL_10_5_NEAT_Speciation.ipynb: More NEAT configuration options

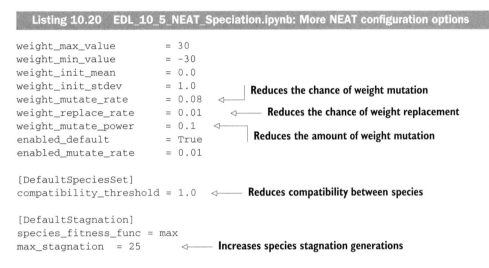

```
weight_max_value       = 30
weight_min_value       = -30
weight_init_mean       = 0.0
weight_init_stdev      = 1.0
weight_mutate_rate     = 0.08    ⟵┐      Reduces the chance of weight mutation
weight_replace_rate    = 0.01    ⟵──── Reduces the chance of weight replacement
weight_mutate_power    = 0.1     ⟵┐
enabled_default        = True          Reduces the amount of weight mutation
enabled_mutate_rate    = 0.01

[DefaultSpeciesSet]
compatibility_threshold = 1.0    ⟵──── Reduces compatibility between species

[DefaultStagnation]
species_fitness_func = max
max_stagnation   = 25            ⟵──── Increases species stagnation generations
```

Next, we look at how the `fitness` evaluation function has been updated to better evaluate the binary classification problem. If you recall, we used MSE for `fitness` evaluation previously. This time, we modify this slightly to better account for incorrect class classification. We could use a function like binary cross-entropy to calculate the error here, but instead, we use a simpler method of calculating the distance from the expected class. Thus, if the expected class is 0 and the network outputs .9, then the error is -.9. Likewise, if the class is 1 and the network outputs .2, the error is .8. Squaring the errors and appending them to the results removes the sign and allows us to use `np.mean` to extract the average error later. The total `fitness` is then calculated by subtracting the max `fitness`, now 1, from the average/mean error, as shown in the following listing.

Listing 10.21   EDL_10_5_NEAT_Speciation.ipynb: Updating `fitness` evaluation

```
results = []
for x, y in zip(X,Y):
  yi = net.activate(x)[0]    ⟵──── Predicts the class value between 0 and 1
  if y < .5:                        Calculates the error for class 0
    error = yi - y
  else:
```

```
    error = y - yi      ←——— Calculates the error for class 1
    print(yi, error)

    results.append(error*error)    ←——┐  Appends the squared error
    fitness = 1 - np.mean(results)  ←——┘
                                       Max fitness(1) – average error
print(fitness)
```

As the notebook is running, scroll down to the evolution code and view the results.
Figure 10.11 shows the results of evolving the network over a few generations. On the
left side of the figure, earlier on in evolution, NEAT is only tracking three species
(groups) of networks. The number of individuals in each species is controlled by
the compatibility_threshold option we saw earlier. Compatibility is a measure of
similarity between networks that may differ by the number of connections, connection
weights, nodes, and so on. Reducing the compatibility threshold creates more species
because the difference in compatibility/similarity between networks is small. Likewise,
increasing this threshold reduces the number of species.

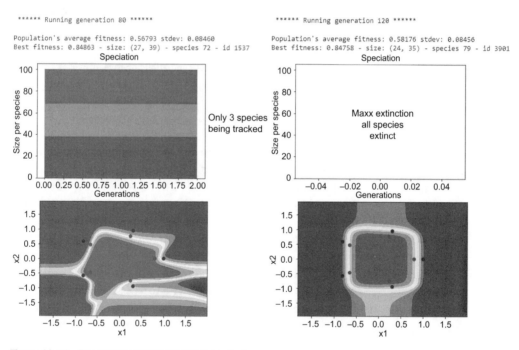

Figure 10.11　The results of training NEAT on circles

NEAT tracks the history of each speciation over the course of the evolutionary process. The max_stagnation option controls how many generations to wait before evaluating the progress of a particular species. After the stagnation period has elapsed,
species are evaluated for progress changes or advances. If at this point, a species
hasn't changed during the stagnation period, it becomes extinct and is removed from

the `population`. In figure 10.11, on the right side of the figure, all species have been marked as extinct. This has happened because the species stagnated, with no discernable changes to improving `fitness`. As it happens, the results of the current winning `genome` look relatively good, so it is likely the `stagnation` period may be too short.

Now it is your turn to go back and explore the various configuration options and see if you can solve the circles problem with greater than `.95 fitness`. Go ahead and make changes to the configuration options file, and after each change, select Runtime > Run All from the menu to rerun the entire notebook.

Go ahead and consult the NEAT-Python configuration options documentation, found here: http://mng.bz/X58E. This document provides further insights and detail into the many options available.

`Speciation` not only provides for increased diversity in `populations`, but it also demonstrates how evolving networks can become stagnant or stuck. The key to NEAT successfully solving complex problems then becomes balancing configuration option tuning. Fortunately, the more you work with NEAT, much like anything, the more you will understand how to turn those dials for better results.

10.5.2 *Learning exercises*

Use the following exercises to improve your understanding of NEAT `speciation`:

1 Increase or decrease the `compatibility_threshold` in listing 10.20 and then rerun the notebook to see what effect this has on the number of species.
2 Increase or decrease the number of maximum `stagnation` generations (`max_stagnation`) in listing 10.20 and then rerun the notebook to see the results.
3 Increase or decrease the `population` size to see what effect this may have on `speciation`. What happens when you use very small `populations`?

In the next chapter, we spend more time with NEAT (NEAT-Python) and explore more interesting and fun problems to solve.

Summary

- NeuroEvolution of Augmenting Topologies (NEAT) is an evolutionary framework that employs numerous techniques from hyperparameter optimization to evolving network architecture. NEAT-Python is an excellent framework that wraps all these complexities into a simple configuration-driven solution. NEAT is an evolutionary self-adapting architecture for DL networks.
- NEAT adapts and evolves the node weights and network architecture over `generations`. Visualizing and inspecting NEAT networks as they change topology can be informative in understanding how the framework functions.
- NEAT can solve various problems, like discontinuous function approximation and other complex classification problems as well as other difficult, closed-form problems.
- NEAT can be used to perform image classification tasks with some limited results.

- `Speciation` is an evolutionary term that refers to classes or subsets of individuals being grouped by similar features. NEAT uses `speciation` to evaluate the performance of groups of `individuals` (species) that may have become stagnant. Stagnant species can then be culled for extinction and removed from the `population` pool. Extinction allows new groups of `individuals` to be established within a fixed `population`.

Evolutionary learning with NEAT

11

This chapter covers

- Introducing to reinforcement learning
- Exploring complex problems from the OpenAI Gym
- Using NEAT as an agent to solve reinforcement learning problems
- Solving Gym's lunar lander problem with a NEAT agent
- Solving Gym's lunar lander problem with a deep Q-network

In the last chapter, we explored NeuroEvolution of Augmenting Topologies (NEAT) to solve common problems we explored in previous chapters. In this chapter, we look at the evolution of learning itself. First, we use NEAT to develop an evolving agent that can solve problems typically associated with RL. Then, we look at more difficult RL problems and provide a NEAT solution for evolutionary learning. Finally, we finish the chapter by looking at how our understanding of learning itself needs to evolve, using a mental model called *instinctual learning*.

11.1 *Introducing reinforcement learning*

Reinforcement learning (RL) is a form of learning based on animal behavior and psychology that attempts to replicate how organisms learn through rewards. If you have ever trained a pet to do a trick using some form of reward, like a treat or praise, then you understand the premise. Many believe the basis for understanding high-level conscience and how we learn is modeled in RL.

Figure 11.1a shows a comparison of three forms of learning covered in this book: supervised learning, representative learning (generative modeling), and RL. There are variations in all three forms of these learning types, from self-supervised learning to deep reinforcement learning.

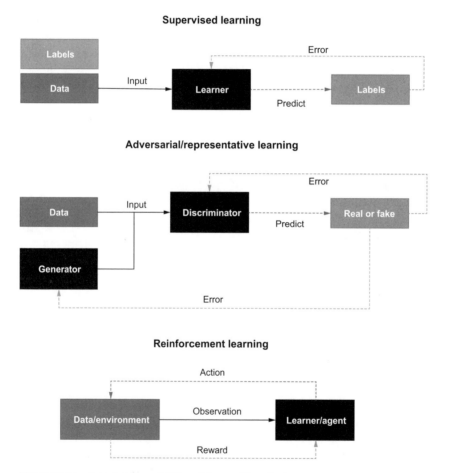

Figure 11.1a   A comparison of different forms of learning

RL works by having the learner, or what is referred to as the *agent*, observe the state of the environment. This observation, or view, of the environment is often referred to as the current state. The agent consumes the observed state and makes a prediction, or action, based on this state. Then, based on that action, the environment provides a reward based on the action at the given state.

This process of observing the environment and the agent performing actions continues until the agent either solves the problem or fails. The agent or learner learns through the accumulation of rewards promoted by the environment, where an action that typically produces a higher reward for a given state is considered more valuable.

The learning process for an RL agent typically involves the agent starting out making random actions. Agents use random actions to probe the environment to find those actions or sequences of actions that produce the most rewards. This type of learning is referred to as *trial and error* or *brute force*.

Trial and error learning vs. executive function

A key criticism of RL is the use of trial and error or brute force learning. This form of learning is repetitive and can be extremely expensive. Often, it requires an agent to execute millions of actions to solve problems. While humans and other animals often learn tasks in a similar fashion, we rarely need millions of iterations to get good at something.

Executive function (EF) is the process of the brain's learning mechanism that allows us to plan and complete complex tasks. While RL can simulate executive function in agents, the mechanism is substantially different. EF allows us to look at complex tasks we have never previously completed and plan a series of actions to successfully complete such tasks. There is ongoing research to uplift executive function into RL agents through a variety of techniques, including evolutionary optimization.

While RL is not without faults, it does provide a mechanism that allows us to solve complex problems we could never consider with supervised or adversarial learning. RL also allows the agent to interact and make changes to an environment, if allowed, causing even more complex problems. To understand how RL works, we look at and solve a first-order problem in the next section.

11.1.1 *Q-learning agent on the frozen lake*

Modern RL is a combination of three algorithmic paths: trial and error, dynamic programming, and Monte Carlo simulation. From that basis, a form of RL called *Q-learning* was derived in 1996 by Chris Watkins. Q-learning has since become a foundational concept to RL and is often taught to students as a first step.

Q-learning works by giving the agent the ability to quantify the quality of a given action for a known state, as shown in figure 11.1b. By being able to measure the quality of a given action, an agent can thereby easily select the correct series of actions to solve a given problem. The agent still needs to fumble around trial and error, probing the environment to derive these action or state qualities.

To see how this works in practice, we start by building a Q-learning agent that can solve a base problem from the OpenAI Gym, called the *frozen lake problem*. The OpenAI

Reinforcement learning

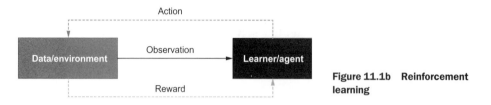

Figure 11.1b   Reinforcement learning

Gym (https://www.gymlibrary.dev/) is an open source project that encapsulates hundreds of different problem environments. These environments range from classic Atari games to basic control problems.

Figure 11.2 shows a diagram of the frozen lake environment we develop for the Q-agent to solve. The environment is a 4-by-4 grid of squares representing a frozen lake, where areas of the lake are frozen solid and safe to navigate across. Other areas of the lake are unstable and have holes that will cause the agent to fall and perish, thus finishing their journey or episode.

Agent start	Frozen	Frozen	Frozen
Frozen	Hole	Frozen	Hole
Frozen	Frozen	Frozen	Hole
Hole	Frozen	Frozen	Reward

Figure 11.2   Frozen lake environment

The goal of the frozen lake problem is for the agent to move across the grid, using the actions up, down, left, or right to traverse. When the agent reaches the bottom-right corner, it is complete and rewarded. If the agent falls through a hole in the lake, the journey is over and the agent is given a negative reward.

Fortunately, building RL agents and environments to test them on has been made easier through the development of the OpenAI Gym. We dive into loading the environment and coding a working Q agent in the next notebook.

Open the EDL_11_1_FrozenLake.ipynb notebook in Google Colab. Refer to the appendix if you need assistance. Run all the cells in the notebook by selecting Runtime > Run All from the menu. The first thing we look at in the following listing is the installation and imports of OpenAI Gym.

Listing 11.1   EDL_11_1_FrozenLake.ipynb: Installing OpenAI Gym

```
!pip install gym          ⟵——— Installs basic Gym

import numpy as np
import gym                ⟵——— Imports the package
import random
```

After that, we look at how Gym is used to create the environment. There are hundreds of environments to select from, and to create one, you just need to pass the name to the gym.make function, as shown in listing 11.2. Then, we query the environment to yield the size of the action and state spaces; these numbers represent how many discrete values are available. The frozen lake environment uses discrete values for both the action and state spaces. In many environments, we use continuous or ranged values to represent either the action, state, or both spaces.

Listing 11.2   EDL_11_1_FrozenLake.ipynb: Creating the environment

```
env = gym.make("FrozenLake-v0")   ⟵——— Creates the environment

action_size = env.action_space.n       ⟵——— Gets the size of the action space
state_size = env.observation_space.n   ⟵┐
print(action_size, state_size)         │  Gets the size of the state space
```

In Q-learning, the agent or learner encapsulates its knowledge or learnings in a table, conveniently called a *Q-table*. The dimensions of this table, its columns, and its rows are defined by the state and available actions. The next step in the code, shown in listing 11.3, is creating this table to represent the agent's knowledge. We construct this table using np.zeros to create an array sized by action_size and state_size values. The result is an array (table) of values, where each row represents the state and each column on the row represents the quality of the action at that state.

Listing 11.3   EDL_11_1_FrozenLake.ipynb: Building the Q-table

```
Q = np.zeros((state_size, action_size))     ⟵———— Creates an array of values, zero
print(Q)

#========== printed Q table
[[0. 0. 0. 0.]          ⟵———— The first row and first state
 [0. 0. 0. 0.]     ⟵
 [0. 0. 0. 0.]          Four actions per row
 [0. 0. 0. 0.]
 [0. 0. 0. 0.]
 [0. 0. 0. 0.]
 [0. 0. 0. 0.]
 [0. 0. 0. 0.]
 [0. 0. 0. 0.]
 [0. 0. 0. 0.]
 [0. 0. 0. 0.]
 [0. 0. 0. 0.]
 [0. 0. 0. 0.]
 [0. 0. 0. 0.]
 [0. 0. 0. 0.]
 [0. 0. 0. 0.]]
```

Next, we look at a set of standard hyperparameters for a Q-learner, shown in listing 11.4. Each journey the agent takes across the lake is defined as an episode. The total_episodes hyperparameter sets the total number of episodes or journeys the agent will take, and the max_steps value defines the maximum number of steps an agent can take on a single journey. Two other values are also used: learning_rate, which is like the learning rate in DL, and gamma, which is a discount factor that controls how important future rewards are to the agent. Finally, the bottom group of hyperparameters controls the agent's exploration.

Listing 11.4   EDL_11_1_FrozenLake.ipynb: Defining hyperparameters

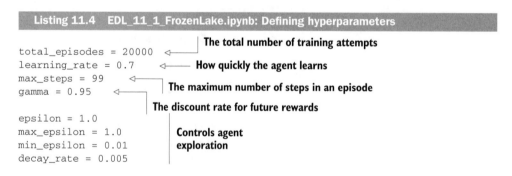

```
                               ┌——— The total number of training attempts
total_episodes = 20000   ⟵————┘
learning_rate = 0.7      ⟵———— How quickly the agent learns
max_steps = 99           ⟵——┐
gamma = 0.95             ⟵—┐ └— The maximum number of steps in an episode
                           └— The discount rate for future rewards
epsilon = 1.0
max_epsilon = 1.0          Controls agent
min_epsilon = 0.01         exploration
decay_rate = 0.005
```

A fundamental concept in Q-learning is the tradeoff between exploration and exploitation, or using the knowledge the agent has gained. When an agent initially starts training, its knowledge is low, represented by all zeroes in the Q-table. With no knowledge, the agent often relies on a random selection of actions. Then, as knowledge increases, the agent can start using values in the Q-table to determine the next best `action`. Unfortunately, if an agent's knowledge is incomplete, always choosing the best `action` may lead to disaster. Instead, we introduce a hyperparameter called `epsilon` to control how frequently an agent explores.

We can see how this exploration and exploitation works by looking at the `choose_action` function, shown in listing 11.5. In this function, a random uniform value is generated and compared against `epsilon`. If the value is less than `epsilon`, the agent randomly selects an `action` from the `action` space and returns it. Otherwise, the agent picks the maximum quality `action` for the current `state` and returns that. As the agent trains over the environment, the `epsilon` value will be reduced or decayed over time to represent the agent's accumulation of knowledge and inclination to explore less.

Listing 11.5 EDL_11_1_FrozenLake.ipynb: Choosing an `action`

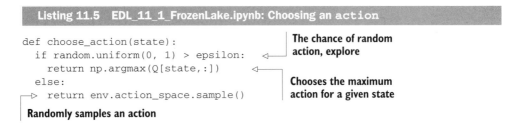

The agent learns through an accumulation of knowledge calculated by the Q-function. Terms within the Q-function represent the current Q-quality values, reward, and application of the `discount` factor gamma. This method of learning is encapsulated in the `learn` function, which applies the Q-learning function, shown in the following listing. We don't cover this function in greater depth here because our focus is on how NEAT can solve the same problem without using the Q-function.

Listing 11.6 EDL_11_1_FrozenLake.ipynb: The `learn` function

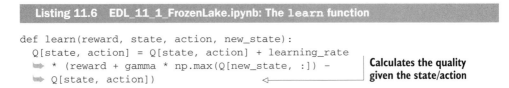

The code to train the agent is split into two loops, with the first looping over the episodes and the second looping over the journey or steps through each episode. At each step, the agent uses the `choose_action` function to select the next `action` and then executes the `action` by calling `env.step(action)`. The output from calling the `step` function is used to update the agent's knowledge in the Q-table by calling the `learn` function. Then, a check is made to confirm whether the episode is complete or incomplete and whether the agent fell into a hole or made it to the end. As the agent loops over the episodes, the `epsilon` value is decayed or reduced, representing the agent's reduced need to explore as time goes on, as shown in the following listing.

Listing 11.7   EDL_11_1_FrozenLake.ipynb: The training function

```
rewards = []
for episode in range(total_episodes):
    state = env.reset()        ◁──────┐ Resets the environment
    step = 0
    done = False
    total_rewards = 0

    for step in range(max_steps):
        action = choose_action(state)                    Selects an action
                                                          and executes on
        new_state, reward, done, info = env.step(action) the environment

        learn(reward, state, action, new_state)   ◁──────┐ Learns and updates
                                                          the Q-table
        total_rewards += reward
        state = new_state
                                            If it is done and the episode
        if done == True:           ◁────── is complete, then it breaks
            break

    epsilon = min_epsilon   ◁─────── Decays epsilon exploration over time
+ (max_epsilon - min_epsilon)*np.exp(-decay_rate*episode)
    rewards.append(total_rewards)


print ("Score over time: " +  str(sum(rewards)/total_episodes))
print(Q)
```

In this example, we train the agent to run over a certain number of episodes, without consideration for improved performance. After the agent has been trained, we test out its knowledge by running the agent through a simulated episode over the environment, as shown in the following listing.

Listing 11.8   EDL_11_1_FrozenLake.ipynb: Exercising the agent

```
for episode in range(5):   ◁────── Loops over 5 episodes
    state = env.reset()
    step = 0
    done = False
    print("***************************************************")
    print("EPISODE ", episode)
                                                  Takes/executes the
    for step in range(max_steps):                 maximum best
        action = np.argmax(Q[state,:])            action for state
        new_state, reward, done, info = env.step(action)

        if done:
            env.render()   ◁────── Renders the environment
            if new_state == 15:
                print("Goal reached 🏆")
            else:
```

```
        print("Aaaah 💀")

      print("Number of steps", step)
      break
    state = new_state
env.close()
```

Figure 11.3 shows the output of running a trained agent over five episodes. From the results, you can see how the agent is able to generally solve the environment within the max allowed steps (99). If you want to go back and try to improve how quickly the

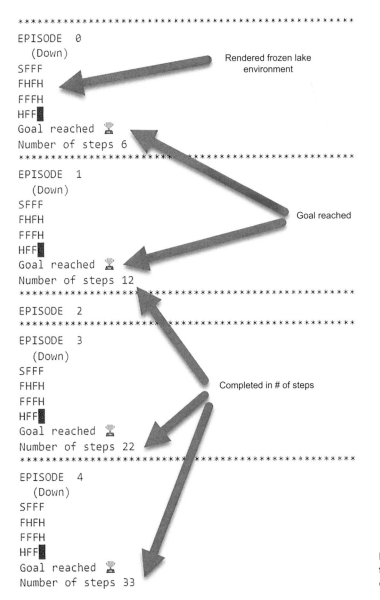

Figure 11.3 The output from simulating an agent on the frozen lake

agent solves the environment consistently, try modifying the hyperparameters and then running the notebook again. The next section showcases some learning exercises that can help improve your knowledge of RL.

11.1.2 *Learning exercises*

Use these exercises to improve your knowledge of the subject material:

1 Change the `learning_rate` and `gamma` hyperparameters from listing 11.4. Observe what effect they have on agent learning.
2 Alter the exploration decay rate, `decay_rate`, from listing 11.4. Observe what effect this has on agent training.
3 Alter the number of training `EPISODES`. Observe what effect this has on agent performance.

Of course, at this stage, we could write an evolutionary optimizer to tune the hyperparameters, as we have done before. However, with NEAT, we can do much better and, in fact, replace the use of RL to solve these types of problems. Before we get to that, though, we look at loading more complex OpenAI Gym environments in the next section.

11.2 *Exploring complex problems from the OpenAI Gym*

The OpenAI Gym provides an enormous collection of training environments designed for improving RL. Before we unleash NEAT on some of those environments, we have some additional prep to undertake to use Colab. In this chapter and the next, we explore various Gym environments, described in the following list:

- *Mountain car*—The goal here is to move a car that starts in the valley of two hills to the top of the target hill. To do this, the car needs to rock itself back and forth until it gets the momentum to climb to the top of the higher hill.
- *Pendulum*—The goal of this problem is to apply force to the rocking arm of a pendulum, so it remains in an upright position. This requires knowledge of when to apply force, depending on the position of the pendulum.
- *Cart pole*—This classic Gym problem requires the balancing of a pole on top of a moving cart. Again, this requires the agent/model to balance the position and velocity of the cart and pole.
- *Lunar lander*—Replicated from an old video game, the goal of lunar lander is to land the moon lander on a flat landing surface. The trick is that the landing velocity of the craft must be low enough to avoid damaging the lander and failing.

In the next quick notebook, we look to set up and explore various Gym environments from the above list.

Open the EDL_11_2_Gym_Setup.ipynb notebook in Google Colab. Refer to the appendix if you need assistance. Run all the cells in the notebook by selecting Runtime > Run All from the menu.

Since Colab is a server notebook, there typically isn't a need to provide UI output. To render some of the prettier Gym environments, we must install some virtual interface drivers and associated helpers, as shown in the following listing. We also install some tools to render our environment outputs and playback as video, which makes our experimentation more entertaining.

Listing 11.9   EDL_11_2_Gym_Setup.ipynb: Installing required packages

```
!apt-get install -y xvfb x11-utils      ⟵── Installs video device drivers

!pip install gym[box2d]==0.17.* \
             pyvirtualdisplay==0.2.* \
             PyOpenGL==3.1.* \
             PyOpenGL-accelerate==3.1.* \
             mediapy \
             piglet -q)
```

- `!pip install gym[box2d]==0.17.*` — **Installs Gym with box2d**
- `pyvirtualdisplay==0.2.* \ PyOpenGL==3.1.* \ PyOpenGL-accelerate==3.1.* \` — **Graphics helpers**
- `mediapy \` — **For playing video/media**
- `piglet -q)` — **The template engine**

We need to create a virtual display and start it. The code to that requires just a few simple lines, as shown in the following listing.

Listing 11.10   EDL_11_2_Gym_Setup.ipynb: Creating a virtual display

```
from pyvirtualdisplay import Display
display = Display(visible=0, size=(1400, 900))      ⟵── Creates a virtual display
display.start()      ⟵── Starts the display
```

After the imports, we can now create an environment and render a frame to the output of the cell. This cell uses a Colab form to provide a list of environment options to choose from. Our goal is to be able to build NEAT agents/solutions that can tackle each of the environments. Visualizing the environments themselves is possible using the `env.render` function and passing in the mode as `rgb_array` for outputting a 2D array. This output can then be rendered using `plt.imshow`, as shown in the following listing.

Listing 11.11   EDL_11_2_Gym_Setup.ipynb: Creating a virtual display

```
#@title Setup Environment { run: "auto" }
ENVIRONMENT = "CartPole-v1" #@param ["CartPole-v1", "Acrobot-v1",
➥ "CubeCrash-v0", "MountainCar-v0", "LunarLander-v2"]      ⟵──

env = gym.make(ENVIRONMENT)      ⟵── Creates the environment

state = env.reset()
plt.imshow(env.render(mode='rgb_array'))      ⟵── Renders a frame and plots it

print("action space: {0!r}".format(env.action_space))
print("observation space: {0!r}".format
➥ (env.observation_space))
```

- **A list of environment names**
- **Prints action/state spaces**

Rendering a single frame is OK, but what we really want is to see how the environment runs or plays through. The next cell we look at, shown in listing 11.12, does just that by creating an environment and then running an agent through the environment. As the simulation runs, the environment renders each frame to a list. That list of frames is then converted to a video and output below the cell. Figure 11.4 shows the output of the lunar lander environment rendered to video output in the Colab notebook.

Listing 11.12   EDL_11_2_Gym_Setup.ipynb: Video render of the environment

```
env = gym.make(ENVIRONMENT)

fitnesses = []
frames = []

for run in range(SIMULATION_RUNS):          Runs for n number simulations
  state = env.reset()
  fitness = 0                                    For the maximum number
  for I in range(SIMULATION_ITERATIONS):         steps in each run
    action = env.action_space.sample()
    state, reward, done, info = env.step        Takes the maximum
    ⮕ (np.argmax(action))                       action and executes
    frames.append(env.render(mode='rgb_array'))
    fitness += reward                            Appends the rendered
  if done:                                        frame to the list
    fitnesses.append(fitness)
    break

mediapy.show_video(frames, fps=30)          Renders the collection
                                            of frames as video
```

If done, this stops the simulation run.

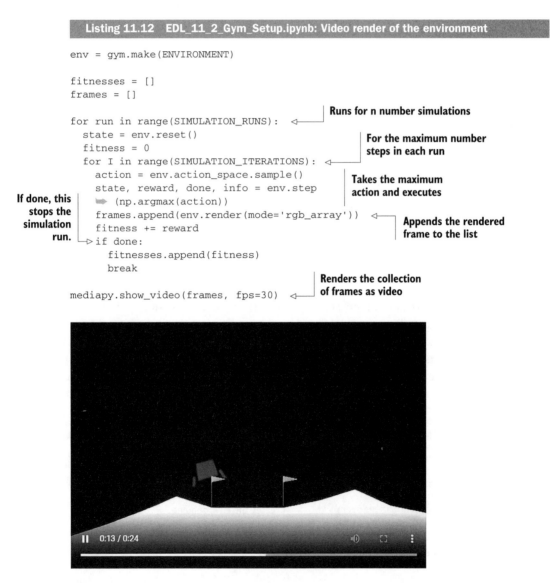

Figure 11.4   Video output of the lunar lander environment

Go ahead and run through the various other environment options to visualize the other possibilities we explore. All these environments are similar in that the state space is continuous and the action space is discrete. We measure the complexity of an environment by the number of possible states.

Figure 11.5 shows each of the environments, the size of the action and state spaces, and the relative complexity. The relative complexity of each environment is calculated by taking the size of the state space and raising it to the power of the action space, given by the following formula:

$$\text{Relative complexity} = \texttt{size\_state\_space}^{\texttt{size\_action\_space}}$$

Take, for example, a version of the mountain car problem, where state_space = 2 and action_space = 3. The relative complexity, then, would be expressed as the following: relative complexity = 2^3 = 2 × 2 × 2 = 8.

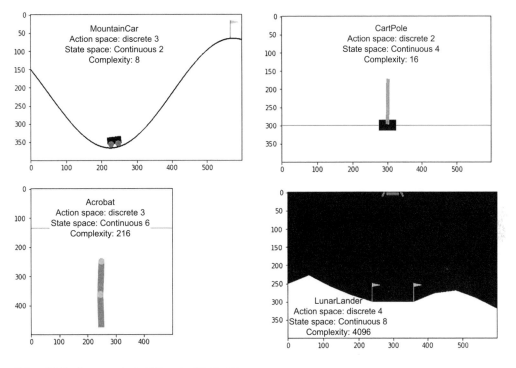

Figure 11.5 A comparison of Gym environments

Typically, the subclass of Box2D environments shown in figure 11.5 is solved using deep reinforcement learning (DRL). DRL is an extension of RL that uses DL to solve the Q-equation or other RL functions. Essentially, DL replaces the need for a state or Q-table with neural networks.

Figure 11.6 shows a comparison between Q-learning and deep Q-learning or deep Q-network (DQN). This DQN model has proven to be very versatile and capable of

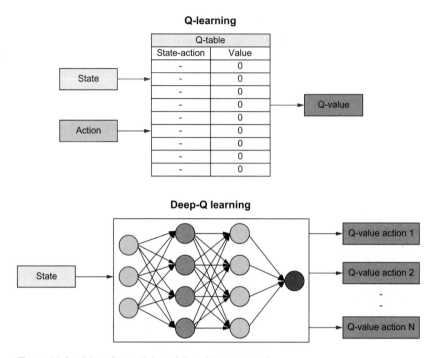

Figure 11.6   Q-learning and deep Q-learning compared

solving a wide variety of RL problems, from classic Atari games to the cart pole and lunar lander problems.

Deep Q-learning works by using the Q-learning function we looked at earlier as the check or supervisor for training a network. That means, internally, a DQN model learns through supervised training, which is provided in the form of the Q-learning equation. The learning exercises in the next section can help reinforce what you have learned in this section.

11.2.1 Learning exercises

Complete the following exercises to improve your understanding of this section's concepts:

1 Open and run all the simulation environments provided in the notebook. Get familiar with each environment's `action` and `observation`/`state` spaces as well.
2 Search the internet for and explore other Gym environments that were either part of the original or have been extended by others. There are hundreds of Gym environments you can explore.
3 Add a new environment to the notebook and demonstrate how an agent can play randomly within this new environment.

Since the development of DQN, there have been many variations and approaches to employing RL with DL networks. In all cases, the basis for the learning is RL in the form of a Q or other derived learning equation. In the next section, we demonstrate how we can raise ourselves above derived RL equations and let the solution evolve itself.

11.3 Solving reinforcement learning problems with NEAT

In this section, we use NEAT to solve some of the difficult RL Gym problems we just looked at. However, it is important to stress that the method we use to derive the network and solve an unknown equation is not RL but, instead, evolution and NEAT. While we do use the RL environments and train the agent in an RL manner, the underlying method is not RL.

Using NEAT and an evolving `population` of NEAT agents is relatively simple to set up, as we see in the next notebook. Open the EDL_11_3_NEAT_Gym.ipynb notebook in Google Colab. Refer to the appendix if you need assistance. Run all the cells in the notebook by selecting Runtime > Run All from the menu.

We just reviewed the setup code, so we can jump straight to the NEAT configuration. The configuration is similar to what we have seen before, but now we define the network `num_inputs` as equal to the `state` or `observation` space size and the `num_outputs` as equal to the size of the `action` space. This means the input into the NEAT agent is the `state`/`observation` and the output is the `action`, as shown in the following listing.

> **Listing 11.13 EDL_11_3_NEAT_Gyms.ipynb: NEAT configuration**

```
inputs = env.observation_space.shape[0]    ←── The size of the state space
outputs = env.action_space.n    ←
                                  │ The size of the action space
config = f'''
[NEAT]
fitness_criterion     = max
fitness_threshold     = 175.0    ←── Defines the fitness threshold
pop_size              = 250
reset_on_extinction   = 0

[DefaultGenome]
num_inputs            = {inputs}    ←── Maps the state space to inputs
num_hidden            = 1
num_outputs           = {outputs}    ←── Maps the action space to outputs
```

Next, we revisit our test genome `fred` to understand how individual fitness is evaluated. We can see how `fred` is created from the `genome` configuration and then instantiated into a network `net`. This network is tested by passing in an arbitrary environment `state` and outputting an `action` set. To execute the `action`, the `np.argmax(action)` is used to extract the `action` index to use when calling `env.step`, as shown in the following listing.

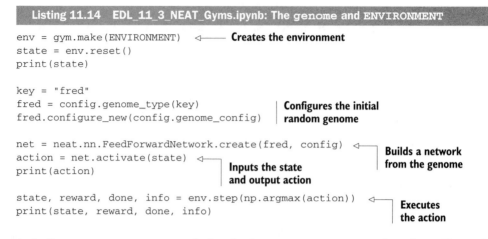

Listing 11.14 EDL_11_3_NEAT_Gyms.ipynb: The genome and ENVIRONMENT

```
env = gym.make(ENVIRONMENT)     ◁——— Creates the environment
state = env.reset()
print(state)

key = "fred"
fred = config.genome_type(key)                    Configures the initial
fred.configure_new(config.genome_config)          random genome

net = neat.nn.FeedForwardNetwork.create(fred, config) ◁——
action = net.activate(state) ◁—                        Builds a network
print(action)               Inputs the state          from the genome
                            and output action

state, reward, done, info = env.step(np.argmax(action))  ◁——
print(state, reward, done, info)                             Executes
                                                            the action
```

As before, we can use fred to derive the base genome evaluate function. The code, shown in listing 11.15, mimics the sample video demonstration playthrough code we already set up. This time, though, the fitness of the genome is calculated based on the accumulation of rewards. That means—and this subtle difference is important—the fitness of a genome is the sum of rewards, but at no time does the agent train/learn how to consume or use those rewards. Evolution uses the rewards to evaluate the agent with the best fitness—the one that can accumulate the most rewards.

Listing 11.15 EDL_11_3_NEAT_Gyms.ipynb: Evaluating genome fitness

```
#@title Simulation Options { run: "auto" }
SIMULATION_ITERATIONS = 200                         The colab form for
SIMULATION_RUNS = 10 #@param {type:"slider", min:1, simulation parameters
➡ max:10, step:1}

frames = []
fitnesses = []
for run in range(SIMULATION_RUNS):
  state = env.reset()
  fitness = 0
  for i in range(SIMULATION_ITERATIONS):     Passes the state to the network
    action = net.activate(state)        ◁——┘ to activate the action
    state, reward, done, info = env.step
    ➡ (np.argmax(action))               ◁——— Executes the step on the environment
    frames.append(env.render(mode='rgb_array'))
    fitness += reward           ◁—
    if done:                    Adds the reward to the fitness
      fitnesses.append(fitness)
      break

print(fitnesses)
mediapy.show_video(frames, fps=30)  ◁——— Replays the simulation runs
```

This simple code can easily be converted into a set of eval_genomes/eval_genome functions, where eval_genomes is the parent function passing the population of genomes and individual genome evaluation is done with `eval_genome`. Internally, the code shown in listing 11.16 works the same as the code we looked at in listing 11.15, without the video frame capture code. After all, we don't need to capture a video of every genome simulation.

Listing 11.16 EDL_11_3_NEAT_Gyms.ipynb: Evaluating genome `fitness`

```
def eval_genome(genome, config):
  net = neat.nn.FeedForwardNetwork.create        Creates the network
    (genome, config)                             from the genome
  fitnesses = []
  for run in range(SIMULATION_RUNS):
    state = env.reset()
    fitness = 0
    for I in range(SIMULATION_ITERATIONS):
      action = net.activate(state)               Passes the state to the network
      state, reward, done, info = env.step       to activate the action
        (np.argmax(action))
      fitness += reward
      if done:
        fitnesses.append(fitness)
        break
  return -9999.99 if len(fitnesses) <            Returns the
    1 else min(fitnesses)                        minimum fitness

def eval_genomes(genomes, config):
  for genome_id, genome in genomes:              Loops through the
    genome.fitness = eval_genome(genome, config) genome population

print(eval_genome(fred, config))   ◁—— Tests the function on fred
```

Now, the code to evolve the `population` becomes quite simple and elegant. The `pop` is created and then the default `statistics` and `out` reporters are added for generating progress updates. After that, we use a new feature called the `neat.ParallelEvaluator` to provide internal multithreaded processing of the evolution. On the free version of Colab, this function has limited use, but if you have a powerful computer, you could try running this code locally for improved performance. Finally, the last line calls `pop.run` to run the evolution and produce a winning `genome`, as shown in the following listing. Figure 11.7 shows the output evolving a `population` of NEAT agents to solve the cart pole Gym environment.

Listing 11.17 EDL_11_3_NEAT_Gyms.ipynb: Evolving the `population`

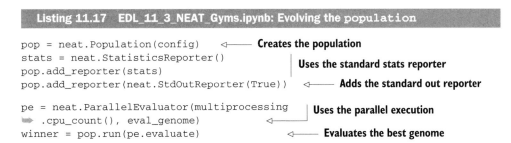

```
pop = neat.Population(config)   ◁—— Creates the population
stats = neat.StatisticsReporter()
pop.add_reporter(stats)                         Uses the standard stats reporter
pop.add_reporter(neat.StdOutReporter(True))   ◁—— Adds the standard out reporter

pe = neat.ParallelEvaluator(multiprocessing     Uses the parallel execution
  .cpu_count(), eval_genome)
winner = pop.run(pe.evaluate)   ◁—— Evaluates the best genome
```

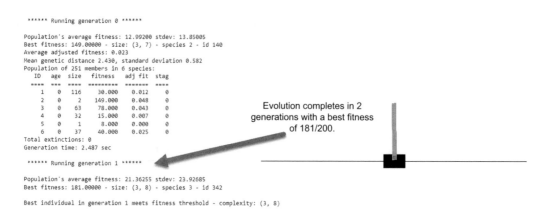

```
****** Running generation 0 ******

Population's average fitness: 12.99200 stdev: 13.85005
Best fitness: 149.00000 - size: (3, 7) - species 2 - id 140
Average adjusted fitness: 0.023
Mean genetic distance 2.430, standard deviation 0.582
Population of 251 members in 6 species:
   ID   age  size  fitness   adj fit  stag
  ====  ===  ====  ========  =======  ====
    1    0   116    30.000    0.012    0
    2    0     2   149.000    0.048    0
    3    0    63    78.000    0.043    0
    4    0    32    15.000    0.007    0
    5    0     1     8.000    0.000    0
    6    0    37    40.000    0.025    0
Total extinctions: 0
Generation time: 2.487 sec

****** Running generation 1 ******

Population's average fitness: 21.36255 stdev: 23.92685
Best fitness: 181.00000 - size: (3, 8) - species 3 - id 342

Best individual in generation 1 meets fitness threshold - complexity: (3, 8)
```

Evolution completes in 2 generations with a best fitness of 181/200.

Figure 11.7   The output of a NEAT agent

While the `fitness` of an agent is correlated with the agent's maximum rewards, it is important to stress that we are not training RL agents. Instead, the evolved networks are evolving their own internal function to accumulate rewards and become more fit. The fact that `fitness` is related to rewards is only a useful metric to describe `individual` performance.

11.3.1   Learning exercises

Use the following additional exercises to help firm your understanding of the content of this section:

1   Try each of the other environments using the NEAT agent to see how well or quickly a solution can be achieved, if at all.

2   Alter the number of `SIMULATION_RUNS` and `SIMULATION_ITERATIONS` and then reevaluate the NEAT agents.

3   Alter the number of hidden neurons in the NEAT configuration, `num_hidden`, from listing 11.13. See what effect this has when rerunning the various environments.

So what type of learning or evolution is this called or described by? Well, we talk about one set of ideas and theories in the next chapter. For now, though, we want to see if we can improve the evolution of the NEAT agent to tackle more difficult problems.

11.4   Solving Gym's lunar lander problem with NEAT agents

Chances are if you ran the last notebook over other RL environments, you discovered that our process only works well for simpler RL environments. In fact, evolving solutions in far more complex environments, like the lunar lander problem, just makes no progress at all. This is because the complexity to evolve a NEAT agent/network using just rewards is not sufficient.

In chapter 12, we look at a further set of strategies that can assist us in solving the lunar lander problem, but for now, we look at a solution example from the NEAT-Python repository examples. NEAT-Python has a nice collection of examples designed to run without notebooks. For convenience, we have converted the lunar lander example to a Colab notebook to demonstrate an improved NEAT solver.

> **CAUTION**   The code in this example demonstrates one possible solution to evolving NEAT networks to solve more complex RL problems. This solution is heavily customized and uses complex mathematical concepts to refine `fitness` evaluation. As stated previously, we look at more elegant solutions in the next chapter, but feel free to review this notebook.

Open the EDL_11_4_NEAT_LunarLander.ipynb notebook in Google Colab. Refer to the appendix if you need assistance. Run all the cells in the notebook by selecting Runtime > Run All from the menu. As always, this notebook has been extended from previous examples and shares a common code base. The key sections we look at in this notebook all center on improvements to the `fitness` evaluation and `gene` operators.

We start by looking at improvements to the `gene` operators and a specialized `LanderGenome` class, as shown in listing 11.18. The core of this class introduces a new parameter called `discount`. The premise of a `discount` parameter is to introduce a factor that reduces rewards over time. *Discounted rewards*, or reducing the influence of future or past rewards over time, is a concept developed in RL. The `gamma` term used in the Q-learning equation represents the decay of future rewards. However, in this solution, decayed rewards do not directly affect the `action` of agents; rather, they are used to better evaluate their `fitness`.

Listing 11.18   EDL_11_4_NEAT_LunarLander.ipynb: Customizing the genome config

```
class LanderGenome(neat.DefaultGenome):
    def __init__(self, key):
        super().__init__(key)            Creates the
        self.discount = None       ◁──   discount parameter

    def configure_new(self, config):
        super().configure_new(config)
        self.discount = 0.01 + 0.98 * random.random()   ◁──   Sets the
                                                              discount value

    def configure_crossover(self, genome1, genome2, config):
        super().configure_crossover(genome1, genome2, config)
        self.discount = random.choice((genome1
        ⮿ .discount, genome2.discount))    ◁──   Crosses over/mates
                                                the discount
    def mutate(self, config):
        super().mutate(config)
        self.discount += random.gauss(0.0, 0.05)
        self.discount = max(0.01, min(0.99, self
        ⮿ .discount))

    def distance(self, other, config):
        dist = super().distance(other, config)
        disc_diff = abs(self.discount - other.discount)
```

Mutates the discount

```
        return dist + disc_diff   ◁──┐  Calculates the
                                      │  genome distance
    def __str__(self):
        return f"Reward discount: {self.discount}\n{super().__str__()}"
```

The `fitness` of a `genome` is now evaluated in a `compute_fitness` function that no longer simulates the agent directly on the environment but, rather, uses a recorded history of `actions`, as shown in listing 11.19. This history of episodes and steps is played back for each `genome`, where the `discount` factor within the `genome` is used to evaluate the importance related to previous agent `actions`. Essentially, the `fitness` of an agent is calculated in comparison to how other agents performed previously. While we can't say this solution uses RL, it does use a normalized and discounted difference between previous agent rewards and future evolved agents.

Listing 11.19   EDL_11_4_NEAT_LunarLander.ipynb: Computing `fitness`

```
def compute_fitness(genome, net, episodes, min_reward, max_reward):
    m = int(round(np.log(0.01) / np.log(genome.discount)))
    discount_function = [genome.discount ** (m - i)
    ➥ for I in range(m + 1)]   ◁──┐  Creates the function to discount

    reward_error = []
    for score, data in episodes:          ◁── Loops over episodes
        # Compute normalized discounted reward.
        dr = np.convolve(data[:, -1], discount_function)[m:]
        dr = 2 * (dr-- min_reward) / (max_reward-- min_reward)-- 1.0
        dr = np.clip(dr, -1.0, 1.0)   ◁──┐ Discounts rewards based on function

        for row, dr in zip(data, dr):   ◁──┐ Loops through episode steps
            observation = row[:8]
            action = int(row[8])
            output = net.activate(observation)
            reward_error.append(float((output[action]-- dr)
            ➥ ** 2))
```
Calculates the difference in reward error

```
    return reward_error
```

There is a lot of code in this notebook that revolves around simulating the agent environment interaction, recording it, and evaluating it across the `population` of genomes. The next key element we look at is the code that runs the simulations: the `simulate` function found within the `PooledErrorCompute` class. Unlike our previous notebook, the agent code that runs through a simulation, shown in listing 11.20, simulates simple exploration based on the current step, giving the simulation the opportunity to add exploratory steps to the simulation data. Each simulation run is added to data to score and extract the most successful runs, where success is still measured in total accumulated rewards.

Listing 11.20   EDL_11_4_NEAT_LunarLander.ipynb: Simulating runs

```
def simulate(self, nets):
    scores = []
    for genome, net in nets:          ◁────── Loops over genome networks
        observation = env.reset()
        step = 0
        data = []
        while 1:
            step += 1                                       Decides to explore
            if step < 200 and random.random() < 0.2:   ◁──┘ or exploit
                action = env.action_space.sample()
            else:
                output = net.activate(observation)
                action = np.argmax(output)

            observation, reward, done, info = env.step(action)
            data.append(np.hstack((observation,
                action, reward)))

            if done:
                break

        data = np.array(data)                   Scores up the best
        score = np.sum(data[:, -1])    ◁──────┘ simulation runs
        self.episode_score.append(score)
        scores.append(score)
        self.episode_length.append(step)
                                                         Appends to the
        self.test_episodes.append((score, data))   ◁──┘ test episodes
```

Appends the step output to the data ┘

This solution does borrow from the RL process and attempts to measure the error in terms of rewards. The total reward error here has a direct influence on `individual fitness`.

Go ahead and review all the rest of the code on your own as the notebook runs—and it will run for quite a while. This notebook can evolve for 8+ hours, and it still may not be able to solve the problem.

As this notebook trains, we see a quick convergence of `fitness`, but then, things quickly plateau. In fact, you may not find any positive rewards or `fitness` being evaluated until 1,000+ `generations` into evolution. The progress is slow, but if you have the patience, a NEAT agent can eventually be evolved to solve the lunar lander environment.

As much as the NEAT agents borrow RL environments and some techniques to help solve the problems, the actual evolution is not something we would refer to as DRL. Instead, we need to consider other evolutionary concepts or ideas that describe how we evolve an agent that self-evolves its own learning function. In essence, we have evolved an agent that evolved its own system of learning or learning function.

While it is unlikely the evolved internal learning function resembles the Q-learning equation, we can confirm it is able to solve complex RL environments. It is the evolution of this learning function that becomes the most interesting and powerful concept we look at in the next and final chapter.

11.4.1   Learning exercises

Performing the following exercises will help you review and improve your understanding of the content:

1   Compare the results of running this notebook against the standard NEAT Gym exercise we explored in the last section. How does an agent perform after that same number of `generations` from each notebook? Is it what you expect?

2   Add a different environment to the notebook to see how the improved `fitness` evaluation increases or decreases the NEAT agent's performance.

3   Implement a different method of exploration. Right now, this notebook uses a fixed exploration rate. Add some variation by implementing a decaying exploration rate, as seen in previous examples.

This section demonstrates the power of NEAT to evolve an `individual` that could internally replicate the Q-learning RL process. In the next section, we look at a baseline DRL implementation called DQN as a comparison to what we have done with NEXT.

11.5   *Solving Gym's lunar lander problem with a deep Q-network*

DRL first made heads turn when it was shown a deep Q-learning model could solve classic Atari games, using just `observation state` as input. This was a dramatic breakthrough, and since then, DRL has been shown to solve many complex tasks far better than humans. In this section's notebook, we look at the classic implementation of DQN as an alternative to solving the lunar lander problem.

> ### Deep Q-networks on Atari
> Solving the classic Atari games using DQN worked, but it took a substantial number of iterations. The number of required training episodes to solve even a basic Atari environment, like Breakout, can be millions of episodes. Improvements in RL methods have since dropped the number of training episodes, but overall, DRL is a computationally expensive endeavor. Fortunately, unlike EC, DRL has been a major beneficiary of the computational enhancements made possible by deep learning.

Open the EDL_11_5_DQN_LunarLander.ipynb notebook in Google Colab. Refer to the appendix if you need assistance. Run all the cells in the notebook by selecting Runtime > Run All from the menu.

This notebook is set up to use the same environments but has the evolution code and libraries removed. Now, our focus is on how the DQN model works on a Gym problem. This means we start with the `DQNAgent` class definition, as shown in the following listing. The `init` function sets up the base hyperparameters and saves the action and observation sizes. It also adds a memory, which is used to store experiences from simulations as well as the agent's brain or model.

Listing 11.21   EDL_11_5_DQN_Gyms.ipynb: The DQN agent

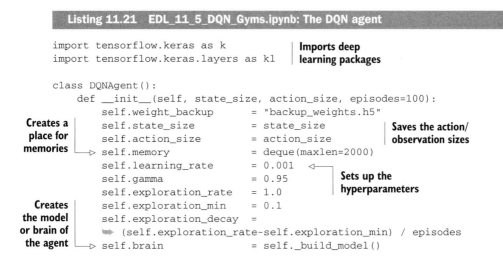

```
import tensorflow.keras as k          Imports deep
import tensorflow.keras.layers as kl  learning packages

class DQNAgent():
    def __init__(self, state_size, action_size, episodes=100):
        self.weight_backup      = "backup_weights.h5"
        self.state_size         = state_size
        self.action_size        = action_size          Saves the action/
        self.memory             = deque(maxlen=2000)   observation sizes
        self.learning_rate      = 0.001
        self.gamma              = 0.95       Sets up the
        self.exploration_rate   = 1.0        hyperparameters
        self.exploration_min    = 0.1
        self.exploration_decay  =
      (self.exploration_rate-self.exploration_min) / episodes
        self.brain              = self._build_model()
```

Creates a place for memories

Sets up the hyperparameters

Creates the model or brain of the agent

The DL model or brain of the agent is defined next in the build_model function. The code in this function creates a three-layer model, taking the state space as input and outputting the action space as output. The model is compiled with mse for loss and an Adam optimizer. Unique to this example is the ability of the model to load a file containing previously trained model weights, as shown in the following listing.

Listing 11.22   EDL_11_5_DQN_Gyms.ipynb: Building the brain

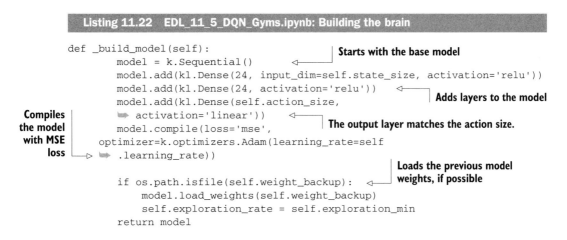

```
def _build_model(self):            Starts with the base model
    model = k.Sequential()
    model.add(kl.Dense(24, input_dim=self.state_size, activation='relu'))
    model.add(kl.Dense(24, activation='relu'))
    model.add(kl.Dense(self.action_size,     Adds layers to the model
      activation='linear'))
    model.compile(loss='mse',      The output layer matches the action size.
    optimizer=k.optimizers.Adam(learning_rate=self
      .learning_rate))
                                        Loads the previous model
    if os.path.isfile(self.weight_backup):    weights, if possible
        model.load_weights(self.weight_backup)
        self.exploration_rate = self.exploration_min
    return model
```

Compiles the model with MSE loss

Before we get to the rest of the DQNAgent definition, let's review the training code. The code, shown in listing 11.23, starts by setting the primary hyperparameters of BATCH_SIZE and EPISODES. It then starts by looping through the number of episodes, simulating the agent until a call to env.step outputs done equals True during each one. If the agent is not done, it inputs the state into the agent.act function to output an `action` prediction, which is then applied to the `env.step` function to output the next `state`, `reward`, and `done`. Next, `agent.remember` is called to add the `action` and consequences to the agent's memory. After each episode, when `done ==` `True`, a call is made to `agent.remember`, which replays all the remembered `actions` and uses the results to train the model.

Listing 11.23   EDL_11_5_DQN_Gyms.ipynb: Training the agent

```
BATCH_SIZE = 256 #@param {type:"slider", min:32,        Sets the primary hyperparameters
➥ max:256, step:2}                              ◁——————————┘
EPISODES = 1000 #@param {type:"slider", min:10, max:1000, step:1}

state_size = env.observation_space.shape[0]
action_size = env.action_space.n
agent = DQNAgent(state_size, action_size, episodes=EPISODES)

groups = { "reward" : {"total", "max", "avg"},
           "agent" : {"explore_rate", "mem_usage"}}
plotlosses = PlotLosses(groups=groups)
total_rewards = 0
for ep in nb.tqdm(range(EPISODES)):
  rewards = []
  state = env.reset()
  state = np.reshape(state, [1, state_size])   ◁——————————┐

  done = False
  index = 0
  while not done:                                          Reshapes the state
    action = agent.act(state)                               for the model
    next_state, reward, done, _ = env.step(action)
    rewards.append(reward)
    next_state = np.reshape(next_state,
➥      [1, state_size])                          ◁————————┘
    agent.remember(state, action, reward, next_state,
➥      done)                          ◁————————┐
    state = next_state                          │ Remembers the action and consequences
  agent.replay(BATCH_SIZE)                       ◁——————┘
  total_rewards += sum(rewards)
  plotlosses.update({'total': sum(rewards),
                     'max': max(rewards),
                     "avg" : total_rewards/(ep+1),
                     "explore_rate" : agent.exploration_rate,
                     "mem_usage" : agent.mem_usage(),
                     })
  plotlosses.send()
```

Predicts and executes the action

Replays actions and trains the agent

Now, we move back to the `DQNAgent` definition and review the `act`, `remember`, and `replay` functions, as shown in listing 11.24. The first function, `act`, evaluates the chance of exploration and responds with either a random `action`, if exploring, or a predicted `action`, if not. Second, the `remember` function stores the experiences of the agent as it simulates through the episodes. The memory used here is a dequeue class that uses a fixed size that automatically throws out the oldest memories as it gets full. Third, the `replay` function extracts a batch of experiences from the agent memory, given there are enough memories. This batch of experiences is then used to replay the agent's `actions` and evaluate the quality of each previously executed `action` (random or predicted). The quality `target` of an `action` is calculated using a form of the Q-learning equation. This calculated value is then used to update the model, using the `fit` function over a single epoch. Finally, at the end of the `replay` function, the chance of exploration—the `exploration_rate`—is updated by the `exploration_decay`, if required.

Listing 11.24   EDL_11_5_DQN_Gyms.ipynb: The `act`, `remember`, and `replay` functions

```
def act(self, state):
    if np.random.rand() <= self.exploration_rate:        ◁─── Selects a random or
        return random.randrange(self.action_size)              predicted action
    act_values = self.brain.predict(state)
    return np.argmax(act_values[0])

def remember(self, state, action, reward, next_state, done):
    self.memory.append((state, action, reward,
    ➦ next_state, done))    ◁─── Appends to the dequeue memory

def replay(self, batch_size):
    if len(self.memory) < batch_size:        ◁─── Checks whether the memory
        return                                     is larger than the batch size
    sample_batch = random.sample(self.memory,
    ➦ batch_size)                             ◁─ Extracts experiences from the memory and trains
    for state, action, reward, next_state, done in sample_batch:
        target = reward
        if not done:
            target = reward + self.gamma *
    np.amax(self.brain.predict(next_state)[0])    Evaluates the target predictions
        target_f = self.brain.predict(state)    ◁─┘ from the Q-learning function
        target_f[0][action] = target
        self.brain.fit(state, target_f, epochs=1, verbose=0)
    if self.exploration_rate > self.exploration_min:
        self.exploration_rate -= self.exploration_decay
```

Figure 11.8 shows the results of training the DQN agent on the lunar lander environment for 1,000 epochs. In the figure, you can see how the agent is able to gradually accumulate rewards as it learns to master the environment.

DQN and DRL are powerful advances in AI and ML that have showcased the potential ability for digital intelligence to solve some tasks better than humans. However, a couple of key challenges for DRL to overcome remain, including multitask, or generalized, learning. We explore how evolution can be used for potentially generalized forms of learning, like DRL, in the next chapter.

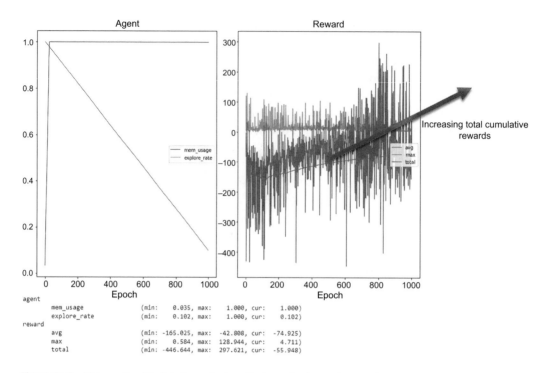

Figure 11.8   The results of training an agent on the lunar lander environment

Summary

- Reinforcement learning is another form of dynamic learning that uses rewards to reinforce the selection of the best appropriate `action` given a current `state`.
- Q-learning is an implementation of RL that uses a `state` or `action` lookup table or policy to provide a decision on the next-best possible `action` an agent should take.
- It is important to be able to differentiate between various forms of learning, including generative, supervised, and reinforcement learning.
- The OpenAI Gym is a framework and tool kit for evaluation and exploring various implementations of RL or other reward/decision-solving models.
- Running the OpenAI Gym within a Colab notebook can be useful for exploring various environments ranging in complexity.
- OpenAI Gym is a common reinforcement learning algorithm benchmark and exploration tool.
- NEAT can be used to solve a variety of sample RL Gym environments by employing typical reinforcement learning.
- A NEAT agent can be developed to solve more complex RL environments using sampling and playback techniques.
- Deep Q-learning is an advanced form of RL that employs DL in place of a Q-table or policy. Deep Q-networks have been used to solve complex environments, like the lunar lander game.

Evolutionary machine learning and beyond

In the last chapter, we looked deeply at how evolutionary solutions like NEAT could be applied to solve RL. In this chapter, we continue with some of those same concepts but also take a step back and look at how evolutionary methods can be applied to expand our understanding of ML. Specifically, looking at what role evolutionary search plays can expand how we develop generalized ML.

DL is tailored for function approximation and optimization that is often designed to solve specific problems. Throughout this book, we have looked at ways

> ## Generalized ML (aka generalized AI)
>
> *Generalized machine learning*, or generalized intelligence, is an area that focuses on building models that can solve more than one task. Typically, in ML, we develop models to classify or regress on a single source of data, training the model iteratively and validating performance with similar data. Generalized ML's goal is to develop models that can predict over multiple disparate forms of data or environments. In data science, you may hear this problem referred to as *cross-domain* or *multimodal*, meaning we are building a model to tackle problems across domains.

of augmenting or improving DL in that respect by taking such steps as improving hyperparameter search, optimizing network architecture, and neuroevolving networks.

In this chapter, we divert our attention from DL and look at examples that use evolution to help generalize the way we solve ML problems. We start by looking at evolving functions and then move on to developing more generalized functions that may solve multiple problems. Expanding on generalization, we then look at an idea that attempts to encapsulate generalized function learning, called *instinctual learning*.

From generalized instinctual learning, we move on to an interesting example that trains an `ant` agent using genetic programming. Then, we explore how a specific agent can be generalized through further evolution. Finally, we finish this final chapter with a discussion of the future of evolution in ML. In the next section, we begin by looking at the core of ML—the function—and how it can be evolved with gene expression programming (GEP).

12.1 Evolution and machine learning with gene expression programming

A function, or a function approximator, is at the core of any ML algorithm. The role of this function is to take in data or input and output a result or prediction. Figure 12.1 shows the various forms of learning we have covered in this book, using DL as the function or function approximator targeted for each type of learning.

In this section, we look at a notebook that builds the actual function, not an approximation using evolution. The benefit here is that evolution removes the need to employ a loss or error function within the learning process. Figure 12.2 shows how this type of learning operates. If you look back to chapter 11, this is the same process we performed with NEAT as a function approximator, replacing traditional DL.

For the notebook in this section, we use Geppy, an extension to DEAP that improves on DEAP implementation of GEP. If you recall, we have already looked at GEP in chapter 3. The work we do here is specific to evolving functions and how this relates to general ML.

Open the EDL_12_1_GEPPY.ipynb notebook in Google Colab. Refer to the appendix if you need assistance. Run all the cells in the notebook by selecting Runtime > Run All from the menu.

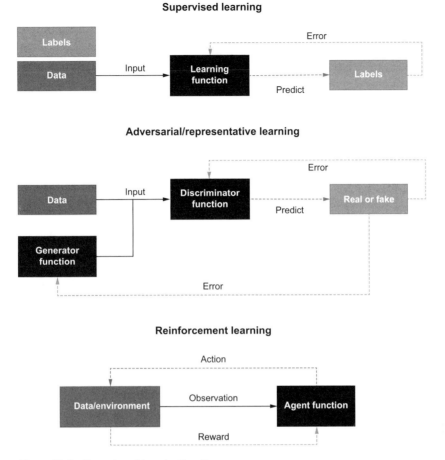

Supervised learning

Adversarial/representative learning

Reinforcement learning

Figure 12.1 **Examples of learning functions**

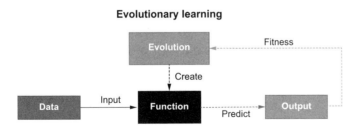

Evolutionary learning

Figure 12.2 **Evolutionary learning**

Since Geppy is an extension of DEAP, most of the code looks very similar to what we have covered previously; as such, we only review new features here. The first code cell block we look at, shown in the following listing, shows the target function we are evolving a solution for. This simple linear function is the target function we want to replicate through evolution.

Listing 12.1   EDL_12_1_GEPPY.ipynb: Defining the target function

```
def f(x1):
    return 6 * x1 + 22   ◁─── A ground truth function
```

This notebook uses a base set of expression operators to generate the expression tree, as shown in the following listing.

Listing 12.2   EDL_12_1_GEPPY.ipynb: Adding expression operators

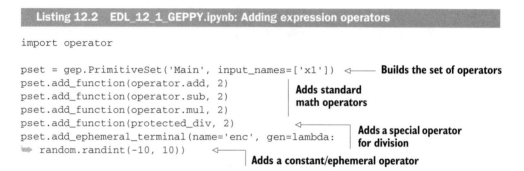

```
import operator

pset = gep.PrimitiveSet('Main', input_names=['x1'])  ◁─── Builds the set of operators
pset.add_function(operator.add, 2)
pset.add_function(operator.sub, 2)          Adds standard
pset.add_function(operator.mul, 2)          math operators
pset.add_function(protected_div, 2)   ◁
pset.add_ephemeral_terminal(name='enc', gen=lambda:   Adds a special operator
                                                      for division
⇨  random.randint(-10, 10))   ◁
                                   Adds a constant/ephemeral operator
```

Next, we jump down to the `evaluate` function, which shows how we determine the fitness of each `individual` in the `population`. The `toolbox.compile` function generates the function from the `individual` gene sequence. Then, the output is generated from the sample `X1` input. After that, the `fitness` is returned by calculating the mean absolute error, as shown in the following listing.

Listing 12.3   EDL_12_1_GEPPY.ipynb: The `evaluate` function

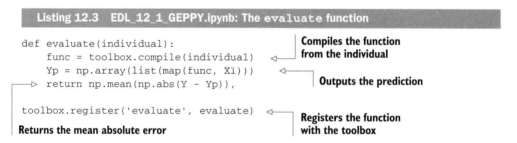

```
def evaluate(individual):                      Compiles the function
    func = toolbox.compile(individual)   ◁──┘  from the individual
    Yp = np.array(list(map(func, X1)))   ◁
─▷  return np.mean(np.abs(Y - Yp)),            Outputs the prediction

toolbox.register('evaluate', evaluate)  ◁──┐
                                            Registers the function
Returns the mean absolute error             with the toolbox
```

The benefit of using Geppy over the base gene expression library from DEAP is that we have access to several helpful extensions and operators relevant to this form evolution. These new operators aid GEP evolution through tweaks in the `mutation` and `crossover` genetic operators, as shown in listing 12.4. The additional `mutation` operators, prefixed with `mut_`, allow the function to be inverted and transposed. Following that, the extra `crossover` operators, prefixed with `cx_`, provide two-point `crossover` and `gene crossover`. Two-point `crossover` allows the `gene` sequence to be split into two locations along a gene sequence. The process of gene crossover allows each gene chromosome to crossover.

Listing 12.4   EDL_12_1_GEPPY.ipynb: Registering custom operators

```
toolbox.register('mut_uniform', gep.mutate_uniform,
➥ pset=pset, ind_pb=0.05, pb=1)
toolbox.register('mut_invert', gep.invert, pb=0.1)
toolbox.register('mut_is_transpose', gep.is_transpose,
➥ pb=0.1)
toolbox.register('mut_ris_transpose',
➥ gep.ris_transpose, pb=0.1)
toolbox.register('mut_gene_transpose',
➥ gep.gene_transpose, pb=0.1)
```
Added for mutation

```
toolbox.register('cx_1p', gep.crossover_one_point,
➥ pb=0.4)
toolbox.register('cx_2p', gep.crossover_two_point,
➥ pb=0.2)
toolbox.register('cx_gene', gep.crossover_gene, pb=0.1)
```
Added for crossover

```
toolbox.register('mut_ephemeral', gep.mutate_
➥ uniform_ephemeral, ind_pb='1p')
toolbox.pbs['mut_ephemeral'] = 1
```
Handles constants/ephermeral operators

Previously, we have usually represented our genetic encoding in a single gene sequence. Geppy works by breaking the gene sequence into components, or chromosomes. Breaking the gene sequence into chromosomes allows complex gene sequences to be isolated into useful parts. Then, through evolution, these parts can be swapped during crossover operations, thereby maintaining useful sections.

We can see how gene chromosomes are defined by looking at the registration of the gene, as shown in listing 12.5. The parameter h represents the number of chromosomes, and the parameter n_genes represents the number of genes in each chromosome. The chromosome template and gene sequence are registered in the toolbox, as we have previously seen.

Listing 12.5   EDL_12_1_GEPPY.ipynb: Defining the gene, head, and chromosomes

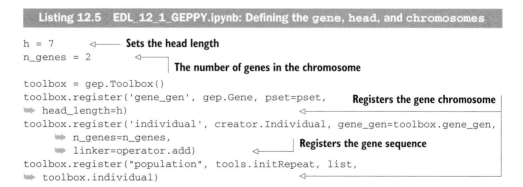

```
h = 7            ⟵  Sets the head length
n_genes = 2          ⟵
                         The number of genes in the chromosome
toolbox = gep.Toolbox()
toolbox.register('gene_gen', gep.Gene, pset=pset,       Registers the gene chromosome
➥ head_length=h)                              ⟵
toolbox.register('individual', creator.Individual, gene_gen=toolbox.gene_gen,
      ➥ n_genes=n_genes,
      ➥ linker=operator.add)      ⟵    Registers the gene sequence
toolbox.register("population", tools.initRepeat, list,
➥ toolbox.individual)                     ⟵
```

The code to evolve the function, shown in listing 12.6, is only a few lines long, starting with creating the population and setting the number of best individuals to track with the HallOfFame class. After that, it's a simple matter of calling gep_simple to evolve the solution over n_gen generations.

Listing 12.6 EDL_12_1_GEPPY.ipynb: Evolving the function

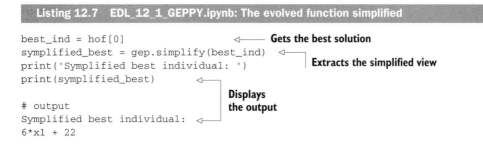

```
n_pop = 100        The parameters for
n_gen = 100        population and generations

pop = toolbox.population(n=n_pop)  ◁──┐  Creates the population
hof = tools.HallOfFame(3)          ◁────  Sets the max number of best

pop, log = gep.gep_simple(pop, toolbox, n_generations=n_gen, n_elites=1,
                        stats=stats, hall_of_fame=
                    ➡ hof, verbose=True)  ◁────  Evolves
```

Since most raw evolved functions have redundant terms or operators, a useful feature offered by Geppy is *simplification*. Calling the gep.simplify function using the best individual generates the top solved function. As you can see from the results in the following listing, the final function matches exactly what the target function was in listing 12.1.

Listing 12.7 EDL_12_1_GEPPY.ipynb: The evolved function simplified

```
best_ind = hof[0]                            ◁──── Gets the best solution
symplified_best = gep.simplify(best_ind)  ◁──┐
print('Symplified best individual: ')        │  Extracts the simplified view
print(symplified_best)  ◁──┐
                           │  Displays
# output                   │  the output
Symplified best individual:  ◁──┘
6*x1 + 22
```

The last cell of the notebook, shown in listing 12.8, renders the raw, not simplified function, using another helpful feature of Geppy. The call to gep.export_expression_tree renders the function in the nice-looking plot shown in figure 12.3. Note that the raw plot you see may look different from that in the figure, but the result—a simplified expression—should be the same.

Listing 12.8 EDL_12_1_GEPPY.ipynb: Displaying an evolved equation

```
rename_labels = {'add': '+', 'sub': '-', 'mul': '*', 'protected_div': '/'}
gep.export_expression_tree(best_ind, rename_labels,
    ➡ 'data/numerical_expression_tree.png')  ◁────┐  Generates an image of
                                                    │  an expression tree
from IPython.display import Image
Image(filename='data/numerical_expression_tree.png')  ◁──┤  Displays the tree
                                                          │  in the notebook
```

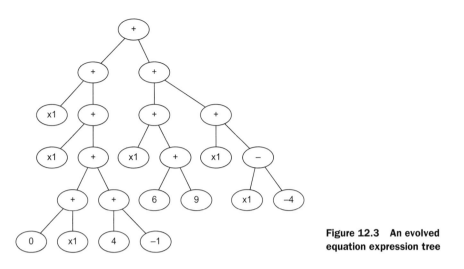

Figure 12.3   An evolved equation expression tree

The point of this notebook is to showcase a useful tool that can derive explicit functions. In this example, the resulting function is identical to the target function, but that won't always be the case. In many cases, the resulting function can provide insight into the data relationships not previously understood, as we see later in the chapter. Before that, though, let's jump into some learning exercises in the next section.

12.1.1   Learning exercises

Use these exercises to help you improve your knowledge of the content:

1   Alter the target function in listing 12.1 and then rerun the notebook. How well does the evolution perform?
2   Modify the `chromosomes` by altering the `head`, `h`, and the number of `genes`, `n_genes`, parameters from listing 12.5. Rerun the notebook to see what effect this had on the evolutionary process.
3   Add or remove expression operators to listing 12.2. You can add operators like `cos` or `sin`, for example—just check the DEAP documentation. Make sure to also update the labels from listing 12.8.

In the next section, we move away from simple examples and on to a classic control problem by revisiting the OpenAI Gym.

12.2   Revisiting reinforcement learning with Geppy

To demonstrate how effective Geppy can be at evolving equations, we look at a class control problem via the OpenAI Gym. The idea is to let Geppy evolve an equation that can drive a couple of the most complex OpenAI Gym environments. This example mirrors what we did with NEAT in chapter 11, and if you need to review some elements, refer to those notebooks.

Open the EDL_12_2_GEPPY_Gym.ipynb notebook in Google Colab. Refer to the appendix if you need assistance. Run all the cells in the notebook by selecting Runtime > Run All from the menu.

> **Potentially unstable**
>
> As mentioned in chapter 11, because of the virtual driver setup and other custom-installed components, these notebooks can be prone to crashing. If the notebook crashes during execution, disconnect and delete the runtime and then restart and rerun. From the menu, select Runtime > Disconnect and Delete Runtime and then Runtime > Run All.

In this notebook, we attempt to solve two `continuous` control problems: the mountain car (continuous) and the pendulum (continuous). The word *continuous* is used to define the `action` and `observation` (state) spaces of the environment. Coincidentally, and slightly confusingly, *continuous* may also refer to the agent receiving continuous rewards. That is, at each step, the environment yields a reward, negative or positive. Setting up the notebooks and rendering their `action` or `observation` spaces is quite simple, as shown in the following listing.

Listing 12.9 EDL_12_2_GEPPY_Gym.ipynb: Rendering the environment spaces

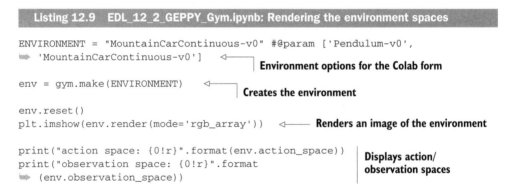

```
ENVIRONMENT = "MountainCarContinuous-v0" #@param ['Pendulum-v0',
    'MountainCarContinuous-v0']          ⟵──┐
                                            │ Environment options for the Colab form

env = gym.make(ENVIRONMENT)     ⟵──┐
                                   │ Creates the environment
env.reset()
plt.imshow(env.render(mode='rgb_array'))   ⟵──── Renders an image of the environment

print("action space: {0!r}".format(env.action_space))    ┐ Displays action/
print("observation space: {0!r}".format                  │ observation spaces
    (env.observation_space))                              ┘
```

Figure 12.4 shows both environments we try to evolve solution equations for. Both environments use a continuous `action` space, while the Gym environments we explored in chapter 11 used discrete `action` spaces. *Continuous* means an `action` can now be a real value within the given range: –2 to +2 for pendulum and –1 to +1 for mountain car. This is perfect, since our derived equation can now just output a value within that range.

The `observation` space for each environment is different, so we must make a slight change to the way we define the `PrimitiveSet`, as shown in listing 12.10. Since the two environments use different `observation` spaces, we need to account for those changes when setting up the base set of inputs. For the pendulum, the `observation` space is the x, y coordinates of the pendulum. Likewise, for mountain car, the `observation` space

```
action space: Box(-2.0, 2.0, (1,), float32)
observation space: Box(-8.0, 8.0, (3,), float32)
```

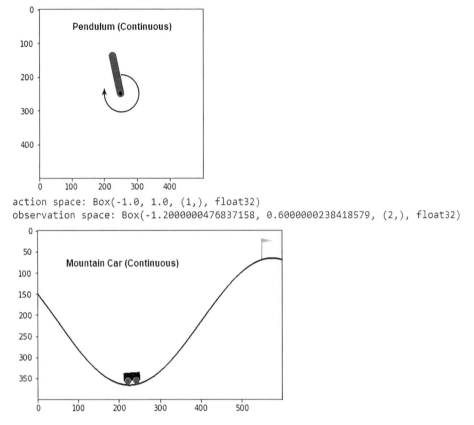

```
action space: Box(-1.0, 1.0, (1,), float32)
observation space: Box(-1.2000000476837158, 0.6000000238418579, (2,), float32)
```

Figure 12.4   Rendering environments and spaces

is the x, y coordinates of the car and its velocity. This means the function for pendulum is f(x, y), and for mountain car, it is f(x, y, velocity).

Listing 12.10   EDL_12_2_GEPPY_Gym.ipynb: Setting the `primitive set`

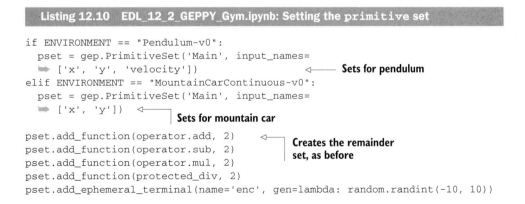

```
if ENVIRONMENT == "Pendulum-v0":
  pset = gep.PrimitiveSet('Main', input_names=
    ['x', 'y', 'velocity'])                          ◁──── Sets for pendulum
elif ENVIRONMENT == "MountainCarContinuous-v0":
  pset = gep.PrimitiveSet('Main', input_names=
    ['x', 'y'])    ◁──────┐ Sets for mountain car

pset.add_function(operator.add, 2)    ◁──────┐ Creates the remainder
pset.add_function(operator.sub, 2)           │ set, as before
pset.add_function(operator.mul, 2)
pset.add_function(protected_div, 2)
pset.add_ephemeral_terminal(name='enc', gen=lambda: random.randint(-10, 10))
```

As we did in chapter 11, we determine the fitness of an individual based on their ability to accumulate rewards. Instead of using a NEAT network to predict the action, though, this time we use the evolved function/equation to calculate the action. In this code block, shown in listing 12.11, two simple functions have been written for each environment. These examples are just used for testing and do not represent the final evolved solution internally. The call to func, depending on the environment, uses the unroll operator * to expand the observed state into arguments to the function. Then, the output of the function, which could be anything, is converted to the appropriate action space of the environment with the convert_to_action and clamp functions.

Listing 12.11   EDL_12_2_GEPPY_Gym.ipynb: Determining individual fitness

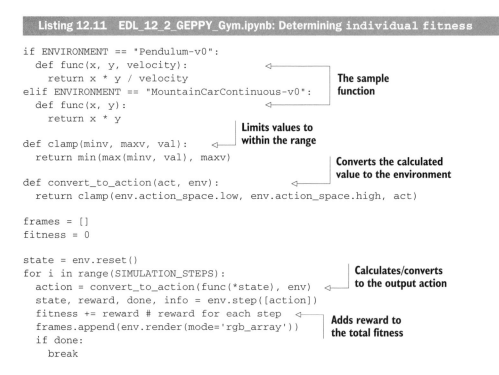

```
if ENVIRONMENT == "Pendulum-v0":
  def func(x, y, velocity):                    ◁──────── The sample
    return x * y / velocity                              function
elif ENVIRONMENT == "MountainCarContinuous-v0":  ◁────
  def func(x, y):
    return x * y
                                       Limits values to
                                       within the range
def clamp(minv, maxv, val):    ◁────────
  return min(max(minv, val), maxv)
                                            Converts the calculated
                                            value to the environment
def convert_to_action(act, env):       ◁──────
  return clamp(env.action_space.low, env.action_space.high, act)

frames = []
fitness = 0

state = env.reset()                            Calculates/converts
for i in range(SIMULATION_STEPS):              to the output action
  action = convert_to_action(func(*state), env)  ◁──
  state, reward, done, info = env.step([action])
  fitness += reward # reward for each step   ◁─
  frames.append(env.render(mode='rgb_array'))    Adds reward to
  if done:                                       the total fitness
    break
```

Now, the real evaluate function, shown in the following listing, can be written from listing 12.11.

Listing 12.12   EDL_12_2_GEPPY_Gym.ipynb: The real evaluate function

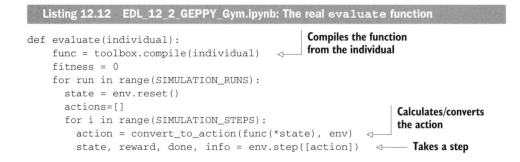

```
def evaluate(individual):               Compiles the function
  func = toolbox.compile(individual)  ◁─ from the individual
  fitness = 0
  for run in range(SIMULATION_RUNS):
    state = env.reset()
    actions=[]
                                                Calculates/converts
    for i in range(SIMULATION_STEPS):           the action
      action = convert_to_action(func(*state), env)  ◁─
      state, reward, done, info = env.step([action])  ◁──── Takes a step
```

```
        fitness += reward        Adds the reward to
        if done:                 the total fitness
            break

    return fitness,

toolbox.register('evaluate', evaluate)        Registers the function
```

The code to run the evolution is quite straightforward, as shown in the following listing.

Listing 12.13 EDL_12_2_GEPPY_Gym.ipynb: Evolving the solution

```
POPULATION = 250 #@param {type:"slider", min:10,
    max:1000, step:5}                              The evolution
GENERATIONS = 25 #@param {type:"slider", min:10,   hyperparameters
    max:250, step:1}

pop = toolbox.population(n=POPULATION)
hof = tools.HallOfFame(3)

for gen in range(GENERATIONS):
  pop, log = gep.gep_simple(pop, toolbox, n_generations=1, n_elites=1,
                        stats=stats, hall_of_fame=
                            hof, verbose=True)        Evolves for a generation
  clear_output()
  print(f"GENERATION: {gen}")
  best = hof[0]                    Shows the performance
  show_best(best)                  of the best individual
```

After each `generation`, we call the `show_best` function to run the `individual` through a simulation and render it to video, as shown in the following listing.

Listing 12.14 EDL_12_2_GEPPY_Gym.ipynb: Showing the fittest

```
def show_best(best):
  func = toolbox.compile(best)        Compiles to the function
  frames = []
  fitness = 0
  state = env.reset()
  for i in range(SIMULATION_STEPS):        Simulates the function over one run
    action = convert_to_action(func(*state), env)
    state, reward, done, info = env.step([action])
    frames.append(env.render(mode='rgb_array'))
    fitness += reward
    if done:
      break

  mediapy.show_video(frames, fps=30)        Renders the recorded sim to video
  try:
    symplified_best = gep.simplify(best)
    print(f'Symplified best individual: {fitness}')        Shows the simplified
    print(symplified_best)                                 form of the function
  except:
    pass
```

Figure 12.5 shows the results of the `mountain car` solution with the simplified equation. The resulting output shows the derived equations being used to get good rewards from the different environments. It is also interesting to note how different each of the equations are, given their similarity in tasks and inputs.

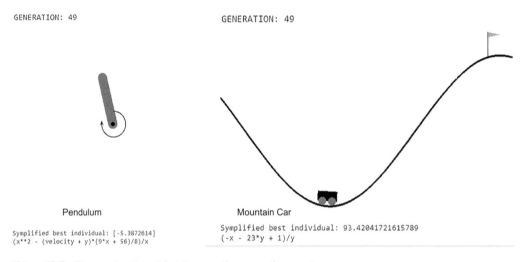

Figure 12.5   The results of evolving the equation on environments

The ability to solve these environments with Geppy evolving an equation is impressive. It demonstrates how effective evolution can be at overcoming control problems. Our goal in this chapter, however, is to look at how more generalized learning solutions may be evolved. We cover this in greater depth in the next section, but for now, let's jump into some learning tasks that can help reinforce this section's concepts.

12.2.1 Learning exercises

Use these exercises to go back over the material and reinforce what you've learned:

1   Search the internet for other potential OpenAI Gym environments we could potentially solve with this technique.
2   Add new expression operators, like `cos` or `sin`, to the set. Rerun the notebook to see if and how these operators are used in the resulting derived equation.
3   Try to obtain the best `fitness` you can with either pendulum or mountain car. This can be done in several ways, including increasing the `population`, increasing the number of `generations` to start, and introducing new expressions.

In the next section, we expand on our understanding of using evolution to evolve more generalized solutions.

12.3 Introducing instinctual learning

Instinctual learning (IL) is a concept developed by the author of this book that attempts to generalize how traits or functions can be both evolved and learned. It is based on biological observations of humans and other organisms and borrows concepts from RL and other behavioral learning methods. In our next notebook, we employ some IL concepts to attempt to evolve a more generalized solution to the example of the last section. Before that, though, let's take a more in-depth look at what IL is.

12.3.1 The basics of instinctual learning

IL is an abstract thought model intended to guide the development of more generalized ML using evolution. The initiative of IL is that if evolution can develop human generalization, it can likewise develop digital life. Of course, evolving some form of generalized digital life is no trivial task, so IL attempts to describe some basic patterns and starting points.

In nature, we observe that many organisms have what we refer to as *instincts*, which describe some form of learned or evolved behavior. For many species, differentiating between learned and evolved instincts may be obvious. A great example of this is the dog, for which some breeds are associated with specific natural behaviors; however, dogs can also learn new behaviors that can become instincts.

A dog typically learns an instinct through behavioral learning, such as reinforcement or rewards-based learning. Initially, training the dog for a task takes a repetitive trial-and-error process, but after some amount of this training, the dog "just knows." That stage where the dog just knows is what we call the *transition to an instinct*. Before we get into how the transition occurs, let's dig a bit deeper into general theories of how a biological mind works in the next section.

THE DUAL-PROCESS THEORY OF THOUGHT

The dual-process theory of thought describes a theory of the higher-order thought process in biological life. The idea is that we have two processes functioning within our brains: one low-level process, called *system 1*, and another more conscious process, called *system 2*. Figure 12.6 shows the key differences between these two processes.

These two processes of thought are generally considered separate, but the thoughts or behaviors from system 2 can be converted to system 1, given enough training and practice. The conscious act of RL is, therefore, a system-2 process that converts to system-1 process, with enough trial and error. We may refer to this transitional process as *conditioning*, originating from Pavlovian conditioning.

Pavlov's dog and Pavlovian conditioning

Ivan Pavlov (1849–1936) was a psychologist who showed through reinforcement (rewards-based) learning that a dog could be conditioned to salivate at the sound of a bell. This conditioned or learned behavior demonstrates the transition from a system-2 process to a system-1 process, where through continued training, the dog instinctually salivated at the sound of a bell.

Dual-process theory of thought

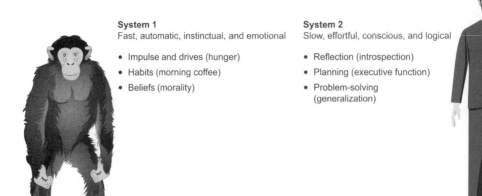

System 1
Fast, automatic, instinctual, and emotional

- Impulse and drives (hunger)
- Habits (morning coffee)
- Beliefs (morality)

System 2
Slow, effortful, conscious, and logical

- Reflection (introspection)
- Planning (executive function)
- Problem-solving (generalization)

Figure 12.6   Dual-process theory

Figure 12.7 depicts dual-process theory in terms of IL. From evolution, an organism derives certain genetic traits or instincts. According to dual-process theory, the organism can think and potentially convert thoughts and actions to instincts.

Figure 12.7   Dual-process theory and instinctual learning

Assuming dual-process theory is accurate, we can also assume evolution developed this process as an efficiency. In other words, we assume at some point in the evolution of higher life, evolution transitioned from building hardcoded instincts to letting organisms develop their own instincts. This means, then, that at some point, an organism evolved the instinct that became what we now call dual-process theory.

IL is the search for the evolutionary foundations that derived this dual process or system-2 instinct. It is about understanding how at some point in the evolution of life, instincts became thoughts. Reinforcement learning is, therefore, an example of a simple form of dual-process theory, and IL is the search for the origins of RL. The notebook example we look at in the next section demonstrates how inefficient evolving generalized instincts (functions) can be.

12.3.2 *Developing generalized instincts*

The next notebook demonstrates how and why organisms may have moved from just developing instincts to higher forms of thought. In the following notebook, we use just evolution to attempt to develop a single equation (instinct) that can solve both Gym problems. In RL, this is called multitask RL and is considered by many to be a difficult problem.

Open the EDL_12_3_GEPPY_Instinctual.ipynb notebook in Google Colab. Refer to the appendix if you need assistance. Run all the cells in the notebook by selecting Runtime > Run All from the menu.

In this notebook, we look at how potentially learned instincts evolved in the last exercise and can be used to generalize learning. The first thing we look at, then, is how those previously developed instincts (aka equations or functions) can be reused, as shown in the following listing. Function `instinct1` is evolved from running the EDL_12_2_GEPPY_Gyms.ipynb notebook on the pendulum environment. Likewise, `instinct2` evolved from the same notebook over mountain car. Refer to figure 12.5 for a review of those generated equations.

Listing 12.15   EDL_12_3_GEPPY_Instinctual.ipynb: Adding the instincts

```
def protected_div(x1, x2):      ⟵—— Avoids division by zero
    if abs(x2) < 1e-6:
        return 1
    return x1 / x2
                                          The function that solved pendulum
def instinct1(x1, x2):      ⟵——┘
  return protected_div((-x1 - 23*x2 + 1),x2)
                                              The function that solved mountain car
def instinct2(x1, x2, x3):                ⟵——┘
  return protected_div(x1**2 - (x3 + x2)*(9*x1 + 56)/8,x1)
```

A primary concept in IL is that instincts or functions are layered and developed or added over time. This notebook attempts to prove how simulated organisms successful in two distinct tasks could be combined to generate a third evolved organism, with this third organism being able to evolve a tertiary, or higher-level, instinct to generalize the solution for both environments.

Next, we look at how these newly defined instincts are added to the `primitive` set, as shown in listing 12.16. For the `PrimitiveSet` definition, we set the inputs to include x, y, and `velocity` as well as a new input, e, that represents the environment. Then, we simplify the possible function operators to only include `add`, `sub`, and `mul`, along with the new instinct operators. The ephemeral constant operators were removed, since the base-level instincts should contain the constants needed.

Listing 12.16   EDL_12_3_GEPPY_Instinctual.ipynb: Completing the `primitive` set

```
pset = gep.PrimitiveSet('Main', input_names=      Generalized inputs
⇨ ['e', 'x', 'y', 'velocity'])      ⟵——————       and environment
```

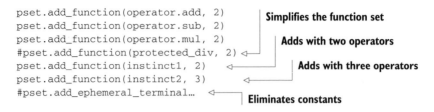

```
pset.add_function(operator.add, 2)        | Simplifies the function set
pset.add_function(operator.sub, 2)        |
pset.add_function(operator.mul, 2)        | Adds with two operators
#pset.add_function(protected_div, 2)
pset.add_function(instinct1, 2)           | Adds with three operators
pset.add_function(instinct2, 3)
#pset.add_ephemeral_terminal…             | Eliminates constants
```

Unlike in previous notebooks, this time we evolve an agent to solve both environments simultaneously. To do this, we create a list of environments we use to evolve the agent on, as shown in the following listing.

Listing 12.17 EDL_12_3_GEPPY_Instinctual.ipynb: Creating environments

```
environments = [gym.make("MountainCarContinuous-v0"),    | A list of environments
    gym.make("Pendulum-v0")]                             | to evaluate on
print(str(environments[1]))          | Converts to a string before printing
```

The next cell block we look at, shown in listing 12.18, contains the `evaluate` function. This time, the function starts by looping over the `environments` list and running a set of simulations for each environment. Input e simply represents the environment index and is fed as the first parameter to the target function. Since each environment has a different `observation` state, when running the pendulum problem with just 2 states, we append a 0 to the `state` space to represent the third input: `velocity`. At the end of the function, the `fitness` values for both environments are averaged and returned.

Listing 12.18 EDL_12_3_GEPPY_Instinctual.ipynb: Building the `evaluate` function

```
def evaluate(individual):
    func = toolbox.compile(individual)   | Loops through
    total_fitness = 0                    | the environments
    for env in environments:
        fitness = []                                  Populates e, based on
        e = environments.index(env)                   the environment index
        for run in range(SIMULATION_RUNS):
            state = env.reset()
            actions=[]
            for i in range(SIMULATION_STEPS):
                if len(state) < 3:
                    state = np.append(state, 0)  ◁── Appends to the state if needed
                state = np.insert(state, 0, e)
                action = convert_to_action(func(*state), env)  ◁── Converts to an action
                state, reward, done, info = env.step([action])
                fitness.append(reward)
                if done:
                    break
        total_fitness += sum(fitness)/len(fitness)
    return total_fitness/2,
```
Returns an average fitness ⎣▷ `return total_fitness/2,`

```
toolbox.register('evaluate', evaluate)
```

The next thing we look at is the updated show_best function, which now combines the simulation runs of the agent over both environments into a single video. This time, the function loops over the environments and simulates the agent on each. Since each environment renders to a different window size, we use the cv2.resize function to make all frames the same size, as shown in listing 12.19. This needs to be done to combine all the frames into a single video. At the end of the function, the expression tree is saved to a file for sidecar viewing. You can view the evolution of the expression tree by opening the system folders on the left side, finding the file in the data folder, and then double-clicking on it to open a side window.

Listing 12.19 EDL_12_3_GEPPY_Instinctual.ipynb: Updating the show_best function

```
rename_labels = {'add' : '+',
                 'sub': '-',
                 'mul': '*',
                 'protected_div': '/',
                 'instinct1': 'I1',      Adds labels for
                 'instinct2': 'I2'}      instinct functions

def show_best(best):
  func = toolbox.compile(best)
  frames = []
  fitness = 0
  for env in environments:        ◁——— Loops over the environments
    e = environments.index(env)
    state = env.reset()
    for i in range(SIMULATION_STEPS):
      if len(state) < 3:
        state = np.append(state, 0)
      state = np.insert(state, 0, e)
      action = convert_to_action(func(*state), env)
      state, reward, done, info = env.step([action])
      frame = env.render(mode='rgb_array')
      frame = cv2.resize(frame, dsize=(600, 400),       Resizes the
                  interpolation=cv2.INTER_CUBIC)   ◁——  captured frame
      frames.append(frame)
      fitness += reward
      if done:
        break

  mediapy.show_video(frames, fps=30)           ◁——— Renders the video
  gep.export_expression_tree(best, rename_labels,
      'data/numerical_expression_tree.png'))   ◁——— Saves the expression tree output
```

Figure 12.8 shows captured output from the generated video running the evolution over 250 generations with 1,000 individuals. You may see the agent solve one or both environments much sooner.

Figure 12.9 shows the final evolved expression tree. If you run this notebook, you may see a different tree, but overall, it will likely be similar. What is interesting about this expression tree is the reuse and chaining of the instinct1 and instinct2 functions.

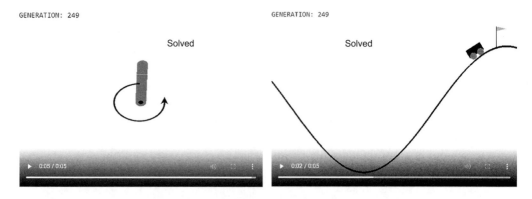

Figure 12.8 **An agent solving both environments simultaneously**

In fact, they become the primary operators in the equation, but they are not used at all the way we would expect. Notice how the inputs, in most cases, don't even align with the instinct's original inputs.

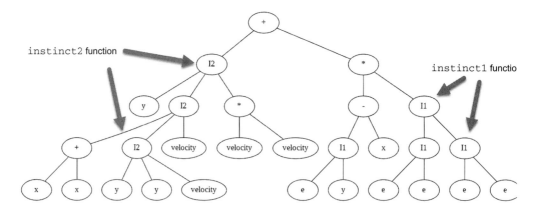

Figure 12.9 **The final evolved expression tree**

At this point, you may be wondering whether we could just let the agent evolve a single function, without the added instinctual operators. This is a fair question, so let's see how it works in the next section.

12.3.3 *Evolving generalized solutions without instincts*

In the following notebook, we take an opposing approach to the last exercise and assume nothing of instincts and IL. This means we allow the agent using evolution to solve both environments by deriving a single equation with no instinctual operators.

Open the EDL_12_3_GEPPY_Generalize.ipynb notebook in Google Colab. Refer to the appendix if you need assistance. Run all the cells in the notebook by selecting Runtime > Run All from the menu.

The only change to this notebook is the definition of the `primitive` set being used to build the expression tree, as shown in listing 12.20. The main change from the IL example is the omission of the instinct operators and the addition of the `protected_div` and `ephemeral` constants. Aside from the extra inputs, this set of operators is the same as the one we used for the base function derivation on a single environment.

Listing 12.20   EDL_12_3_GEPPY_Generalize.ipynb: Setting up the `primitive` set

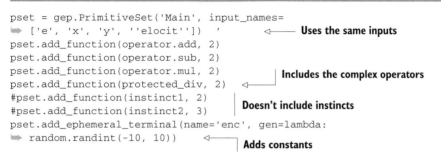

```
pset = gep.PrimitiveSet('Main', input_names=
  ['e', 'x', 'y', ''elocit''])           ⟵——  Uses the same inputs
pset.add_function(operator.add, 2)
pset.add_function(operator.sub, 2)
pset.add_function(operator.mul, 2)                    Includes the complex operators
pset.add_function(protected_div, 2)   ⟵——┘
#pset.add_function(instinct1, 2)
#pset.add_function(instinct2, 3)        Doesn't include instincts
pset.add_ephemeral_terminal(name='enc', gen=lambda:
  random.randint(-10, 10))   ⟵——┐
                                 └ Adds constants
```

The rest of the notebook is the same as we saw previously, so just sit back and watch the evolution—or, perhaps, lack thereof. Indeed, by running this example over multiple environments, you will find that, at best, the agent converges to only getting close to solving a single environment. Figure 12.10 shows an example of the video output displaying this failure.

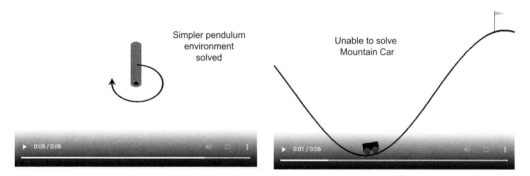

Figure 12.10   The failure of an agent to generalize across both tasks

So what's going on? How is it possible that reusing previously developed functions or instincts as operators in a new function derivation is more successful than deriving a new equation? The simple answer to the problem is limiting complexity and choices. Reusable instincts reduce complexity and choices when evolving new functions.

This concept of reuse and development of reusable code and functions is a cornerstone of today's software development best practices. Today, coders build applications from numerous previously developed components or functions. What has evolved today in the software industry could very well just be mimicking an evolutionary best practice developed millions of years ago.

Figure 12.11 shows how instincts may evolve over time, using an example of cephalopod (octopus) evolution. Early on, the organism may have evolved hardcoded instincts not unlike what we did in the EDL_12_2_GEPPY_Gyms.ipynbnotebook. Through another stage of evolution, the organism then may evolve a tertiary instinct that allows itself to use both instincts at the same time. Finally, at the last stage of evolution, the cephalopod develops a new type of instinct: a system-2 instinct, or an instinct that allows itself to think.

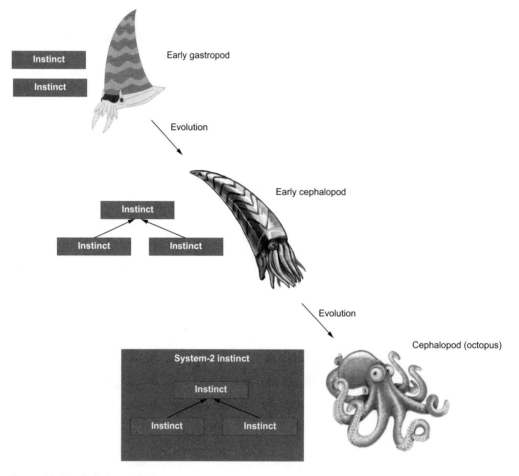

Figure 12.11   IL during evolution

In the next section, we look at one possible approach to modeling, developing, and evolving a dual-process system level-2 instinct. Before that, though, let's look at some helpful learning examples that will help your recall.

> ### Cephalopod (octopus) evolution
>
> The octopus is an incredible creature that shows advanced intelligence in the form of tool use and conscious behavior. What makes the octopus especially unique is that its evolutionary path is far removed from what we normally consider higher life forms to have developed from. It is also unique in that it has no central nervous system or brain, and it is believed that much of an octopus's thoughts are generated throughout its body. Understanding how cephalopods evolve will likely provide us with incredible insight not only into the validity of IL but how all conscious thought may have evolved.

12.3.4   Learning exercises

Use the following exercises to improve your understanding of the material and perhaps even develop new tricks and techniques on your own:

1   Remove one of the base instincts from the `primitive` set of notebook example EDL_12_3_GEPPY_Instinctual.ipynb and then run the exercise again. Are you getting similar results using only a single instinct?

2   Go back and run the EDL_12_2_GEPPY_Gyms.ipynb notebook to derive new equations that use different operators. Try adding new operators, like `cos` or `sin`. Next, use those equations in notebook EDL_12_3_GEPPY_Instinctual .ipynb to see the results.

3   Add more operators to the EDL_12_3_GEPPY_Instinctual.ipynb, including the instincts, and see what effect this has on agent generalization.

In the next section, we continue looking at ways to generalize learning by looking at another approach to developing dual-process system-2 instincts.

12.4   Generalized learning with genetic programming

Genetic programming is the basis for the GEP techniques we have been exploring with GEPPY. With GP, it is possible to develop structured code that can emulate decision-making processes with Boolean logic, for instance. Not only is GP a powerful ML technique capable of developing interesting solutions, but it can also illuminate how a system-2 thought process or instinct can be evolved.

In this section, we look at a classic genetic programming example: the genetic ant. In the example, an `ant` agent evolves to search through an environment to find and consume food. This example was derived from the standard DEAP examples and modified here to demonstrate important concepts and show how the `ant` could be generalized to eat from multiple different environments.

Open the EDL_12_4_DEAP_Ant.ipynb notebook in Google Colab. Refer to the appendix if you need assistance. Run all the cells in the notebook by selecting Runtime > Run All from the menu.

This notebook uses the GP components from DEAP, and as such, the example is somewhat different, but much of the code is the same as we have seen several times previously. GP is very similar to GEP and uses a `primitive` set to define the main set of functions, as shown in listing 12.21. Unlike GEP with GEPPY, the functions in GP are not expression trees but actual code implementations. If you scroll down to the setup of the primitive set, you can see how the base functions are added. Notice how `PrimitiveSet` is constructed to accept no inputs. This is because the generated code pulls the needed inputs on its own as it runs. Next, we see the addition of three primitive binary or tertiary operators followed by terminal node functions. These functions are executed when the GP expression tree or code routine is executed.

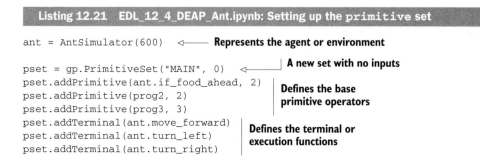

Listing 12.21   EDL_12_4_DEAP_Ant.ipynb: Setting up the primitive set

```
ant = AntSimulator(600)   ◁——— Represents the agent or environment

pset = gp.PrimitiveSet("MAIN", 0)   ◁———| A new set with no inputs
pset.addPrimitive(ant.if_food_ahead, 2)   | Defines the base
pset.addPrimitive(prog2, 2)                | primitive operators
pset.addPrimitive(prog3, 3)
pset.addTerminal(ant.move_forward)   | Defines the terminal or
pset.addTerminal(ant.turn_left)      | execution functions
pset.addTerminal(ant.turn_right)
```

Now, we can look at the definitions of the primitive operators used to define the ant agent's logic. The set up of these functions uses the partial function—a helper that allows base functions to be wrapped and exposes variable input parameters. The three operators used by ant are prog2, prog3, and if_then_else, but notice how, internally, each function executes the terminal input it is passed, as shown in the following listing. That means the higher-level operators consume Boolean logic for operation. As a result, the terminal functions, which we look at shortly, return True or False.

Listing 12.22   EDL_12_4_DEAP_Ant.ipynb: Setting up the logic functions

```
def progn(*args):   ◁——— The base partial function
    for arg in args:
        arg()

def prog2(out1, out2):          ◁——— The operator accepts two inputs
    return partial(progn,out1,out2)

def prog3(out1, out2, out3):          ◁——— The operator accepts three inputs
    return partial(progn,out1,out2,out3)

def if_then_else(condition, out1, out2):   ◁——— The conditional operator
    out1() if condition() else out2()
```

The terminal functions are written into the AntSimulator class, as shown in listing 12.23. Don't be too concerned about the actual code within each function. This code deals with the ant agent's position, movement, and facing on a grid environment. It is interesting to note that these terminal functions take and express no outputs.

Listing 12.23   EDL_12_4_DEAP_Ant.ipynb: Terminal functions

```
def turn_left(self):          ⟵——— Turns the ant to face 90 degrees left
    if self.moves < self.max_moves:
        self.moves += 1
        self.dir = (self.dir - 1) % 4

def turn_right(self):         ⟵——— Turns the ant to face 90 degrees right
    if self.moves < self.max_moves:
        self.moves += 1
        self.dir = (self.dir + 1) % 4

def move_forward(self):       ⟵——— Moves the ant forward and consumes any food
    if self.moves < self.max_moves:
        self.moves += 1
        self.row = (self.row + self.dir_row[self.dir]) % self.matrix_row
        self.col = (self.col + self.dir_col[self.dir]) % self.matrix_col
        if self.matrix_exc[self.row][self.col] == "food":
            self.eaten += 1
            self.matrix_exc[self.row][self.col] = "empty"
        self.matrix_exc[self.row][self.col] = "passed"
```

From the terminal functions, we move on to look at the one-operator custom function the ant implements. Again, the code within the function checks the grid to determine whether the ant senses food ahead of itself and the direction it is facing. The sense_food function, shown in the following listing, is what detects whether the ant is currently facing food.

Listing 12.24   EDL_12_4_DEAP_Ant.ipynb: Custom operator functions

```
                              | Custom operator functions
def sense_food(self):    ⟵——
    ahead_row = (self.row + self.dir_row[self.dir]) % self.matrix_row
    ahead_col = (self.col + self.dir_col[self.dir]) % self.matrix_col
    return self.matrix_exc[ahead_row][ahead_col] == "food"
                                    | The internal terminal helper function
def if_food_ahead(self, out1, out2):    ⟵——
⟶    return partial(if_then_else, self.sense_food, out1, out2)
```
Uses the predefined operator function if_then_else

The evaluate function, called evalArtificalAnt here, used to determine individual fitness is simple. It starts by first converting the individual gene sequence to compiled Python code using gp.compile. The output routine is run using the AntSimulator run function. After that, the fitness of the ant is output, based on the number of food squares the ant consumed, as shown in the following listing.

Listing 12.25   EDL_12_4_DEAP_Ant.ipynb: The fitness evaluate function

```
def evalArtificialAnt(individual):
    routine = gp.compile(individual, pset)    ⟵——— Compiles to Python code
⟶  ant.run(routine)
    return ant.eaten,    ⟵——— Returns the fitness based on the food eaten
```
Runs the script routine

The run function of the `AntSimulator` is where the resulting expression code tree is executed. Before executing that, though, the environment is reset, as is typical. Then, if the ant agent has remaining moves, it executes a move by calling the generated or evolved `routine` function, as shown in the following listing. You can think of this as some form of conscious decision-making thought process, described in dual-process theory as system 2.

Listing 12.26 EDL_12_4_DEAP_Ant.ipynb: Running routines

```
def run(self,routine):              Resets the simulation environment
    self._reset()      ◄──────────
    while self.moves < self.max_moves:    ◄────── Checks if there are moves remaining
        routine()
```
Executes the GP code

Unlike the Gym environments we looked at previously, the `AntSimulator` can load an arbitrarily described environment, as shown in the following listing. The first environment we try to evolve an `ant` to be successful in is from the original DEAP example.

Listing 12.27 EDL_12_4_DEAP_Ant.ipynb: Defining the environment

```
%%writefile santafe_trail1.txt     ◄────── Writes the file to the file system with a name
S###.........................      ◄──────
...#.........................              S represents the starting location.
...#.....................###....
...#.....................#....#..
...#.....................#....#..
...####.#####........##..........    ◄────── # is food.
..........#.................#..
..........#.......#..........
..........#.......#..........#..
..........#.......#..........
..................#..........
..........#.................#..
..........#..................
..........#.......#.....###...
..........#.......#..#........
..................#..........
..................#..........    ◄────── . is empty space.
..........#.......#..........
..........#...#..........#....
..........#...#..............
..........#...#..............
..........#...#..........#.....
..........#...#.....#......
..................#..........
...##..#####....#............
.#..............#............
.#..............#............
.#......#######..............
.#.....#.....................
.......#.....................
..####.......................
.............................
```

This example is very quick to run, and after it completes, you get to witness how the best ant moves through the environment in real time, as shown in figure 12.12. As you watch the ant, notice how it moves through the grid space.

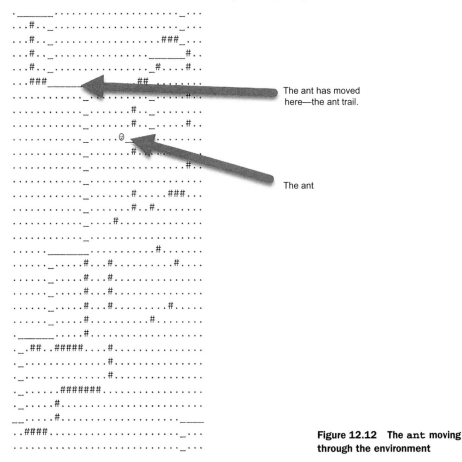

The ant has moved here—the ant trail.

The ant

Figure 12.12   The ant moving through the environment

This is a fun example to run and explore. It also demonstrates the power of genetic programming for creating code, but more importantly, it exposes a method to create that instinctual system level-2 thought process. To further demonstrate this capability, let's continue with the same notebook.

Continue with the EDL_12_4_DEAP_Ant.ipynb notebook in Colab. Assuming the notebook has completed execution, we just review the remaining cells to see how an ant can be evolved to generalize across environments. Figure 12.13 shows the two additional environments we load into the AntSimulator with the hope the evolved ants can generalize across environments. Next, we look at the code to add those environments to the ant simulator, shown in listing 12.28.

```
1  %%writefile santafe_trail2.txt          1  %%writefile santafe_trail3.txt
2  S###............................        2  S...............................
3  ...#.............2nd.............        3  ...........3rd environment......
                  environment
4  ...#............................        4  ................................
5  ...#............................        5  ................................
6  ...#............................        6  ................................
7  ...#########....................        7  ................................
8  ............#...................        8  ................................
9  ............#...................        9  ..............###############...
10 ............#...................        10 ...........################....
11 ............#...................        11 ...........################....
12 ............#...................        12 ...........#....................
13 ............#...................        13 ............########............
14 ............#...................        14 ..........#.....................
15 ............#...................        15 ..........#.....................
16 ..........#########.............        16 .....###############............
17 ..........#########.............        17 .....###############............
18 ..........#########.............        18 ......#...........###...........
19 ..........#########.............        19 .....###############............
20 ............#...................        20 ...........#....................
21 ............#...................        21 ...........#....................
22 ............#...................        22 ...........#....................
23 ............#...................        23 ...........#....................
24 ............#...................        24 ...........#....................
25 ............#...................        25 ...........#....................
26 ......######....................        26 ................................
27 ......#.........................        27 ................................
28 ......#.........................        28 ................................
29 ......########..................        29 ................................
30 ................................        30 ................................
31 ................................        31 ................................
32 ................................        32 ................................
33 ................................        33 ................................
```

Figure 12.13 Adding two environments

Listing 12.28 EDL_12_4_DEAP_Ant.ipynb: Adding environments to the simulator

```
ant.clear_matrix()                          ◁─── The clear existing environment
with  open("santafe_trail2.txt") as trail_file:
    ant.add_matrix(trail_file)    ◁──┐
                                      │ Adds environment 2

with  open("santafe_trail3.txt") as trail_file:
    ant.add_matrix(trail_file)    ◁──┐
                                      │ Adds environment 3
```

Without performing any further evolution, we can test the current best ant on these new environments by simply running the visual_run function, as shown in the following listing. As we can see from running the ant on these two new environments, they don't perform very well. We can improve on this by evolving the ant in all three environments simultaneously.

Listing 12.29   EDL_12_4_DEAP_Ant.ipynb: Testing the ant

```
ant.visualize_run(routine)     ◁──── Visualizes the ant on new environments
```

Evolving the ant on all three environments is now just a matter of adding the specific environments to the simulator and rerunning the evolution. Internally, an ant evaluating the call to the reset function puts the ant into an environment chosen at random. Since the ant is now randomly switching to different environments, the resulting code routine must account for a better search for food, as shown in the following listing.

Listing 12.30   EDL_12_4_DEAP_Ant.ipynb: Generalizing the ant

```
ant.clear_matrix()     ◁──── Clears existing environments

with  open("santafe_trail1.txt") as trail_file:
  ant.add_matrix(trail_file)                          ◁─┐

with  open("santafe_trail2.txt") as trail_file:          Adds new
  ant.add_matrix(trail_file)                          ◁─ environments

with  open("santafe_trail3.txt") as trail_file:
  ant.add_matrix(trail_file)                          ◁─┘

GENERATIONS = 100 #@param {type:"slider", min:10, max:1000, step:5}
algorithms.eaSimple(pop, toolbox, 0.5, 0.2,
⇒ GENERATIONS, stats, halloffame=hof)     ◁──── Evolves the ant
```

After the evolution has completed, you can visualize how well the ant now performs by, again, running the ant.visualize_run function call. This exercise demonstrates how well genetic programming can be used to generalize an agent to solve for multiple environments. It does this by separating the lower-level terminal functions, or what we may call *activities* or *instincts*, from the higher-level Boolean logic that may represent thought. As a result, the ant agent doesn't just derive a single core function or expression tree but, rather, two distinct systems of operation or thought.

Genetic programming is, therefore, a potential path in the search for the instinct or process that describes the dual-process system's level-2 thought. But keep in mind that one system of thought may not resemble others, and it still needs to be determined if this can lead to higher forms of generalization and consciousness in AI. We discuss evolution and the search for a higher form of AI and ML in greater depth in the next section. Before that, though, let's explore some learning exercises.

12.4.1 Learning exercises

Use the following exercises to expand your knowledge of genetic programming and the genetic ant problem:

1 Add a few new environments for the `ant` to explore and evolve on. Make sure these new environments have roughly the same number of food squares.

2 Think of ways you could alter or add to the terminal functions. Perhaps, you can add a `jump` or `fly` function that moves the `ant` several spaces in the direction it is facing.

3 Add a new operator `sense` function, like `sense_food`, that could be used to sense food, or anything else, at distances.

Genetic programming gives us a potential base for potentially finding a higher-order, dual-process system level-2 function or instinct. We discuss the potential future of IL and EDL in the next section of the book.

12.5 The future of evolutionary machine learning

In this section, we look into the future of evolutionary search for the application of improving ML and, of course, DL. While our focus in this book has been on DL, evolutionary search has far-reaching applications in other forms of ML. Evolutionary search has the potential to help guide us to new forms of learning or sublearning methods, like IL. We start our journey toward what may be possible with evolution search in the next section with a discussion on whether evolution itself may be broken.

12.5.1 Is evolution broken?

In recent years, our understanding of the evolutionary process has come under harsh scrutiny. Now, evolution being scrutinized is nothing new, but this time the critics are evolutionists themselves. Evolutionists claim our current understanding of the evolutionary process does not account for the dramatic changes we see between steps in evolution.

Darwin himself questioned his theory of evolution for 2 decades for very similar reasons. He wrestled with the uneasy feeling that mutation, the cornerstone of evolutionary change, could not develop something so complex as the human eye. Over time and with enormous statistical and fossil evidence, mutation-driven evolution became accepted.

You may have also had similar feelings toward evolution if you have run through many of the longer-running exercises in this book. Some of those exercises simulated `mutation`-based evolution over a thousand `individuals` for thousands of `generations`, only producing very minor changes. It is certainly easy to question `mutation` as the primary director of change, but what else could there be?

12.5.2 *Evolutionary plasticity*

Evolutionary plasticity, derived from the concept of phenotypic plasticity, attempts to describe possible genetic changes without mutation. The basic concept is that genetic changes may occur within an organism during its lifetime, and these changes then get passed on to future `generations`. The changes are not random, as they are in mutation, but a direct result of interacting with other organisms and the environment.

Our modern and rapid innovations in DNA research and the understanding of our and other species' genomes have changed our understanding of what is possible. No longer do we need to perform selective breeding to enforce genetic changes, but rather, we can now directly modify genomes and let those modifications pass on to future `generations`. What has also been shown is the ease at which those changes can be undertaken—which also brings to question our understanding of evolution.

> **CRISPR technology**
>
> *Clustered regularly interspaced short palindromic repeats* (CRISPR) is a very new technology that allows humans to modify ourselves and other species by essentially performing gene splicing. In some cases, this means removing bad genes, and in others, it simply means replacing genes to produce some new effect, like glowing. What makes this technology so impressive is that it provides a low tech means to alter the genome of a species. You can, for instance, buy CRISPR kits on the internet that allow you to alter bacteria or even frogs' DNA.

What comes into question, then, is whether a genome can be altered through very specific environmental changes and how we account for such changes in evolution. For a traditional evolutionist, this may just be another form of mutation, and mutation can describe those changes effectively enough. However, for us digital evolutionists, this presents some interesting opportunities for other forms of simulation.

Either way, evolutionary plasticity likely indicates our understanding of evolution is subject to change and, with it, the application of digital evolutionary search, where instead of driving evolution through slow and rare mutation, we use other genetic operators that provide quicker, selectively driven changes. In the next section, we look at our final notebook, which demonstrates evolution with plasticity.

12.5.3 *Improving evolution with plasticity*

In the notebook in this section, we revisit one of our original examples that initially demonstrated GA trying to replicate images, like the *Mona Lisa*. We make a single and simple change here that implements a new `plasticity` operator that could be used to enhance digital evolution. The implementation of this operator is just one interpretation of how a `plasticity` operator may function.

Open the EDL_12_5_Genetic_Plasticity.ipynb notebook as well as EDL_2_6_Genetic_Algorithms.ipynb, for comparison. Go ahead and run both notebooks via Runtime > Run All from the menu.

Review the code for both notebooks. We only focus on the implementation of the `plasticity` operator here. In biology, plasticity assumes that any environmental change is positive for the organism, so to simulate a `plasticity` operator, we first determine `individual` fitness as a baseline, as shown in the following listing. Then, we enforce a 100% chance of `mutation` of a new `individual` and determine the changed `fitness`. If the change improves `fitness`, the modified `individual` is returned; otherwise, we keep the original.

Listing 12.31   EDL_12_5_Genetic_Plasticity.ipynb: The genetic `plasticity` operator

```
def plasticity(individual):
    original = individual.copy()      ◁————  Makes a copy to keep the original
    f1 = fitness(individual)          ◁
    indvidual = mutation(individual, 1.0)    Determines the fitness before
    f2 = fitness(individual)          ◁       and after the change
    if f1 < f2:
        return individual             ◁———  Returns the more
    else:                                    fit individual
        return original               ◁

plasticity(pop[parents[0]])
```

Enforces the mutated change — points to line `indvidual = mutation(individual, 1.0)`

Figure 12.14 shows the results of the evolution for the original genetic operator's example from chapter 2 and the new one that includes `plasticity`. The output was generated by evolving a `population` of 300 `individuals` over 10,000 `generations` in both notebooks.

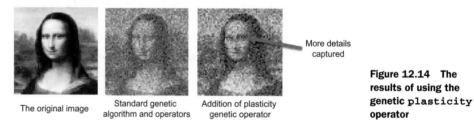

The original image   Standard genetic algorithm and operators   Addition of plasticity genetic operator

More details captured

Figure 12.14   The results of using the genetic `plasticity` operator

Computationally, the implementation of this form of `plasticity` is expensive. If you run the notebooks side by side, you will clearly notice this difference. However, computational differences aside, what is evident is how well this new `plasticity` operator improves on the finer details. Perhaps ironically, the eyes in the improved notebook are the first to become clearly recognizable.

The `plasticity` operator developed for this example is an example of how evolution can be improved using a slightly modified form of `mutation`. This new operator does perform better, as we have seen in this isolated example. Because of the added computational expense and the yet unproven theory of plasticity, we have not used it in the examples in this book. However, it does pose an interesting question about the future of both biological and digital evolution. This example does showcase, however, how limiting computation is when using evolutionary search, which is something we explore in the next section.

12.5.4   *Computation and evolutionary search*

One of, perhaps, the key limiting factors in using evolutionary search for optimizing DL or ML is the additional cost of the computation. This is something we witnessed and struggled to accommodate in several examples in this book. It also becomes a key limiting factor in the practical application of evolutionary search.

DL has reaped the benefits of advances in the gaming industry that allowed it to use fast GPUs to reduce computational costs immensely. It is because of those computational advancements that DL has the edge to become a key AI and ML technology of the future. But what if computationally evolutionary search could also be improved upon using distributed computing or perhaps even quantum computers?

In this book, DEAP has been applied with Google Colab, which limits the use of the framework-distributed computational abilities. For any serious projects, though, using distributed computing would likely alleviate much of the additional computational cost. Unfortunately, not a lot of work has been done in this area yet, so how effective this is remains to be seen.

However, if the cost or time of evolutionary search can be reduced, then this opens further possibilities for more expensive exploration. Techniques like IL or using evolution to search for new learning methods may be more practical. Instead of researchers spending hours developing new algorithms, the search could potentially be performed by evolution. In the next and final section of this book, we explore a technique using IL and DL.

12.6   *Generalization with instinctual deep and deep reinforcement learning*

In this final section, we look at a notebook that demonstrates IL being applied to DRL to generalize an agent across multiple environments. This exercise mimics the IL generalization example we developed previously but this time applied through DRL. DRL networks like the one we used for the DQN example are quite simple and make a good foundation for an application of IL.

Figure 12.15 shows how a pair of DQN DRL networks are used to solve two different environments. However, the middle layer of each network has been split into three distinct shareable instinct slots, where the goal of generalizing the learning for both networks is to find a shared base set of instincts: the instinct pool.

We can also see in figure 12.15 that shared instincts don't have to be in the same position in either network. Again, as we saw in the exercise with Geppy, reused instinct function operators are often mixed and matched to solve both environments. However, unlike with Geppy, we strictly limit the placement of these instincts and how they operate, even going a bit further and allowing the top and bottom layers of each network to be trained specifically to the environment.

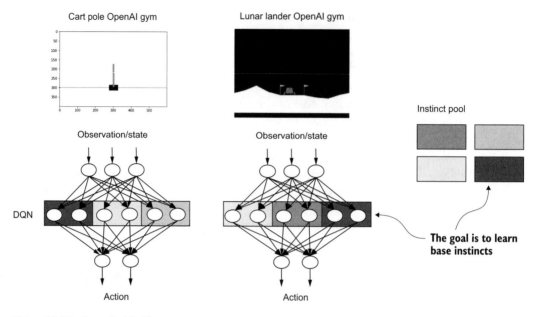

Cart pole OpenAI gym

Lunar lander OpenAI gym

Instinct pool

Observation/state

Observation/state

DQN

The goal is to learn
base instincts

Action

Action

Figure 12.15   IL applied to DL

Open the EDL_12_6_Instinctual_DQN_GYMS.ipynb notebook. Go ahead and run both notebooks via Runtime > Run All from the menu. This notebook has been extended from EDL_11_5_DQN_GYMS.ipynb, so if you need a review on DQN or DRL, refer to section 11.5.

The first thing we look at is the modification of the DQNAgent class_build_model function, as shown in listing 12.32. To slice the network up into functional chunks (instincts), we use the Keras functional API, which allows a DL network to be described in terms of functions. That also means each layer section can be treated as a function. So instead of building the model from a static set of layer or function definitions, we pass in a block of layers in the instincts list. The first and last elements of this list are layers defined specifically for the environment, and the middle layers or functions are the reusable instincts. Figure 12.16 explains how the build_model function is converted from a standard DL network to an instinctual one.

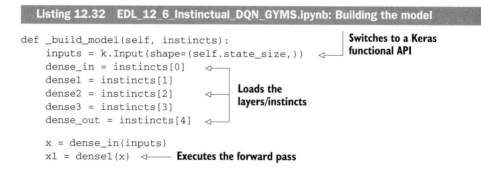

Listing 12.32   EDL_12_6_Instinctual_DQN_GYMS.ipynb: Building the model

```
def _build_model(self, instincts):                          Switches to a Keras
    inputs = k.Input(shape=(self.state_size,))         ◁──┘  functional API
    dense_in = instincts[0]    ◁─┐
    dense1 = instincts[1]
    dense2 = instincts[2]      ◁── Loads the
    dense3 = instincts[3]          layers/instincts
    dense_out = instincts[4]   ◁─┘

    x = dense_in(inputs)
    x1 = dense1(x)    ◁──── Executes the forward pass
```

```
x2 = dense2(x)
x3 = dense3(x)
x = kl.concatenate([x1, x2, x3])          Concatenates
                                          the instincts
outputs = dense_out(x)
model = k.Model(inputs=inputs, outputs=outputs)    Builds/compiles and
                                                   returns the model
model.compile(loss='mse',
 optimizer=k.optimizers.Adam(learning_rate=self.learning_rate))
return model
```

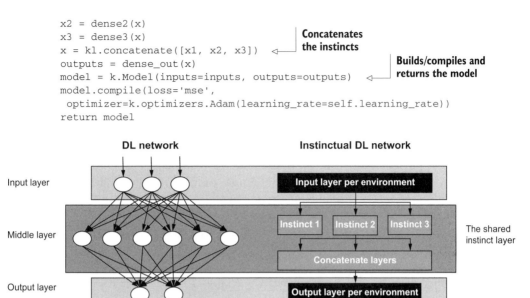

Figure 12.16 Converting to IL

The notebook contains several example cells that demonstrate how the instincts list of layers is populated and then used to create the DQNAgent. Here, we focus on how the instinct layers are created for training or finding instincts in multiple environments, as shown in listing 12.33. This code creates the base set of instincts in the shared layer pool—in this case, a standard Dense layer with 8 nodes, using ReLU activation. Then, we create environment-specific layers for inputs and outputs as well as a memory dequeue for each environment. In this example, we use just two environments, so a pool of four layers will work. If you are applying this technique to more than two environments, you may want to increase the size of the shared pool.

Listing 12.33 EDL_12_6_Instinctual_DQN_GYMS.ipynb: Creating layers

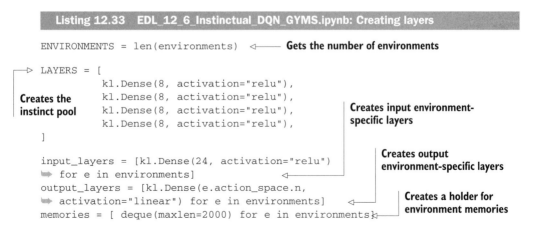

```
ENVIRONMENTS = len(environments)    ◁── Gets the number of environments

LAYERS = [
           kl.Dense(8, activation="relu"),
           kl.Dense(8, activation="relu"),
           kl.Dense(8, activation="relu"),
           kl.Dense(8, activation="relu"),
]

input_layers = [kl.Dense(24, activation="relu")
 for e in environments]        ◁
output_layers = [kl.Dense(e.action_space.n,
 activation="linear") for e in environments]    ◁
memories = [ deque(maxlen=2000) for e in environments]
```

Creates the instinct pool

Creates input environment-specific layers

Creates output environment-specific layers

Creates a holder for environment memories

Now, to find how the base instincts (functional layers) are shared and reused to solve both environments simultaneously, we, of course, use evolutionary search, reverting to our old friend: GAs with DEAP. Since we only use three instincts per environment, a simple gene sequence can be built with three genes per environment, where each gene represents an index into the shared instinct layer pool. Figure 12.17 shows how the gene sequence is constructed, where each environmental model describes a set of indexes that link back to the shared layer pool.

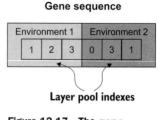

Gene sequence

Figure 12.17   The gene sequence of an individual

We can see how this all comes together in the evaluate function. The code starts by looping over each environment and converting the gene sequence to layer indexes. This then constructs the set of specific and shared layers to pass into the model. Then, a new agent model is constructed and evaluated for each environment. Notice how the training is blocked until the evaluate function is called with train=True in the following listing—we get to why this is shortly.

Listing 12.34   EDL_12_6_Instinctual_DQN_GYMS.ipynb: The evaluate function

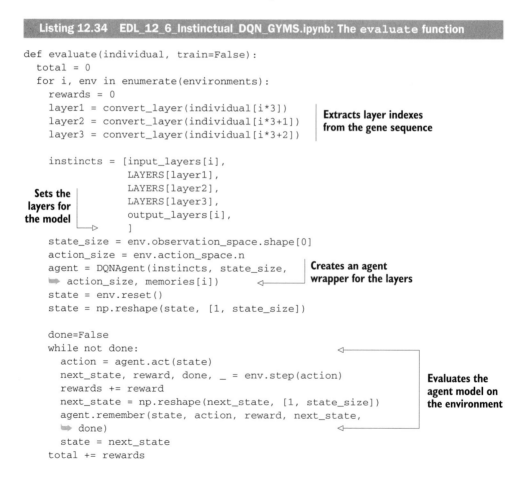

```
def evaluate(individual, train=False):
  total = 0
  for i, env in enumerate(environments):
    rewards = 0
    layer1 = convert_layer(individual[i*3])
    layer2 = convert_layer(individual[i*3+1])      Extracts layer indexes
    layer3 = convert_layer(individual[i*3+2])      from the gene sequence

    instincts = [input_layers[i],
                 LAYERS[layer1],
                 LAYERS[layer2],
                 LAYERS[layer3],
                 output_layers[i],
                 ]
    state_size = env.observation_space.shape[0]
    action_size = env.action_space.n
    agent = DQNAgent(instincts, state_size,         Creates an agent
    ➡ action_size, memories[i])                     wrapper for the layers
    state = env.reset()
    state = np.reshape(state, [1, state_size])

    done=False
    while not done:
      action = agent.act(state)
      next_state, reward, done, _ = env.step(action)
      rewards += reward                              Evaluates the
      next_state = np.reshape(next_state, [1, state_size])   agent model on
      agent.remember(state, action, reward, next_state,      the environment
      ➡ done)
      state = next_state
    total += rewards
```

(Sets the layers for the model)

```
    if train:
        agent.replay(32)   ◁──── Only trains when required

  print(total/len(environments))
  return total/len(environments),   ◁──── Returns the average fitness
```

The reason we don't train the derived model and the specific and shared layers for every `individual` is that this can cause internal conflicts or duality. We saw this when we tried to train a single model in both environments without using instincts. Instead, our goal is to only train the best agent for each `generation`. That means all layers are only trained or updated on the best `individual` once per evolutionary `generation`. If we were trying to adhere to a strict evolutionary search, we would never do this. But if we were to borrow the concept of `plasticity`, covered earlier, we could accept this training process is a reactionary improvement or `mutation` from the environment.

That means when evolving the environment, we now perform training of the DL layers on the best current `individual`, as shown in listing 12.35. Notice that no other training is performed, which means updating or tuning the weights of the model is specific to the models' instincts, which can vary. Because of this near randomness of our DQN agent, we remove any exploration or randomness in training. You can see this if you look at the `DQNAgent.act` function.

Listing 12.35   EDL_12_6_Instinctual_DQN_GYMS.ipynb: Evolving the instincts

```
for g in range(NGEN):                                          Performs a generation
  pop, logbook = algorithms.eaSimple(pop, toolbox,     ◁──┐   of evolution
            cxpb=CXPB, mutpb=MUTPB, ngen=RGEN, stats=stats, halloffame=hof,
  ➥ verbose=False)
  best = hof[0]                                    │  Runs evaluate on the
  best_fit = evaluate(best, train=True)    ◁──┘  best and does training
```

This example has now been simplified for explanation over performance, where appropriate. It can produce a generalized set of instincts that can be used to solve both environments, but evolution and training take time. A more robust instinctual deep learner would likely use smaller and a larger number of instincts, perhaps even sharing instincts for both input and output layers.

The primary goal of IL is to find the base set of instincts or functions that can be reused on disparate tasks to generalize a model. The goal is to allow reusing functions (instincts) to excel in the way systems generalize learning. IL's secondary goal is finding the function (instinct) that can dynamically reorganize these instincts by process or thought.

IL is still early in its development, yet it is getting close to solving its primary goal. There are still several alternative DL network types, applications, and evolutionary search methods that can be applied. It is my hope that researchers and students embrace the path to finding these base instinct functions shared amongst networks.

Summary

- Evolution can be applied to many other forms of ML and provides new opportunities for expanding our knowledge.
- Geppy and gene expression programming are extensions to GAs that work by writing coherent code or functions. Geppy can be an excellent tool for generating readable functions for complex function approximation problems.
- Geppy can be applied to evolutionary search on a DRL problem as a function approximation tool to generate single readable functions. Generated functions can then be used to apply and solve complex control environments from the OpenAI Gym tool kit.
- IL is a pattern of combining evolutionary methods with DL to find new methods for modeling and solving complex problems.
- Fundamental to IL is the instinct, or the core learned behavior of a model or organism:
  - In nature, biological life develops instincts to solve tasks, like eating or walking. The number, size, and complexity of instincts tend to diminish the more complex a life form becomes.
  - Instead, the life form often must learn to control its base instincts to accomplish basic or complex tasks.
- The concept of evolution and our understanding of evolution itself may adapt and evolve to allow us to evolve ML and DL further. Theoretical concepts like evolutionary plasticity—that organisms may be able to evolve outside of reproduction—may have interesting applications in EC and EDL.
- The basic premise of IL can be demonstrated by breaking down a DQN agent network into instincts and then letting an agent train those instincts against multiple tasks. An agent that can generalize to multiple tasks using IL can be shown to approach more generalized models across tasks.

appendix

A.1 Accessing the source code

The source code for the book is located at https://github.com/cxbxmxcx/
EvolutionaryDeepLearning. You are not required to download any code to your
local machine for this code; all the code will run on Google Colaboratory, or Colab
for short. To open your first notebook, follow these steps:

1 Navigate to https://github.com/cxbxmxcx/EvolutionaryDeepLearning, and
  open one of the sample notebooks by clicking the link shown in figure A.1.

Figure A.1 Clicking a notebook link in the repository code view

2 This will open a view of the notebook. At the top will be a Colab badge (figure A.2). Click on the badge to open the notebook in Colab.

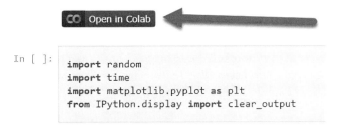

Figure A.2 A view from a sample notebook

3 Once the notebook is open, you can follow along with the rest of the book
  exercise.

325

> **Google Colab Pro**
>
> Over the years, Colab has gone from being an excellent free platform for doing Python computation to something more commercially driven. While it still is an excellent platform, access to GPU resources is now limited for free users. As such, if you find yourself heavily using Colab, it may be beneficial to acquire a Colab Pro license.

A.2   Running code on other platforms

Colab can also connect to a secondary Jupyter runtime, either hosted locally or on another cloud resource. This is only beneficial if you have the configured computing/ GPU resources and the ability to mirror the setup of Colab. You can access this option and further instructions by clicking the runtime drop-down menu located in the top-right menu bar (figure A.3).

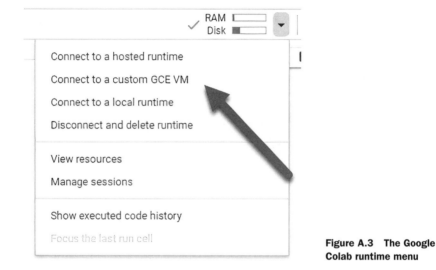

Figure A.3   The Google Colab runtime menu

Of course, another option is to convert the code to Python and run it outside a notebook. To do that, simply use the feature within Colab to download the notebook as a Python file. You can access this feature from the menu by navigating to File > Download > Download .py as shown in figure A.4.

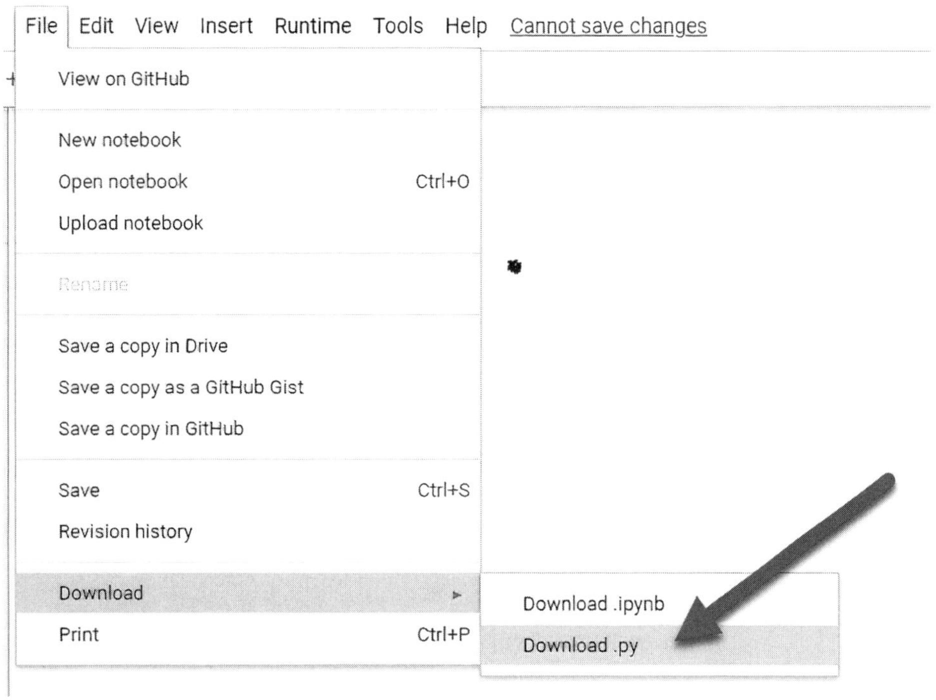

Figure A.4 Downloading a notebook as a Python file

index

H

I